PUBLIC SPEAKING
FOR PERSONAL SUCCESS

FIFTH EDITION

MICHAEL S. HANNA

PROFESSOR OF COMMUNICATION

UNIVERSITY OF SOUTH ALABAMA

JAMES W. GIBSON

PROFESSOR EMERITUS OF COMMUNICATION

UNIVERSITY OF MISSOURI-COLUMBIA

PEARSON CUSTOM PUBLISHING

Cover Photo © Stephen Marks/The Image Bank

Printed in the United States of America

10 9 8 7 6 5 4 3 2 1

Please visit our website at www.pearsoncustom.com

ISBN 0–536–02336–0

BA 990111

PEARSON CUSTOM PUBLISHING
160 Gould Street/Needham Heights, MA 02494
Pearson Education Company

DEDICATION

Our wives, Nancy Hadden Hanna and Joanne McNamee Gibson, have seen us through production of five iterations of this book. It is truly as much theirs as it is ours. So we fondly dedicate this fifth edition to them.

CONTENTS

PART 1
Speaking and Listening   1

CHAPTER 1 INTRODUCTION   3

Objectives   3
Outline   4
Abstract   4
Imagine   5
Introduction   5
  Purpose of the Book   5
  Definitions of Terms   6
    Public Speaking   6
    The Public Speaking Course   7
Why We Speak   8
  To Express Ourselves   8
  To Provide Information   9
  To Persuade Others   9
  To Entertain an Audience   9
Ethics of Speech Making   10
  Ethical Issues in Public Speaking   11
  Ethical Standards in Public Speaking   11
The Process of Public Speaking   12
  Why the Audience Is Gathered   12
  When You Speak   12
  Where You Speak   13
  Events that Precede and Follow
    Your Speech   13
    Source/Encoder (Speaker)   13
    Channels   14

Messages   14
Decoder/Receiver (Listener)   14
Noise   15
Feedback   15
Public Speaking Separated from Other
    Communication Behavior   16
  Structure   16
  Formality   16
  Anxiety   17
Text Goal and Overview   17
Summary   19
Key Terms   20
Application Questions   20
It's More Fun to Know   20
Self-Test for Review   21
Suggested Readings   22
Notes   22

CHAPTER 2 PLANNING THE FIRST
            SPEECH   23

Objectives   23
Outline   24
Abstract   24
Imagine   24
Introduction   25
  What kinds of first speaking assignments
    are most likely?   26
  What can I do about my feelings of
    anxiety?   26
  What can we suggest to alleviate
    the fear of speaking in public?   30

How can I avoid making
common mistakes?   32
How should I go about developing the
first speaking assignment?   32
Step 1. Select a topic.   32
Step 2. Determine the purpose.   33
Step 3. Organize the ideas.   34
Step 4. Build support for the ideas.   36
Step 5. Practice carefully.   38
Is there a preferred style of delivery for
the first speaking assignment?   38
Summary   39
Key Terms   42
Application Questions   42
It's More Fun to Know   42
Self-Test for Review   43
Suggested Readings   44
Internet Activities   44
Example Speeches   45
Notes   46

CHAPTER 3 LISTENING   47
Objectives   47
Outline   48
Abstract   48
Imagine   48
Introduction   49
Model of the Listening Process   49
Sensing   50
Attending   50
Understanding   50
Remembering   50
Sensing Problems   51
What To Do About Sensing
Problems   51
Attending Problems   52
Selective Perception   52
Poor Attention Habits   52
Attitudes and Needs That Interfere
with Attending   52

Low Message Intensity   53
What to Do about Attending
Problems   53
Understanding Problems   54
What to Do About Misunderstanding
Problems   54
Remembering Problems   55
What to Do About Memory Problems   56
Problems with Empathy and
What to Do About Them   56
How to Develop Your Personal Listening
Skills   57
Concentrate on the Message and the
Speaker   57
Identify With the Speaker   58
React to the Speaker   58
Be Objective About the Speaker's
Message   58
Work Hard at Remembering   58
Summary   59
Key Terms   60
Application Questions   60
It's More Fun to Know   60
Self-Test for Review   61
Suggested Readings   61
Notes   62

PART 2
Designing the Speech   63

CHAPTER 4 SELECTING AND NARROWING
YOUR TOPIC   65
Objectives   65
Outline   66
Abstract   66
Imagine   66
Introduction   67
Selecting a Topic   68
Select a Topic Based on What You
Already Know   69

Select an Idea That Will Interest and
Appeal to Your Listeners 71

Narrowing the Topic 72

Sample Speech 76

How to Develop the Thesis Statement 81

How to Test the Thesis Statement 82

Summary 83

Key Terms 84

Application Questions 84

It's More Fun to Know 84

Self-Test for Review 85

Suggested Readings 87

Internet Activities 87

Notes 87

CHAPTER 5 AUDIENCE ANALYSIS 89

Objectives 89

Outline 90

Abstract 90

Imagine 91

Introduction 91

Audience Setting and Occasion as
Rhetorical Field 93

When You Speak 93

Where You Speak 93

The Occasion 94

Events Surrounding Your Speech 94

Conducting an Audience Analysis 94

Analyzing Your Classroom
Audience 94

Inferential Audience Analysis 98

Meeting Audience Expectations and
Adapting to Where They Stand 103

Summary 104

Key Terms 105

Application Questions 105

It's More Fun To Know 105

Self-Test for Review 106

Suggested Readings 106

Internet Activities 107

Notes 108

CHAPTER 6 THE PROCESS OF PROVING:
DISCOVERING AND DEVELOPING
IDEAS FOR A SPEECH 109

Objectives 109

Outline 110

Abstract 110

Imagine 111

Introduction 112

How to Support Ideas with
Argument 112

Inductive Argument 112

Deductive Argument 113

The Process of Proving 119

How to Construct an Argument 120

How to Support a Knowledge Claim
With Arguments 124

How to Build Speaker Credibility 124

How to Support Arguments with
Evidence 126

Summary 131

Key Terms 132

Application Questions 132

It's More Fun to Know 132

Self-Test for Review 133

Suggested Readings 134

Internet Activities 135

Notes 135

CHAPTER 7 HOW TO GATHER
SUPPORTING MATERIALS 137

Objectives 137

Outline 138

Abstract 138

Imagine 139

Introduction 140

A Word About Ethics in Scholarship 140

How to Locate Information by Interviewing
and Corresponding with Your Network
of Friends and Acquaintances 141

Information-gathering Interview   141

Gathering Information Through
    Correspondence   141

How to Use the Library   143

Finding Your Way Around the
    Library   143

How to Use Some of the More Useful
    Computerized Databases in the
    Library   146

How to Conduct a Key-Word Search   147

How to Use Various General and
    Specialized Indexes in Your Library
    (Paper-based or Computer-based)
    and on the Internet   149

How to Use Reference Works   149

Atlases and Gazettes   151

Biographical Aids   151

Dictionaries   152

Encyclopedias   152

How to Use the Internet for Research   153

Search Engines   153

Use the Library as a Metaphor for
    Your Research On Line   156

Bookmark Interesting Web Sites   156

Examine Specialized Resources
    First   157

Reference Sources   157

Evaluate Internet and Other Research
    Documents Carefully   158

Make Careful and Complete Notes the
    First Time   160

Use Note Cards or Half-Sheets   160

Establish a Standard Form of
    Entry   160

Use One Card Per Entry and One
    Entry Per Card   160

Take Plenty of Notes   161

Do Not Plagiarize, Even by
    Accident   161

Develop a Working Bibliography   162

Use Your Note Card File to Plan
    a Speech   162

Summary   163

Key Terms   164

Application Questions   164

It's More Fun to Know   165

Self-Test for Review   166

Suggested Readings   167

Notes   168

PART 3
Organizing the Speech   169

CHAPTER 8   ORGANIZING THE BODY
             OF THE SPEECH   171

Objectives   171

Outline   172

Abstract   172

Imagine   172

Introduction   173

Why Organization Is Important   173

Characteristics of Good
    Organization   174

Clear and Simple   174

Few Main Points   175

Logical Development   176

Organizing the Body of Your Speech   176

Time   176

Space   178

Problem to Solution   178

Causal Order   178

Topical Divisions   181

Motivated Sequence   184

Organizational Links   186

Transitions   187

Signposts   187

Internal Summaries   188

Summary   188

Key Terms   189

Application Questions   189

It's More Fun to Know   189

Self-Test for Review   190
Suggested Readings   191
Notes   191

CHAPTER 9 OUTLINING THE SPEECH   193
Objectives   193
Outline   194
Abstract   194
Imagine   194
Introduction   195
  How to Develop a Planning Outline   195
    Label the Major Parts of the
        Outline   196
    Use A Standard Outline Format   201
    Write the General Purpose, the
        Specific Purpose, and the Thesis
        Statement   201
    Support the Thesis Statement With
        Main Ideas and Subpoints   203
    Consistently Follow an
        Organizational Pattern   203
    Write Simple Sentences with
        Action Verbs   210
    Plan Organizational Links   211
    Include Appropriate
        Documentation   212
  How to Develop A Speaking Outline   212
Summary   218
Key Terms   219
Application Questions   219
It's More Fun to Know   219
Self-Test for Review   220
Suggested Reading   221
Internet Activities   221
Sample Outlines   222
  Model Speaking Outline   222
  Model Speaking Outline with
      Annotations   224
Notes   225

CHAPTER 10 INTRODUCTIONS
            AND CONCLUSIONS   227
Objectives   227
Outline   228
Abstract   228
Imagine   229
Introduction   229
  The Introduction   229
    Purposes of the Introduction   229
    Strategies for Introductions   230
The Conclusion   237
  Purposes of the Conclusion   237
    Strategies for Conclusions   237
    Summary   239
    Quotation   239
    Reference to the Introduction   239
    Call for Action   240
    Combinations   240
Summary   240
Key Terms   242
Application Questions   242
It's More Fun to Know   242
Self-Test for Review   243
Suggested Readings   244
Internet Activities   244
Notes   244

PART 4
Delivering the Speech   245

CHAPTER 11 LANGUAGE: THE KEY TO
            SUCCESSFUL SPEAKING   247
Objectives   247
Outline   248
Abstract   248
Imagine   248
Introduction   249

Language: Sharing Reality and
    Meaning   249
    Language Creates Reality   250
    Language Carries Meaning   251
Using Language Well   255
    Use Appropriate Language   256
    Use Simple Language   257
    Use Clear Language   258
    Use Vivid Language   258
Use Accurate and Unambiguous
    Language   260
Summary   261
Key Terms   262
Application Questions   262
It's More Fun to Know   262
Self-Test for Review   263
Suggested Readings   264
Internet Activities   265
Notes   265

CHAPTER 12 SUPPORTING IDEAS
            VISUALLY   267
Objectives   267
Outline   268
Abstract   268
Imagine   269
Introduction   270
    Why Don't People Use Visual Aids?   270
    Why Should You Use Visual Aids?   271
    When to Use Visual Aids   272
        To Simplify Complexity   273
        To Help Listeners Organize Your
            Ideas   273
        To Control Audience Attention   274
        To Help Listeners Understand Abstract
            Ideas   274
        To Help Listeners Remember   275
        To Help You Remain Organized While
            Speaking   277
    What to Support with Visual
        Materials   278

Steps in Developing a Visual Aid
    Program   278
    Think About The Key Ideas   278
    Develop a Rough Plan for the Visual
        Program   280
    Design Thumbnail Sketches of Each
        Visual Aid   281
Choose the Visual Media for the
    Program   282
    Convenience of Use   282
    Costs Versus Benefits   282
    Communication Power   284
Produce Rough Visual Aids for
    Practice   284
Produce the Finished Visual Aids for
    the Program   284
How to Make a Two-Dimensional
    Visual Aid   285
    The Rule of Thirds   286
    Straight Lines and Curved Lines   288
    The Balance of Triangles   288
    Eye Movement and Negative
        Space   288
    Sketches and Illustrations   290
    Language and Lettering   291
Review and Revise the Final
    Program   293
How to Use Visual Materials: Matters
    of Delivery   294
Summary   295
Key Terms   298
Application Questions   298
It's More Fun to Know   298
Self-Test for Review   299
Suggested Readings   300
Internet Activities   300
Notes   301

CHAPTER 13 DELIVERY   303
Objectives   303
Outline   304

Abstract   304

Imagine   305

Introduction   305

   Choosing a Method of Delivery   306

      Manuscript Delivery   306

      Memorized Delivery   308

      Extemporaneous Delivery   309

      Impromptu Delivery   310

   Differences Between Written and Oral Styles   311

   The Speaking Voice   312

      Rate   313

      Pitch   314

      Volume   315

   Nonverbal Messages   315

      Gestures   316

      Eye Contact   318

      Personal Appearance and Behavior   319

   Practice Your Speech   319

Summary   320

Key Terms   322

Application Questions   322

It's More Fun to Know   322

Self-Test for Review   322

Suggested Readings   323

Internet Activities   324

Notes   324

PART 5
Common Types of Speeches   325

CHAPTER 14 INFORMATIVE SPEAKING   327

Objectives   327

Outline   328

Abstract   328

Imagine   329

Introduction   329

Ways of Characterizing Informative Speeches   329

   The Speaker's Intention   331

   Function of the Information   331

   Listeners' Perception   332

   Types of Informative Speeches   332

Guidelines for Informative Speaking   338

   How to Generate Attention and Interest   338

Summary   346

Key Terms   348

Application Questions   348

It's More Fun to Know   348

Self-Test for Review   349

Suggested Readings   350

Internet Activities   351

Notes   351

CHAPTER 15 PERSUASIVE SPEAKING   353

Objectives   353

Outline   354

Abstract   354

Imagine   354

Introduction   355

Ethical Considerations   356

Theories of Persuasion   357

   Aristotle and Artistic Proofs   357

   Intensification/Downplay Model of Persuasion   358

   Evoked Recall Model of Persuasion   358

   Beliefs and Values   359

      Beliefs   359

      Changing Beliefs   361

      Values   362

Characteristics of the Effective Persuasive Speech   364

   Speaker Credibility   364

   Message Credibility   364

      Fact   366

      Value   368

      Policy   369

Message Strategies   369
  One-Sided Versus Two-Sided
    Arguments   369
  Explicit Versus Implicit
    Conclusions   371
  Evoked Recall Appeals   372
  Organizing in a Motivated
    Sequence   375
Summary   376
Key Terms   377
Application Questions   377
It's More Fun To Know   378
Self-Test for Review   378
Suggested Readings   379
Internet Activities   380
Notes   380

CHAPTER 16 SPEECHES FOR SPECIAL
            OCCASIONS   381
Objectives   381
Outline   382
Abstract   382
Imagine   382
Introduction   383
  Speeches of Praise and Tribute   383
    Introductory Speeches   384
    Presentation Speeches   386
    Acceptance Speeches   386
    Eulogies   388
  Inspirational Speeches   390
    Commencement Speeches   390

Keynote Speeches   391
  Welcoming Speeches   391
  Speeches for the Sake of Humor   394
    After-Dinner Speeches   395
Summary   398
Key Terms   400
Application Questions   400
It's More Fun to Know   400
Self-Test for Review   401
Suggested Readings   402
Internet Activities   402
Notes   403

APPENDIX A SAMPLE SPEECHES   405
Never Give Up: The Power of
  Perseverance   405
The American Red Cross: Public Relations
  and Communication   409
American Sport at Century's End:
  An Overview   413
Women And Men Communicating: Who's
  from Mars?   418
Journalism: Words from a Dinosaur   423
Hawaii—Land of Volcanoes   425

APPENDIX B TROUBLESHOOTING GUIDE   427

APPENDIX C POSSIBLE SPEECH TOPICS   437

APPENDIX D GLOSSARY   443

APPENDIX E INDEX   451

PREFACE

This fifth edition of *Public Speaking for Personal Success* is written for students enrolled in a first public speaking course. We have tried to present a blend of theory and practice students and teachers will enjoy. And we have illustrated the ideas in this book with many real examples drawn from our classroom and our consulting experience. We have no doubt that this approach works best in the classroom.

Much of this edition is new material. All of it has been updated to reflect the changes in communications technology that have characterized the intervening years. For example, the materials on using the library reflect the fact that most libraries are now computerized. These changes reflect our determination to keep our book fresh and timely.

The title of this book is intended to convey the book's applicability. We are convinced that a direct relationship exists between a person's success and that person's ability to speak clearly, articulately, and persuasively. The skills involved can be learned and practiced. The purpose of this book is to provide the materials students need to learn those skills.

We are also convinced that people learn by example. To that end we have included a large number of carefully developed examples and illustrations. Many of these have been drawn from public speaking classrooms. Many more have been drawn from our consulting experience. A few have been created for instructional effect. Our aim has been to show students how the knowledge, skills, and abilities taught in a public speaking class carry into the world of work and into a person's personal life, as well.

In 1968, Jim Gibson and his colleagues began an ongoing investigation of the basic public speaking course sponsored by the Undergraduate Speech Instruction Interest Group of the National Communication Association. In 1974 Mike Hanna joined that effort. The findings of that longitudinal study have been published in 1980, 1985, and 1990. The most recent installment appeared as the lead article in Lawrence W. Hugenberg, ed. *Basic Communication Course Annual 11* (Boston: American Press, 1999). We have based this text, including the changes reflected in all its iterations, on the findings from that ongoing study. This edition is not an exception. Readers may be sure the topics discussed in this book, all the changes in the current edition, and all the information presented reflect the best thinking of basic public speaking course teachers and scholars around the country.

NEW FEATURES

The chapter sequence and materials in this book have been carefully designed to fit public speaking classes as they are generally taught today. Decisions about how to revise and upgrade the fifth edition have all been driven by a desire to keep the book current. Certain new features have resulted from this effort.

We have increased our emphasis on diversity. The examples, names of student speakers, sources, photographs, and the like, celebrate the rich diversity of the American people. Moreover, we have taken care to assure that women and men not only have an equal share of superior and subordinate relationships in our examples and illustrations, but also equal representation. We have also done our best to write gender-neutral language that does not leap off the page.

We have increased our emphasis on ethics. In addition to the already strong essay in the first chapter, we have integrated ethical considerations throughout the book where they have seemed relevant and appropriate. Moreover, to call reader attention to the ethics of public address, at each location where an ethical issue rises out of our discussion we have raised that issue in a side bar. Our intention has been to ask students to consider their own ethical responsibilities—for example, as they design visual materials, or as they choose emotional appeals to support persuasive speeches.

We have increased our emphasis on technology. Throughout the book, where technology has become relevant since the last edition, we have mentioned and described its relevance. For example, in the chapter on organizing ideas we tell students about the organizing functions of various word processors and presentation managers. End matter to each chapter includes two or three, and sometimes more, Internet exercises designed to get students onto the WWW and to find relevant and useful websites there. We are aware this strategy can backfire—web sites don't always stay "up" for the duration of a book's edition. However, we have taken pains to select sites we believe will be available through the life of this edition. And in any case, we firmly believe that learning to use the Internet is a critical intellectual skill for all college students.

We have simplified information retrieval for the student who uses our book. Where possible we have pared lengthy essays and put the essential material into tables and exhibits. Most chapters now include lists of pointers that extract the "How to do it" suggestions from the text material and locate them in one place. Research shows that students often rely upon such pedagogical devices.

We have strengthened the research and theory grounding for each of our suggestions in each of the chapters, but without slowing down the student with a huge increase in the number of specific citations. Instead, at the end of each chapter we have produced a brief essay, called "It's More Fun to Know," that describes the theory and research on which the chapter is grounded. This new feature responds to feedback from basic course directors who are frustrated with the apparent disregard in basic texts of the theoretical and research underpinnings of the basic course.

Each chapter begins with an opening scenario, called "Imagine." This narrative illustrates the importance of the materials in the chapter and sets the focus for the chapter. Students who read these narratives will find reason to study the chapter.

SPECIFIC FEATURES OF THE FIFTH EDITION

Chapter 1. Introduction to Ethical Public Speaking

In examining the context of a public speech event we introduce the idea of "rhetorical field"—the physical, temporal, social, psychological environment in which communication takes place. This idea helps the student make sense out of the notion that a speaker must adapt to the overall speaking situation, and that these choices usually have ethical implications. It becomes the central consideration in Chapter 5, "Analyzing the Audience."

Chapter 2. Planning the First Speech

Teachers usually have their students up and speaking in the first week or two of the course—a fact that gives many students serious pause. We have moved our appendix on communication anxiety into this second chapter. The treatment has been streamlined, revised, and updated. We have also laid the groundwork for the remainder of the text by highlighting materials from the book throughout this chapter. Students who study this chapter will approach the first speaking assignment with much less trepidation. Two annotated sample speeches appear at the end of this chapter to provide models for students to follow.

Chapter 3. Listening

We have strengthened the focus of this chapter on how a speaker can help audience members listen. The chapter builds on a model of listening that shows four subprocesses—attending, perceiving, comprehending, and remembering. Each of these subprocesses presents opportunities for speakers to increase the rhetorical impact of their speeches.

Chapter 4. Selecting and Narrowing Your Topic

Chapter 4 has been thoroughly revised and updated. In addition to the more traditional suggestions usually found in public speaking textbooks, this chapter now gives thorough treatment to various on-line resources available for help in selecting and narrowing a topic.

Chapter 5. Analyzing the Audience

A speech occurs in a rhetorical field—the combination of context, setting, and occasion in which an audience understands itself to exist. We describe this field as a means of helping readers understand which arguments and ideas will seem relevant to a particular audience in a particular context. This new focus makes it possible to tell students how they can meet or adapt to listener expectations in a way that makes much more sense to them.

Chapter 6. The Process of Proving: Discovering and Developing Ideas for a Speech

Chapter 6 is largely new, much less theoretical, and much more practical than in previous editions of this book. We describe and illustrate the commonly occurring kinds of arguments and make specific suggestions about how to test the quality and strength of these arguments. Toulmin's basic model of persuasive arguments shows readers how to build arguments and determine the types and quality of evidence needed to support them.

Chapter 7. How to Gather Supporting Materials

This well received chapter has been updated to include use of computers both in libraries and on the Internet. The first iteration of this chapter was written with the close help of the University of South Alabama library staff. Those men and women have helped us in each revision of the text. Their help with this chapter has made it one of the strongest sources anywhere of information on how to gather supporting materials.

Chapter 8. Organizing the Body of the Speech

Chapter 8 has been simplified for this edition and the illustrative material greatly increased. The new, more numerous examples make it easier for students to learn how to organize ideas.

Chapter 9. Outlining the Speech

The entire chapter has been updated with new examples and with reference to various software and on-line resources students can use as they plan and organize their speeches. We have placed new emphasis on the value of outlining for all planned discourse.

Chapter 10. Introductions and Conclusions

Speeches often fail because of ill conceived or poorly developed introductions and conclusions. This chapter explains the functions and purposes of both parts, and tells the reader how to develop them.

Chapter 11. Language: The Key to Successful Speaking

Our discussion of denotative, connotative, and relational meaning leads the reader into materials about how to use language well. This chapter is rich with illustrative materials that reflect life at the turn of the millennium.

Chapter 12. Supporting Ideas Visually

Through the first four editions of Public Speaking for Personal Success, this chapter has been one of the most highly praised. But changes in communications technology—both software and hardware—have required that the chapter be completely revised and refreshed. While this chapter retains earlier ideas on two-dimensional design and appropriate choice of visual media, we have updated the examples and added new material to describe how to use computers to make visual supporting materials. For example, we have added new material on graphics and photographs, font sizes, and the like.

Chapter 13. Delivery

Methods of delivery haven't changed much, and neither has this chapter. We have tightened the prose to make the information easier for students to retrieve. We have also talked about how technological advances have changed some of the assumptions and techniques people make about speech delivery.

Chapter 14. Informative Speaking

New and updated examples and illustrations freshen this already well-received chapter and place infomative speaking in all walks of adult life in the United States.

Chapter 15. Persuasive Speaking

The chapter revolves around four theories and models of persuasion, clearly identified: (1) Aristotle's artistic proofs—*ethos, logos, pathos,* (2) Hugh Rank's emphasis/downplay model, (3) the evoked recall model that originated with Tony Schwartz and Vance Packard, and (4) Roheache's structure of beliefs and values. Readers will learn to develop speaker and message credibility. New tables and examples make this chapter easy for students to use.

Chapter 16. Speeches for Special Occasions

This chapter heightens student awareness of how often special occasions occur in life, and how commonly they involve epideictic speeches. In combination, the examples and the pedagogical materials in the chapter make it easy for students to quickly and easily prepare speeches for special occasions.

LEARNING AIDS

Chapter Opening Pedagogy

Each chapter has been designed to give students the clearest possible impression of what lies within and why. The **Chapter Objectives** point to the most important themes in a chapter and call out the behaviors a student should be able to exhibit after having studied carefully. These objectives also serve as the basis for study and review in preparation for exams because they tell students what materials in each chapter are important to know and understand. The **Chapter Outline** includes the heading within the text. Students can tell at a glance how the chapter is organized and what it includes.

End of Chapter Pedagogy

Several helpful learning tools follow each chapter. These include a carefully worded **Summary** of the chapter's key ideas. The **Key Terms** are each defined in the chapter and again in the glossary. These are the essential concepts the students should retain. **Application Questions** ask students to apply what they have learned to real-life situations. They encourage students to practice both analytical and performance skills introduced in the chapters. A brief essay called **It's More Fun to Know** summarizes theory and research on which the suggestions in the chapter are based. Students have suggested they are more likely to read this material than the footnotes. A keyed **Self-test for Review** lets the student test how much of the chapter material he or she has grasped. Included in the **Suggested Readings** is a brief, annotated bibliography of classical and contemporary works. **Internet Activities** at the end of each chapter take the learner to relevant Internet sites where directly relevant and helpful materials may be found. Each chapter ends with **Notes** and citations referenced within the chapter. Chapter 2 follows the notes with two annotated sample speeches to serve as models for students to follow.

Ethics Side Bars

From time to time throughout the text, students will discover sidebars that raise questions about ethical considerations they may encounter. Both students and faculty will enjoy the discussions these ethical questions stimulate.

End of Book Pedagogy

Readers will find the end-of-book material especially helpful. **Sample Speeches** have been chosen on the basis of their teaching value and on topic interest. Students need to be exposed to various levels of speaker experience. To that end, the samples include both student work as well as more mature and experienced work.

The **Trouble Shooting Guide,** pioneered in the first edition, has continued to be well received because of its value to readers. The guide is organized around questions most commonly asked by students within several broad categories. The student's question leads to various places in the text where the question is addressed. For example, the question might be, "What visual aids do I need?" This question appears in the trouble shooting guide as "What should I support with a visual aid?" The guide refers the reader to answers in the text.

The **Glossary** defines every key term in the text, and in terms used in the body of the text. In addition, the glossary carries a few terms, closely related to text discussions, that are not defined in the chapters. The glossary can stand alone as a dictionary of every key concept in public speaking. The **Index** provides further access to the materials discussed in the book.

ACKNOWLEDGMENTS

Over the years many people have helped us by reading our work critically. They have helped us greatly to improve this book through its first four editions. We express our continuing gratitude to the following individuals who made valuable suggestions for the fourth edition:

John Bee, University of Ackron; Robert Dunbar, City College of San Francisco; Beth Ellis, Ball State University; Anne Holmquest, Augsburg College; Michael Ingram, Whitworth College; Patti Kalanquin, William Rainey Harper College; John Meyer, University of Southern Mississippi; Barbara Mollberg, Rochester Community College; John Muchmore, William Rainey Harper College; Lawrence Rifkind, Georgia State University; Ann Scroggie, Santa Fe Community College; Wayne Silver, Mohegan Community College; Todd Thomas, Indiana University-Bloomington; Beth Waggenspack, Virginia Poly Institute and State University; John Williams, California State University-Sacramento.

And we acknowledge our debt to the following people who reviewed the first three editions of our text:

Martha Atkins, Iowa State University; Phil Backlund, Central Washington University; David Branco, University of Nebraska–Omaha; Larry Caillouet, Western Kentucky University; Isaac Catt, California State University–Chico; Martha Cooper, Northern Illinois University; Roseanne Dawson, University of Southern Colorado; Elizabeth Faries, Western Illinois University; Suzanne Fitch, Southwest Texas State University; James Floyd, Central Missouri State University; Thurman Garner, University of Georgia; Kathleen German, Miami University; Dennis Gouran, Pennsylvania State University; Gail Hankins, North Carolina State University; Susan A. Hellweg, San Diego State University; Kelly Huff, University of South Alabama; Larry Hugenberg, Youngstown State University; Diane Ivy, North Carolina State University; Robert Jackson, Ball State University; Fred Jandt, California State University–San Bernardino; Lcdr. Keith Maynard, U.S. Naval Academy; Linda Medaris, Central Missouri State University; Kathleen Morgenstern, California State University–Fresno; Mark Morman, Southern Utah State College; Greg Olson, Marquette University; Patricia Palm, Mankato State University; Mary Pelias, Southern Illinois University; Robert L. Phillips, Longview Community College; Steve Rendahl, University of North Dakota; Michael Schliessman, South Dakota State University; Larry Schnoor, Mankato State University; Bill Seiler, University of Nebraska; Paul Shaffer, Austin Peay State University; Mark Shilstone, University of Missouri; Lee Snyder, Kearney State University; James Stewart, Tennessee Technological University; Cathy Thomas, Morehead State University; Susan Thomas, University of Illinois; Nancy Wendt, California State University–Sacramento; Donald Wolfarth, University of Wisconsin–Eau Claire.

Authors do not write books. We write manuscripts. When a manuscript arrives at a publishing house, editors turn it into a book. All great books have been "worked on" by a great book team of editors, designers, and production people. We therefore thank the book team who get credit for the beautiful book you are holding in your hands.

Terry Brennan, Executive Editor, has worked tirelessly with us from the moment we signed the contract for this edition. We also want to thank:

Sheila Meyer, Vice President Development, Production and Manufacturing

Ellen Bedell, Development Manager

Deborah Shaw, Rights and Research Manager

Peter Schiller, Production Manager

Christian Stolte, Art Manager

Michael S. Hanna, Professor, University of South Alabama

James W. Gibson, Professor Emeritus, University of Missouri-Columbia

PART 1

Speaking and Listening

CHAPTER 1

INTRODUCTION

OBJECTIVES

After reading this chapter you should be able to:

1. Name three areas of your life in which public speaking skills can contribute to your success, and explain how improved speaking skills can make those contributions.

2. Explain how a course in public speaking requires self-disclosure.

3. Differentiate among ethical, unethical, and ethically neutral speaking behaviors, and provide examples of each.

4. Explain what a model is, and specify the defining features of a process model of communication.

5. Identify, define, and explain the following elements in the process model of communication: physical and emotional context, source/encoder, channels, verbal and nonverbal messages, decoder/receiver, physical and psychological noise, and feedback.

6. Name and explain the three features that set public speaking apart from other forms of communication.

OUTLINE

Objectives
Outline
Abstract
Imagine
Introduction
  Purpose of the Book
  Definitions of Terms
    Public Speaking
    The Public Speaking
    Course
Why We Speak
  To Express Ourselves
  To Provide Information
  To Persuade Others
  To Entertain an Audience
Ethics of Speech Making
  Ethical Issues in Public
    Speaking
  Ethical Standards in Public
    Speaking
The Process of Public Speaking
  Why the Audience Is
    Gathered
  When You Speak

Where You Speak
Events that Precede and
  Follow the Speech
    Source/Encoder (Speaker)
    Channels
    Messages
    Decoder/Receiver
    (Listener)
    Noise
    Feedback
Public Speaking Separated
  from Other Communication
  Behavior
  Structure
  Formality
  Anxiety
Text Goals and Overview
Summary
Key Terms
Application Questions
It's More Fun to Know
Self-Test for Review
Suggested Readings
Notes

ABSTRACT

Skill in public speaking can contribute to personal and professional success. Ability to speak well contributes to leadership and self-confidence. This fact implies certain ethical responsibilities inherent in public speaking activity. You must know what you are talking about, reject fraud and deception, measure your limits carefully and honestly, know and understand your position on controversial issues, and adopt a standard of honor. Public speaking skills grow with understanding how the constraints and influences of a particular context, setting and occasion require a speaker to adapt.

IMAGINE

"So, what are you going to take this term?" asked the young woman's father. He was proud his oldest child was about to begin her college career, and as usual, Dad had a lot of questions.

"Well, they have a fairly straight-forward set of general education requirements. You know, English, math, history, science and physical education. And they have a public speaking requirement. I'm signed up to take public speaking, and I'm a little nervous about it."

""Yes. I was too." Then Dad said, thoughtfully, "You know, in retrospect, that was one of the most useful courses I ever took."

INTRODUCTION

Congratulations. Your decision to take this public speaking course was wise. People who know how to communicate typically have greater success than those who do not. They know how to share knowledge, to persuade, to motivate. They seem to have control of their lives. They are trusted and sought out by others.

In this course, you will learn how to get your ideas across, how to inform and persuade an audience, how to stimulate and motivate people. Speaking skills are relevant in small groups and whenever you are trying to persuade. Some are relevant to one-on-one discussions with a colleague or even when you are talking on the telephone. People who seem successful, who sell themselves and their ideas to others, who exercise power, and who have influence, know how to use the techniques you will practice day after day in this course.

Public speaking skills can help you attain personal success in three areas: (1) your private life, (2) your professional life, and (3) your public life outside work. As you increase your public speaking skills, you will gain self-confidence. In turn, this strengthened image will cause other people to place greater confidence in you. [1]

Purpose of the Book

The two-fold purpose of this book is to provide a thorough description rich with examples of how to make a successful public speech, and how to solve the various problems involved in learning to make an effective presentation.

Definitions of Terms

In order to assure a common ground of understanding, we will define a number of terms throughout this chapter and this text. You will find a glossary at the end of the text, as well, that compiles all of these definitions.

Public Speaking

Public Speaking is oral communication in a one-to-many setting, usually occurring face-to-face. Your private life can be powerfully affected by increased self-confidence in your ability to express yourself. To illustrate, one student tried three times to give a speech in his first public speaking class. He was so nervous and unsettled that he could not push himself through the classroom door when his name appeared on the speaking schedule. His avoidance behavior also extended to other important areas of his life. He reported having difficulty meeting people. He once made an appointment for a job interview but could not make himself go to it. He had a difficult time asking women for dates and found criticism nearly intolerable. He seldom asked for help, even when he was lost, preferring to wander aimlessly until he found his way. He said that blaming others and expressing anger were strategies he used to hold people away.

Even so, this student finally completed his public speaking course. In a brief "exit essay" for use in helping other students, he wrote:

> *I can't believe it. A year ago, even three months ago, I would never have thought it possible to get through this course. Each time I got through a speech, I felt like I'd done something impossible. In time, as I learned how to do it, I began to feel easier. I sure wasn't wonderful, but I sure feel wonderful now.*

His experience is a testimonial to the value a public speaking course can have in your private life.

If you are one who experiences some discomfort thinking about making a speech, it may help you to know you are not alone. In a timeless survey, people were asked to identify their greatest fear or anxiety. Of the more than 2500 people surveyed, 41 percent listed public speaking as one of their greatest fears. Only 18 percent identified death as one of their greatest concerns.[2]

In addition to affecting your private life, public speaking skills can have a tremendous impact on a developing career. Effective presenters tend to become visible people. Visibility generates opportunities. Public speaking skills call attention to the speaker's thinking and reasoning, to the quality of the speaker's thought. They advertise without bragging. They lend credibility. They make it possible to contribute reserves of energy and knowledge in many different settings. Generally, people who are perceived as more powerful become more powerful.[3] To illustrate, two graduates entered a large paper company in the same month, right out of college. One learned to apply the public speaking skills she learned in college to a variety of business contexts, and she could really persuade. The other student, a young man, had similar intelligence but lacked communication skills. The woman used her public speaking skills every day; the man avoided such opportunities. After six years, the woman was in a high-ranking management development position, while the man's climb up the corporate ladder was nowhere near as rapid. In a letter to one of the authors the woman wrote:

We have many opportunities to speak in public. © David Young-Wolff/ PhotoEdit

> I volunteered to give an update speech concerning a quality committee I am a part of. (I would never have considered it before your course.) I gave the speech. I was hardly nervous, and since you weren't there, I'll have to tell you, I was great. I was the only speaker who didn't hang on the podium; I went into the audience. I used no notes—only the overheads I'd made. I used the techniques you taught in Public Speaking.
>
> There were about two hundred people in attendance, and over the next few days, it seemed that at least half of them complimented me. The vice president in charge of technology congratulated me and asked my supervisor for details about my career.
>
> It was fun and rewarding. I have the invaluable lessons you teach about speaking to thank.[4]

Numerous social groups provide opportunities to speak. For example, PTA, Kiwanis, church groups, the community garden club, and countless other gatherings provide opportunities to contribute what you know—and to practice speaking skills. In these contexts, if you can make an effective presentation, your ability to make a contribution to others increases. As you gain recognition and respect, your ideas take on greater persuasive force.[5]

The Public Speaking Course

The Public Speaking Course is the course which focuses most or all of its attention on the public speaking activity. In a public speaking course you will learn to present yourself and your ideas by building on the commonsense knowledge you already possess. For example, you already know much about what constitutes effective speech making. You can tell when a speaker holds your attention or successfully meets your criteria for a good speech. You also know when a speech does not go anywhere, lacks focus, or seems shallow and unsupported.

In a public speaking course you will use your common sense knowledge to work hand in hand with your instructor and with the other students. While the course will draw on your knowledge and experience, it also will ask you to tie new information to what you already know.

Your instructor will help you develop a clearer sense of purpose, organization, and style, and will be glad to answer your questions. In addition, your instructor will provide comments and suggestions about your classroom presentations. Make a point of getting to know this person, who is a valuable learning resource.

This book will help, too. It includes many examples drawn from students and from consulting experience. In some cases, the illustrations have been invented. Yet, each one *shows* you as well as tells you how to improve your speech making. Even so, effective public speaking requires hard work. The payoff from taking this course is directly related to how much effort you put into it.

WHY WE SPEAK

People give speeches for at least four general reasons: (1) to express themselves, (2) to provide information, (3) to persuade others, and (4) to entertain an audience.

To Express Ourselves

We often talk to make our feelings known. The way we feel about rap music, the Academy Award movie or some celebrity's private life is something we often like to share. It is our way of saying, "This is me, and this is what I like."

Many speeches are self-expressive. In public speaking classes, teachers often assign a self-expressive speech early in the term in order to provide students an opportunity to talk about topics with which they are most comfortable.

To Provide Information

Sharing information is the way people learn. All people are both teachers and learners! Speeches to inform have the main goal of passing information to the listeners.

Information is critical to our decision-making processes, too. Speakers serve an important function when they provide information that will help others to arrive at informed decisions.

To Persuade Others

Persuasion is the process of influencing other people—trying to change attitudes or behavior. Speakers commonly attempt to persuade their listening audiences. These arguments, all taken from student speeches illustrate student speakers trying to persuade their classmates:

1. Ford's products are more innovative than General Motors'.
2. Women are far more socially sensitive than men.
3. The International Monetary Fund helps reduce the likelihood of financial disaster around the world.
4. Portugal is one of the best-kept secrets for an ideal European vacation.
5. The nine justices of the Supreme Court do not practice equal opportunity.

To Entertain an Audience

People often speak to entertain, not only in public, but in small groups and one-to-one situations as well. Their goal is to hold listener attention agreeably, and to divert or amuse the listeners. Speeches to entertain do not require that listeners must be doubled over with laughter. We can be entertained and amused without such overt behavior. Three speech titles suggest the approach some students have taken to assigned speeches to entertain:

1. What is Santa Hiding Behind that Beard?
2. Why do Doctors and Lawyers Always Practice their Professions?
3. Hammers, Nations, Streams, Departments, and Showers Have Heads. Why don't they have Feet?

ETHICS OF SPEECH MAKING

Public speaking skill implies certain ethical responsibilities. **Ethics** refers to the study of moral values, of rightness or wrongness. Ethical questions arise often when people plan for and deliver speeches. For example, is it right to influence another person's behavior? Are right and wrong absolutely opposite? Or do they range along a continuum of behavioral choices? Do a speaker's worthy goals ever justify the means used to achieve them? When you set out to change attitudes or behaviors, when you inspire people to adopt a new course of action, your motives come into question. Unfortunately, ethical decisions are rarely easy to make.

To illustrate, Paul Johnson chose to present his ideas on financing the government to his public speaking class. In his research Paul discovered there are billions of dollars in the "underground economy." That represents a huge revenue loss in uncollectable taxes. Paul found that individual income taxes could be reduced by about 20-percent if many of the "cash businesses" in the United States paid the taxes they owe.

Paul had a problem. One of his good friends operates a local roofing business that offers "discount for cash work." Their regular price for roofing a house is $1.00 per square foot, or $2,000 for a 2,000 square foot house. But if the customer pays in cash the charge is only $1,700. The discount is possible because Paul's friend does not report or pay income or social security taxes for his employees when he is paid in cash.

Paul had planned to say he felt money from all business and personal sources should be taxed. He was going to use the government's financial problems as the basis for this argument. But after talking with his friend, he discovered that the IRS does not treat all taxpayers alike. Paul decided the taxes his friend pays, although not as much as he would pay if he reported his cash business, are at least a "fair share." As a result, Paul redesigned his speech to argue that all people and business should pay their fair share of taxes, but no more than their fair share. He avoided talking about the particulars of the federal and state tax laws related to his friend's cash business, but he did quote the IRS's own statements that the tax laws do not treat all taxpayers equally.

What do you think? Was it ethical for Paul to ignore the legal features of the problem, only to focus on what he and his friend defined as a "fair share?" Was it ethical for Paul to advocate civil disobedience?

Ethical Issues in Public Speaking

Richard Johannesen identified some basic ethical issues that every speaker should consider:[6]

1. Can ethical standards be flexible, or must they be absolute?
2. Is it okay to follow a minimum standard, or must we always shoot for the highest possible ethical level?
3. Do the ends justify the means? Are questionable persuasive techniques permissible when a worthwhile goal can be achieved?
4. Is it ever permissible to lie? What constitutes a lie?
5. Is it ever permissible to create intentional ambiguity—to cloud an issue?
6. Is television advertising that clouds the truth in vagueness and ambiguity unethical?
7. Is propaganda ethical? Is persuasion propaganda? Is, then, persuasion ethical?
8. Is name-calling ethical?
9. Is the masculine assumption in language adequate to describe the hopes and dreams of both men and women?
10. Is there an ethic involved in matters of taste?

Think through your ethical choices carefully. If you violate the ethical code your audience subscribes to, and if anyone in the audience discovers this violation, your credibility and your ability to influence the listeners will surely suffer, not only for the short term but for the long term as well.

Because public speaking can influence others, and because public speaking always takes a listener's time and energy, you have an obligation to *be prepared every time you speak*. Know your subject, examine the evidence, and develop solid and sensible arguments. Assume your classroom audience has the same motives as any other important group. Prepare thoroughly—it's your best guarantee of success.

Preserve your listeners' choices. Listeners have a right to know all the critical information related to a decision you want them to make. As a general rule, you would be wise to provide it.

Ethical Standards in Public Speaking

In summary, you have an ethical responsibility to follow these time-honored standards of appropriate behavior:

1. Play it straight. Do not try to deceive.
2. Do not try to keep critical information from your audience.

3. Test your evidence carefully.
4. Avoid exaggeration.
5. Present information as accurately and honestly as possible.
6. Know what you are talking about.
7. Learn how to measure your limits.
8. Reflect on your position on controversial issues and have clear reasons for your points of view.
9. Take care that you do not dishonor yourself or anyone else.
10. Value human diversity.

THE PROCESS OF PUBLIC SPEAKING

Public speaking happens at a particular time, to a particular audience that has gathered in a particular place for a particular purpose. Public speaking occurs in a rhetorical field. **Rhetorical Field** refers to the combination of context, setting, and occasion in which an audience understands itself to exist. The members of the audience understand that they constitute an audience. They understand why they have assembled, and they understand that certain rules control what communication behavior is okay and what is not in that context. The members believe in these rules and subscribe to them. So, if you want your speech to succeed, you must conform to listener expectations within the physical, social, psychological, and temporal environment of the speech.

Why the Audience Is Gathered

Every audience knows it is an audience! The members know why they have gathered and they know what is appropriate and inappropriate behavior for their situation. For example, members of a symphony concert audience know it is inappropriate for people to carry on private conversations during the performance. That is why people who do so are considered rude, and why other members of the audience may very well ask the talkers for silence—or demand it.

Clearly, why the audience is gathered controls what its members expect to gain from their membership in it!

When You Speak

When you speak is as much a part of the rhetorical field as what you may say. Will you present your ideas in the morning? People should be rested then. Will your presentation occur in the afternoon? People may be drowsy and tired. Will you present in the evening? Before a meal? Following a meal? Prior to the high point of the event? Following the high point of the event? Early in the program? In the middle of the program? Late in the program? Each of these questions about when you will speak has important implications for your success in presenting your ideas. Each one points to an important part of the context.

Where You Speak

Will you present out of doors? Inside? Will the speech occur in a small space in which everyone can hear you if you speak in normal tones? Or will you present in a large space requiring a public address system? If you are indoors, will the air be conditioned for the comfort of your listeners? Warm enough? Cool enough? Will the air be fresh or stale? If you are outdoors, will the temperature create a problem for your listeners? Will the weather hold? Will there be enough light? Will the listeners be seated or standing?

Events that Precede and Follow Your Speech

What is going to occur before and after your presentation? What comes before will set the mood of the listeners and may be so powerful that the listeners have difficulty paying attention to you unless you help them. What follows your speech can dampen its impact.

Thus, context plays an important part in communication success because it controls how people experience an event. Context can also influence a person's ability to listen, to be heard, or even to care. If a lecture hall is too warm or stuffy, for example, even the most motivated students will have difficulty concentrating on the lecture. **Physical context** refers to the physical and temporal surroundings in which a communication event occurs. **Emotional context** refers to the social and psychological portion of the communication event.

Exhibit 1.1 attempts to show the relationships among the component parts of a public speaking process during a single moment. The large box is the rhetorical field—the context, setting and occasion— in which the speech occurs.

Source/Encoder (Speaker)

The speaker is both **source** and **receiver** of information. The speaker gets an idea, then translates it into **codes** that allow the idea to take shape and to have substance. Thus, another term for speaker is **source/encoder.**

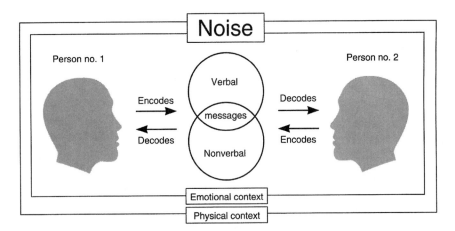

Exhibit 1.1 A Model of the Public Speaking Process

Channels

Speeches go through channels to listeners. **Channels** are the means of transmission, the vehicles through which messages are sent. In public speaking the term *channels* refers to sound waves (your words traveling through the air) and light waves (the visual messages presented by your gestures and posture). The channels are understood to exist in this model as part of the rhetorical field. The arrows in the model illustrate communication flow, but not channels, per se.

Messages

Whatever information a speaker sends into the rhetorical field is called a **message.** Messages in public speaking occur verbally as spoken words and words printed in visual materials, and nonverbally as visual and auditory signals such as gestures and tone of voice. Some are intended; others are sent accidentally. When information is available to listeners they can interpret it, and so the information is called messages.

Speakers always send more than one message at a time—the words and the way the words are presented. Listeners use *how* speakers say things to interpret *what* speakers have said. That's why speakers must sound like they care and look like they care, if they want their listeners to care.

Decoder/Receiver (Listener)

An audience is a group of individual listeners. Each listener decodes and interprets the messages he or she selects from the available package. The speech is part of that available package, but so is any stimulus material that comes from anywhere else in the rhetorical field. Thus, each listener is also a **decoder/receiver. Decoding** is the process of drawing information from the rhetorical field and then interpreting that information. People do not always decode skillfully, a fact which has created many interesting and perplexing communication problems between speakers and listeners.

Noise

Anything that interferes with the fidelity of message exchange between two people is called **noise.** Noise that occurs in the channels is called **physical noise.** (Example: Loud talking and laughter immediately outside the classroom door.) Noise that occurs inside people is called **psychological noise.** (Example: A listener's particular way of using language that's different from yours.) See Exhibit 1.2 for more examples.

Feedback

Feedback refers to messages listeners send back to speakers. In the process model of communication shown in Exhibit 1.1 feedback is represented by arrows. Feedback allows people to correct and control errors in how they understand and interpret each other. To illustrate, a puzzled look tells you your friend is having a difficult time understanding you, so you repeat yourself and give an example.

EXHIBIT 1.2

EXAMPLES OF PHYSICAL AND PSYCHOLOGICAL NOISE	
Physical Noise	*Psychological Noise*
Just as the professor writes a key statistics formula on the chalkboard, the lights go out. You cannot read the formula. Just as your friend begins to tell you how to get to her house, static in the phone line keeps you from understanding the directions.	A speaker uses very strong language to describe his feelings about your favorite political candidate. You resent it and begin to think of ways to respond to the speaker. Thus focused, you miss what the speaker says next. You respond with a strong emotion when your friend tells you about her illness. It shows on your face. She takes your response to mean that you do not want to hear about the illness, so she changes the subject.

PUBLIC SPEAKING SEPARATED FROM OTHER COMMUNICATION BEHAVIOR

The communication process model in Exhibit 1.1 can be used to describe all kinds of communication events. What, then, makes public speaking different from other kinds of events? Three characteristics set public speaking apart: (1) the structure of the event, (2) the level of formality, and (3) the degree of anxiety involved.

Structure

A public speech is highly structured. The parts of a good speech join smoothly together and are designed to form a single entity with a specific purpose, clearly identified arguments, and relevant supporting evidence.[7] The speech can be presented within certain time constraints. Listeners rarely talk, depending instead on the speaker to have organized ideas they can follow and grasp easily.

A conversation rarely flows so smoothly. One speaker interrupts the other, sometimes introducing entirely new and unrelated topics. People begin, stammer, and begin again. Arguments are rarely presented in a reasoned structure. People say what they think, talk around their ideas, and inject bits and pieces of evidence as they exchange information. Over time the arguments may emerge, but often, they are not specifically and clearly stated. Instead, the participants just seem to understand that they have reached an agreement without ever having stated what it is.

Three characteristics set public speaking apart from other forms of communication: (1) the structure of the event, (2) the level of formality, and (3) the degree of anxiety involved. © PH School

Formality

A speech is more formal than a conversation. Listeners expect a speaker to take control and to develop ideas critically and fully. In addition, listeners demand certain standards of behavior from speakers that would not apply to casual conversations. Public speakers try to adhere to more careful standards of grammar and of appropriate dress.

Anxiety

Anxiety also separates public address from casual conversation. Even the most experienced speakers may develop fairly high levels of anxiety before and during a speech. Listeners, too, feel greater anxiety in a public speaking situation than in a conversation. For example, when you listen to an important classroom lecture, you may experience more anxiety than when you are discussing the same material with your friends after class.

TEXT GOAL AND OVERVIEW

This text aims to help you identify and learn to use the skills that will make you an effective public speaker. Each chapter focuses attention on some critical set of public speaking skills and abilities. For example, many public speaking teachers like to have their students speaking right away. Your teacher may assign you to give a brief speech early in the term. **Chapter 2**, "Planning the First Speech," provides an overview of what to do and what to avoid. You will learn a little about choosing a subject and purpose, and what you can do to manage any communication anxiety you may feel.

Effective speakers understand of how people listen and of some of the common problems they have as listeners. **Chapter 3**, "Listening," explains how to work with the most common listening problems audience members are likely to encounter. Reading this chapter will also help you improve your own listening skills.

In **Chapter 4**, "Selecting and Narrowing Your Topic," you learn how to select exciting ideas for your speeches and how to focus those speeches on a single goal. You will also learn how to test your ideas to discover if they are right for a particular audience and rhetorical field.

Chapter 5, "Audience Analysis," carries the idea of how to adapt to listeners much further. You will learn to estimate what listeners already know about your subject and to adapt features of your speech to a specific audience group. Learning to analyze an audience is the most important part adapting to the situation. The skill with which you adapt to a particular group, gathered at a particular time and place for a particular purpose, will determine whether your ideas will seem credible to those listeners.

Chapter 6, "Supporting Ideas with Argument and Evidence," shows you how the evidence and argument you present work together with what an audience expects. You can't succeed if your audience doesn't have confidence in your ideas. This chapter will help you increase the credibility and strength of your arguments.

In **Chapter 7**, "Gathering Supporting Materials and Using the Library," you learn how to gather materials for a speech. All kinds of sources are available to you. You are surrounded by experts. Your school library—and the massive and wonderful on-line library called the Internet—hold nearly all the information available in the world! This chapter will show you how to use your library, your computer, and people around you to find relevant facts and opinions on almost any topic you can imagine.

Chapter 8, "Organizing the Body of the Speech," tells you how to organize the information you gather. This process clarifies and strengthens ideas and helps the listeners follow and remember your ideas.

Chapter 9, "Outlining the Speech," shows how to develop two kinds of outlines. A full-sentence planning outline helps you to study the structure of a speech to assure your ideas are complete and convincing. A speaking outline provides notes, including key words and phrases, reminders, marginal notes, and indications where your visual program fits into the speech. Use these notes as you deliver your presentation.

Chapter 10, "Beginning and Ending a Speech," identifies the purposes and types of a speech introduction and conclusion. Getting off to a good start and ending well can be the difference between a successful speech and one that does not succeed.

Chapter 11, "Language: The Key to Successful Speaking," shows you how to use language well. There is no substitute for careful choice of language, for it can determine whether the images you create in other people stimulate them. Further, language choice determines whether or not people understand you.

In **Chapter 12**, "Supporting Ideas Visually," you learn when to use visual supporting materials, what to support with visual aids, how to select the visual medium most likely to help you achieve your speaking goals, and how to design and use two-dimensional and computer-generated visual aids.

Chapter 13, "Delivery," focuses on both the verbal and nonverbal aspects of effective delivery. You learn about how different delivery methods, vocal control, and your nonverbal messages, such as gestures, eye contact, and personal appearance and behavior, affect how listeners perceive you and your message.

After you work through **Chapter 14**, "Informative Speaking," your speeches will be clearer, simpler, and more concrete and specific than you ever thought possible. You will understand how to get your ideas across, and your speech making will show it.

Chapter 15, "Persuasive Speaking," teaches you how to influence the attitudes, beliefs, and behaviors of listeners. Persuasion works when you and your message are credible and when your message appeals to both the rational and emotional needs of listeners. You will find very powerful tools in this chapter.

Although you may not deliver many special occasion speeches in your public speaking course, much of your life after college will involve such speech making. In **Chapter 16**, "Speeches for Special Occasions," you learn how to plan and present speeches of praise or tribute, inspirational speeches, and speeches for the sake of humor. This chapter will be useful long after you graduate.

This text tries to teach by example, with many current and relevant Exhibits and illustrations in every chapter. In addition, a number of annotated sample speeches have been collected into appendix A at the end of the book. The editorial and critical comments found in the margins of these sample speeches show you at a glance what the speakers were trying to do and whether or not they were successful. Use the sample speeches for models as you plan your own.

If you have a problem or a question about how to prepare, plan, or deliver a speech, or how to understand or adapt to your listeners, turn to appendix C, the "Troubleshooting Guide" at the end of the book. There you will find references to particular passages in the text that give time-tested and research-based advice.

SUMMARY

Your lifetime will offer many opportunities to speak in public. But even if you never give another speech in your life after this course, your study will pay you valuable dividends.

Improved public speaking skills increase your personal power. Along with increased power comes increased ethical responsibility. However, if you prepare carefully, strive to meet standards of honesty and accuracy, build arguments on sound evidence, and realistically assess your strengths and weaknesses, you will find that you can meet the expectations and motivations of a listening audience. You can use the power of public speaking to make important contributions that less skillful people cannot hope to make.

You already have a basic idea of what constitutes a good speech, but you may need help in expanding on and structuring that knowledge. Begin by thinking of public speaking as two-way phenomenon that occurs in a rhetorical field. The components of the communication process (source/encoder, channels, messages, decoder/receiver, noise, and feedback) each play an important part in your overall speaking success.

Public speaking is generally more formal and more carefully structured than other forms of talk and often produces greater anxiety. Yet, your overall speaking effectiveness is likely to improve with practice.

KEY TERMS

Channels	Ethics	Process model
Code	Feedback	Psychological noise
Context	Message	Receiver
Credibility	Model	Rhetorical field
Decoder/receiver	Noise	Source
Decoding	Physical context	Source/encoder
Emotional context	Physical noise	

APPLICATION QUESTIONS

1. If you were going to develop an original communication model, would you develop a linear model? A process model? What elements would you include? Why? With a few of your classmates, develop a communication model that represents the public speaking situation.

2. What criteria help you to judge possible candidates? Would you include John Kennedy? Winston Churchill? Jesse Jackson? Ronald Reagan? Why or why not? Would you include Oprah Winfrey? Hillary Rodham Clinton? With two or three of your classmates, develop a list of the twentieth century's greatest speakers. Compare your list to those of other groups of classmates. Are the lists similar? Did the groups use similar criteria?

3. Name two successful people. What measures of success do you apply when making this decision? Have you ever heard either of these people give a speech? With a classmate, create a list of three or four successful people who you know. Then ask these people about their public speaking experiences. How often do they speak in public? Do they find it useful? Report your findings to the class.

IT'S MORE FUN TO KNOW

Public speaking has been an acknowledged skill, essential in humans since ancient times. Aristotle, Cicero, and Quintilian wrote extensively on this skill and established the basis for our modern studies. The contributions of other ancients is well described by J.W. Wills, "Speaking Arenas in Ancient Mesopotamia," *Quarterly Journal of Speech,* 56, (1970).

Wilbur Schramm developed one of the earliest and widely accepted models of communication in his work, "How Communication Works," in Wilbur Schramm (ed) *The Process and Effects of Mass Communication,* (Urbana, IL: University of Illinois Press, 1954). Since then, scholars have worked on refining and developing further these theories.

Because honesty and the ethical dimension is at the heart of all effective communication, the outstanding book on the role of ethics in communication by Clifford Christians and Michael Traber (eds) *Communication Ethics and Universal Values,* (Thousand Oaks, CA: Sage Publications, 1997) warrants examination by any serious public speaker.

We know how central effective communication is in theory, but recent studies have identified it as one of the major traits employers seek. Mimi Collins, "Who They Are and What Do They Want?", *Journal of Career Planning and Employment*, 57:1 (Fall 1996) 41, identifies communication skills as a primary skill which employers in the service, managerial, sales, and social service occupations must possess.

SELF-TEST FOR REVIEW

1. Name three areas of your life in which public speaking skills can contribute to your success.

   a. _____

   b. _____

   c. _____

2. Public speaking requires self-disclosure. Place a check mark ✓ next to each of the following statements that explains why:

   _____ a. Speech making requires you to talk about your beliefs and about the things, people, and events in your life.

   _____ b. Anyone who has ever listened to a speech knows if it is a good speech.

   _____ c. When you make an argument, you display your thinking.

3. Mark the following as either E (ethical), U (unethical), or N (ethically neutral):

   _____ a. Falsifying evidence

   _____ b. Rejecting ideas that seem doubtful because of a lack of evidence

   _____ c. Appealing to a listener's psychological needs

   _____ d. Deceiving listeners about your purposes and intentions, even when it is for their own good

4. Match the following terms and definitions:

   _____ a. Source/encoder

   _____ b. Channels

   _____ c. Decoder/receiver

   _____ d. Messages

   _____ e. Context

   _____ f. Feedback

   _____ g. Noise

   1. Any sign, symbol, or combination of signs or symbols that function as stimuli for a receiver

   2. Any source of interference or distortion in message exchange

   3. The location of an idea; the originator of a message

   4. Messages sent from receiver to source for correction and control of error

   5. The physical, social, psychological, and temporal environment in which a communication event occurs

   6. The means of transmission; vehicle through which messages are sent

   7. The mechanism or agent that translates messages into meaningful, comprehensible units

5. Name three features that set public speaking apart from other forms of communication.

a. _____

b. _____

c. _____

Answers: 1. a. Private life, b. Professional life, c. Public life outside work. 2. a, c. 3. a. U, b. E, c. N, d. U. 4. a. 3, b. 6, c. 7, d. 1, e. 5, f. 4, g. 2. 5. a. Structure of the event, b. Level of formality c. Degree of anxiety.

SUGGESTED READINGS

Foss, Sonja K., Karen A. Foss, and Robert Trapp. *Contemporary Perspectives on Rhetoric.* Prospect Heights, Ill.: Waveland Press, 1985. This one book constitutes your best source for insights into the thinking of I. A. Richards, Richard M. Weaver, Stephen Toulmin, Chaim Perelman, Ernesto Grassi, Kenneth Burke, Michel Foucault, and Jürgen Habermas—the dominating scholars in modern rhetorical thinking.

Littlejohn, Stephen W. *Theories of Human Communication.* 4th ed. Belmont, Calif.: Wadsworth, 1992. This book is a rich source of facts and ideas, and it is a virtual annotated bibliography of important research and theory about meaning, information processing, language use, and conflict.

Rybacki, Karyn, and Donald Rybacki. *Communication Criticism: Approaches and Genres.* Belmont, Calif.: Wadsworth, 1991. This book will help you to become a much more discriminating consumer of communication. This is not an easy read, but is well worth the struggle if you want to improve your performance skills since it also shows how discriminating listeners are likely to receive your ideas.

NOTES

1. The research literature about how self-esteem relates to personal success has become a virtual torrent since about 1970. Start with the most complete current work on self-esteem by Nathaniel Branden, *The Six Pillars of Self-Esteem* (New York: Bantam Books, 1995) for a thorough grounding.

2. See David Wallechinsky, Irving Wallace, and Amy Wallace, *The Book of Lists* (New York: Bantam Books, 1977), p. 314. More recently, see Howard Liebgold, *Curing Phobias, Shyness and Obsessive Complusive Disorders,* (Rocklin, CA: Prima Publishing Co., 1997), and "Ten Most Common Fears" at *http://www.tigerx.com/trivia/fears.htm*

3. For a substantial analysis of this thesis see Roderick M. Kramer, *Power and Influence in Organizations,* (Thousand Oaks, CA: Sage Publications, 1998); Mats Alvesson, *Communication, Power and Organization,* (New York: Walter de Gruyter, 1996), and, Theodore O. Prosise, *Bridging Chasms and Filling Gaps: Toward a Practical Social Theory of Symbolic Power,* MA Thesis, San Diego State University, 1996.

4. Virginia Silver, Personal letter, 5 November 1989. Printed by permission.

5. For one of the best discussions, see Charles U. Larson, *Persuasion: Reception and Responsibility* (8th ed) (Belmont, CA: Wadsworth Publishing Co., 1998)

6. Richard L. Johannsen, *Ethics in Human Communication,* 4th ed, (Prospect Heights, IL: Waveland Press, 1996)

7. See Robert A. Cocetti, "Understanding the Oral Mind: Implications for Speech Education," Paper presented at the Annual Meeting of the Central States Communication Association, (Chicago, 11-14 April 1991)

CHAPTER 2

PLANNING THE FIRST SPEECH

OBJECTIVES

After reading this chapter you should be able to:

1. Name and explain some common first speaking assignments.

2. Name and explain six fears surrounding the public speaking experience, and describe what you can do about any feelings of speech anxiety you may have.

3. Describe how you can relax the major muscle groups in your body, and name those major muscle groups.

4. Name and describe the most common mistakes speakers make and explain how to avoid making them.

5. Describe how to develop the first speaking assignment.

6. Compare and contrast general purpose, specific purpose, and thesis statement.

7. Explain how to organize a speech to inform and a speech to persuade, and describe how to organize a speech introduction and a speech conclusion.

8. Describe how to choose an appropriate style of delivery, and how to practice for a speech.

OUTLINE

Objectives
Outline
Abstract
Imagine
Introduction
What kinds of first speaking
assignments are most
likely?
What can I do about my
feelings of anxiety?
What can we suggest to
alleviate the fear of public
speaking?
How can I avoid making
common mistakes?
How should I go about
developing the first
speaking assignment?
Step 1. Select a topic.
Step 2. Determine the
purpose.

Step 3. Organize the ideas.
Step 4. Build support for
the ideas.
Step 5. Practice carefully.
Is there a preferred style of
delivery for the first
speaking assignment?
Summary
Key Terms
Application Questions
It's More Fun to Know
Self-Test for Review
Suggested Readings
Internet Activities
Example Speeches
Sample 1. My Personal Hero:
Aristotle
Sample 2. Speech of
Introduction
Notes

ABSTRACT

Speech teachers generally have two goals in mind when they assign the first speech: (1) they want students to practice and experience speech making as soon as possible, and (2) they want to know how they can best help their students—whether any students will require special instruction for particular speaking problems. This chapter will help you plan and develop your first speaking assignment. It will help you answer such questions as "What kinds of first speaking assignments are most likely?" "What topic should I speak about?" "What do I want from my listening audience?" "How should I organize my ideas?" "Should I use visual materials?" "What should I do about delivery?" and "Are there any recommended methods for practicing most effectively?"

IMAGINE

Morning Light Sanchez was surprised when, on the second meeting of her public speaking class, the teacher assigned a three-minute speech

Successful speakers take the time to think their speeches through, and they practice. © James L. Shaffer

to be given during the following week. She felt very anxious about it. Morning Light had been avoiding the required public speaking course for over a year, but now she had to complete it or she would not be allowed to take upper division courses. The assignment was to describe a personal hero, so it was easy for her to select her topic. Morning Light's aunt had raised her after her own mother had died when Morning Light was three years old. The title of her speech was, "I Call My Aunt My Mother." The speech was a rousing success because Morning Light knew so many wonderful things to say about her aunt. She talked about her aunt's courage and her generosity, and how these features of her personality had helped Morning Light follow the trail through childhood and adolescence.

INTRODUCTION

Experience shows that many students share Morning Light Sanchez's concerns when they have to make their first speech. The purpose of this chapter is to help alleviate those concerns by answering several questions beginning speech students ask. In a sense, this chapter is a brief summary of the remainder of the book. The advice you will find here is well grounded in communication research and practice. You will find the ideas presented here are developed more fully in coming chapters. This chapter provides brief answers to the following questions:

What kinds of first speaking assignments are most likely?

What can I do about my feelings of anxiety?

How can I get over fear of speaking in public?

How can I avoid making common mistakes?

How should I go about developing the first speaking assignment?

What kinds of first speaking assignments are most likely?

The first speaking assignment in a public speaking class is likely to be a brief one. The teacher wants to provide students an early opportunity to get up and give a speech. Most likely, the assignment will come before you will have had much opportunity to study such things as how to select a topic and how to organize the speech. This suggests your first speech will probably be an informative speech.

You may be asked to teach the listeners something about yourself, or about someone else whom you admire. Or you may be asked to tell a story—perhaps a family story that has come to be part of your family culture. You will probably be asked to talk about something you already know much about, although you may well also be expected to back up your ideas. Exhibit 2.1 shows some common first assignments and suggests how you might go about preparing.

What can I do about my feelings of anxiety?

Old fashioned anxiety—sometimes called "stage fright" and sometimes called "communication apprehension" or "communication anxiety"—remains one of the most intimidating parts of the first assignment for many students. This chapter will help you understand, manage, and use any communication apprehension you may experience. Indeed, that's where the chapter begins. If you do not want to read this material about communication anxiety, turn immediately to page 32.

To get over fear of speaking in public, be sure exactly what you are worrying about. The word *anxiety* refers to a generalized state of apprehension: distress or worry caused by perceived or anticipated danger or misfortune. When you experience feelings of dread similar to fear, and cannot put a finger on why, you are said to be anxious.

EXHIBIT 2.1

SOME COMMON FIRST SPEAKING ASSIGNMENTS		
Assignment	*Suggestions*	*Examples*
Tell a family story	Think about a story you heard often. Interview a relative asking to hear the story again. Ask the relative to help you identify the theme—the key idea—that underlies the story. Find a way to make that key idea important to the listeners.	One family tells each new generation the story of how a young man with no education and little money walked from Connecticut to Illinois as a young man, opened a blacksmith shop, and from that humble beginning, founded the company that still supports the family.
Describe your personal hero	A hero is someone admired for his or her courage, strength, ability, etc. Your personal hero might be living or dead, or, even some character from literature. Identify the features you admire, then show the listeners how these admirable features are important to you.	Ghandi, your parent, Harry S. Truman, Philip of Macedonia, Napoleon, a favorite teacher, the protagonist in your favorite novel.
Tell about your vocation or avocation	What you do for fun or for profit can make for very interesting listening. Do you play ball? Work as a lifeguard? Wait tables? Are you a weekend rodeo rider? Do you aspire to become a scientist? Musician? Do you play in a band?	See exhibit 2.5
Introduce your best friend	Get permission from your friend. Interview him or her. Think of the reasons why your friendship is so strong. What are the friend's features of personality and character that endear him or her to you? Present those to your listeners.	"Ladies and gentlemen, today I wish to introduce my best friend, Connie Esteph. She can't be with us today, but she's certainly here in spirit and in my mind. Three things stand out when I think of Connie Esteph . . . ."
Introduce a classmate	Interview the classmate. What organizations does she belong to? What does he do for fun? For work? What are her hopes and dreams? What are his immediate goals and aspirations? Why is she taking the course? What motivates him to do his best? What do you and your classmate share in common?	"Today it's my privilege to introduce our classmate, Bernie Esser, a sophomore from Boulder, Colorado. I was impressed with two things about Bernie when I interviewed him last Wednesday."

Continued

Exhibit 2.1 *continued*

Assignment	Suggestions	Examples
Introduce yourself	Try to imagine someone else making the introduction. What they would do is tell the things they think would make you attractive to the class. You can do the same thing without sacrificing your modesty. What features of your personality and style make you fun to be around? What makes you a good friend? Tell about those things.	"Today I'd like to tell you about a feature of my character that I think makes me a good friend. When it comes to loyalty, I . . . ."
Describe a favorite trip (or book, or town, etc.)	Stories about places you have been and things you have done make for very interesting narrative because they work at two levels: (1) they tell about you, and (2) they tell about the world you find interesting. Similarly, the things you read, the movies you see, the people you associate with, the organizations you belong to, are all excellent subject matter for narratives. Try to tell a story. And remember you don't really have a story unless you have some kind of tension and resolution.	The canoe trip that almost went sour because of an accident. The trip to the Grand Canyon that never was completed because you found a more interesting place along the way. The book you might have written yourself because you had a similar experience. The first time you jumped from the high dive at the pool. Your experience on the bunny slope. The day you learned females can play football, too. How you got into the school band.

A more specific type of anxiety—*communication anxiety*—sometimes occurs when certain people approach a communication situation they do not fully understand.[1] Possible unknowns include:

1. They do not know much about the audience.
2. They are uncertain about what is expected of them.
3. They are unsure how their ideas or their presentation will be received.
4. They feel ill prepared.

Anxiety is fear—fear of being hurt or fear of loss. The feelings are the same whether there is a real reason or merely an imagined one for the fear. Fortunately, nervousness can be managed.[2] And a very good case has been made for the value of a public speaking course as a means to the end of reducing communication anxiety. Indeed, Rubin, Rubin and Jordan[3] reconfirmed what other scholars have argued for years: there exists a clear relationship between communication competence and communication anxiety—the greater the competence the less the anxiety.

Six modern-day fears surround the public speaking experience for most people, and each one has implications for your choices of behavior. Exhibit 2.2 names those fears and describes certain implications.

EXHIBIT 2.2

SIX MODERN DAY FEARS	
Fear	*Implications*
1. Fear of being in the spotlight.	This fear relates to the nature of public speaking. The situation is designed to focus attention on the speaker. Audience members give you feedback as you speak. They nod, frown, smile, and so on. That puts you in the spotlight, but also provides you the best information you have about whether the audience is following your ideas. No matter how you think "the audience" is responding, remember individual members are listening to and enjoying your remarks.
2. Fear of performing badly.	In reality, speakers rarely embarrass themselves or come off as incompetent. If something unusual happens while you are speaking, you have only two choices for handling it. (1) Decide the situation is horrible, then come unglued. This does not seem a viable option. (2) You can decide to accept the unusual and adapt to it. If you decide the second, your audience will adapt, too—and will appreciate your leadership.
3. Fear of the audience.	Audiences want speakers to take control of the situation. Use the fact that audiences pull for speakers. If you get stuck, ask the listeners for help! For example, if you ask "Where was I? I just lost my place," an audience member will tell you, and be glad you asked.
4. Fear that your ideas are not good enough.	There are no uninteresting subjects—only uninterested people. Your real job is to tie your ideas to the world the listeners live in—their needs and feelings. People are always interested in the ideas they believe are relevant to themselves.
5. Fear that you, personally, are not good enough.	Everyone is human, therefore everyone has both strengths and limitations. An audience does not especially care about the whole story of your life. They care if you have something for them. From the listeners' point of view, you're good enough if what you have to say is relevant to them and worth their time to listen.
6. Fear of the unknown.	Reduce your uncertainty about the situation and the audience as much as you can. Count on the fact that this fear lessens with experience, and seek as many opportunities as possible to gain experience.

What can we suggest to alleviate the fear of speaking in public?

Learn as much about your audience as you can. Find out what is expected of you.

To assure a positive reception of your ideas, be sure they are relevant to your audience and well organized.

Prepare carefully, both by planning and by practicing until you feel prepared.

You should probably focus more on the content—subject matter and organization of ideas—than on the actual physical presentation of the speech. Your teacher expects you to be a little nervous, and probably will be more concerned with whether you understand how to put a speech together than your delivery skills. Those delivery skills will come as you practice and as you gain experience.

If you have any feelings of nervousness, try to relax and accept them, knowing that your teacher—and your classmates—will understand what you are going through.

Most importantly, try to accept the situation and let your personality show. People who like you in an interpersonal event will like you in a public speaking event too. Tell yourself you are okay, just the way you are.

You can also learn to control your nervousness, and to use those feelings to improve speech making. Here are some suggestions:

Keep your fear to yourself. Nervousness does not usually show. Moderate trembling is almost invisible. Do not apologize for your feelings, and do not try to force them to go away. Rather, accept your nervousness as normal, then concentrate on helping your listeners get your ideas. Try to channel the extra energy your nervousness generates into making contact with the listeners.

Visualize yourself being successful. Imagine yourself standing before a group who are enthralled with you and your ideas. Engage in positive self-talk.[4]

Practice working with your body. If you experience, as many students do, pounding heart, trembling hands and knees, rapid, shallow breathing, flushed face, and a combination of constricted throat and that "cotton mouth" sensation, say to yourself: "This is a normal, although unpleasant experience, but I can get my point across."

Teach yourself to relax. (When you are relaxed, negative feelings are unlikely.) Develop a systematic procedure for relaxing yourself, then learn to use it. First, identify your major muscle groups. Then practice tensing and relaxing these major muscle groups. At the same time, practice deep breathing exercises. Draw in a deep breath, then exhale slowly and completely. Continue these activities for about 15 minutes each day. Within a week or so you will be able to achieve deep levels of relaxation quickly. Exhibit 2.3 lists the major muscle groups in our body. Try to concentrate on each group as you work on relaxing.

EXHIBIT 2.3

A LIST OF MAJOR MUSCLE GROUPS

Feet and ankles
Calves, knees, and thighs
Pelvic girdle
Small of the back—the lumbar region
Abdominal muscles
Chest and upper back
Shoulders, upper back, and back of the neck
Upper arms, elbows, and forearms
Wrists and hands
Neck muscles
Muscles of the face—around the mouth, cheeks, eyes, frown muscles of the
   forehead.

Surround yourself with notes. Do not try to hide them. Use note cards, visual materials, etc. But do not become dependent on your notes. Use your notes to guarantee yourself you will not "get lost" during your speech.

Know and understand your listeners. Try to find out what the audience members already know about your subject and what they need to know.

Don't look for problems that don't exist. The audience is not out to get you. Sometimes members whisper to each other, stare at the ceiling, shuffle their feet, and even talk to each other, but this does not mean they are bored. It could mean they are listening intently, and are excited about your ideas.

Check out all arrangements carefully. Be sure you are comfortable with the layout of the room; that every piece of equipment is there and working. You are more-or-less in charge of the space. If you don't like something, you can probably arrange to get it changed, but only if you check out the arrangements in advance of the speech.

Talk only about things you know and care about. Then remember you are the expert on your subject matter. You know your speech better than anyone in the room does. You have prepared carefully. You have a clear, well supported point of view.

Prepare carefully and practice a lot. Practice until you are confident you know what you want to say and do.

Remind yourself that nervousness is normal. Pretend you are confident, even if you are not. Imagine yourself being confident. Tell yourself you are confident—your nervousness is normal, and can even be helpful.

Pause briefly before you start. A few beats give you the opportunity to collect yourself. They also give listeners a little time to adjust to the fact you are standing there and have something to say. You are building image and rapport with listeners when you take this pause.

There is no substitute for practice if you want to learn a new skill. © James L. Shaffer

Use your audience. Establish eye contact as much as you can. Talk **with** the audience rather than at them. Include the audience with words like "you and I," and "we."

Give yourself permission to make mistakes. You are not perfect—neither is anyone else. You are willing to give other people permission to make mistakes—why not give yourself the same permission?

How can I avoid making common mistakes?

The most common mistakes people make in public speaking revolve around a single theme. They do not think deeply enough about the needs of their listeners. Notice how all the common mistakes work together. If you make a change for the better in one area, you automatically improve all the rest. Exhibit 2.4 describes the most common mistakes, identifies the common listener response to the mistakes, and then suggests what to do. Each of these mistakes is easy to avoid.

Use Exhibit 2.4 for pointers as you plan and prepare for your first speaking assignment. If you do, most of the anxiety will go away and your speech should be a rousing success for you.

How should I go about developing the first speaking assignment?

The first speaking assignment can be easily developed if you follow a planned sequence of events. (1) Select the topic, (2) determine the purpose, (3) organize the ideas, (4) build support for the ideas, (5) practice carefully.

Step 1. Select a topic.

The best way to select a topic is to draw on what you already know. Sort through your life experiences for moments and activities that bring you greatest pleasure. (These are the topics you know well.) Choose a topic you can tie to your audience's interests and needs. Listeners must be at the center of your concerns. The critical question is, "What difference does this topic make to the listeners?" Exhibit 2.5 presents a checklist of questions you can ask that will help you select an appropriate topic for your speech. And Appendix D, on page 445 lists many speech topics that your listeners will find interesting.

Exhibit 2.4

THE MOST COMMON MISTAKES IN PUBLIC SPEAKING		
Mistake	*Listener Response*	*How to Avoid Making the Mistake*
1. Purpose of speech is not clear	"I can't figure out what the speaker wants from me."	Tell the listeners exactly what you want from them, and do so both at the beginning and end of the speech.
2. Speech is not relevant to listeners.	"I can't figure out why I should listen to this speech."	Tie the speech to the listeners' wants, needs, and interests. (See Chapter 5, Audience Analysis.)
3. Speech is badly organized.	"I can't follow the logic from one point to another."	Develop a clear outline, then make the transitions clear to the listeners. (See Chapters 8 and 9, Organization and Outlining.)
4. Speech includes unimportant or irrelevant detail.	"I can't process all the technical and meaningless details."	Include only the "need to know" materials. Provide necessary technical details in writing—both in visual aids and in a handout. Take the time to help the listeners by going through the details, using examples, metaphors, and the like, to help listeners understand.
5. Speech does not contain enough supporting material.	"I'd be more likely to believe if these ideas were backed up with stories, examples, and other evidence."	Provide examples, stories, quotations, and facts and figures to support your knowledge claims. (See Chapter 7, Supporting Materials.)
6. Delivery is boring.	"I can't pay attention to monotonous voice, sloppy speech, listless posture and gestures. This speaker doesn't seem to care—why should I?"	Practice. Think of the listeners as individuals. Try to talk with the listeners rather than at them. Use visual materials to help listeners pay attention.

Step 2. Determine the purpose.

A speech is a success when audience members respond by giving the speaker what she or he wants. Yet many speeches fail because the speaker does not know the purpose of the speech. Successful speakers

EXHIBIT 2.5

QUESTIONS THAT MAY HELP YOU SELECT A TOPIC

1. What is your favorite recreational activity?
2. What has been your most interesting experience since you began college?
3. What kind of job do you have? What kind of job did you have last summer? What kind of job do you hope to have after you complete your education?
4. What is the most important event in your life?
5. What is the most unusual feature of the neighborhood where you grew up? That you currently live in?
6. Who is the most unusual, most outstanding, most interesting, most important, or most powerful person you have ever met?
7. How, if at all, can listeners use information about this topic?
8. Does the subject matter make a difference the listeners don't know about?
9. Can you tie your topic to something listeners already know and understand?
10. Would you like any particular behavior or action from your listeners?

must be able to differentiate among (1) a *general purpose*, (2) a *specific purpose*, and (3) *a thesis statement*. The clearest—hence, most helpful—specific purposes focus on listener *behavior* rather than listener attitude. Exhibit 2.6 compares these three elements.

When you know what observable behavior you want from your listeners, everything else about effective speech making seems to fall into place naturally. In your early speeches we suggest you tell the listeners exactly what you want from them in your introduction. The sample thesis statements in Exhibit 2.6 show how to do this.

Step 3. Organize the ideas.

In large measure, what you want from your listeners controls how you should organize your ideas. In general, if your general purpose is to persuade, then you probably should consider either a problem-solution or motivated sequence pattern for organizing your ideas. If your general purpose is to teach or inform, then the subject matter will probably suggest an organizational pattern. Some of the easiest-to-use possibilities include (1) natural divisions of the topic, (2) time or sequence, and (3) spatial relationships.

Two of the easiest organizational patterns to follow, when you want some kind of change in policy are (1) problem-to-solution and (2) the motivated sequence. Exhibit 2.7 displays these organizational patterns side by side.

Your first speaking assignment will probably be a speech to inform. Typically, you can organize informative speeches by identifying and using the natural divisions of the subject matter. Some speeches lend themselves well to a time sequence. For example, if you were to teach listeners how to do something you might say: "First, . . . Second, ..." And so on. Other speeches can be organized by looking for the spatial relationships among the ideas. For example: describing

EXHIBIT 2.6

COMPARISON OF GENERAL PURPOSE, SPECIFIC PURPOSE AND THESIS STATEMENT

General Purpose	Specific Purpose	Thesis Statement
The broad intention that motivates a speech: to inform, to entertain, to persuade.	*The particular action goal of the speech. What you want the listeners to do, or be able to do, as a result of the speech.*	*Something you say in the introduction of your speech that gives the most important point or purpose of the speech.*
I want to inform the listeners about something they don't already know. (Inform)	I want my listeners to know (be able to describe) how to make gunpowder.	"You can make gun powder from materials you have in your home or can easily get."
I want to change what my listeners feel or believe. (Persuade)	I want the listeners to believe they should not wait for the newest technology to come out before they buy a computer.	"It makes no sense to wait until the newest technology comes out before you buy a computer."
I want to get the listeners to do something. (Persuade)	I want my listeners to contribute at least one hour's salary each month to the United Way.	"I'd like you to pledge one hour's salary each month to the United Way by filling out this pledge card."
I want to amuse or relax my listeners. (Entertain)	I want my listeners to anticipate a good time.	"I know you're going to enjoy your stay here at the Grand Hotel."
I want my listeners to believe something. (Persuade)	I want my listeners to believe inflation is worse than depression.	"Nothing could be worse for America than unbridled inflation."
I want my listeners to know something. (Inform)	I want my listeners to be able to trace the rise and fall of Russian communism from 1917 to 1992.	"The Russian revolution lasted seventy-five years."
I want my listeners to understand something. (Inform)	I want my listeners to be able to explain the root causes of tension between Israel and the Arab states.	"The tension in the Middle East has its roots in two things: religion and geography."
I want my listeners to support federal aid to Brazil. (Persuade)	I want my listeners to sign this petition I will send to our senators and representatives.	"Ladies and gentlemen, Brazil needs your help and your support."

EXHIBIT 2.7

PROBLEM-SOLUTION AND THE MOTIVATED SEQUENCE	
Problem-Solution	*Motivated Sequence*
1. A problem exists	1. Gather the attention of the listeners.
2. The problem is serious	
3. The problem is relevant to the listeners	2. Argue the need case (an abbreviated version of the first three items in the left-hand column).
4. This plan will solve the problem	3. Show how doing what you ask or suggest will satisfy the listeners' need or solve their problem.
5. The means are available to implement the plan	
6. The plan will not cause new, serious problems.	4. Visualize how it will be in the future—either following listener adoption of your proposal or if the listeners do not adopt your proposal.
	5. Call for action.

Is it ever ethical to claim to know something when you really don't?

how a structure is built or how to get from one place to another. Exhibit 2.8 will help you choose an effective pattern to organize such a speech.

In addition to a clearly organized body, every speech needs a beginning and an end. The introduction is important because it is when you gather listener attention and set them up for the speech. The conclusion is important because it is when you summarize your key ideas and leave the listeners thinking about what you want from them. So it is important to organize the introduction and conclusion carefully— and it is easy to do. Exhibit 2.9 shows how to organize an effective introduction and conclusion, and provides examples. The results from using this approach will not be elaborate or fancy, but they will work every time you give a speech.

Step 4. Build support for the ideas.

Each idea and argument in a speech must seem credible to your listeners. In addition, you will want your listeners to identify emotionally with what you are saying. These audience responses depend on the quality of supporting materials you use. **Supporting material** includes any verbal or nonverbal material you use to develop your credibility or to win acceptance for your knowledge claims. A **knowledge claim** is any statement suggesting you know something. In the sample introduction above the knowledge claims are:

EXHIBIT 2.8

QUESTIONS FOR CHOOSING AMONG THREE WAYS TO ORGANIZE INFORMATIVE SPEECHES

Natural Divisions of the Topic

1. Does the thing have parts—hands, arms, feet, legs, head, body?
2. Does the thing have related systems—respiratory, circulatory, skeletal?
3. Does the thing have departments or components—production, marketing, sales, legal, personnel?
4. Can you use a metaphor—roots, trunk, limbs, leaves?
5. Can you use natural elements or ingredients—flour, salt, sugar, milk, eggs, yeast?

Time or Sequence

1. Does the thing you want to teach suggest steps in a sequence—first, second, third?
2. Is there a natural sequence of events through time—morning, noon, mid-afternoon, evening?
3. Does the process include a series of steps—step one, step two, step three?

Spatial Relationships

1. Would it help to show directions—north, south, east, west?
2. Does the topic suggest inside-outside relationships?
3. Can you use top to bottom, near to far, or left to right as an organizational motif?
4. Does a geographical figure (star, triangle, square) suggest an organizational pattern?

1. We have a problem.
2. Mobile Bay is in danger of dying because of pollution.
3. The problem faces us all, and in many different ways.
4. Our health is at risk.
5. Our economy is at risk.
6. Nothing will be changed if we do not insist on the changes.

Two likely questions from the listeners tell you exactly what you must do to support the knowledge claims in a speech. The questions are: (1) How do you know? and (2) What difference does this make to me?

Suppose you want to support the argument "Mobile Bay is in danger of dying because of pollution." The listener question, "How do you know" fairly demands both expert testimony, and physical and scientific evidence of the extent and nature of pollution in the bay. The listener question, "What difference does this make to me" tells you to show the relevance of the problem to the listeners, and stimulate their emotional identification and involvement. And remember: a listener

Exhibit 2.9

Suggested Organization for an Introduction and a Conclusion

Steps in an Introduction	Steps in a Conclusion
1. Greet the listeners 2. Say who you are 3. State your topic 4. Say how your topic is important to the listeners	1. Summarize the main ideas 2. Add a final, motivated, up-beat comment that gives the speech to the listeners and lets them know you are through.

Example

"Good evening, ladies and gentlemen. My name is Demetrius Bell, and I am a life-long resident of this town. We have a problem I want to talk about. Mobile Bay is in danger of dying because of pollution. That's a problem that faces us all, and in many different ways. Our health and our economy are both at risk. And nothing will be changed if we—you and I and every other concerned citizen—do not insist on the changes."

Example

"So what have I shown you tonight? I think I've proved that Mobile Bay is dying from pollution. I have shown you how this situation puts us at risk, both economically and in terms of our general health. I have shown what must be changed, and that we must be the ones who insist on that change. Ladies and gentlemen, let us insist before it is too late. Let us insist now, tonight."

. . . Here the speaker circulated a petition.

has to see as well as hear a problem in order to identify with it. Show the listener by using vivid descriptions or photographs of the problem details—dead birds and fish floating on the surface, sludge washing ashore.

Step 5. Practice carefully.

Nothing substitutes for practice. Successful public speaking depends on practice. The pointers in Exhibit 2.10 are based on both research and experience.

Is there a preferred style of delivery for the first speaking assignment?

Good delivery is invisible. It does not call attention to itself. Listeners should not notice the delivery choices a speaker has made. Rather, the listeners should be concentrating on the ideas of the speech.

Choose carefully when you select a style of delivery—the physical aspects of presenting a speech. There are four styles of delivery: (1) manuscript speaking, (2) memorized speaking, (3) impromptu speak-

EXHIBIT 2.10

HOW TO PRACTICE FOR A SPEECH

1. Distribute your practice over many brief sessions, rather than spending the same amount of time in only one session.
2. Keep practice sessions brief. Two or three run-throughs each time will do the trick.
3. Practice in different contexts and settings—empty classroom, your living room, under a tree, while walking from one class to another.
4. Practice using any visual aids. Touch every switch, flip every chart. Work the bugs out of your visual aid program during practice sessions, not during the speech.
5. Use your notes to remind you of key ideas, but do not read from a manuscript, and do not try to memorize your speech.

ing, and (4) extemporaneous speaking. In general, extemporaneous speaking is much to be preferred because it provides many advantages over the others and few of the disadvantages. However, there are occasions when you might prefer to memorize the speech or read from a manuscript. Both of these styles are difficult to master. In general, you would probably be wise to avoid them.

Sometimes you simply can't avoid giving an impromptu speech. For example, you might be called upon without notice during a planning group meeting to describe the results of your past week's work.

Exhibit 2.11 will help you select the most appropriate style of delivery.

SUMMARY

Speech teachers ask students to give speeches early in a term in order to get them on their feet for practice, and to find out how they can best help individual students who may need extra attention. But having the first speech assignment due early in the term creates problems for students who have not had much experience with speech making. For example, discovering what to talk about may be problematic. Organizing the ideas and finding supporting materials might also present problems. And many students feel anxious about giving a speech. This chapter provided suggestions and examples for managing the most common problems speech students experience.

EXHIBIT 2.11

HOW TO SELECT THE MOST APPROPRIATE STYLE OF DELIVERY

Style 1. Manuscript Speaking   A style of delivery in which the speaker reads from a written document.

Advantages

1. Provides control over exact choice of language.
2. Allows control of sequence of ideas.
3. Allows exact timing.
4. Allows opportunities for cueing technical assistants

Disadvantages

1. Eye contact may be restricted to the manuscript.
2. The speech may sound stilted because of differences between spoken and written language, and because of reading skills.
3. Speaker may appear "wooden" because the manuscript "ties" the speaker to a particular spot and inhibits physical movement and any deviation from what's written.

Implications

1. Read the manuscript aloud many times.
2. Know how to pronounce every word.
3. Have at least one dress rehearsal during which you flip every switch, show every visual, turn every page.
4. Try to make the speech sound as though it is occurring to you for the very first time.
5. Concentrate on making and maintaining eye contact.

Style 2. Memorized Speaking   A style of delivery in which the speaker commits the speech to memory and delivers a word-for-word progression of ideas.

Advantages

1. Provides control over exact choice of language.
2. Allows control of sequence of ideas.
3. Allows exact timing.
4. Allows opportunities for cueing technical assistants

Disadvantages

1. Possible memory loss can lead to embarrassing silence.
2. Speech may sound memorized because of a lack of vocal variety, emphasis, and changes in rate.
3. Discourages audience response or interaction.
4. May increase speaker apprehension.
5. May increase listeners' apprehension about the speech.
6. Inhibits flexibility in idea development or change to meet the demands of the moment.

Continued

Implications
1. Practice fully.
2. Prepare a key-word outline to assist in memory.
3. Work on vocal variety.
4. Encourage audience interaction if that is appropriate, and be sure to look for nonverbal signs the listeners wish to interact (hands raised, eyebrows raised, head movements, etc.)
5. Learn the speech in parts so that you can re-arrange the parts to meet audience needs.

Style 3. Impromptu Speaking   A style of delivery that involves speaking without preparation or advance planning.

Advantages	Disadvantages
1. Allows immediate response to another's ideas without advanced planning.	1. Ill-planned remarks may be difficult for listeners to follow.
2. Speaker can take advantage of unexpected opportunities to make a point.	2. Possible loss of credibility because speaker seems inarticulate or less knowledgeable about a topic.
	3. Possible memory loss may inhibit full explication of ideas "on the fly."

Implications
1. Take a moment to organize your thoughts. Ask for this time and take it.
2. Make a few notes.
3. Begin with the four-step introduction outlined, above. (See page 38.)
4. Consider organizing around one of these simple, repetitive patterns:
   - "Tell them what you're going to tell them, tell them, then tell them what you told them."
   - Past—Present—Future
   - State idea—Explain idea—Support idea—Summarize
   - Three reasons: First—Second—Third

Style 4. Extemporaneous Speaking   A style of delivery that uses careful preparation but minimal notes—and is neither memorized nor read from a manuscript.

Advantages	Disadvantages
1. Encourages flexibility and audience adaptation.	1. Requires extra preparation.
2. More direct and spontaneous than either manuscript speaking or memorization.	
3. Speaker is free to interact with audience members.	
4. Listeners are more likely to view the speech as an interpersonal event that involves them as individuals.	
5. Increases speaker confidence.	

Implications
1. Prepare visual aids carefully—they are beneficial to both speaker and listener.
2. Focus on the audience. Think in terms of an interpersonal, interactive event where appropriate. Actually invite and take comments or questions from the listeners.

KEY TERMS

Anxiety
General Purpose
Specific Purpose
Thesis Statement
Problem-Solution Organizational Pattern
The Motivated Sequence
   Organizational Pattern
Natural Divisions of the Topic
   Organizational Pattern

Time Sequence Organizational Pattern
Spatial Relationships
   Organizational Pattern
Supporting Material
Knowledge Claim
Manuscript Style of Delivery
Memorized Style of Delivery
Impromptu Style of Delivery
Extemporaneous Style of Delivery

APPLICATION QUESTIONS

1. If people did not engage in public speaking, what effect would this have on society? Would society be better or worse? In what ways, and why do you think so?

2. Can you recall listening to a speaker who did not consider the audience? What effect did this have on the presentation and on the audience? How did you feel as you listened to the speaker?

3. Attend a speech on campus or in your community. Listen for evidence that the speaker is really trying to connect with the listeners. What did the speaker do to make you think he or she was trying to connect? How can you apply your insights as you plan and present your own speeches?

IT'S MORE FUN TO KNOW

The first speech often seems a daunting experience to students. Available evidence clearly shows that speakers who have negative thoughts about the experience before they speak are more nervous during the speech. Additionally, we know that positive thinking and seeing yourself as successful helps determine success. (Joe Ayres, "Coping With Speech Anxiety: The Power of Positive Thinking," *Communication Education*, 37:4 (October 1988), 289–296.)

Additional convincing evidence shows that positive thinking, relaxation activity, and preparation help reduce the level of anxiety in speakers (David Kondo, "Strategies for Reducing Public Speaking Anxiety in Japan," *Communication Reports*, 7:1 (Winter 1994), 20-26.)

Because our heart rate and blood pressure both increase with the approach of the speech, it is not surprising we feel uncomfortable. (See Michael J. Beatty and Ralph R. Behnke, "Effects of Public Speaking Trait Anxiety and Intensity of Speaking Task on Heart Rate During Performance," *Human Communication Research*, 18:2 (December 1991) 147–176, and, Charles H. Tardy, Michael T. Allen, Walter R. Thompson, and Mark P. Leary, "Social Anxiety and Cardiovascular Responses to Interpersonal Communication," *Southern Communication Journal*, 57:1 (Fall 1991), 25–34.)

This information helps us conclude that thorough preparation and practice, as outlined in this chapter, will help to reduce the physical and psychological anxiety that is typical in the first speech.

SELF-TEST FOR REVIEW

1. Name four reasons why people give speeches:
   a. _____
   b. _____
   c. _____
   d. _____

2. Why do so many speech teachers make early term speaking assignments?

3. Match each statement in the left-hand column with the number of the entry in the right hand column that best describes the statement.

   _____ a. "I want my listeners to know how to make gun powder."

   _____ b. "I want to change what my listeners believe."

   _____ c. "I'd like you to pledge one hour's salary each month."

   _____ d. "I want my listeners to believe they should buy a computer now."

   _____ e. "The time has come for you to buy a computer."

   _____ f. "I want my listeners to believe that inflation is worse than depression."

   _____ g. "Nothing is worse for a nation than unchecked inflation."

   1. General Purpose
   2. Specific Purpose
   3. Thesis Statement

4. Match each statement in the left-hand column with the number of the entry in the right-hand column that best describes why the listener is having a problem.

   _____ a. "I can't pay attention. This speaker doesn't seem to care about what she's saying."

   _____ b. "I can't tell what this speaker wants from me."

   _____ c. "I doubt this argument."

   _____ d. "I'm lost in all this jumbled up detail."

   _____ e. "I can't follow this argument."

   _____ f. "What does this speech have to do with me?"

   1. Purpose not clear
   2. Speech not relevant
   3. Irrelevant or unimportant details
   4. Not enough support
   5. Boring delivery
   6. Speech badly organized.

5. Mark the following statements: 1 = Good advice about practicing
                                    2 = Bad advice about practicing

   _____ a. All you really need to do is run through the speech one time.

   _____ b. Keep your practice sessions brief.

   _____ c. Always practice in the same place.

_____ d. Practice using your visual aids.

_____ e. Write out your speech and read from a manuscript.

Answers: 1. a. To express themselves, b. To inform, c. To persuade, d. To entertain. 2. To encourage practice and to diagnose any student speaking problems that must be addressed. 3. a = 2, b = 1, c = 3, d = 2, e = 3, f = 2, g = 3. 4. a = 5, b = 1, c = 4, d = 3, e = 3, f = 6, f = 2. 5. a = 2, b = 1, c = 2, d = 1, e = 2

SUGGESTED READINGS

Gass, Robert H. and John S. Seiter. *Persuasion, Social Influence and Compliance Gaining.* Boston: Allyn and Bacon, 1999. An excellent and quite practically written work on the basic processes of persuasion, replete with highly effective illustrative material. This is a first-rate source for understanding persuasion.

Jaffe, Clella. *Public Speaking: Concepts and Skills for a Diverse Society.* Belmont, CA: Wadsworth Publishing Co, 1998. This introductory text very effectively addresses student concerns and the most effective ways to prepare for the initial public speaking experience.

MacIntyre, Peter D. and J. Renee MacDonald, "Public Speaking Anxiety: Percieved Competence and Audience Congeniality." *Communication Education*, 47:4 (October 1998) 359-365. A most interesting study which has clear implications for students preparing for their first speech. The most anxious students perceived the audience as most friendly. These same students saw themselves as improving the most in their speaking performance.

INTERNET ACTIVITIES

You will find a lot of help for preparing your first speaking assignment on the Internet. Here are three good places to start.

1. The University of Kansas maintains a "virtual presentation assistant" at the URL: *http://www.ukans.edu/cwis/units/coms2/vpa/vpa.htm* Go there and browse through the links.

2. The library staff at O'Keefe Library, St. Ambrose University, have suggested a series of very likely speech topics at the URL: *http://www.sau.edu/CWIS/INTERNET/WILD/Hot/hotindex.htm#top* Each topic is linked to resource materials about that topic.

3. The broad diversity in our society is a wonderful source of strength and wisdom. The CLNet Diversity Page at the URL: *http://clnet.ucr.edu/diversity1.html* includes links to (1) Guides to Electronic Resources on the Internet, (2) African American, (3) Asian American, (4) Latinos, (5) Native American, (6) Multicultural and National WWW Service, (7) Women, and (8) Gay & Lesbian Studies. Any of these links will take you to a rich resource of information.

EXAMPLE SPEECHES

SAMPLE 1

MY PERSONAL HERO: ARISTOTLE

Introduction

Greeting and speaker's name. Speaker's qualifications to give the speech

Thesis statement.

Body

Aristotle's credentials

Clarifies the permanence and quality of Aristotle's contribution

Self-promoting

Conclusion

Summary

Kicker

INTRODUCTION

Good morning. My name is Martin Rousso. I'm a Political Science major in my second year. My personal hero has always been the classical Greek philosopher, Aristotle.

Aristotle lived 62 years, from 384 to 322 B.C. He was a member of Plato's academy for twenty years, and he was Alexander the Great's teacher. He founded a school in Athens called the Lyceum. But these are not my reasons for honoring him. Aristotle was the greatest thinker of his time, and his influence has never diminished.

BODY

Aristotle was the greatest thinker of his time—perhaps of all time. But he was not a writer. He was a teacher. What we know of his thinking comes in the form of notes that he made for his lectures. They weren't really edited into texts until some time in the first century by a Roman named Andronicus.

But what lectures they must have been. And what a far-reaching mind. Aristotle taught philosophy, science, logic, physics, biology, psychology, metaphysics, ethics, politics, poetics, and rhetoric. In each of these fields, his influence lasted for centuries. Even today, in the textbook for this course, you'll find references to Aristotle.

So Aristotle was, I think, the ultimate role model. I'd love to be like him. If it sounds conceited, nevertheless, I'd like to have fame and fortune, and to gain these things as a result of my good works and the quality of my thought. That's what Aristotle did. He was famous and wealthy even in his own time, and his contribution to western thought has lasted more than two thousand years.

CONCLUSION

You can meet Aristotle in nearly every department on our campus. He is there, in the textbooks, on the walls, and in the excitement that the teachers have for the long tradition of western thought.

Aristotle was the greatest thinker of his time or any time, and a personal role model for me. There's no doubt about it. He is my personal hero.

Thank you.

SAMPLE 2
SPEECH OF INTRODUCTION

Greeting and	Good morning, ladies and gentlemen.
Speaker's name and qualifications	My name is Ellen Cambridge, and I am a student here at Colorado State College.
	It is my privilege and pleasure to introduce Mr. William McKinley, our keynote speaker.

BODY

Clear statement of opinion	I have known Bill McKinley for the past twelve years. I have worked for him as one of his employees, and I have worked with him as a colleague on three environmental protection projects. I can assure you that Mr. McKinley has clear and firm ideas about how we should protect our environment.
Further qualification of speaker as expert	Bill has a bachelor's, a master's, and a doctor's degree in the areas of marine geology and microbiology. He has written two college textbooks on these subjects, and he has published more than fifty scholarly articles in the area. But you probably know him best as the author of the popular book *Save the Earth Now, or Never.*
Appeal to common interest	I know that you are concerned about the quality of our own environment here in Colorado. That's the focus of this conference. I am pleased that this is also what Bill McKinley wants to talk about.

CONCLUSION

So, it's my pleasure and privilege to introduce my friend and our keynote speaker.

Ladies and gentlemen, may I present Mr. Bill McKinley?

NOTES

1. Terri Freeman, Chris R. Sawyer, and Ralph R. Behnke, "Behavioral Inhibition and the Attribution of Public Speaking Anxiety," *Communication Education* 46 (July 1997), 175. See, also, Rebecca B. Rubin, Alan M. Rubin, and Felecia F. Jordan, "Effects of Instruction on Communication Apprehension and Communication Competence," *Communication Education* 46 (April 1997), 111.

2. Philip M. Ericson and John W. Gardner, "Two Longitudinal Studies of Communication Apprehension and Its Effects on College Students' Success," *Communication Quarterly* 40 (Spring 1992): 127. See, also, Lynne Kelly and James Keaten, "A Test of the Effectiveness of the Reticence Program at Pennsylvania State University," *Communication Education* 41 (October 1992), 361.

3. Rubin, Rubin and Jordan, *op. cit.*, 105–114.

4. A massive and growing literature support these recommendations. See Matthew McKay and Patrick Fanning, *Self-Esteem: A Proven Program of Cognitive Techniques for Assessing, Improving, and Maintaining your Self-Esteem* (Oakland, CA: New Harbinger Publications, 1987). See, also, Joe Ayres and Tim Hopf, "Visualization: Reducing Speech Anxiety and Enhancing Performance," *Communication Reports* (Winter 1992).

CHAPTER 3

LISTENING

OBJECTIVES

1. You should be able to name four subprocesses in listening.

2. You should be able to name the problems for listeners within each of the four subprocesses in listening.

3. You should be able to specify how a speaker can use the information about listener problems to adapt to the audience while giving a speech in order to help the audience members listen more effectively.

4. You should be able to describe how to improve your own listening behavior.

OUTLINE

Objectives
Outline
Abstract
Imagine
Introduction
   Model of the Listening Process
     Sensing
     Attending
     Understanding
     Remembering
   Sensing Problems
    What to Do About Sensing
      Problems
   Attending Problems
    Selective Perception
    Poor Attention Habits
    Attitudes and Needs That
      Interfere with Attending
    Low Message Intensity
   What to Do About Attending
     Problems
   Understanding Problems
    What to Do About Misunder-
     standing Problems

Remembering Problems
   What to Do About Memory
    Problems
Problems With Empathy and
   What to Do About Them
How to Develop Your Personal
   Listening Skills
   Concentrate on the Message
    and the Speaker
   Identify with the Speaker
   React to the Speaker
   Be Objective About the
    Speaker's Message
   Work Hard at Remembering
Summary
Key Terms
Application Questions
It's More Fun to Know
Self-Test for Review
Suggested Readings
Notes

ABSTRACT

This chapter describes the listening process and identifies the most common listening problems. It explains how to develop your personal listening skills, but its focus is primarily on how, as a speaker, you can help your audience listen more effectively. Most audience members do not acknowledge any personal responsibility for listening well. If you want them to get your message, you have to help them.

IMAGINE

A conversation overheard on campus.
   Girlfriend: "I've got a class coming up in 20 minutes. Man, I really hate to go to that class."

Boyfriend: "Why? It's your art history class, isn't it? I thought you loved art history."

Girlfriend: "I did, last term. But this term I have a prof who just can't seem to get it across. I mean, she speaks in a monotone, and she never turns the lights on—not even between the slides. And I don't think I can stand to look at another early Renaissance painting of saints and angels. It's impossible to listen in there, and I keep falling asleep."

Boyfriend: "Well, then, let's go to the beach."

Girlfriend: "Yeah! Sure! And make an F on the first midterm quiz? No way! I guess I'll just go in there and suffer."

INTRODUCTION

More than half of human communication behavior is listening. It is the primary way we gain information and receive impressions. Unfortunately, most people are not efficient or effective listeners because they lack certain listening skills. The fact that most people are not effective listeners creates an interesting challenge for public speakers. If you want your speech to be received by audience members, you have to help them listen more effectively. You can do that by studying the most common listening problems and then compensating for the effects of those problems.

Does careful control of what audience members listen to constitute an ethical problem?

Model of the Listening Process

Exhibit 3.1 presents a useful model of the listening process. It helps to identify the areas in which most listening problems occur, and by implication, suggests what you can do that will help audience members to listen more effectively.

As indicated by the model, the listening process goes on inside an individual, but always within a context (represented by the outer box in exhibit 3.1). **Context** refers to the physical, social, psychological, and temporal environment in which communication takes place. In a public speech, the context includes the room, plus everything in the room—people and their reasons for being there, furniture, noise, temperature, etc. This also includes everything the people brought with them. Thus one listener's toothache is part of the context. Another's tension is part of the context. Still another's emotional state is part of the context.

The inner box in exhibit 3.1 represents one individual listener in a particular context and shows the four internal elements of the listening process: (1) sensing, (2) attending, (3) understanding, and (4) remembering. Both the context and the listener determine how effec-

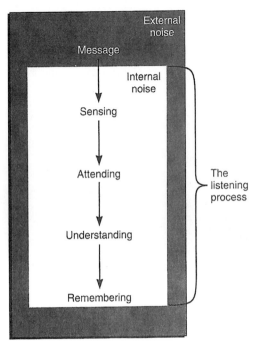

EXHIBIT 3.1 Components of the Listening Process

tively the listener performs in these four listening tasks. These listening process elements are also the areas in which most audience members are likely to make listening mistakes.

Sensing

The first element of the listening process is called **sensing,** which means receiving stimuli through the senses. People can hear us, see us, and touch us. If we are close enough, they can smell us. When we see people, talk to them, and then shake their hands, we are sensing them. We use all these sensory data to help us interpret what a speaker has said. However, if we have a problem with one or more of our sensory mechanisms, or if we're not paying full attention, we may overlook some important nonverbal signal and thus distort what a speaker has said.

Attending

Attending refers to the process of selecting and then focusing on certain stimuli. Because we are continually bombarded with billions of stimuli, we cannot process them all. We select some and ignore others. This attending process is unique to each person. Listeners, including audience members, pay attention according to what seems relevant and important to them in that particular context, and at that particular time. The speaker's task, of course, is to try to call listener attention to the truly important ideas in a speech.

Understanding

Understanding, the third element of the listening model, means interpreting and evaluating what comes in through our senses. Clearly, each individual understands what she or he hears in a private and personal way. If one of them creates a meaning different from the speaker's intended messages, miscommunication occurs. Thus the speaker's task is to do as much as possible to create shared meaning.

Remembering

For many people, remembering is the hardest part of listening. **Remembering** means bringing back to consciousness those things that are stored in our minds.

Because remembering is easy for some people and difficult for others, part of a speaker's task is to think of ways to help audience members remember the key ideas in a speech.

As you study listening problems in greater detail you will begin to understand how your choices as a public speaker can make a difference to your audience. You will also begin to see ways of improving your own listening behavior.

Sensing Problems

Problems with sensing are the result of either (1) damage to the sensory system or (2) noise. For example, some people have hearing and vision losses. People who cannot hear

Listeners communicate to speakers by giving feedback. What information could the speaker draw from these listeners? © Billy E. Barnes/Stock Boston

well may adjust by using a hearing aid or by sitting closer to the speaker. Someone who cannot see well may buy glasses to correct the problem. These simple choices are the responsibility of the listener, but some listeners do not make them.

People also may not be able to see or hear you well due to **noise,** which is any source of interference or distortion in message exchange. For example, outside sounds coming from open windows may make it more difficult for listeners to hear you, or poorly planned seating arrangements may make it more difficult for listeners to see you.

What to Do About Sensing Problems

Listeners depend on the speaker to help them compensate for such sensing problems. Wise speakers accept this responsibility both before and during the time they are making their presentations.

Train yourself to think about sensing problems. For example, to help correct for listeners' visual impairments, be sure that the lighting is adequate and that you are standing or sitting in the light. Use a good visual aids package. In a setting where there is external noise, ask someone to correct it.

Occasionally, some audience members talk so loudly that other listeners cannot hear the speaker. If this should happen while you are speaking, politely ask noisy audience members for quiet. Or consider asking the talkers to control themselves: "I'd appreciate it if you'd give me a chance to make my statement. It's hard for me to think when you're speaking so loudly, and I know some others can't hear." Other times, a simple request to the talkers, such as, "Please hold it down now so we can get our business managed, OK?" will do the job.

The best overall advice for beginning speakers who want to compensate for the sensory impairments of audience members is to speak up, slow down, and repeat yourself. Plus, consider using well-designed visual materials. If you speak loudly enough to be heard, are sure that you are talking slowly enough to be understood, repeat your message several times, and make sure listeners can see as well as hear your ideas, you will help your audience overcome most sensing problems.

Attending Problems

Listeners are more likely to have problems with attention than with sensing, primarily because attention problems are more universal and subtler. Four primary attention problems include: (1) selective perception, (2) poor attention habits, (3) attitudes and needs that interfere with attention, and (4) low message intensity.

Listeners can find it difficult to pay attention if the speaker does not help them.
© Bob Daemmrich/Stock Boston/PNI

Selective Perception

When we choose, unconsciously, to focus on one idea or one person to the exclusion of others, we engage in **selective perception.** Our experiences and interests cause us to listen carefully to some ideas and to ignore others.

Poor Attention Habits

Listeners generally have poor attention habits. Some listeners fake attention, others avoid hard listening, while some listen just for facts. For example, sometimes you may pretend to be listening to your instructor. Instead, you are thinking mainly about what you are going to do on the weekend.

Attitudes and Needs That Interfere with Attending

Some people listen to a message based on their attitude toward the subject. For example, strong feelings about AIDS, abortion, or gays in the military, may keep people from paying much attention to a speech on one of these topics.

Thus negative attitudes may decrease a person's ability to pay attention. On the other hand, positive attitudes increase attention. We pay attention to listeners who support our positions.

Our needs sometimes prevent us from paying attention to a speaker. For example, listeners might be too hungry or too sleepy to pay attention. Similarly, a speech that stimulates listeners' insecurity without providing any resolution creates a difficult listening problem. Or a listener's self-concept may prevent him or her from paying attention.

For example, students occasionally believe that they "can't do math." They avoid taking courses in mathematics, which sets up a self-fulfilling prophesy. Low self-esteem regarding math abilities would certainly influence these students' attitudes about a speaker's argument that all students should be required to pass at least two courses in statistics.

Low Message Intensity

A speech in which the speaker talks in a monotone, stresses nothing, and plods on at the same rate and pitch creates low message intensity. Most people find such low-intensity, "flat" messages impossible to listen to.

Speakers who do not seem interested in their own words also lack message intensity. Listeners find it very hard to give the speakers' ideas much credibility. On the other hand, some speakers stress nearly everything as "important." When this happens, nothing seems important because the listeners cannot identify the significant ideas. Thus, ironically, the stress-every-idea approach results in low message intensity.

What to Do About Attending Problems

Give people *reasons to listen*. We listen to ideas that seem tied to our lives. We want to know why we should pay attention to your words. Simply put, we must understand what is in it for us.

Listeners will be more likely pay attention if you are *a credible speaker*. Act and sound like you understand your subject and your mission. People are more likely to listen to a speaker who:

* Acts energetic and interested.
* Has good command of the subject.
* Supports ideas with examples and evidence.
* Is well organized.[1]

When strong feelings interfere with your listening, are you violating an ethical standard?

Understanding Problems

Understanding involves **shared meaning:** Both speaker and listeners have a similar perception of an idea or an object. Often, however, speakers and listeners do not share meaning. Understanding occurs only when both parties get the same meaning from the language. To illustrate, Exhibit 3.2 presents cases of misunderstanding. What the speaker said is not necessarily what the listener heard.

What to Do About Misunderstanding Problems

People understand ideas better if you put the ideas into a familiar framework or if the ideas deal with strong listener needs and wants. For example, assume that an audience is composed of factory workers, most of whom never went to college. If a politician tries to persuade this group using examples from the banking industry, the speech might fail because the listeners lack a familiar framework into which they can place the speaker's arguments. A wiser politician would use examples from the factory life that the audience members live every working day.

Similarly, an idea that bears on listeners' needs and wants will seem easier for listeners to understand than an idea that has no relationship to them. The same audience of factory workers would have little basis for listening to, paying attention to, or remembering a speech about economics theory, but they would have little trouble understanding and remembering a talk about changes in the way their pay would be calculated.

The context or setting also affects a listener's desire to understand. Consider how the following situations "set" listeners to understand certain ideas, and perhaps to ignore or misunderstand others:

EXHIBIT 3.2

SAMPLE MISUNDERSTANDINGS	
What was said:	*What was heard:*
1. "You need to be flexible in your approach."	Don't take a stand on anything.
2. "The Cardinals are an inexperienced team."	The Cardinals are a pushover this year.
3. "The only sensible weight-control program is to eat less."	You have to starve yourself to lose weight.
4. "Regular studying is the best way to get good grades."	Bookworms get the high marks.

1. Spring break on the beach in Florida
2. Student government meeting where a tuition increase is the topic for discussion
3. A rally to demonstrate opposition to the death penalty
4. A debate in the U.S. Senate on the right to filibuster
5. Japanese-American talks on ways to correct the trade imbalance

A speaker, then, must adapt to and be consistent with the context or setting in which a presentation occurs or risk that the listeners will misunderstand.

The attitudes people bring to a speech also affect their understanding. For example, in a student government meeting, a message opposing a tuition increase probably would be understood and accepted by most listeners. However the tuition increase might also be appealing to some listeners if it could be tied to additional student benefits.

Be brief, and organize carefully. A speaker who is brief and well organized is easier for people to follow. Use vivid language. Listeners are also likely to be more interested if the speaker uses vivid language, descriptions, or examples. For example, here's how one student used vivid language:

"When Mark McGwire hit 70 home runs in a single season he demolished the best known record in baseball. And he broke Babe Ruth's record in fewer games than it took the Babe to set it."

"If you want to see raw beauty, travel to Alaska. In just two days or so, you will see killer whales, eagles nesting, so many salmon spawning that the water appears to boil, a vast, wooded, and natural wilderness."

Make it easy for listeners to know when important ideas are coming. Such cueing devices as, "My second point is . . ." or "The best example of this situation I know is . . ." help listeners to know what is important.

Use simple language. For example, use the word *everywhere* instead of *ubiquitous*. Ideas can be impressive without using fancy words and phrases. Lincoln's Gettysburg Address uses simple language, but the message is profound and easy to understand.

Finally, fill your speech with examples, illustrations, and specific details. Many listeners reason from examples. They "perk up" when they hear the words *for example* because they know the material is much more likely to be interesting and concrete. Such examples make it easier for listeners to understand.

Remembering Problems

Most people have difficulty remembering. Some "have no head for figures." Others "can't remember names." Others "can't seem to recall the details." Others, still, lose key ideas. Indeed, a large body of scholarship makes clear we may forget more than 90 per cent of a message within 24 hours of hearing it![2] Why do we have so much trouble remembering?[3]

What to Do About Memory Problems

You can do a lot to help your audience remember your ideas. Listeners retain material that is (1) useful and interesting, (2) striking or out of the ordinary, (3) organized, and (4) visual.[4] These four elements tell you, in part, how to render speech ideas more memorable. Tell and show your listeners how your ideas are useful to them. Cast those ideas in terms, narratives, and examples your listeners can relate to and understand in a personal way—relevant stories, clear and vivid examples, compelling visual materials. Tie ideas to something your listeners find important or emotionally engaging.[5] People retain material best if they understand it the first time they hear it.[6]

Repetition also helps listeners to remember. Repeat every important idea more than once, and provide the repetition through more than one channel. For example, use a visual aid or tell a story that highlights the point. In your summary, state the point still again.

Develop a metaphor that will help listeners to associate your idea with something they know. Put your idea into a context listeners care about.

A touch of humor can help audiences remember.[7] For example, in a speech about southern hospitality, one student taught her classroom audience to treat everyone as though they were special. "Don't try to make them feel at home," she said. "If they wanted to feel at home, they would have stayed at home." This student's light touch made it easy for her listeners to remember her central idea.

Problems with Empathy and What to Do About Them

Listeners often find it hard to empathize (to identify mentally or physically) with the speaker. They may not agree with the speaker's position, or the message might not be consistent with what listeners believe.

As a speaker, this does not mean that you have to give up your ideas or your controversial position. It does mean, however, that you must find ways to present your position so that it is more likely to be accepted by your listeners.

Empathy also involves feedback. Most listeners are unwilling to interrupt a speaker, believing that such behavior is rude. Thus, as the speaker, you must pay attention to the nonverbal messages that listeners send while you are speaking. For example, listeners may nod, smile, frown, or touch their ear to indicate that they cannot hear you. These messages may be the most accurate feedback you will receive from your audience.

Occasionally, you may not be sure what some of the nonverbal messages from listeners mean. Ask questions if it appears that audience members are confused. You could say, "You seem to be confused about that last idea. Would you like me to repeat and explain it?" No one is likely to be offended. Do not allow poor use of feedback to result in a listening breakdown where listeners have lost all feelings of empathy with the speaker.

In an effort to create ongoing empathy with your listeners, *ask them to think about your ideas after you finish speaking.* Tell them what you want them to take away and remember.

In summary, speakers can do a lot to help audience members listen more effectively. By keeping in mind the most likely problems listeners have in sensing, attending, understanding, and remembering, and by taking overt action to help audience members overcome these likely problems, you can greatly increase the likelihood your ideas will get across to your listeners.

How to Develop Your Personal Listening Skills

If it's true that audience members sometimes have difficulty listening, it is also true that you, personally, may have similar difficulty in listening. All of us experience such difficulties from time to time.

Here, then, are some suggestions you can use to develop your personal listening skills.

Concentrate on the Message and the Speaker

Determine to listen and then concentrate your mind. Determine not to allow yourself to wander to another subject, and if you do find yourself wandering, come back to the speaker and the ideas. Concentrate. **Paraphrasing** (putting another's ideas into your own words) will help you check your understanding of the speaker's message. The speaker may say, "Procrastination is at the root of most of the problems the average college student faces." A paraphrase of that statement might be, "I must stop putting things off or I'll have more problems."

Take notes if that will help you concentrate. Ask yourself: "What is this speaker trying to tell me?" Translate the speaker's words and ideas into your own language. Identify—and highlight in your notes— the key ideas. Summarize to yourself often. Ask yourself: "What is the key idea here?" "What is the support for this key idea?" Such active participation on your part will help you concentrate more fully on what is being said.

Identify With the Speaker

Try to empathize with the speaker. **Empathy** involves trying to identify with the other person and to respond appropriately (as the other person perceives appropriate) to that person. Suspend your personal judgment and listen to ideas from the speaker's point of view. How does the speaker feel about the subject? What are the reasons for this feeling?

Think about the speaker's needs instead of your own! This will give you a different outlook and should help you listen more effectively.

React to the Speaker

Get and give feedback. Get involved. Nonverbal reactions, such as nodding, smiling, or shaking your head, give speakers an indication of how you feel about their ideas. If you cannot paraphrase what the speaker is saying, use nonverbal signals to show the speaker that the message is not clear. Shake your head or move your hands to show that you do not understand and that you want some clarification.

Be Objective About the Speaker's Message

Suspend personal biases and mental sets. Your position on a subject is important, but you will listen more effectively if you listen to the other side without arguing in your mind. Do not mentally debate each idea you hear. Your interest in the subject should aid, not interfere, with your reception of the message. Ask yourself:

* What has this speaker said?
* What is the major point?
* How clearly and well is it supported?

Try to listen with an open mind and to judge statements on their own merits. Summarize the speaker's ideas in your own mind.

Work Hard at Remembering

To commit a speaker's ideas to your short-term memory :

1. Take brief notes. Use key words so you will not miss any ideas and will be able to recall the information later. Try to use the speaker's organization in organizing your notes.
2. Consciously strive to set aside any distractions that tend to "jump out" in your mind during the message.
3. Put aside your personal motives so that you do not mentally argue with the speaker.

If you want to put information into "long-term storage," you may need to practice.

1. After twenty-four hours, go over your notes about a speaker's message.
2. Review them again after a week, a month, and after six months.
3. Write down all that you can remember and then compare this information with your notes from the listening event. You will be surprised by how much of the material you have retained.

SUMMARY

Because most people are not efficient or effective listeners, you will have to help them listen.

How effectively a listener performs in these four listening tasks (1) sensing, (2) attending, (3) understanding, and (4) remembering, depends on the context, the listener's skill, and on the speaker's ability to help the audience listen. Each of these listening tasks can be made easier when the speaker understands them and adapts to them.

Enhancing your personal listening skills requires (1) concentrating on the message and the speaker, (2) identifying with the speaker, (3) reacting to the speaker, (4) staying objective about the speaker's message, and (5) working hard at remembering.

To compensate for listeners' sensory impairments, speak up, slow down, and repeat yourself. Attending problems are best addressed by giving audience members reasons to listen. People will understand your ideas better if you put the ideas into a familiar framework or if the ideas deal with strong listener needs and wants. Help listeners remember your message by making your ideas useful or interesting, striking, organized, and visual. Repeat main ideas and associate ideas with something important or emotionally involving to listeners. Help listeners to empathize by tailoring your presentation them. Encourage their feedback. Of course, your audience will be able to listen more effectively if you know your subject well.

KEY TERMS

Attending	Remembering	Shared meaning
Empathy	Selective perception	Understanding
Noise	Sensing	

APPLICATION QUESTIONS

1. How important is feedback to you when you speak? Do you change what you say when you see how listeners react? How accurate is your perception of listeners' responses?

2. Some people believe that they can listen only part of the time and still receive the entire message. How true do you think this statement may be? How does your answer apply to your role as a listener?

3. What steps can a speaker take to help listeners attend to and remember a speech? Who is most responsible for reception of a message? Why?

IT'S MORE FUN TO KNOW

Although many people think that listening is something we "just naturally do and do well," there is much evidence to the contrary. The modern study of listening began in 1926 when Paul Tory Rankin ("The Measurement of the Ability to Understand Spoken Language," Ph.D. Dissertation, University of Michigan) studied the frequency of listening in our everyday lives. His finding that adults spend over 42 percent of their total verbal communication time listening was a startling discovery for early researchers.

Ralph Nichols began the study of listening in the field of communication with his emphasis on the effort needed to listen well, stressing that listening is not a passive activity. (Ralph G. Nichols, "Listening Is A 10-Part Skill," *Nation's Business*, 45: (1957), 56–58.)

More recently, the Sperry Corporation (a division of UNISYS) concluded that it was so important to improve employee listening that they initiated an advertising campaign on the rewards of listening and spent $10 million on listening research and an advertising campaign (Stacey Lucas, "Skills: Listening Is A Learned Art," *Working Woman*, August 1983, p. 45). We also know that many of the employees in large corporations spend nearly 60 percent of their day listening (Leland Brown, *Communicating Facts and Ideas in Business*, (Englewood Cliffs, NJ: Prentice-Hall, 1982), p. 380).

Research has revealed that intelligent people do not necessarily listen well (Robert N. Bostrom, *Listening Behavior: Measurement and Application* (New York: The Guilford Press, 1990). The advice of Ebling that we should train systematically so as to learn to listen effectively (A.O. Ebling, *Behavioral Decisions in Organizations* (Glenview, IL: Scott, Foresman, 1970) is pertinent today and provides us with a rationale for studying and working to improve our listening skills.

SELF-TEST FOR REVIEW

1. List the four internal elements of the listening process, as identified in the model in exhibit 3.1.

    a. _____

    b. _____

    c. _____

    d. _____

Mark each of the following as either true (T) or false (F).

2. To sense is to select and give attention to selected stimuli.   T   F

3. For many people, attending is the hardest part of the listening process.   T   F

4. A primary problem in attending involves selective perception. T F

5. When you say that a speaker is "flat," you are referring to the speaker's intensity level.   T   F

6. Empathic listening means that you listen to ideas from the speaker's perspective.   T   F

7. Note taking interferes with good listening.   T   F

8. A credible speaker increases the likelihood that audiences will pay attention.   T   F

Answers: 1. a. sensing, b. attending, c. comprehending, d. remembering. 2. F; 3. T; 4. T; 5. T; 6 T; 7. F; 8. T.

SUGGESTED READINGS

Wolff, Florence I., and Nadine C. Marsnik. *Perceptive Listening.* 2d ed. Orlando, FL.: Harcourt Brace Jovanovich, 1992. This book is written for all levels: students, businesspeople, and professionals. It is a very practically oriented and easily read work that stresses contemporary applications, the values of listening, and general guides for rapid improvement in listening skills.

Wolvin, Andrew, and Carolyn Gwynn Coakley. *Listening.* 5th ed. Dubuque, IA: Brown & Benchmark Publishers, 1995. This is probably the most comprehensive study of listening behavior available today. It combines all the relevant research findings and discusses at length the elements of the listening process. This is a must reading for anyone interested in listening.

NOTES

1. The most thorough source for information on this topic is James B. Stiff, *Persuasive Communication* (New York: Guilford Press, 1994), pp. 90–102.

2. See "Conversational Memory: The Effects of Time, Recall, Mode and Memory Expectancies on Remembering of Natural Conversations," *Human Communication Research*, 14:6 (Winter 1987), 203–229.

3. Consider Steven Golen, "A Factor Analysis of Barriers to Effective Listening," *Journal of Business Communication*, 27 (1990), 29-35.

4. For an intruiging exploration see Geoffrey Cowley and Anne Underwood, "Baby Boomers Attempt to Retain Memories As They Grow Older," *Newsweek*, 131:24 (June 15, 1998), p.49.

5. For a fascinating discussion read "When Fond Memories From Your Kid's Past Don't Even Ring A Bell," *Wall Street Journal,* October 28, 1998, p. B1.

6. See, for example, Michael Venturino, "Interference and Information Organization in Keeping Track of Continually Changing Information, *Human Factors*, (December 1997), 39:4, p. 532.

7. See Charles R. Gruner, *Understanding Laughter: The Workings of Wit and Humor*, (Chicago: Nelson-Hall, 1978), pp. 218–220.

PART 2

Designing the Speech

CHAPTER 4

SELECTING AND NARROWING YOUR TOPIC

OBJECTIVES

1. You should be able to name and explain four criteria that control selection of a speech topic.

2. You should be able to describe four techniques for generating speech topics based on what you already know.

3. You should be able to explain how to narrow a speech topic down to manageable limits, and specify why narrowing a topic in this way is essential to the success of a speech.

4. You should be able to define, describe, and differentiate among general purpose, specific purpose, and thesis statement.

5. You should be able to produce in writing an example of general purpose, specific purpose, and thesis statement for any topic about which you are knowledgeable.

OUTLINE

Objectives
Outline
Abstract
Imagine
Introduction
  Selecting a Topic
    Select a Topic Based on What
      You Know
      Brainstorm Your Ideas
      How to Brainstorm
        Your Ideas
    Select an Idea That Will
      Interest and Appeal to
      Your Listeners
      Examine Your Personal
        Library for Ideas

Look Through Your
    Personal Calendar or
    Daybook
  Narrowing the Topic
  Sample Speech: Give Blood
    for Tommy
How to Test the Thesis
  Statement
Summary
Application Questions
It's More Fun to Know
Self-Test for Review
Suggested Readings
Internet Activities
Notes

ABSTRACT

Public speakers must be able to select and narrow a speech topic so that it will (1) be appropriate for the occasion, (2) fit within time constraints, (3) meet audience expectations and abilities, and (4) be consistent with their own intellectual limits. To discover many potential speech topics, you should, brainstorm, search your personal knowledge, examine your personal library, and look through your personal calendar. Then narrow the topic and bring it into focus.

Narrow a speech topic by turning a general purpose (inform, persuade, entertain) into a specific purpose that tells what single, observable goal you want listeners to accomplish. Then develop and test a thesis statement. Selecting and narrowing a speech topic may be the most difficult and most important part of speech preparation.

IMAGINE

Temetra was having difficulty identifying a topic for her speech. "I just don't have any ideas," she said. Her professor suggested she open the dictionary to the first page under A to see how many topics she might find interesting. She wrote this list:

AA, Alcoholics Anonymous

AAA, Amateur Athletic Association

AAAL, American Academy of Arts and Letters

Aachen, a city in Germany

Aalto, a Finnish architect and furniture designer

AAM, air to air missile

Aar, a river in central Switzerland

Aaron, the brother of Moses

ABA, American Bar Association

Abacus, a device for making arithmetic calculations

Then the professor suggested: "Let's get on the Internet to see if we can find any topics that might interest you." Temetra and her professor clicked on the web browser icon on his computer screen and the computer displayed this image:

Temetra looked at the computer screen briefly and then allowed she could find many topics from this screen alone.

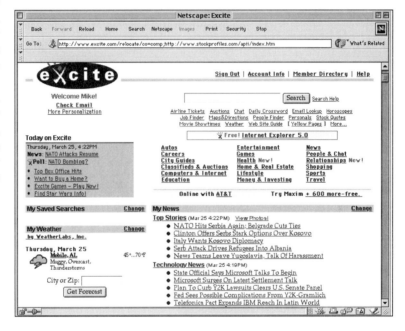

INTRODUCTION

Perhaps one of the most difficult tasks for beginning speech students comes when they must select and focus a topic. "What can I talk about? I don't know anything that will be interesting to my classmates." These concerns soon go away as students begin to think more clearly about the assignment. Likewise, the same students don't realize or believe that they can make their speech-

Marketers use survey research to help them identify important issues. © R. Sidney/Image Works

es far more interesting and effective if they focus and narrow down the ideas, then talk about interesting details.

The purpose of this chapter is to explain, step by step, how to select an interesting and provocative speech topic from things you already know, and then how to focus that topic clearly.

Selecting a Topic

A worthwhile, important, and interesting topic will sustain you as you plan, research, and organize your ideas. It will also motivate your audience members to listen to your speech. Four criteria should determine your topic selection. Choose wisely. Select a topic that:

Is it okay to "pick up" a topic from a list like the one in Appendix C, Possible Speech Topics, that begins on page 439?

1. you know about,
2. will interest and appeal to your listeners,
3. fits the occasion, and
4. can be discussed within the time constraints of your speech.

Exhibit 4.1 displays and describes these four criteria.

EXHIBIT 4.1

CRITERIA FOR SELECTING A SPEECH TOPIC	
The Criteria	*Explanation*
1. You are knowledgeable about the topic.	The more you know about a topic the less time you will have to study it, the more varied and interesting the "angles" you can take, and the more likely are you to make a successful speech.
2. The topic will be interesting and appealing to your listeners.	Some topics appeal more to men than women, more to young than old, more to liberal than conservative. Analyze your audience (See Chapter 5) to decide if your topic will be interesting and appealing to your listeners.
3. The topic fits the occasion.	Is the occasion formal or informal? Is the occasion ceremonial? Does the occasion suggest a topic? Does the occasion eliminate the topic you are thinking about?
4. The topic can be discussed within the time constraints of your speech.	Determine—ask—how much time has been planned for your presentation. Your topic must be manageable within that time limit. If you need 40 minutes to explain something, that topic will not be suitable for a 10-minute presentation.

Each of these criteria, in turn, guides your thinking about the topics you select for speech making. The following pointers and techniques will help.

Select a Topic Based on What You Already Know

Your speech topics should be based on what you know. Never talk about a subject you do not know well. This does not mean you have to be an expert on the subject. Rather, you should select topics about which you already have information. Then, if you do not know it well enough to give a speech, do some research. Exhibit 4.2 shows four techniques for selecting a speech topic based on what you already know.

Brainstorm Your Ideas

Brainstorming is a timed procedure for generating a large number of ideas quickly. You can brainstorm alone or with other people. Before brainstorming for a speech topic, be sure you have the necessary tools at hand—paper and something to write with. Here are two techniques for brainstorming for speech ideas.

EXHIBIT 4.2

FOUR TECHNIQUES FOR GENERATING SPEECH TOPICS BASED ON WHAT YOU ALREADY KNOW	
Technique	*Description*
1. Brainstorm you ideas.	Brainstorming is a procedure for generating a large number of ideas quickly. Set a time limit—say 5 minutes. Work quickly. Jot down as many ideas as occur to you, but don't make any judgments about the value or quality of the ideas until after the time limit has elapsed.
2. Search your personal storehouse of knowledge.	Think about the things you personally enjoy or find interesting. Work quickly. Jot down as many of these as you can within a time limit—say 5 minutes.
3. Examine your personal library.	The printed material you have personally collected suggest the things you find interesting and useful. Scan through them for ideas.
4. Look through your personal calendar or daybook.	If you keep a calendar or "day book," you have a record of how you spend your time. Chances are good you spend most of your time in activities you find personally relevant, interesting, and enjoyable. They make good topics for speeches.

EXHIBIT 4.3

TWO BRAINSTORMING TECHNIQUES

Related Lists

On a blank sheet of paper and draw six columns and label them who, what, when, where, why, and how. Then begin to write down whatever enters your head about each category. Then randomly draw lines that connect entries in the several columns. Since the columns occurred to you, and the entries within the columns occurred to you, you should be able to generate a number of possible speech topics from this activity.

Example

A LIST OF TOPICS BY POSSIBLE CATEGORIES

WHO	WHAT	WHEN	WHERE	WHY	HOW
Minister	Guns	Exam time	Home	To make war	Submarines surface.
Tenants	Airplanes	Spring	New York	For peace	Wine is aged.
Cops	Stereos	Evening	France	To study	Experience affects behavior.
Military	Music	Birthday	Superdome	For profit	Rumors are spread.
Friends	Income tax	Rainy days	The office	To learn	Exams are failed.
Models	Television	Vacation	Library	To pray	Exercise works.
Athletes	Classes	February 14	The park	For health	The body burns food.
Dentists	Books	Mardi Gras	The Mall	For pleasure	
Students	Vocabulary	Martin Luther King Day	Downtown	To remember	

Thought mapping

A visual pattern will help identify possible speech topics. Put your name in the center, draw several lines out from the center, then ask, "what do I like?" Working as rapidly as you can, jot down on each line whatever pops into your head. Then, within each category, jot down what occurs to you. Continue expanding the thought map in this way—without criticizing yourself or your work—for the planned time period. You will soon find many speech topics based on what you know.

Example

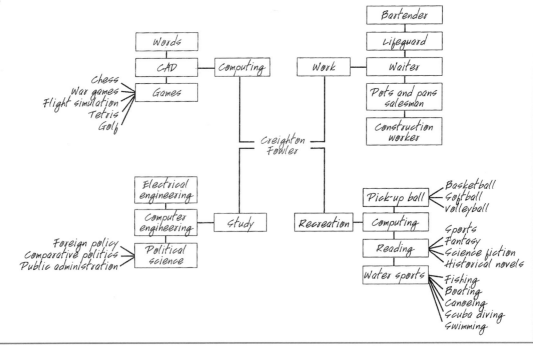

How to Brainstorm Your Ideas

Two related techniques have been especially helpful to students as they begin to brainstorm for speech ideas. One of these involves the use of related lists. The second involves thought mapping. Exhibit 4.3 shows how to use these two effective techniques.

Other combinations spring to mind. Try "Morning, Noon, Night." Try "North, South, East, West." Try "Family, Friends, Colleagues at work." Try "Favorite courses." Each of these—and many more combinations that will occur to you can provide the starting place for selecting and narrowing a speech topic.

Select an Idea That Will Interest and Appeal to Your Listeners

Have you noticed how people go to some movies you like, but stay away from others? Some students pay more attention in some classes than in others, and seem to enjoy them more. Some people don't attend sporting events while others never miss going. At least three factors, possibly more, account for these facts: (1) audience attitudes, (2) audience knowledge, and (3) audience interests. Keep these three factors in mind as you consider your speech topic in greater detail. How is your audience likely to react to your speech? Exhibit 4.4 should help. Chapter 5, "Audience Analysis," discusses this matter of adapting speech topics to the audience in greater detail. On line you

EXHIBIT 4.4

MAKE IDEAS INTERESTING AND APPEALING TO LISTENERS	
1. audience attitudes	Listener attitudes toward a topic will tell you how to handle your ideas. For example, a supportive audience is less likely to be critical than a hostile audience. If you knew in advance your audience was likely to be hostile, you probably would want to take extra care with the quality and depth of your supporting materials.
2. audience knowledge	People tend to take greater interest in things that are familiar to them than to things they don't know much about. They also tend to want to learn about things that interest them. So you would want to estimate how much the listeners are likely to know about your topic in order to help you settle on an approach.
3. audience interest	When they can make a choice, people generally spend time doing what interests them. In a classroom situation they don't always have that choice. If you can discover the audience's most probable interest level you can make adjustments accordingly. Show how your topic is relevant and important to them, and get them involved. Use vivid language and lively examples. Use carefully visual materials, etc.

will find a number of detailed and interesting sites on the Internet concerning audience analysis. To illustrate, go to the URL *www.AltaVista.com* and type "audience analysis" into the search window. You will get over twenty pages of links!

Examine Your Personal Library for Ideas

The reading materials you own and use suggest areas of your personal interest. Look at the magazines and books you have on your shelves. Do you find any common themes? For example, one student reported how she had not thought to give a speech about walking, although she reads widely about the subject and takes cross-country walks for exercise and because the activity helps her unwind. Her personal library included three books on cross-country walking, and she subscribes to a fitness magazine that usually carries interesting articles about the health benefits of walking. When asked why she hadn't though about this interesting topic before she said: "It just seems so ordinary."

Look Through Your Personal Calendar or Daybook

Many students keep track of their appointments and activities in a calendar or daybook. After a while, such a book begins to develop patterns that point to the owner's interests. To illustrate, Kim leBlank was willing to show her personal appointment calendar to one of the authors. Every Tuesday afternoon during the fall semester, Kim had scheduled an hour for cards with three of her friends. When asked, "What kind of card games do you like?" Kim said "We play stud poker for pennies." What an interesting idea for a speech.

Wise speakers get the help of others in focusing and narrowing their ideas. © Henley & Savage/Stock Market

Narrowing the Topic

Once you discover a topic that suits you and seems relevant and appropriate to the audience, the occasion, and the time constraints, you are ready to begin the real work of speech making. More speeches fail because they lack focus than for any other reason. Exhibit 4.5 provides a quick overview on how to narrow a speech topic. It is followed by more detailed explanations and examples for determining the specific purpose and for developing and testing a thesis statement.

EXHIBIT 4.5

HOW TO NARROW A SPEECH TOPIC	
Follow these Steps	*Explanation*
1. Specify the general purpose of the speech	(1) to inform, (2) to persuade, (3) to entertain
2. Determine the specific purpose of the speech	**TO INFORM** To know To understand To discriminate To comprehend To discern To perceive To conclude **TO PERSUADE** To believe To value To want To hope To request To urge To demand To feel To act **TO ENTERTAIN** To amuse To delight To charm To please To laugh To smile
3. Develop the thesis statement	Write out a complete declarative sentence, not a question. Now try it aloud. Does it convey what you want to say to your audience?
4. Test the thesis statement	1. Is the statement expressed in one, simple, declarative sentence? (It should not be a question.) 2. Does the statement summarize the purpose and main ideas of the speech? 3. Does the statement specify or at least clearly imply what you want listeners to remember after the speech? 4. Is the statement free of judgmental and figurative language?

Pointers for Narrowing a Speech Topic

1. Write a complete sentence, not a sentence fragment.
2. Write a sentence that includes the audience and a specific behavior you want from the audience.
3. Avoid judgmental statements and figures of speech.
4. Be sure the specific purpose sentence includes only one goal.
5. Specify a goal your listeners can give.

Exhibit 4.6 provides examples that compare topics, general purposes and specific purposes. Exhibit 4.7 shows how to make a specific purpose observable by using action language. Once you know what you want your listeners to do—observable behavior—everything else seems to fall naturally into place.

EXHIBIT 4.6

	COMPARING TOPICS, GENERAL PURPOSES AND SPECIFIC PURPOSES	
Topic	General Purpose	Specific Purpose
Music as a part time job	To inform	I want my listeners to know how they can use what they love to do as a part-time job.
End the workday with a workout	To persuade	I want my listeners to use the gym.
How to work with volunteers	To inform	I want my listeners to know three things about working successfully with volunteers.
Treat yourself to rest	To persuade	I want my listeners to get at least eight hours of bed rest each day.

Examine Exhibit 4.7 carefully. You will see that, in each case, the more observable specific purpose suggests what the speaker should do. For example, in order to assure the listeners could actually speci-

EXHIBIT 4.7

	MAKING THE SPECIFIC PURPOSE OBSERVABLE
Evaluation	Specific Purpose
Not specific	I want my listeners to know how they can use what they love to do as a part-time job.
Better	I want my listeners to specify at least three ways they can use what they love to do in a part-time job.
Not specific	I want my listeners to know three things about working successfully with volunteers.
Better	I want my listeners to specify three ways to help volunteer workers succeed.
Not specific	I want my listeners to participate in the blood drive.
Better	I want my listeners to give blood at the University Center this afternoon.
Not specific	I want my listeners to use the gym.
Better	I want my listeners to sustain an elevated heart rate for at least thirty minutes.

fy three ways to help volunteer workers succeed, the speaker would want to name the three ways, develop each one (including reference to the research that makes the suggestion credible), then repeat the three ways. The speaker might wish to use a visual aid to show the listeners the three ways. How much more interesting than "to know three things about working successfully with volunteers."

A complete sentence is a complete thought. A sentence fragment is a thought fragment. Fragments may pinpoint a speech topic, but they do little to indicate the specific or general purpose of a speech. Thus it is better by far to write out a complete sentence. Exhibit 4.8 compares complete sentences and fragments.

One way to assure your purpose is clear is to include your listeners when you write the purpose statement. The easiest way to do that is to write out what you want them to do, or be able to do, after hearing your speech—even if you never ask them for the behavior during the speech. Try to imagine the effect your speech will have on the listeners.

A simple case illustrates these ideas. One student speaker decided to talk about the annual on-campus blood drive.

Topic: The annual on-campus blood drive
General purpose: To persuade

Now the student needed a single, observable behavior she would like from audience members. "After giving this speech, I want my listeners to give blood in the on-campus blood drive." This effort to focus and narrow her idea resulted in a relevant and interesting topic with

EXHIBIT 4.8

COMPARING COMPLETE SENTENCES TO FRAGMENTS

Evaluation	Specific Purpose
Fragment	Violins and fiddles
Sentence	"I want my audience to be able to specify the differences between violins and fiddles."
Fragment	The larva of the butterfly
Sentence	"I want my listeners to be able to explain the process of metamorphosis."
Fragment	The speech mechanism
Sentence	"I want my listeners to be able to list the parts of the speech mechanism that are contained in the mouth."

EXHIBIT 4.9

Evaluation	Specific Purpose
INCLUDING THE AUDIENCE AND SPECIFYING LISTENING BEHAVIOR	
Not specific	"I want my audience to know about the French origins of many English words."
Problem	This statement does not specify what the speaker wants the listeners to do.
Better	"I want my audience to be able to explain how French words, such as *parliament, sermon, scarlet, chair, conversation, logic,* and hundreds more, came into the English language at the time of the Norman Conquest."
Not specific	"I want to inform my audience about how the word *crucifix* came into English."
Problem	The statement does not specify an action goal for listeners.
Better	I want my audience to be able to explain how the term *crucifix* came into English."
Not specific	"I want my audience to agree that the university should change to the semester system."
Problem	Agreement cannot be observed. What does the speaker want audience members to do? The speaker must work to achieve clarity and specificity, or listeners are not likely to figure it out.
Better	"I want my listeners to vote in the upcoming Student Government Association referendum on the proposed switch to the semester system."

a specific purpose the student could manage within the assignment's three-minute time limit:

Topic: The annual on-campus blood drive
General purpose: To persuade
Specific purpose: To persuade my listeners to give blood during the blood drive this afternoon

Here is the speech the student produced.

SAMPLE SPEECH

GIVE BLOOD FOR TOMMY
by
Carmen Maes

Good morning, classmates. As you probably know, my name is Carmen Maes. I thought you might like to meet a friend of mine this morning. He can't be with us here in the classroom, although I am sure he would rather be here than in his hospital room. Tommy is nine. He's a bright kid who is interested, more than anything else, in becoming an astronaut. And he has a good chance, too—even though he has something called pre-leukemia. He has intelligence, curiosity, wit, charm, and amazing self-possession for a nine-year-old.

Tommy has enormous brown eyes that seem to look beyond you. He smiles quickly and often. He seems at ease with people of every age. He is full of fun, and he is full of hope. What he doesn't have, and what he needs most, is your help. He needs blood, lots of it. And that can only come from people.

And not only Tommy. There are many people who need blood in this community every day, and there is only one place where they can get it.

Today, all day long, in the University Center, they're having a blood drive. They've come here, to our campus, because they know that a college campus is the best place to find a large number of healthy adults who have more blood than they need, and more caring and concern for their fellow man than anywhere else.

They've come here knowing that all they have to do to get help for Tommy is to ask you. They know that you've been helpful in the past. In fact, last year at this time, you gave about half the blood that they collected, citywide, in their whole campaign. In doing that, you gave back the lives, for a while, at least, to over a hundred patients who needed your help.

And now they're asking for your help again. I am asking for your help, too, for my friend Tommy. He needs you. He really, really needs you, and he knows you'll help. Will you walk with me, right now, over to the University Center—for Tommy and for yourself?

Do you think Carmen really thinks of Tommy as a friend? Would you find an ethical problem if she merely invented Tommy for persuasive effect?

Judgmental statements and figures of speech (metaphors, similes, analogies, personification, and so on) create confusion in a purpose statement, and they often seem trite. In addition, they usually do not specify an action goal. Exhibit 4.10 will help you avoid judgmental statements and figures of speech when writing specific purpose statements.

A specific purpose statement that includes more than one goal tends to confuse both the speaker and the listeners. Arguments and supporting materials are likely to go in two directions, and listeners are likely to be uncertain what the speaker wants from them. Be sure your specific purpose statement does not include connecting terms such as *and, but, however*, and such connecting punctuation as commas and semicolons. These are often indicators the sentence contains two or more ideas. Exhibit 4.11 illustrates the problem.

Finally, you should always seek a goal your listeners can give you. Otherwise you simply cannot succeed. In the examples provided in

EXHIBIT 4.10

AVOID JUDGMENTAL STATEMENTS AND FIGURES OF SPEECH IN A SPECIFIC PURPOSE STATEMENT	
Evaluation	*Specific Purpose*
Judgmental	"I want my listeners to believe that the Student Government Association president is a jerk."
Problem	Although the judgment tells what the speaker thinks, it does not specify what the speaker wants from listeners. Also, the statement would be clearer if the speaker had written an observable action.
Better	"I want my listeners to sign this petition to recall the Student Government Association president."
Judgmental	"I want my audience to know that the Greek-letter system on campus is corrupt and should be abolished."
Problem	"Know" seems misleading. The speaker probably means "believe." Even so, the statement does not specify what the speaker wants from the audience. Notice, also, that the statement includes two goals, neither of which is an action goal. The word *and* gives the clue.
Better	"I want my listeners to believe that the Greek-letter system on campus should be abolished."
Problem	Although the focus is better in this attempt, and although belief is a legitimate persuasive goal, what does belief look like? The goal is not observable, so developing the speech will be more difficult.
Still Better	"I want my listeners to join the Student Coalition for a Greek-Free Campus."
Trite Metaphor	"I want my listeners to know that the movement on campus to abolish our football team is *dead as a doornail.*"
Better	"I want my listeners to be able to describe the status of the Abolish Football movement on campus."

exhibit 4.12, audience members could only give the response requested in the last example. They could write a letter.

Thus you can see how five guidelines will help develop clear and specific purpose statements. Exhibit 4.13 is a checklist you can use as you evaluate your own specific purpose statements.

EXHIBIT 4.11

INCLUDE ONLY ONE GOAL	
Evaluation	*Specific Purpose*
Two Goals	"I want my listeners to agree with me that they should support student theater productions on campus, and buy a ticket to next week's play."
Better	"I want my listeners to believe that they should support student theater productions on campus."
Still Better	"I want each of my listeners to purchase a ticket to next week's student theater production."
Two Ideas	"I want my audience to know *and* believe . . ."
Three Ideas	"I want my listeners to know *and* believe *and* act . . ."
Better	"I want my audience to explain . . ."
Still Better	"I want my listeners *to be able to define* each term in the model."

EXHIBIT 4.12

SPECIFY AN ACHIEVABLE GOAL	
Evaluation	*Specific Purpose*
Not achievable	"The university library should be expanded."
Problem	Who can do this? Can the audience do this? Can the listeners expand the library? A student group could not. The Board of Regents could. Check to see if the goal lies beyond what audience members can give. Specify an achievable goal. What does *expand* mean? More money? More space? More books?
Much Better	"I want my listeners to write to the university president to ask that the library's undergraduate collection be enlarged."

The general purpose motivates a speech. The specific purpose is the particular action goal of your speech. The thesis statement, made in the introduction, gives the most important point or purpose of the speech. Exhibit 4.14 compares and contrasts general and specific purposes for student speeches on a variety of topics.

EXHIBIT 4.13

SPECIFIC PURPOSE CHECKLIST •

1. Does the specific purpose fulfill the assignment? (For example, if the assignment is to inform, are you trying to persuade?)
2. Is the specific purpose focused on the audience? (Does the purpose statement name and include the listeners?)
3. Does the specific purpose specify something for audience members to do? (Does it name an observable action—even if you do not plan to call for the action ["After this speech, I want my audience to be able to . . . "]?)
4. Is the specific purpose within listeners' capability? (They may not be able to change the system, but they can contribute to the cause, vote, sign a petition, make phone calls, and so on.)
5. Does the specific purpose matter to listeners? (Think about the listeners' perspective. What will they consider relevant and important?)
6. Is the specific purpose too trivial for listeners? (Topics that diminish anyone in the audience only give offense. A speech on how to wash the clothes, or how to sweep a room, or the best kind of paper clip tend to put listeners down.)
7. Is the specific purpose too technical for listeners? (How to run a regression analysis, what's wrong with today's camera lenses, how to select the right band width for your multimedia application, and celestial navigation in the south Atlantic may all seem overwhelming to your listeners.)
8. Can the specific purpose be accomplished within the time limits of the assignment? (You could not teach listeners how to play jazz music on a sax in one six-minute classroom speech. You could not even teach them how to finger the sax in that length of time. However, you might be able to teach them how to vibrate the reed.)

HOW TO DEVELOP THE THESIS STATEMENT

The **thesis statement**, made in the introduction, gives the most important point or purpose of the speech. Think of a specific purpose statement as planning and the thesis statement as something you say while you are giving the speech.

Specific purpose statements point to the planning a speaker has to do to accomplish the speaking goal. For example, if you wish to teach listeners how to make gunpowder, you need to discover, and then tell the audience, what materials to use, in what proportions, and where to find them. These considerations suggest the main ideas of the body of the speech. In the actual introduction, give your thesis statement: "You can make gunpowder from materials you have in your home or that you can get easily." Point to the main idea you are trying to get across. Exhibit 4.15 illustrates the difference.

Once you have prepared the thesis statement for your presentation, the last step is to test it. Good speakers test the phrasing when they plan a thesis statement.

EXHIBIT 4.15

SPECIFIC PURPOSES AND SAMPLE THESIS STATEMENTS

Specific Purpose	Thesis Statement
"I want my listeners to vote in this afternoon's Student Government Association election."	"You must vote in the Student Government Association election this afternoon."
"I want my listeners to think of buying a computer as they think of buying a car."	"Now is the time to buy your first computer."
"I want my listeners to write Representative Calahan in support of his handgun legislation."	"Representative Calahan wants to hear from you."
"I want my audience to make two changes in essay exam procedures: (1) provide a clear and accurate study guide and (2) return a hypothetical 'A' answer with each student paper."	"Two valuable improvements in essay exam procedures will help your students without inconveniencing you."
"I want my audience to be able to describe how to make gunpowder."	"You can make gunpowder from materials you have in your home or that you can get easily."

HOW TO TEST THE THESIS STATEMENT

Four questions will help you test the phrasing of a thesis statement:

1. Is the statement expressed in one, simple, declarative sentence? (It should not be a question.)
2. Does the statement summarize the purpose and main ideas of the speech?
3. Does the statement specify or at least clearly imply what you want listeners to remember after the speech?
4. Is the statement free of judgmental and figurative language?

The sample thesis sentences in Exhibit 4.16 illustrate the problems implied in each of these questions and show how to improve them. Each of the "Better" examples tells, in one sentence, the speaker's main idea, focuses listeners' attention on this main idea, and prepares listeners for what is coming in the rest of the speech.

EXHIBIT 4.16

IMPROVING THESIS STATEMENTS	
Evaluation	*Thesis Statement*
Wrong	"How much should you pay for a personal computer?"
Problem	The question might work as an attention-getting device in the introduction, but it does not carry any information. The main thrust of the speech is not clear. What the speaker wants from listeners cannot be determined from a question.
Better	"You can get a computer for about $1,000 that will run every kind of business software."
Wrong	"Federal government entitlements are wrecking our economy."
Problems	This claim is too general. An audience would not know what to do with it. There is no indication that the speaker has the audience in mind. What action goal, if any, does this statement point to?
Better	"Write to your congressperson and ask for a bill to end all farm subsidies above $25,000."
Wrong	"This is a good time for entrepreneurship."
Problems	This statement hides the main idea from listeners. Also, it does not suggest or imply any observable behavior.
Better	"This is a good time to borrow venture capital."
Wrong	"I want you to be able to explain how well built the new fine arts building is."
Problem	The goal is not clear. Listeners know that the speaker is asking them to learn, but what? What does the speaker want them to take away from the speech? Even such a direct sentence can confuse listeners.
Worse	"The new fine arts building is built like a battleship."
Problem	The figurative language seems trite, and the metaphor does not fit the situation. It raises the confusing question: Why would anyone build a building like a battleship?
Better	"The new fine arts building has an earthquake-proof foundation."

SUMMARY

There are millions of good speech topics, and you already know about thousands of them. Selecting a topic is not so difficult. Rather, the problem lies in selecting a topic that you are knowledgeable about, that relates to the audience, that fits the occasion, and that can be discussed within the given time constraints. Bringing the topic into focus around a clear action goal is the second part of the challenge.

Your speech topics should be based on what you know. Brainstorm ideas, search your personal storehouse of knowledge, look through your personal library, and examine your appointment calendar. The demographic makeup of the audience also often suggests and eliminates topics, as does the occasion and time constraints. All of these sources help you to locate a topic that you know and can care about.

What remains, then, is the task of narrowing the topic down to manageable limits. Begin with the general purpose of the speech. Do you want to inform, to persuade, or to entertain? This information tells you the mind-set that will help you most. For example, if your general purpose is to inform, the most helpful mind-set is that of a teacher. If your general purpose is to persuade, then in your mind, you must become an advocate or salesperson.

Regardless of the general purpose, the easiest and best way to determine the specific purpose of a speech is to think in terms of audience behavior. What single, observable behavior do you want from listeners? Guidelines for developing clear and specific purpose statements include writing a complete sentence that includes the audience and a specific behavior you want from the audience, avoiding judgmental statements and figures of speech, and specifying only one goal, a goal that listeners can achieve. When your specific purpose is stated in terms of one observable goal, everything else about speech making seems to fall into place. Know your specific purpose and know your audience, and you will know what you must do in the rest of the speech.

A specific purpose statement is part of speech planning, whereas a thesis statement is stated during the actual speech. State the thesis in the introduction as part of your effort to prepare listeners for what is coming. The thesis statement should be one, simple, declarative sentence, not a question. It should summarize the purpose and main ideas of the speech, as well as specify or clearly imply what you want listeners to remember after the speech. The thesis statement also should be free of judgmental and figurative language.

KEY TERMS

Brainstorming
general purpose
to entertain
to inform

to persuade
Specific purpose
thesis statement

APPLICATION QUESTIONS

1. Either alone, or preferably with one or more of your classmates, attend a speech on campus or in your community. Try to determine if the speaker has a clear purpose in mind. What is the topic? What is the specific purpose? Does the speaker have a thesis statement? How do you assess the quality of the speech? Do you think that the quality and effectiveness of the speech has anything to do with the speaker's focus? In your opinion, are the speech topic and focus appropriate to the audience and occasion? If not, why not? What changes could you suggest?

2. Visit the courthouse in your community or county during a jury trial. As you listen to the proceedings, can you identify how the bits and pieces of evidence and argument fit together? Can you infer how they relate to the attorney's specific purpose?

3. Drive down one of the busier commercial streets in your community. Let the things you see stimulate your thinking. Have a friend riding with you write down every possible speech topic that occurs to you as a result of this trip (or you can do this yourself after you park the car). What insight, if any, does this excursion generate in you about the number of potential speech topics?

IT'S MORE FUN TO KNOW

Here is a "picture" captured from the Communication Institute for Online Scholarship (CIOS) of Professor Dan O'Keefe's argument that explicitness is directly related to the persuasiveness of an argument.

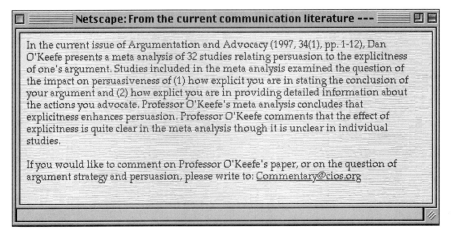

Netscape: From the current communication literature ---

In the current issue of Argumentation and Advocacy (1997, 34(1), pp. 1-12), Dan O'Keefe presents a meta analysis of 32 studies relating persuasion to the explicitness of one's argument. Studies included in the meta analysis examined the question of the impact on persuasiveness of (1) how explicit you are in stating the conclusion of your argument and (2) how explicit you are in providing detailed information about the actions you advocate. Professor O'Keefe's meta analysis concludes that explicitness enhances persuasion. Professor O'Keefe comments that the effect of explicitness is quite clear in the meta analysis though it is unclear in individual studies.

If you would like to comment on Professor O'Keefe's paper, or on the question of argument strategy and persuasion, please write to: Commentary@cios.org

"O'Keefe's article arrives at slightly different conclusions than do the writings of Robert H. Gass and John S. Seiter in *Persuasion, Social Influence, and Compliance Gaining* (Boston: Allyn and Bacon, 1999) pp. 183-184, in which they believe the evidence, at this point, is inconclusive on the issue of effectiveness of explicitness versus implictness. Perhaps these differences in perspective are best understood by the fact that Gass and Seiter examined a series of individual studies, rather than dealing with the issue in meta analysis."

SELF-TEST FOR REVIEW

1. List four guidelines for selecting a topic.

   _____

   _____

   _____

   _____

2. Which of the following items influence whether a speech topic is appropriate to an audience or an occasion? (Check the correct answer.)

   _____ a. The occasion.

   _____ b. The weather.

   _____ c. The time limits.

   _____ d. The clothes you are wearing.

   _____ e. Features of the audience.

   _____ f. Your personal knowledge.

3. An old friend of your parents is offering you unsolicited advice about your speech class. Which of the following is good advice? Place a "✓" mark next to each piece of good advice.

   _____ a. "Ask the person who invited you to speak what she wants you to talk about. Talk about that subject no matter what. Otherwise, you're bound to miss the audience."

   _____ b. "It's okay to wing it sometimes, if you aren't sure what you're talking about. Most of the time the listeners won't know your subject anyway."

   _____ c. "A good way to find a topic is to search through your own library. You are what you read, you know!"

   _____ d. "If you keep a daybook or diary, you'll have no difficulty finding a topic. All you have to do is look at that to see how you spend your time. With some thinking, you'll locate a lot of speech subjects there."

   _____ e. "You can develop about one main idea per minute, so if you have a ten-minute time limit for your speech, you can introduce and develop about ten main ideas."

   _____ f. "You always have to have at least two main ideas. Remember the rule about outlining? If you have an A, you must have a B."

   _____ g. "It's not wise to have more than one specific purpose for a speech."

4. Match each statement on the left with the stage of speech planning on the right to which it applies.

    ____ a. Think in terms of observable behavior.

    ____ b. Inform, persuade, or entertain.

    ____ c. Be sure that your statement points to the main idea you are trying to get across.

    ____ d. Does the statement summarize the purpose and main ideas of the speech?

    ____ e. Write down the intention that motivates the speech.

    ____ f. Write a complete sentence, not a sentence fragment.

    ____ g. Check to see if the statement expresses one, simple idea in a declarative sentence.

    ____ h. Make this statement in the introduction, while you are giving the speech.

1. Specifying the general purpose.

2. Determining the specific purpose

3. Developing and testing a thesis statement.

5. Which of the following is the best definition of a thesis statement? (Circle the correct response.)

a. A statement in the introduction of a speech that specifies the most important point

b. A statement designed during the planning stages of the speech that tells what you want from listeners

c. A general goal for a speech

d. A specific purpose statement that tells what the speech is all about

6. Write an appropriate thesis statement for each of the following specific purposes.

a. "I want my listeners to vote in the Student Government Association elections tomorrow."

b. "I want my listeners to sign this petition in support of abolishing the foreign language requirement."

c. "I want my listeners to be able to describe how it is possible for a sailboat to sail upwind."

7. List the four questions you can use to test a thesis statement. Then use these questions to check the thesis statements you wrote for question 6.

a. _____

b. _____

c. _____

d. _____

Answers 1. Adapt to the occasion, to the audience, to time constraints, to what you know. 2. a, c, e, f. 3. c, d, g. 4. a-2, b-1, c-e, d-3, e-1, f-2, g-3, h-3. 5. a. 6. a. "Vote in the Student Government Association elections tomorrow." b. "We must work together to abolish this unnecessary, arbitrary, and harmful requirement." "I'm going to ask you to put your name on a petition that would abolish the foreign language requirement." c. "The laws of physics make it possible for a sailboat to move upwind." "Sailboats really do move against the wind." 7. a. Is the statement expressed in one, simple, declarative sentence? b. Does the statement summarize the purpose and main ideas of the speech? c. Does the statement specify or imply what you want listeners to remember after the speech? d. Is the statement free of judgmental and figurative language?

SUGGESTED READINGS

If you are stumped in attempting to come up with an appropriate topic for a speech, consult Kathryn Lamm, *10,000 Ideas for Term Papers, Projects, Reports and Speeches* (Third Edition) (New York: Macmillan, Inc., 1991).

Freeley, Austin J. Argumentation and Debate: Critical Thinking for Reasoned Decision Making. 9th ed. Belmont, Calif.: Wadsworth, 1996. This is a classic work. The first edition appeared in 1961. Acceptance for this work has lasted through eight editions because it is so helpful. See, especially, chapters 3, 4, and 5, "Stating the Controversy," "Analyzing the Controversy," and "Exploring the Controversy." If you understand these chapters, you will never have a question about how to focus a speech idea.

Warnick, Barbara, and Edward S. Inch. Critical Thinking and Communication: The Use of Reason in Argument. 3d ed. New York: Macmillan, 1998. This text is extremely useful for help in focusing ideas.

INTERNET ACTIVITIES

1. Go to the Internet Public Library reference section and find "dictionaries." The URL is: *http://www.ipl.org/ref* Scroll through the list, taking note of the wide range of dictionaries available to you. At the bottom of the "page" you will find a search window. Type in the word "speech." There you will find links to texts of many of the world's greatest speeches. See if you can find two or three drafts of Lincoln's *Gettysburg Address*. Which draft did you study when you were in high school?

2. Suppose you wish to give a speech about working with volunteers. Go to the AltaVista search engine at URL: *http://www.altavista.digital.com* Type in the words "working with volunteers" and press return. Among the top five entries you will find as much information as you could use to develop the topic.

3. Go to the URL: *http://speeches.com* In the drop-down menu choose "visit the speech library" and click on "GO." There you will find a number of categories. Choose one, locate a couple of example speeches within the category, and see if you can identify the thesis sentence.

NOTES

1. You may wish to consult the following recent articles to understand better how several demographic characteristics have an effect on listeners. See Jane D. Brown and Laurie Schulze, "The Effects of Race, Gender, and Fandom on Audience Interpretations of Madonna's Music Video's," *Journal of Communication* (Spring 1990), 40:2, pp. 88–102; James G. Cantrill and Michelle D. Masluk, "Place and Privilege as Predictors of How the Environment is Described in Discourse," *Communication Reports*, (Winter 1996) 9:1, pp. 79–84; Heidi M. Reeder, "A Critical Look at Gender Differences in Communication Research," *Communication Studies*, (Winter 1996), 47:4, pp. 318–330; Rebecca Cline J. Welsh and J. Nelya, "Sex Differences in Communication and the Construction of HIV/AIDS," *Journal of Applied Communication*, (1994), 22:4, pp. 322–337.

CHAPTER 5

AUDIENCE ANALYSIS

OBJECTIVES

1. You should be able to name and describe the four features of an audience as a rhetorical field.

2. You should be able to describe the three elements of an audience setting and explain how these elements affect the role of speaker.

3. You should be able to explain the relationship between audience perceptions and expectations, on one hand, and speaking objectives on the other.

4. You should be able to describe two methods of conducting an audience analysis: direct-access audience analysis and inferential audience analysis.

5. You should be able to define demographic profile, and explain how demographic characteristics can affect how audience members feel about and react to a speech.

6. You should be able to develop a demographic profile of an audience.

7. You should be able to perform an accurate and usable audience analysis using the information gained through a demographic profile.

OUTLINE

Objectives
Outline
Abstract
Imagine
Introduction
  Audience Setting and
    Occasion as Rhetorical Field
  When You Speak
  Where You Speak
  The Occasion
  Events Surrounding Your
    Speech
  Conducting an Audience
    Analysis
  Analyzing Your Classroom
    Audience

Ask direct questions
Develop and use a
  questionnaire
Inferential Audience Analysis
Meeting Audience
  Expectations and Adapting
  to Where They Stand
Summary
Key Terms
Application Questions
It's More Fun to Know
Self-Test for Review
Suggested Readings
Internet Activities
Notes

ABSTRACT

Every audience group understands itself to be special in some way. Its members know why they have assembled and what they should expect. They share some common purpose, and they agree on what would constitute "good reasons." Because these things are true, every audience group may be understood as a "rhetorical field." Success as a public speaker depends on how well you relate to your listeners within this rhetorical field. By developing a demographic profile, you learn listeners' characteristics, such as their age, gender, and socio-economic status. This information makes it possible for you to infer their needs and perceptions accurately, and to predict how they are likely to react to your speech. It suggests the dimensions and nature of the gathering in which you find them, and therefore, the group's sense of what constitutes good reasons. Thus, audience analysis helps you to estimate what the audience already knows about your subject, suggests how to adapt features of your speech to specific groups of listeners, and predicts what kind of speech will have a maximum effect on an audience. This chapter discusses the process of audience analysis and examines those kinds of analyses that will help you to achieve a higher level of success with your target audience.

IMAGINE

Debra Grelen's idea of how to analyze her classroom audience was to count the number of men and women and to notice about how old they were on average. She knew she had to be aware of the number of minority group members represented in her audience. But she wasn't sure why she needed all this information. About three weeks into her course on public speaking, during a classroom discussion on the matter, the teacher asked her, "What will you do with the information?" Debra knew to answer, "Adapt to the audience."

"But," persisted the teacher, "how will you use the information in order to know what adaptations to make?"

That question stumped Debra Grelen as it has so many public speaking students, even though it is the most important question to be asked about audience analysis.

INTRODUCTION

The purpose of this chapter is to describe how you can gather information about a listening audience, then easily and accurately use that information to make decisions about how best to adapt to that audience.

Audience analysis is the process by which a speaker tries to identify and understand the major characteristics of a group of listeners and the features of context and setting that render the group an audience. As a result of this analysis you should be able to adapt more intelligently to the listeners and to the situation in which you find them. Audience analysis serves three goals: (1) To help you make choices that will cause key listeners to believe you are credible as a person and qualified to give the speech. (2) To help you focus upon and set a speaking goal you can hope to achieve with a particular audience. (3) To help you identify and use arguments, evidence, and persuasive appeals most likely to attract a favorable response from your target audience.

Audience analysis begins with **demographic analysis**—the statistical study of a population's vital characteristics, including income, marital status, age, sex, socioeconomic status, educational level, political background, and so on. Demographic information allows you to draw inferences and make predictions about how listeners are likely to respond.

Speakers who understand their listeners are much more likely to succeed in gathering and maintaining their attention, interest, and good will. © Michael Newman/PhotoEdit

A cautionary note seems appropriate. Demographic analysis tells you about a group in general, but not about the individual members of the group. Audience members are not all alike and often have different opinions on the same subject. Nevertheless, all assembled groups share certain common features. (1) They know they have boundaries or limits—that they are part of a particular audience. (2) They share some sense of purpose. They have some common goal or goals. (3) They understand that certain rules control the kinds of talk that are appropriate. (4) Their discourse conforms to those rules. Thus it is sensible to think of an audience as a rhetorical field.[1]

Inferential analysis is the process of drawing inferences from demographic data about how listeners are likely to respond to a speech. This analysis results in educated guesses about such things as what a target audience is likely, already, to know or feel about a subject, or where the target audience is likely to stand on an issue. Inferential analysis aims to help you understand a target audience's motivations for gathering, and therefore, the kinds of arguments and appeals to which they are most likely to respond. Thus, inferential analysis attempts to assess the rhetorical field so you, the speaker, can make appropriate rhetorical choices.

Remember, even though the word "audience" refers to a group, an **audience** is a collection of individual, unique human beings. These individual members may range anywhere from enthusiastic support of your ideas to fairly active opposition.

One goal of your analysis is to determine, so far as possible, which subgroups exist in a particular audience. After you have identified the subgroups you can anticipate their probable motivations and reactions. **Motivation** refers to the needs and desires that drive or impel people to act as they do in their effort to achieve certain specific goals.

So, a speaker will increase the likelihood of success by performing a demographic analysis, and drawing careful inferences about what the listeners know already, what their likely positions are on the subject, and what motivates those positions. In addition, the setting and occasion of a speech—the rhetorical field—tell the listeners what to expect and what to accept.

Audience Setting and Occasion as Rhetorical Field

One key concern for every speech is the **audience setting,** or the speaking environment. Another is the occasion. The three elements that make up the audience setting are: (1) *when* you plan to speak, (2) *where* you will be speaking, and (3) the *events that precede and follow* your appearance. The **occasion** refers to *why* the audience is gathered. In combination, these four elements constitute the **rhetorical field** in which the speech is given.

All audience groups come together for some purpose. For example, a group may gather to celebrate a person's birthday, or to honor a sport figure for setting a new world record. Likewise, a group may gather to hear a political figure or to learn about a new product line. Your public speaking class comes together to share in the teaching and learning process—to develop their analytical and performance skills. Thus, they, too, are a rhetorical field. (1) They know they have boundaries or limits—that they are part of a particular audience. (2) They share some sense of purpose. (3) They understand that certain rules control the kinds of talk that are appropriate. (4) Their discourse conforms to those rules.

When You Speak

When a speech is scheduled can be a very important consideration. Audience attention is higher at some times of the day than at others. To illustrate, after-lunch speakers face a formidable challenge: Listeners are tired, their stomachs are full, and they have a tendency to doze off. Likewise, speakers who must make their presentations just before a meal face listeners who may be distracted because their stomachs are empty. Speakers with midmorning engagements on a Tuesday or Wednesday, however, are much more likely to find listeners who are alert, and have a good energy levels.

Where You Speak

Where a speech is scheduled can require a speaker to make adjustments. For example, a high level of noise may require you to take action to eliminate as much of it as possible. Or if the problem cannot be reduced, to determine how to overcome it. Will the speech be presented in a large auditorium with a public address system? Will you be talking in a gym with poor acoustics? What types of audience adjustments will be necessary if you are speaking in a quiet church or synagogue? If you are speaking outside and audience members have to stand, you want to be brief because their legs will tire soon. Similarly, if audience members have to sit on hard, wooden chairs, they will get restless in a hurry.

Speaking in a classroom has its own set of challenges: Students might be making noise in the hall, or a campus maintenance worker could be mowing the grass outside the classroom. Some students may have difficulty paying attention to your speech because they are concentrating on their own presentation coming up. Thus, where you speak may very well require you to make adaptations.

The Occasion

Why a group is gathered influences how its members listen and behave. For example, an audience at a political rally probably already supports the candidate whose rally it is. Their response to their favorite candidate is likely to be enthusiastic. An audience gathered to be entertained—say, the audience in a comedy club—will react differently in that context from how the same people might behave during a classroom lecture.

Events Surrounding Your Speech

The events surrounding a speech affect listeners and therefore require speaker adaptation. For example, in a classroom setting, if you are the first speaker, your classmates will be interested in how you manage the situation. You set the tone for the rest of the speeches that day. Similarly, if you are one of the last speakers, the audience reaction to you will be affected by the three or four people who went ahead of you. Listeners are conditioned to expect good performances from everyone who follows a successful presentation. Speakers usually rise to the challenge and succeed.

You cannot always predict what events will affect your speech. Remember, whatever happens before you talk will affect how listeners react to you. Thus, you cannot ignore when and where you speak, nor the events surrounding your speech and the occasion for which a group has gathered. They constitute a rhetorical field, so the choices you make as you plan to speak must be consistent with the requirements and expectations of that rhetorical field.

Conducting an Audience Analysis

Analyzing Your Classroom Audience

A public speaking class provides a unique opportunity to polish audience analysis skills. The people in your classroom audience—the rhetorical field—will be the same throughout the course, so you can come to know them rather well. You can ask people questions.

Through discussions, you can determine people's attitudes, goals, interests, and preferences. You can experiment with different kinds of arguments to see what they will accept and what they will not. Always seize opportunities to get information directly from these important listeners.

Even though your classmates are a "captive" audience (attendance is usually required and they do not feel free to leave whenever they choose) that does not mean that their needs can be ignored. A classroom audience is a real audience. And its nature provides many opportunities to study audience analysis in a rhetorical field where mistakes are expected and even encouraged.

Ask direct questions

Begin analyzing your classroom audience by asking people questions in interviews. First, work at obtaining general information about audience reaction to your topic, then focus on more particular details that may be relevant. Exhibit 5.2 describes and provides examples of

EXHIBIT 5.2

OPEN AND CLOSED QUESTIONS FOR INFORMATION GATHERING		
Question Type	*When To Use the Type*	*Examples*
Open questions seek broad, general information.	1. To relax the interviewee. 2. When the question is easy to answer. 3. To discover what the person thinks is important. 4. To discover what the person knows. 5. To discover the person's values or feelings.	
Highly open questions suggest a general topic but allow almost complete freedom of response		1. Tell me about _____. 2. What do you think about _____? 3. Do you have a view about _____? 4. How do you feel about _____? 5. What position do you take on _____?

Continued

Exhibit 5.2 *continued*

Question Type	When to Use the Type	Examples
Moderately open questions produce a more focused answer.		1. Tell me why you chose to fly Northwest Air Lines? 2. How have you responded to the delays? 3. What do you expect to be the air line's response to your complaint?
Closed questions narrow response options to some specific area of interest.	1. When you want to have control over both the questions and the answers. 2. When you need specific information and the time for interviews is short. 3. When you plan to code or tabulate answers from repeated interviews. 4. When you don't care about the "why" of a person's answer, or the person's feelings are not particularly relevant.	
Moderately closed questions ask the respondent to supply particular information.		1. What other airlines have you flown? 2. How many times have you flown on Northwest in the past six months? 3. How many times were your flights delayed more than 15-minutes?
Highly closed questions severely limit the response options.	When you are using a survey.	1. Objective-type, multiple choice and true-false test questions are all highly closed questions. 2. On a scale of one to five, where five is best, how would you rank _____?

various levels of open and closed questions, and makes suggestions about when to use them. Such questions can quickly yield an amazing amount of information about the people in your audience.

Develop and use a questionnaire

While the general information presented in Exhibit 5.3 is useful, you may also need more specific information in order to adjust your organization and ideas. Try developing a short questionnaire. You then will have a standard approach for getting detailed information from all your listeners. Exhibit 5.3 shows a sample questionnaire a student asked classmates to complete on the security of the U.S. banking system.

Exhibit 5.4 illustrates and describes advantages and disadvantages of different types of questionnaire items. You can use this exhibit as you develop a questionnaire for use in your classroom.

EXHIBIT 5.3

SAMPLE QUESTIONNAIRE FOR TOPIC:
THE SECURITY OF THE U.S. BANKING SYSTEM

1. Do you know how secure your money is in a national bank?
   Yes ___ No ___ Not sure

2. Can you estimate how many U.S. banks failed last year?
   Yes ___ No ___ Not sure

3. Are U.S. banks more secure than banks in other countries?
   Yes ___ No ___ Not sure

4. How much money was lost as the result of bank failures last year?
   A huge amount _____\ Very little

5. To what extent is the public aware of the crisis in the U.S. banking system?
   Not at all _____\ Quite aware

6. How do you think the federal government should become more involved in the security of U.S. banks?

EXHIBIT 5.4

ADVANTAGES AND DISADVANTAGES OF DIFFERENT TYPES OF QUESTIONNAIRE ITEMS		
Type of Question	*Examples*	*Advantages/disadvantages*
Forced choice	"Do you know the size of the national debt?" [yes or no] "Is Somalia in Asia?" [yes or no]	Limits the type of answer. Gives information but very little detail.
Scale item	"How worried are you about getting AIDS?" [Very worried, somewhat worried, uncertain, not very worried, unconcerned] "The income tax system in the United States is unfair." [Strongly agree, agree somewhat, neutral, disagree slightly, disagree strongly]	Shows the strength of feeling and the nature of attitude. Questions must be written carefully to avoid creating bias in the answers.
Open-response item	"What do you think should be done with Social Security?" "How do you believe we can become a more energy-efficient country?"	Gives a great deal of information. Some of the information may not be useful.

Inferential Audience Analysis

Sometimes a speaker does not see the audience until a few minutes before a speech begins. In these situations, you have to draw inferences about the rhetorical field. This process is called **inferential audience analysis** because audience characteristics are *inferred* from information already known or gathered about the audience. When you lack firsthand information about your listeners, you can conduct an inferential audience analysis by using one or more of the following methods:

1. Ask the person who invited you to speak to describe the audience and the features of the rhetorical field. (A) Why are they to be gathered? (B) What sense of purpose do they share? What are their common goals? (C) What rules control the kinds of talk that are appropriate?

2. Select demographic categories provided in Exhibit 5.5 that are relevant to your topic, and ask for this information from the person who invited you to speak. Ask this person for the names and telephone numbers of one or two people who will attend the event, and for the names of one or two people who have addressed the group in the past.

3. Ask the potential members of the audience to help you estimate the crucial characteristics of the rest of the group.

4. Ask the people who have spoken to this audience before to describe the audience.

These methods yield a demographic profile of an audience. Then, based on the information you have gathered, you must make careful, educated guesses about the characteristics and attitudes of audience members. Do notice that there is no complete nor perfect list of demographic features. Every new speaking situation demands its own relevant list of demographic features. Exhibit 5.5 lists and explains how to use some of the most commonly named demographic features of a listening group.

EXHIBIT 5.5

SAMPLE DEMOGRAPHIC CATEGORIES

(Pointer: Try these categories in computerized key-word searches to discover if any research findings bear on your situation. See Chapter 7 for more information on conducting research on line and using the library.)

Demographic category	What you may want to know	What to do with the information
Gender	Is gender critical to the rhetorical field? How many men? Women? What is the gender "mix"?	You can see the impact that gender has had upon the rhetorical field. It now is a crucial component. To see how far it reaches into the field of communication go to (*http://www.excite.com/*) and in the Search box type "gender differences." The results will illustrate the extent of the relationship.
Age	Is age critical to the rhetorical field? How old are the listeners? Range of ages? How is age distributed?	The ages of listeners often influence their attitudes and interests.[3] Be sure you take into account the distribution of ages in your listeners as you think about the arguments and appeals you will use.
		A massive research literature on age-related variables is available both on the Internet and through your college library. For example go to the ERIC index through your library or on the Internet, and search for the words "age differences" in a variety of different sub-indexes.
		One clear finding runs through this massive research literature: age profoundly affects what people are interested in, and what they think and feel about the topics that interest them.

Continued

Exhibit 5.5 *continued*

Demographic category	What you may want to know	What to do with the information
Educational level	Is educational attainment critical to the rhetorical field? How many high school graduates? How many college graduates? Any relevant special educational or training background? (such as music, engineering, military training focused on your topic)	The educational level of your audience will provide an indication of how much information they can understand and accept regarding your topic.[4] Similarly, specialized training can bear directly on what a group knows, feels, or thinks. Indeed, some groups form just to stimulate each other intellectually. For example, book clubs, investment clubs, etc., form for specific intellectual stimulation. Attained educational level is not, however, a reliable indicator of intelligence. Even so, people with less education tend to have a narrower range of interests.
Political affiliation	Is political affiliation critical to the rhetorical field? Is the group primarily of one party or the other? Do audience members represent all elements of the political spectrum? How strongly do they hold their political views?	Do not use the political affiliations of your audience members to jump to conclusions about their attitudes or opinions. Instead, combine political preference with other demographic features for a more accurate and complete picture. For example, in general, people tend to think of Republicans as more "conservative" than Democrats, wealthier, and older. These stereotypes are simply not accurate. Many Democrats think of themselves as conservative, and many Republicans are young, and not particularly wealthy.
Socioeconomic status	Is socioeconomic status critical to the rhetorical field? Are listeners wealthy? Do they range from wealthy to poor? What is the mix?	Low-income people have different attitudes and wants than high-income individuals.[5] And the middle-class group has a different agenda of interests and information than other elements of the socioeconomic spectrum. Be realistic about these differences as you choose and build upon your speech topics.
Religious affiliation	Is religion a special feature of the rhetorical field? Do listeners hold a dominant religious belief or do they represent many different views? How strong is their religious commitment?	Be sensitive to religious preferences among audience members. Avoid topics that stereotype any religious group. Also, check your calendar before you speak to be sure of any religious holiday that may coincide with your presentation. Diverse religious beliefs may bear on some topics and have nothing whatsoever to do with others. Also, you cannot reliably assume that members of a religious group necessarily subscribe to all of that group's dogma and traditions. Again, use religious affiliation in context with other demographic indicators as you draw inferences about your target listeners.
Race or Ethnic Identification	Is race or ethnic identification critical to the rhetorical field? What is the racial or ethnic composition of the listeners? Does one race or ethnic group predominate?	Discover whether racial or ethnic identification is relevant to your topic. If so, how? An audience of African Americans may be more likely than whites to know and understand issues that face U.S. American inner cities, but not necessarily. Native Americans may know about the problems of rural poverty, but not necessarily. Be sensitive to differences that flow from ethnic and racial diversity. Do not give offense by assuming a stereotypical view. Rather, ask someone. Do your research.

Continued

Exhibit 5.5 *continued*

Demographic category	What you may want to know	What to do with the information
Occupation	Is occupation important to the rhetorical field? In what field do listeners work? How much experience do they possess? White collar? Blue collar? Gold collar? Is their work related to their education?	Knowing how listeners are employed will begin to tell you what general kinds of information they have, but do not assume everyone in the same general field has the same amount of, or the same kind of information.[6] Occupation can be a very helpful indicator of what listeners are likely to know. For example, a loan officer learns quickly what to look for in an application form, and a police officer learns to see through flimsy alibis.
Organization memberships	Are listeners members of professional, social, or service organizations? Are they "joiners"? Is organizational membership critical to the rhetorical field?	Organizational memberships point to interests and the type of information people may have. Examples: Members of the Chamber of Commerce are likely to be interested in business. Members of the League of Women Voters are likely to be up-to-date about local political candidates, or at least, politically aware. People volunteer to join groups because they are interested in the goals and activities of the groups.

The demographic characteristics you select will depend upon the topic you intend to discuss. Suppose, for example, the topic is noise pollution and your argument is that individual water craft, sometimes called water skis, should be banned from the public waterways in your state because they create too much noise. *Gender* probably would not be a relevant demographic feature. *Age* might be, however. Younger people might be more tolerant of the noise generated by personal water craft than older people.

Political affiliation would probably not be very important—although you might try to tie your position to an over-all party position on pollution control. *Socioeconomic status* seems largely irrelevant to the topic. Although these craft are expensive to own and rent, the issue is about having to share the space with them, not about owning or using them.

Religious affiliation seems irrelevant, but may not be! A clever speaker might figure out a way to tie noise pollution to the religious attitudes and convictions of some listeners. The *racial or ethnic identification* of the listeners would probably not bear on the topic. However, the *occupation* and the *organizational memberships* of the audience might be directly relevant. For example, an audience of water-sports equipment sales persons would likely have a view on the subject.

There are no uninteresting subjects, but there are disinterested people. Find a way to relate your interests to your listener's needs and wants. © PhotoDisc

You would need to discover these important questions about the rhetorical field in order to make arguments the audience members would be likely to accept.

The point is, you have to select the *relevant* demographic features of an audience, and understand how these characteristic features bear upon your speech. You have to meet the audience's expectations within the rhetorical field in which you find them.

EXHIBIT 5.6

INFERRING AUDIENCE REACTION TO YOUR TOPIC	
What You Should Ask	*Why You Need to Know*
Ask: How much, and what kind of information do listeners have on my topic?	Listeners may range from having no information to knowing a lot about the topic. They may have biased information. How can you adapt your remarks, or choose and focus on the needs of a target subgroup in the larger audience without this relevant information about them?
Ask: How important is this topic to my audience?	A group that doesn't care much about the topic needs a different approach from a group that thinks the topic is very important. You may need to teach them why the topic is important by showing them how the topic bears upon their lives.
Ask: Does the speech appeal to the common interests of my audience members?	If you can't find a common thread among all the members of an audience, then you must tailor the speech to the needs of the most relevant subgroup in the larger audience. Perhaps certain parts of a topic are more relevant than others. Perhaps you can find a way to build a common ground with the audience.
Ask: How do audience members feel about this topic?	A group with strong negative feelings about your topic will need a different speech than a group that does not care either way. An audience that is eager to hear about the topic needs still a different approach.
Ask: What level of language would be appropriate for this audience?	In general, listeners are more comfortable with language levels of difficulty and formality that "fit" their ability and expectations. Refer to Chapter 11, beginning on page 247, to read further about this important feature of speech making.
Ask: What is the occasion of this speech?	People gather for reasons. A speech must seem consistent with the listener's reasons for attending. For an obvious example, listeners gathered at a loved one's funeral would be unlikely to accept an after-dinner speech as appropriate.
Ask: How long should the speech be?	Audiences always have expectations. Time constraints always exist for a presentation, so you should determine what those time constraints actually are.

Meeting Audience Expectations and Adapting to Where They Stand

A group always has a sense of what constitutes "good reasons." Listeners tend to apply different standards to various situations. Since this is so, wise speakers plan carefully to meet audience expectations. Exhibit 5.6 displays some questions you might attempt to answer, based on the demographic data you have gathered. Your work with these questions will go a long way toward helping you meet audience expectations.

Even though the word "audience" refers to a group, the individual, unique human beings tend to distribute themselves anywhere from enthusiastic support of your ideas to fairly active opposition. Exhibit 5.1 illustrated this key idea. Here, in Exhibit 5.7, we add to that illustration. When your analysis suggests the audience distribution, your best plan will be to direct your remarks to the most important or largest audience subgroup. For example, if you believe most of your listeners are opposed to your idea, you know they will not be persuaded by a speech designed to stimulate them to action in favor of your own position. Rather, this audience group needs to be entertained in the same sense you would entertain someone in your home. Do what you can to help them feel comfortable and at east. Provide them an opportunity to get to know you and become comfortable with you.

As the target audience group moves to the right on this continuum, they will be more likely to listen to and consider information about your subject matter and your position on the matter. If you find your largest target group is somewhere in the middle of this continuum—say, they are mostly neutral on the matter—then your speech might be designed to change them from neutral toward belief in favor of your idea.

If the target group believes in your ideas to some extent, then your speech might best be designed to convince them they are right and to begin to stimulate them to act in some way favorable to your position.

How far can you go in adapting to an audience before you reach an ethical bind? Can you tell listeners what they want to hear, even if you don't agree with what you are saying?

EXHIBIT 5.7

ADAPTING A SPEECH TO THE NEEDS OF AN AUDIENCE, BASED UPON THE POSITION THEY TAKE				
If the audience is:				
Opposed to the idea		Neutral		In favor of the idea
You should:				
Entertain	Inform	Change belief	Convince	Stimulate to Action

SUMMARY

Your success as a public speaker depends on how well you and your listeners relate to each other. It is useful to think of the audience and its setting as a rhetorical field, characterized by four features. (1) They know they have boundaries or limits—that they are part of a particular audience. (2) They share some sense of purpose. They have some common goal or goals. (3) They understand that certain rules control the kinds of talk that are appropriate. (4) Their discourse conforms to those rules.

Even though we think of audiences as a group, each audience is a collection of individual, unique human beings with particular characteristics, interests, attitudes, and information. Audience analysis is the process by which speakers try to identify and understand the major characteristics of a group of listeners so as to better adapt their message to the audience.

Audience analysis should involve looking at the four elements that make up the rhetorical field—your speaking environment: (1) when you plan to speak, (2) where you will be speaking, (3) the events that precede and follow your appearance, and (4) the purpose for which the audience is assembled. Audience analysis also includes determining what image listeners have of you, themselves, and the occasion. This information helps you to make speaking an audience-centered process.

There are two methods of conducting an audience analysis, and the method of choice depends on your access to the audience you plan to address. In direct-access audience analysis, you go directly to your audience and gather information by asking questions, listening to discussions, conducting interviews, and asking audience members to complete questionnaires.

In inferential audience analysis, you do not have direct access to your audience and must instead rely on alternate sources for information about listeners' characteristics and attitudes. You then draw inferences about your listeners by describing them in terms of a demographic profile. Demographic characteristics that you might want to explore include gender, age, educational level, political affiliation, socioeconomic status, religious affiliation, race, occupation, and organizational memberships.

The purpose of all this analysis is to adapt to the motivations of the listeners, and to find the arguments and appeals the audience is likely to accept.

KEY TERMS

Audience
Audience analysis
Audience setting

Demographic analysis
Demographic profile
Direct-access audience analysis

Immediate audience
Inferential audience analysis
Rhetorical field

APPLICATION QUESTIONS

1. Suppose you have been assigned to speak on the subject of abortion. Working alone, perform an inferential demographic analysis, using your class as the target audience. Use table 5.5 to guide your research. Bring your notes to class. Then, working together as a class, perform a direct-access audience analysis. Compare and contrast your inferences about the audience with the actual findings of direct-access analysis. What were the similarities and differences? Why? Did other class members analyze the classroom audience in the same way you did? How do you account for the differences?

2. With two or three other members of your class, attend a public speaking event. For example, go to a church or temple and listen to the sermon, or attend a political rally and listen to the key speaker, or attend a PTA meeting or one of the weekly meetings of the Kiwanis Club or The Junior League. Do you think the principal speaker at this event conducted an audience analysis? Why or why not? Be as specific as you can in discussing these questions with your classmates.

3. Working with two or three other classmates, select any event in which a group gathers itself into an audience. Analyze that audience as a rhetorical field, and come to class prepared to describe (1) the boundaries or limits they know they have, (2) the sense of purpose they share (their common goal), (3) the particular rules controlling the kinds of talk that are appropriate in that event, and (4) how discourse conforms to those rules.

IT'S MORE FUN TO KNOW

The audience is central to every speech. An effective speaker should spend considerable time determining the interests, attitudes, and basic characteristics of the listeners. In the "Imagine" section of this chapter, our character, Jeff, could have profited from reading James G. Cantrill and Michelle D. Masluk, "Place and Privilege as Predictors of How the Environment is Described in Discourse," *Communication Reports,* (Winter 1996) 9:1, pp. 79–84. The gender composition of the audience also is a major consideration since women have different interests and aptitudes than men, as pointed out in the article by Heidi M. Reeder, "A Critical Look at Gender Differences in Communication Research," *Communication Studies,* (Winter 1996), 47:4, pp. 318–33. This substantial difference also is emphasized by Rebecca Cline J. Welsh and J. Nelya, "Sex Differences in Communication and the Construction of HIV/AIDS," *Journal of Applied Communication,* (1994), 22:4, pp. 322–337. The differences in audience attitude and knowledge based on environmental and employment issues also are spelled out in detail in the "Notes" section of this chapter. The prudent speaker will concentrate on understanding the audience before collecting and structuring ideas.

SELF-TEST FOR REVIEW

Mark each of the following as either true (T) or false (F).

1. The audience's image of you as a speaker can have a significant effect on the success of your speech.   T   F

2. An audience is a single group and, for speaking purposes, should be treated as a group.   T   F

3. Gender is a reasonably accurate predictor of the attitudes and knowledge of listeners.   T   F

4. Factors that make a difference in how an audience reacts to a message (age, sex, race religion, and so on) are called demographic variables.   T   F

5. The primary purpose of audience analysis is to discover the standards and guidelines the group uses to evaluate arguments and appeals.   T   F

6. How you organize and present your speech may depend on the outcome of your audience analysis.   T   F

7. Inferential audience analysis involves interacting directly with your audience to obtain information.   T   F

8. Organizational memberships and occupation rarely are important demographic variables.   T   F

9. Open questions seek more particular information than closed questions.   T   F

10. If you have direct access to your audience and want to determine audience attitude and information before a speech, ask audience members to answer scale items and open-response questions on the topic.   T   F

Answers: 1T, 2F, 3F, 4T, 5T, 6T, 7F, 8F, 9F, 10T

SUGGESTED READINGS

Kiyosaki, Robert T. and Sharon L. Lechter. *Rich Dad, Poor Dad: What the Rich Teach Their Kids About Money That the Poor and Middle Class Don't.* Paradise Valley, AZ: Techpress, 1997. An intriguing examination of the preparation and attitude development of children from wealthy homes vs. middle class and poor homes. It provides interesting clues to the knowledge and attitudes of all income groups and is especially useful in inferential audience analysis.

Mitchell, Susan. *The Official Guide to American Attitudes.* Ithica, NY: New Strategist Publications, 1996. An exciting work that reveals the attitudes that shape such issues as marriage, love, race, work, money, and personal outlook. Based on information drawn from the National Opinion Research Center, this work is a MUST READ for any speaker interested in the attitudes of listeners.

Russell, Cheryl. *The Official Guide to Racial and Ethnic Diversity: Asians, Blacks, Hispanics, Native Americans, and Whites.* Ithica, NY: New Strategist Publications, 1996. A splendid and comprehensive examination of the trends that drive advertisers and marketers in their efforts to reach all segments of our diverse population. The author translates raw data into graphs and tables which are comprehensible and useful to anyone interested in the specific interests and needs of each race and ethnic group in this nation.

Seybold, Patricia with Ronni T. Marsh. *Customers.com.* New York: Random House, 1998. Although this work is written to enable merchants to find ways to make purchases more easily, it is highly appropriate for the study of audience analysis. Seybold emphasizes the importance of tailoring the message (the service or product) to the needs and interests of the buyer (the audience). This work provides an interesting and eminently useful approach to analyzing material from the "buyer's perspective."

INTERNET ACTIVITIES

1. Suppose you are not an African American, but you wish to understand something of the African American experience as part of your analysis of a classroom audience. Explore these hyperlinks, then report what you found to your class.

   www.naacp.org

   www.black-collegian.com

   www.rain.org / ~kmw / aa.html

   www.afamnet.com / NationalPage / index.html

   www.afroam.org

   www.blackenterprise.com

   www.melanet.com

   www.netnoir.com

   www.theconduit.com

2. Try to develop a similar list of hyperlinks to Internet sites that provide information about Hispanic People, Native American People, Chinese American People, and so on. Which of these Internet search engines provide you the quickest access to the information you seek? *www.yahoo.com, www.AltaVista.com, www.excite.com*

3. What happens when you go to *www.yahoo.com* and type the words "demographic analysis" into the search block? Do you believe all those business, academic and governmental pages and web sites would exist if audience analysis were not an important tool for communicators?

4. Find and click on a link to an Internet survey—many of these will have popped up when you performed Activity #3. Evaluate the questionnaire based on the suggestions in this chapter. What kinds of questions do you find? Are any of the questions too hard for you to answer? Were the instructions clear and easy to follow? Come to class prepared to discuss the implications of your findings for your public speaking classmates.

NOTES

1. The idea of audience as "rhetorical field" has a rich history. It begins with Stephen Toulmin's *The Uses of Argument* (Cambridge: Cambridge University Press, 1958). See, also, Stephen Toulmin, Richard Rieke, and A. Janik, *An Introduction to Reasoning* (New York: Macmillan, 1979). See, also, M. W. Shelton and Enid S. Waldhart, "Dreams of fields: The basic public speaking course as an argument field." Paper presented to the National Communication Association Conference, New York, 1998.

2. You may wish to consult the following recent articles to understand better how several demographic characteristics have an effect on listeners. See Jane D. Brown and Laurie Schulze, "The Effects of Race, Gender, and Fandom on Audience Interpretations of Madonna's Music Video's," *Journal of Communication* (Spring 1990), 40:2, pp. 88–102; James G. Cantrill and Michelle D. Masluk, "Place and Privilege as Predictors of How the Environment is Described in Discourse," *Communication Reports,* (Winter 1996) 9:1, pp. 79-84; Heidi M. Reeder, "A Critical Look at Gender Differences in Communication Research," *Communication Studies,* (Winter 1996), 47:4, pp. 318–330; Rebecca Cline J. Welsh and J. Nelya, "Sex Differences in Communication and the Construction of HIV/AIDS," *Journal of Applied Communication,* (1994), 22:4, pp. 322–337.

3. For example, see "X'ers vs. boomers" *The Futurist*, 32:7 (October 1998), 8; Sara J. Czaja and Joseph Sharit, "Age Differences in Attitudes Towards Computers," *The Journals of Gerontology, Series B*, 53:5 (September 1998) 239; and Jeffrey F. Milem, "Attitude Change in College Students: Examining the Effect of College Peer Groups and Faculty Groups," *Journal of Higher Education*, 69:2 (March-April 1998, 117.

4. These sources are instructive. Carol Schlagheck, "Newspapers Reading Choices by College Students," *Newspaper Research Journal*, 19:2 (Spring 1998), 74, and Adria Steinberg, "From School to Work: Making the Transition," *Current*, 394 (July-August 1997, 9.

5. You might wish to examine "Who We Are At Work," *Workforce* (November 1998): Joan F. Morton and Joanne E. Guthrie, "Diet-Related Knowledge, Attitudes, and Practices of Low-Income Individuals with Children in the Household," *Family Economics and Nutrition Review*, 10:1 (Winter 1997), 2; Donna Strobino, Virginia Keane, Elizabeth Holt, Nancy Hughart and Bernard Guyer, "Parental Attitudes Do Not Explain Underimmunization," *Pediatrics*, 98:6 (December 1996), 107.

6. Useful information on this matter can be found in Katherine T. Beddingfield, "My Brilliant Interim Career," *U.S. News and World Report* (October 26, 1998), 78; J. D. Bakos, "Communication Skills for the 21st Century," *Journal of Professional Issues in Engineering Education and Practice*, 123:1 (January 1997), 14; and Anna M. Miller and Victoria L. Champion, "Attitudes About Breast Cancer and Mammography; Racial, Income, and Educational Differences," *Women and Health*, 26:1 (Winter 1997), 41.

CHAPTER 6

THE PROCESS OF PROVING:
DISCOVERING AND DEVELOPING
IDEAS FOR A SPEECH

OBJECTIVES

After reading this chapter, you should be able to:

1. Explain how to support your ideas with seven kinds of argument: (a) inductive argument, (b) deductive argument, (c) argument from sign, (d) argument from cause, (e) argument from example, (f) argument from analogy, and (g) argument from authority.

2. Explain how to test each kind of argument for accuracy and credibility.

3. Name and define four kinds of evidence:

   (a) testimony,

   (b) definition and explanation,

   (c) statistics, and

   (d) examples.

4. Explain how to evaluate evidence in terms of the competency of the source and the believability, consistency, verifiability, and currency of the evidence itself.

OUTLINE

Objectives
Outline
Abstract
Imagine
Introduction
   How to Support Ideas with
     Argument
     Inductive Argument
       How to Test Inductive
         Argument
     Deductive Argument
       How to Test Deductive
         Argument
       How to Test Arguments
         from Sign and Cause
       How to Test
         Arguments from
         Example
       How to Test
         Arguments from
         Authority
   The Process of Proving
     How to Construct an
       Argument
     How to Support a
       Knowledge Claim with
       Arguments

How to Build Speaker
   Credibility
How to Support Argu-
   ments with Evidence
   The Types of Evidence
   How to Test the Quality
     of Evidence
     Applying the Stan-
       dards to Testimony
     Applying the Stan-
       dards to Examples
     Pointers on Using
       Examples
       as Evidence
Summary
Key Terms
Application Questions
It's More Fun to Know
On Uses of Evidence
On Source Credibility
Self-Test for Review
Suggested Readings
Internet Activities
Notes

ABSTRACT

This chapter is about the process of proving. It shows you how to develop arguments, how to support arguments with evidence, and how to test the quality of the arguments and evidence.

Arguments take many forms. Inductive argument works from a range of specific cases in order to draw a general conclusion. Deductive arguments begin with the general conclusion and reason toward specific cases. Arguments from sign, cause, example, analogy, and authority are the most common forms of reasoning. The process of proving is a process of presenting arguments and evidence of sufficient strength and value to compel listeners to accept arguments.

Stephen Toulmin developed an influential model for constructing arguments based on how people reason in their daily lives. Learning to use his model involves learning how to identify when, and what kind of argument and evidence is needed.

Proving also involves learning how to identify and support knowledge claims, how to build speaker credibility, and how to support arguments with evidence. The chapter ends with a thorough description of not only how to test the quality of evidence, but also how to use four types of evidence (testimony, definition and explanation, statistics, and example).

IMAGINE

The people in the office were in disagreement. Fred kept saying, "I know I got a good deal when I bought my car. I paid fifty dollars over dealer cost." Marsha countered, "I got an ever better deal because I paid the invoice price." Beth was adamant, "I know I did best because I paid the dealer's cost and then I got a $300 incentive deal too."

Charlie, the real dealmaker, cut through the fog. "Look, there's only one way to get the best deal. First, you have to determine how much the dealer actually paid for the car, not just his invoice price. That amount is the dealer invoice price less any additional money that the manufacturers pay the dealers for each car they sell. You can get that information on the Internet from places like Autobytel.com or Edmunds.com. Second, you have to decide how much profit is appropriate for the dealer before you go to the showroom. Do you think the dealer should sell the car for $100 over his cost or should it be $500 over his true cost? Remember, there is a cost to doing business, such as advertising, turning on the heat and lights, and servicing vehicles. Once you make that decision, you're ready to go shopping and then we'll see who gets the best deal."

Nearly everyone left the meeting, convinced they paid more for their car than necessary. But no one could quarrel with the sensibility of Charlie's arguments.

Supporting materials can be found in the library, on the Internet, and in the heads of people. It takes time to conduct effective research, so wise speakers start early. © PhotoDisc

INTRODUCTION

Successful speaking depends greatly on how you formulate your ideas and arguments and on how you support your positions with proofs and evidence. This chapter introduces the different types of arguments and shows how to use them. You also will learn about artistic proofs—speaker credibility and reputation, emotional appeals, and rational appeals—that give listeners the reasons they should support your position. The chapter also offers suggestions about using evidence effectively to enhance a presentation.

Some people argue without first thinking their arguments through. But it's easy to make an argument compelling, once you know how. The purpose of this chapter is to show you how to do it.

How to Support Ideas with Argument

The word **argument** refers to a situation in which one person presents a position and supports that stance with various types of reasoning. According to S. Morris Engel, "an argument is a piece of reasoning in which one or more statements are offered as support for some other statement." [1]

The statements used for support are called **proofs.** In a successful argument, the speaker puts together various items of proof in order to make a convincing case on one side of an issue. The proofs give listeners a reason for accepting the speaker's argument.

Several different types and kinds of argument are available to public speakers. The two broad types of arguments are (1) inductive argument and (2) deductive argument. Within these two broad categories you will find five commonly used patterns or "kinds." They are: (1) argument from sign, (2) argument from cause, (3) argument from example, (4) argument from analogy, and (5) argument from authority.

Inductive Argument

Inductive arguments work from a series of individual cases to a conclusion. Induction, then, moves from specifics to a generalization. While you cannot say with certainty that anything will happen, you can use induction to look at cases from the past and to indicate the *probability* of a problem or situation in the present or future. Exhibit 6.1 provides examples of inductive argument. Use inductive argument when you want to show that an event will probably occur, or that something probably took place.

EXHIBIT 6.1

EXAMPLES OF INDUCTIVE ARGUMENT

Case 1: IBM has reduced the size of its work force.

Case 2: General Motors has cut back on its number of employees.

Case 3: United Technologies has permanently laid off many employees.

Case 4: AT&T has had a large work force reduction.

Generalization: Major U.S. corporations are downsizing to become profitable.

Case 1: In 1890, the U.S. center of population was just outside Cincinnati, Ohio.

Case 2: In 1940, the center of population for the United States was in western Indiana.

Case 3: n 1960, the population center of the United States was in west central Illinois.

Case 4: In 1990, the U.S. population center was in southeast Missouri.

Generalization: The population center of the United States is gradually moving westward.

How to Test Inductive Arguments

The first example of inductive argument suggests major U.S. companies are reducing the number of employees to become more efficient. The second example implies the U.S. population center is moving westward. These generalizations cannot be made with absolute certainty. But if (1) you choose a sufficient number of cases, (2) those cases are representative, and (3) the generalization comes from the cases, then the conclusion will likely be valid. Exhibit 6.2 provides a checklist by which you can test an inductive argument.

Deductive Argument

Deductive argument follows an opposite sequence from inductive argument. When you reason deductively, you proceed from a general conclusion and identify the specific instances that establish the con-

EXHIBIT 6.2

A CHECKLIST FOR TESTING INDUCTIVE ARGUMENT

_____ 1. Are there enough cases to suggest a probable trend?

_____ 2. If the conclusion is about a local or regional situation, are the cases sufficient?

_____ 3. Are the cases used to support the conclusion truly representative of the conclusion?

_____ 4. Does the conclusion flow logically from the cases?

clusion. A variation on the classical syllogism you learned in grade school provides a somewhat strained illustration of the deductive process. As you read it, notice the word "all" in the major premise. Deductive arguments rest on "the allness assumption." The generalization assumes and includes all members of the class. Here's how it works. First, you have to come to a general conclusion.

General conclusion: All people die.

How do you know? Because

Case 1: Socrates died.

Case 2: Plato died.

Case 3: Julius Caesar died.

Case N: Everyone in history, except currently living individuals, died.

Now you are ready to reason from the general conclusion.

(Major Premise): All people die.

(Minor Premise): Helen is a person.

(Conclusion): Helen will die.

The following is an example of reasoning by deduction:

(Major Premise): All college students need to develop computer skills.

(Minor Premise): You are a college student.

(Conclusion): You need to develop computer skills.

(Major Premise): All consumer product or service companies spend a great deal of money on advertising.

(Minor Premise): Procter & Gamble is a consumer product company.

(Conclusion): Procter & Gamble spends a great deal of money on advertising

Deductive argument is especially useful when listeners do not know much about the subject and would not be able to provide the specific cases on their own. The specific cases or elements of a deductive argument provide the information needed to arrive at a certain conclusion.[2]

To illustrate, a young man made this claim in a speech to the Mobile City Council: "The City of Mobile needs to develop the vacant land on the water front into a public park in order to prevent it from being developed inappropriately." Following this statement he gave numerous specific examples of what he believed were inappropriate waterfront land use. Then he said: "Waterfront property is always developed if it is not protected. Right now the vacant land next to the foot of Government Street is not protected. It will certainly be developed if you don't protect it." Then he asked them to consider his proposal.

There are never any guarantees of success. One of the risks to this approach is that listeners may be "put off" by either the initial claim or by one or more of the examples. If that happens, they begin, in their minds, to argue with the claim rather than to listen to the speaker. For example, the young man believed and argued that the coal terminal on the Mobile waterfront is an inappropriate use of the land. "It's dirty," he said. "It pollutes the water, and it creates a coal-dust problem in downtown Mobile. And it keeps the citizens of Mobile away from their waterfront."

The argument failed. One of the members of the City Council was an executive with the State Docks—the agency that administers the coal terminal. The Mayor was happy to draw port-tax money from the ships that come to and go from the coal terminal. So, instead of listening to the speaker's appeal for the city's general good and welfare, these people were thinking of objections to one of the details in his speech.

How to Test Deductive Arguments

Four simple questions will test the truth of a deductive argument:

1. *Is the general statement true?*

2. *Is there enough evidence to support the general statement?*

3. *Is the specific statement (the minor premise) also true?*

4. *Is there enough evidence to show the minor premise is true?*

The example about college students needing computer skills shows why deductive arguments require testing:

(Major Premise): All college students need to develop computer skills.

(Minor Premise): You are a college student.

(Conclusion): You need to develop computer skills.

Do all college students need to develop computer skills? How do you know all of them do? Perhaps one or two do not need computer skills. You would be hard pressed to prove that all college students need to develop computer skills. How would you prove that? The answer lies in the minds of the receivers.

Most arguments work inductively, and most take predictable form. Exhibit 6.3 provides a quick overview of the most commonly occurring kinds of argument.

Just as inductive and deductive arguments should be tested, so should arguments from sign, cause, example and authority be tested.

How to Test Arguments from Sign and Cause

To check the strength or validity of an arguments from sign or cause, ask:

1. Is the sign infallible? Does the sign always lead to the conclusion?

2. Is there a real connection between the cause and the effect?

EXHIBIT 6.3

THE MOST COMMONLY OCCURRING KINDS OF ARGUMENT		
Kind	*Explanation*	*Illustration*
Argument from sign	The existence of a feature, condition, or characteristic provides evidence for another feature, condition, or characteristic with which it is associated.	There are water puddles standing on the road and in the field. I guess it rained.
Argument from cause	A condition or event causes or contributes to the occurrence of another condition or event.	When they increased the speed limit to 70 the number of traffic deaths increased dramatically.
Argument from example	What is true of the example is true of the entire class.	When we installed insulation in Mr. Bernson's attic his energy bill dropped 50-percent. If it worked for him it will work for you.
Argument from analogy	Because two things resemble each other in certain known ways, they will resemble each other in unknown ways, too.	The Lexus and the Chevy both have four wheels and an engine. They both use gas and oil. They have about the same wheel base. They have the same creature comforts. So you might as well buy the Chevy. They're both the same, anyway.
Argument from authority	It is true because a person presumed to be knowledgeable about the matter says it is true.	More doctors recommend aspirin than any other pain relief medicine. So aspirin must be the best pain relief medicine.

3. Could any other cause produce the observed effect?
4. Has anything prevented this cause from operating?
5. Is this cause sufficient to produce the effect?

Infallible signs are rare, so the more signs you can introduce the greater the likelihood your argument is sound. Be sure to present enough cases so the listeners can have confidence in your conclusion. Exhibit 6.4 presents examples that show the difference between fallible and infallible signs.

EXHIBIT 6.4

FALLIBLE AND INFALLIBLE SIGNS		
Sign	*Conclusion*	*Quality of the Sign*
Ice on the lake	Water temperature is at least 32° F or colder.	Infallible
They drive a Rolls Royce.	They are wealthy.	Fallible
The person took out a key, opened the door, climbed into the car, and drove away.	The car belongs to the person.	Fallible
Listeners make eye contact and nod their heads.	Audience members are interested in and agree with the speaker.	Fallible

Causal argument assumes that something happened because of an earlier event. The following are examples of effect-to-cause arguments:

* The ground is wet. There are puddles in the road. It must have rained.
* The empty car rolled backward out of its parking place and smashed into a second car parked across the street. The brakes must have failed.

The following examples show cause-to-effect arguments:

* I don't feel that I know how to answer many of the questions on the final exam. Because I failed the midterm, I'll probably fail the course.
* The plane I'm supposed to catch at 7:30 is an hour late in Memphis. I'll probably miss my connection in Dallas-Fort Worth.

Causal arguments can create weird logical problems, especially if you reason from effect to cause. Cause rarely exists in a single chain of events. Rather, events are the result of many causes.

To test the validity of arguments from cause ask the following questions:

1. *Is there a real connection between the cause and the effect?* Do not be misled into believing that a result occurred because of something that preceded it. When Aunt Sally comes to visit and it begins to rain, you might say, "You certainly brought bad weather." However, there is no real connection between the visit and the weather change.

2. *Could any other cause produce the observed effect?* Usually, a single cause is not the basis for the observed effect. Instead, the effect probably is the result of several causes. For example, if someone asked you, "Why did you decide to major in economics?" you might say, "Because I liked Econ 101." While that might have been one element in your decision, there probably were others as well. You may have liked some of the faculty in the economics department, job possibilities in economics may have been attractive, and/or your parents may have encouraged you to consider economics as you tried to choose a major. As a speaker, be sure the causal relationship is strong enough for listeners to believe it.

3. *Has anything prevented this cause from operating?* A car with an empty gas tank has no fuel, and a driver cannot make the car go by putting the key in the ignition and turning it. When you examine a causal relationship, be sure that nothing (empty gas tank) has prevented a cause (turning the key) from producing the desired effect (starting the car).

4. *Is this cause sufficient to produce the effect?* To your roommate's question: "Why didn't you read the history assignment?" you might reply: "Because I couldn't get to the library tonight." Is this enough of a cause to prevent reading the history assignment? Maybe yes, and maybe no. Be sure that the cause is sufficient to produce the effect before you accept or present an argument.

How to Test Argument from Example

An **argument from example** involves comparing something known and understood (the example) to something less well known, then arguing that the two things are similar in important ways. This kind of argument is sometimes called "argument from analogy." For practical purposes, although there are some subtle differences between example and analogy, you can treat both kinds the same. An argument from example (or analogy) must satisfy three tests:

1. *Is the example typical of the class it represents?* Does the example truly illustrate the category?

   To illustrate, suppose a speaker wants you only to buy American made products. He says: "American quality is second to none in the world. For example, look at the shirts sold downtown at the Gap." Because you read the papers, you know the example doesn't illustrate the category. The papers report that many of the shirts sold at the Gap are made by Chinese laborers in a sweat shop in Saipan.[4]

2. *Do the points of comparison outweigh the points of difference?* Example: "Enlarging the airport in St. Louis will help the city's general economy because enlarging the airports in

Dallas and Newark had a positive effect on both cities."
For this argument from analogy to be valid, the similarities between the cities mentioned must be shown to be greater than the differences. For example, the cities' economic bases, sizes, networks of available highways, and transportation requirements are important issues of comparison. The similarities among the cities must outweigh the differences if the argument is to be accepted.

3. *Are the points of comparison relevant?*

The items that are compared may be alike in ways that are not relevant to the argument. Example: "My cousin is as good a basketball player as Shaquille O'Neal. He can run the court just as fast, he can lead the fast break, he's murder on the backboards, and he is a 'franchise' player. He also went to Louisiana State University."
The argument from analogy fails in this case, because there is more to being a star basketball player than the characteristics listed. The cousin's athletic prowess does not make him the equivalent of one of the premier NBA centers. Star players must have many other crucial attributes in addition to being able to run the court, control the backboard, and attend LSU.

How to Test Argument from Authority

Argument from authority says something is true if an expert says it is true. The key to understanding such arguments is consistency—consistency between the authority's expertise and the subject at hand, consistency between the authority's behavior and the statement he or she makes, consistency between the authority's statement and known fact. To test the quality of an argument from authority, ask questions about consistency:

1. *Is the authority qualified to make the statement?*
2. *Is the authority's behavior consistent with his or her statements?*
3. *Is the authority's statement consistent with what is already known?*

The Process of Proving

The process of proving is the process of attempting to establish the truth of something in the minds of receivers. The process sometimes involves selecting and using evidence you hope will compel the receivers. Sometimes it involves psychological appeals. Either way, proof is always about what people will accept. For public speakers, then, proving must always be an audience-centered activity. Four ideas bear directly on the process of proving:

1. The credibility of an idea, an argument, evidence, or the person giving it, is never a characteristic of the idea, argument evidence or the speaker! It is a characteristic attributed by receivers.

2. Credibility depends on variables related to the context, time, and situation in which the event occurs. For example, if the President scores a foreign policy victory, his credibility ratings go up. If the news media report the President is involved in a scandal of some kind, his credibility ratings go down.

3. Source credibility is more important when people cannot personally check and verify statements.

4. Listeners attribute some degree of credibility based on what you say ("derived credibility") and also based on their perceptions of what kind of a person you are ("initial credibility").

Speakers are sometimes tempted to invent evidence to support their arguments. Can you imagine a situation in which inventing evidence would be ethical?

So, how do you go about proving something? First, you must construct an argument, then support the argument with evidence and other arguments, then cause listeners to identify with the arguments and evidence—and with you. You cannot prove something, therefore, unless you understand your listeners well enough to select the right arguments and evidence.

How to Construct an Argument

Stephen Toulmin, a British philosopher, developed a model of the kind of persuasion most people usually encounter. His work, *The Uses of Argument*[5] is among the most influential books about argument and persuasion ever written. While Aristotle described formal argumentative structures called "syllogisms" and "enthymemes," Toulmin's contribution is a description of everyday encounters. Even though his ideas are jargon-bound, they are fairly simple to understand if you don't let the jargon put you off. And the ideas are very useful, indeed, when you set out to prove something to a listening audience.

Any argument can be divided into three basic parts: Claim, Data, and Warrant. A **claim** is any expression of an opinion or conclusion that a speaker wants accepted. **Data** means evidence, or grounds for accepting a claim. A **Warrant** is the line of reasoning that connects the data and the claim. Exhibit 6.5 shows the relationship among these parts as it is usually presented in textbooks.

The argument illustrated here seems compelling. Of course we should take her to the hospital. But the argument is nonetheless incomplete. How would the speaker know to make the statements in the warrant? Toulmin's system provides three more elements: Back-

EXHIBIT 6.5

TOULMIN'S BASIC MODEL OF PERSUASIVE ARGUMENTS	
DATA	**CLAIM**
My granddaughter accidentally rode her tricycle off the front porch. She has a deep cut on her jaw that is bleeding profusely, and another on her head. She is pale, she has a low-grade fever, and she says she is very sleepy.	We should take her to the hospital where they can clean and stitch up the cuts, and give her some medicine to fight any infection. Then we should take her home and keep her quiet—in bed, if possible—for several hours.

WARRANT

If the cuts aren't stitched up expertly, the wounds may heal with bad scars. Moreover, injuries of this kind often result in infection.

ing, Qualifier, and Reservation. **Backing** refers to any additional evidence and argument that supports the principle in the warrant. The **qualifier** tells how much confidence the speaker has in the claim. **Reservations** are any statements that might undermine or diminish the claim. Exhibit 6.6 shows the complete model as it is usually presented in texts about argumentation.

The key to using this model lies in the question: "How do you know?" Consider Grandfather's statement: We should take her to the hospital. If we were to ask him, "How do you know?" Grandfather might actually say out loud what he was thinking: "If the cuts aren't stitched up expertly, the wounds may heal with bad scars. Besides, injuries of this kind often result in infection."

> How do you know that, Grandfather?
>
> "I've seen this before. Plus, I've studied a little about scars and infections."

Now notice Grandfather's reservation. He is allergic to penicillin. We can suppose he suffered from a reaction to the drug—a reaction bad enough for him to worry about the possibility of passing his allergy down to his granddaughter. But his reservation cannot overcome the strength of his conviction that the granddaughter needs medical care.

EXHIBIT 6.6

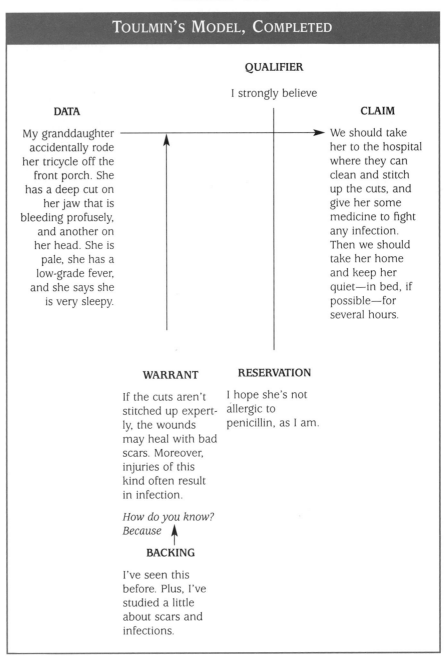

TOULMIN'S MODEL, COMPLETED

QUALIFIER

I strongly believe

DATA

My granddaughter accidentally rode her tricycle off the front porch. She has a deep cut on her jaw that is bleeding profusely, and another on her head. She is pale, she has a low-grade fever, and she says she is very sleepy.

CLAIM

We should take her to the hospital where they can clean and stitch up the cuts, and give her some medicine to fight any infection. Then we should take her home and keep her quiet—in bed, if possible—for several hours.

WARRANT

If the cuts aren't stitched up expertly, the wounds may heal with bad scars. Moreover, injuries of this kind often result in infection.

How do you know?
Because

BACKING

I've seen this before. Plus, I've studied a little about scars and infections.

RESERVATION

I hope she's not allergic to penicillin, as I am.

This is exactly the kind of mental/emotional process we go through when people try to persuade us. It is exactly the kind of mental/emotional process audience members go through when you try to prove something to them, too! And so the model tells you where and how to

EXHIBIT 6.7

USING TOULMIN'S MODEL TO CONSTRUCT AN ARGUMENT	
You think:	*You imagine the listener's response:*
Claim: *State your position.*	
The United States should guarantee the sovereignty of NATO nations with military force.	That's quite a claim! How do you know?
Data: *Make an argument that justifies the claim.*	
When NATO nation sovereignty is at risk, US interests require US military involvement.	Hummm. How do you know this to be true?
*(**Needed:** Evidence that will show the direct tie between NATO nation sovereignty and US interests).*	Okay
Warrant: *Support for the Data*	
The US is the only nation currently powerful enough to guarantee the sovereignty of other NATO nations.	I'm skeptical. How do you know?
*(**Needed:** Evidence that will show the US is the only NATO nation powerful enough to make the guarantee.)*	I'm not sure it is the responsibility of the United States. How do you know?
Reservation: *Statements that might undermine or diminish the claim.*	
But the Unites States should not assume sole responsibility for policing the world. We should urge the other NATO nations to join us.	
*(**Needed:** Evidence to show US responsibility for involving itself in the affairs of NATO, including the treaty details that show all NATO states share responsibility.)*	
Qualifier: *What is your level of confidence.*	Hummm. I have no doubts about this conclusion.
I have no doubts about this conclusion.	

use evidence and arguments. Coupled with careful audience analysis, it also suggests how much and what quality of evidence may be needed. Exhibit 6.7 suggests the sequence of events to follow when constructing an argument.

Would you trust a speaker or the speech if you discovered she or he had left out evidence which might have weakened the argument?

How to Support a Knowledge Claim with Arguments

To discover and use arguments, ask the question: What can I say that would be most likely to move my audience to feel or think or do as I want? From the listener's point of view, a speech must answer three questions: (1) What are you trying to tell me? (2) How do you know? (3) What difference does it make to me? The answers to these three questions are your arguments. Exhibit 6.8 shows how to use these three questions:

A knowledge claim—what you are trying to tell the listeners—can take three forms. In Exhibit 6.8 you undoubtedly noticed the terms fact, value, and policy. Exhibit 6.9 shows how to establish the credibility of these three kinds of knowledge claims.

How to Build Speaker Credibility

Research shows that listeners perceive speakers as credible when they meet three criteria: (1) expertise, (2) trustworthiness, and (3) attractiveness. Research also shows that listeners will not readily accept arguments from speakers they do not believe are credible. So it makes sense, a part of the process of proving, to learn how to build your credibility with the listeners. Exhibit 6.10 defines these three

Exhibit 6.8

Questions to Help Discover Needed Arguments	
Listener's question	*The argument you need*
What are you trying to tell me?	*Fact:* Something is.
	Value: Something is good, right, important, more, etc.
	Policy: Someone should or ought to do something.
How do you know?	The evidence says so.
Why does this matter to me?	This matters to you because . . . .

component parts of speaker credibility and makes suggestions for meeting the criteria. Notice how closely speaker credibility is tied to

EXHIBIT 6.9

	HOW TO ESTABLISH THE CREDIBILITY OF THREE KINDS OF KNOWLEDGE CLAIMS		
Kind	*Examples*	*What is needed*	*Test*
Fact	Andrea is an expert. Madhu is a graduate student in the Communication Department. That used to be a functioning unit.	Enough evidence and argument to cause listeners to believe the claim.	Is there enough evidence to establish this claim?
Value	That's a good idea. We've really screwed up this time. I just don't think there's enough collateral to support this loan application.	Arguments, supported by sufficient evidence, that establish the evaluative criteria as the right ones, followed by appropriate application of the criteria to the claim.	Are these the right criteria? Are there additional criteria needed to establish this claim? Do the criteria apply to the claim? Do the criteria establish the claim?
Policy	We should approve this loan application. You ought to tenure this faculty member. They should buy the john boat rather than the skiff. We ought to go to the movies tonight.	Argument and evidence that say the policy is needed in order to address some harm, and that the policy proposed will solve or resolve the harm.	*(The stock issues)* Is there a harm? Is the harm serious? Is the harm relevant to the audience? Will the proposal solve or resolve the harm? Are the means available to implement the proposal? Will the proposal generate new serious problems?

EXHIBIT 6.10

HOW TO BUILD SPEAKER CREDIBILITY		
Criterion	*Definition*	*Suggestions*
Expertise	Skillful; having much training and knowledge in a specific field	Become as skillful and knowledgeable as possible, then either have someone else tell them, or you tell your listeners of this expertise and your qualifications before and during the presentation.
Trustworthiness	Trust means having firm belief or confidence in the honesty, integrity, reliability, justice, etc., of another person. We trust people whose behavior we can predict, and whom we believe have our best interests at heart.	Behave honestly, justly, reliably. Make yourself predictable by consistently stating your intentions openly, then by following through on your intentions and honoring your commitments.
Attractiveness	The degree to which an audience admires and identifies with the source. Somewhat related to neat appearance. Closely related to how much psychological space the source can command.	Study your audience. Find the common ground with them, then claim the ground as your own. Act and speak confidently. As they say in theatre, "take the stage" when you make an entrance. Provide leadership and calm assurance. Look your best.

ethical behavior.

How to Support Arguments with Evidence

Evidence is the basic material of the argument, the data that are used as a base for an argument. Evidence refers to any informative statement that, because it is believed by a listener, can be used as a means for gaining the listener's support.[6]

The Types of Evidence

Several types of evidence are examined here, including testimony, definition and explanation, statistics, and examples. Exhibit 6.11 defines and provides an explanation of each type.

How to Test the Quality of Evidence

Several types of evidence—testimony, definition and explanation, statistics, and examples—have been discussed in this section. With all of these evidence types, test the evidence to be sure that it meets your standards. Ask the following questions about any evidence you plan to use:

EXHIBIT 6.11

THE TYPES OF EVIDENCE		
Criterion	*Definition*	*Explanation or expansion*
Testimony	Using the words of another person to support your argument.	Testimony from a prominent, qualified individual is called **expert testimony. Lay testimony** is testimony from the "man in the street." **Personal Testimony** or first person testimony, says "I was there, I saw; here were my experiences," and is sometimes used as a kind of eye witness testimony.
Definition and explanation	The formal statement of the meaning or significance of a word or phrase. To determine the nature and limits of a concept.	Two kinds of terms need definition: (1) very technical terms or jargon that only a specialist would understand, and (2) familiar terms that we use every day, but that, because of their various connotative meanings, convey different thing to different people.
Statistics	The use of numbers to support ideas. A shorthand method of summarizing a large number of cases.	Guidelines for using statistics include: 1. Round off complicated statistics. 2. Use representative statistics. 3. Explain what the statistics mean to the listeners. 4. Use visual aids to help explain statistics. 5. Do not use too many statistics. 6. Do not use sloppy statistics.
Examples	Something selected to show the nature or character of the rest; a typical instance.	A real example is a presentation of something that actually happened. Hypothetical examples are invented by speakers to represent reality when actual examples are not available.

This person is using statistics as supporting material. Notice how clearly the visual aid communicates those statistics. © Jose Palaez Photography/Stock Market

1. *Is there enough evidence to make your point believable?*

Exercise personal judgment here. Include enough high-quality evidence that a reasonable person will decide that your point has been supported convincingly.

2. *Is the evidence consistent with what is already known?*

Listeners are more likely to believe your evidence if it corresponds to what they already believe or know. Such evidence as "a fifty-five pound infant" or a "raccoon that dresses itself" clearly does not match up with listeners' previous experience. They already know that infants do not weigh that much and that animals do not dress themselves. Introduce evidence that reinforces already acquired information.

3. *Can you verify the evidence?*

Be sure that your evidence agrees with other sources. Select evidence that others can see and determine is valid. If your evidence is not verifiable, your credibility is damaged.

4. *Is the source of the evidence competent?*

This criterion applies to people as well as to publications. Sources who are "degreed," who have an MD, JD, Ph.D., or Ed.D. automatically have believability, although listeners want to know, when you refer to "doctor," whether you mean a physician, a veterinarian, or a college teacher. People with recognized reputations in their field are highly credible. Introduce them by demonstrating their level of competency.

Standards of competency also apply to published sources. Among the widely respected, nationally circulated newspapers are such publications as the *Wall Street Journal,* the *Des Moines Register,* the *Los Angeles Times,* and the *New York Times. Time Magazine, Newsweek,* and *US News & World Report* are weekly magazines that meet the tests of believability.

5. *Is the source of the evidence biased or prejudiced?*

Introduce evidence from impartial sources that do not profit from the information itself. Sources that look at all the information objectively do not reach biased conclusions.

6. *Is the evidence current?*

Sometimes the situation may call for evidence that shows historical development, but in most cases, your evidence should be fresh and up-to-date. In cases where you are presenting a particular person's view, remember that that person's position may have changed over time. Use information that honestly shows how the person feels now. The same standard applies to an issue like the national debt as a percentage of the gross national product. Be certain that you present the current picture, as well as perhaps provide a historical perspective.

Applying the Standards to Testimony

To apply the standards of evidence to testimony ask yourself:

1. *How consistent is the testimony?*

Does the information correspond to what listeners believe is reality? Is the information consistent within itself? Is it consistent with what we know about the world? Does the speaker get into contradictory positions or statements? If the answer to any of these questions is "yes," look elsewhere for testimony to support your ideas.

2. *Does the source have preconceived biases?*

Many people have an ax to grind. Is your source prejudiced or open-minded? Listeners respect a person who sees both sides of the issue more than a prejudiced source.

3. *Does the testimony agree with other expert?*

Look for consistency and representativeness in testimony. Everyone does not agree on every issue. However, sources who are at odds with everyone else may have questionable believability or motives. Check to see if your sources are in the mainstream of the field. If they are pioneers in their field, their testimony may be controversial, and you should inform listeners of possible controversy when you introduce your sources' testimony.

Would you ever try to hide the bias of a source from an audience?

Applying the Standards to Examples

To apply the standards of evidence to examples ask:

1. *Is the example typical?*

   Examples should represent events or situations that are typical—common in the experience of the listeners.

2. *Are the examples sufficient in number?*

   Do not rely upon a single example to establish your argument. Provide at least two examples to show listeners that you have a common position that is understandable. If you can, follow up with a credible statistic. Remember, statistics are short-hand summaries of long lists of examples.

3. *Are the examples recent?*

   Unless you are talking about historical matters or can show a reason for introducing old data, present examples chosen from recent events. Time changes society, and listeners want up-to-date support that recognizes situations of today.

Pointers on Using Examples as Evidence

1. Use real examples when you can.
2. Build the strength of an idea by stacking up brief examples, then following up with statistics to show the brief examples are not isolated cases.
3. Use hypothetical examples only when you can't find a real example. Be sure the hypothetical example seems consistent with what the listeners already know, and truly illustrates the idea you are trying to explain.
4. Use many examples. They may be the most powerful forms of supporting material.

This speaker is using testimony by referencing a source that is acceptable to his listeners. © Gary Conner/PhotoEdit

Appendix A, "Sample Speeches," contains a speech that applies evidence well. The speech, by Amy Olson of Bradley University, uses evidence to prove to listeners that a problem exists in the movement to recycle paper.

SUMMARY

Successful speaking depends greatly on how speakers present and support their ideas and arguments. This chapter examines the different types of arguments, artistic proofs, and evidence.

An argument is a piece of reasoning in which one or more statements are offered as support for some other statement. Inductive arguments work from a series of individual cases to a conclusion, while deductive arguments proceed from a general conclusion and then identify the specific instances that establish the conclusion. Arguments from sign observe that characteristic features or symptoms suggest a state of affairs. An argument from cause is based on the assumption that something happened because of an earlier event. An argument from analogy involves comparing a known and understood set of facts to less well-known ones and then arguing that the two sets of facts are similar.

While the statements used to support an argument are called proofs, proofs can also be more generally defined as artistic elements that provide a reason for supporting the speaker's position. Aristotle identified three categories of artistic proofs: ethos, pathos, and logos. Speaker credibility, an essential element in any communication, is an element of ethos. Pathos involves emotional appeals, such as feelings of fear, pride, pity, concern, and courage. Logos includes two types of rational appeals: the syllogism and the enthymeme.

Effective arguments must be supported by evidence that backs up the speaker's claim. Expert testimony, lay testimony, personal testimony, definitions and explanations, statistics, and real and hypothetical examples are all effective categories of evidence. All evidence should be evaluated in terms of the competency of the source and the believability, consistency, verifiability, and currency of the evidence itself.

KEY TERMS

Argument	Credibility	Expert testimony
Argument from sign	Deductive argument	Inductive argument
Argument from cause	Definition and explanation	Lay testimony
Argument from example	Evidence	Statistics
Argument from authority	Examples	Testimony

APPLICATION QUESTIONS

1. Arguments occur all around you. Spend half a day making notes each time you hear or see some examples of argument. Try to classify the arguments as inductive or deductive, or as an argument from cause, sign, analogy or authority. Compare your notes with your classmates' findings. Based on this informal research, which kinds of arguments seem most common? Why do you suppose that is?

2. Bring to class a magazine that you purchased before reading this chapter. With a group of your classmates, page through the magazine and study the advertisements. You will find that every ad in the magazine makes an argument. Can you classify the arguments you find? Do the advertisers offer any supporting proofs for their arguments? How do the proofs stand up to the tests of evidence?

3. What is your position on the following controversial issues?

    Euthanasia

    Assisted suicide

    Guaranteed minimum annual cash income for every American citizen

    The next U.S. president being a Republican

4. How much evidence, and what kinds, would someone have to provide in order to persuade you to change your mind? What insights does this give you about argumentation?

IT'S MORE FUN TO KNOW

A massive literature supports the claims of this chapter.

On uses of evidence:

In 1969 James C. McCroskey published "A Summary of Experimental Research on the Effects of Evidence in Persuasive Communication" in *Quarterly Journal of Speech*, 55 (1969), p. 169. Thomas B. Harte tied the perception of source credibility to the effects of evidence in his essay, "The Effects of Evidence in Persuasive Communication" *Central States Speech Journal,* 27 (1976), pp. 42–46. R. Glen Hass reviewed and summarized the literature on source credibility in his essay "Effects of Source Characteristics on Cognitive Responses and Persuasion," in *Cognitive Responses in Persuasion,* Richard E. Petty, Thomas M. Ostrom, and Timothy C. Brock, eds. (Hillsdale, NJ: Lawrence Erlbaum Associates, 1981), pp. 141–172.

In 1983 Rodney Reynolds and Michael Burgoon published a review of the research that ties belief, reasoning and evidence together. They concluded there is a massive correlation between assertions that seem to report data and changes in attitudes. Among other things, they argued: (1) use of evidence produces more attitude change than not using evidence, and more than simple assertions. (2) If a speaker is low on credibility, he or she should use highly relevant evidence from well-respected sources. If the speaker cites the evidence clearly his or her credibility rises. Plus, the clearer the evidence cited the greater the perception that both the evidence and the speaker are credible. (4) The use of evidence produces attitude change in receivers who don't have prior knowledge of the evidence. It increases attitude change over time regardless of whether the speaker seems credible, but only when the receivers hold strong attitudes on the subject. (5) Receivers evaluate the evidence they hear through the frame of reference of their own attitudes, and this is true no matter the quality of the evidence.

On source credibility:

The three criteria of expertise, trustworthiness, and attractiveness have emerged from much research. As early as 1969, David K. Berlo and his colleagues asked audiences to describe what they find credible. (See "Dimensions for Evaluating the Acceptability of Message Sources" *Public Opinion Quarterly,* 33, pp. 563–576.) In the early 1950s Hovland, Janis, and Kelley conducted a massive study at Yale University, concluding the credibility of any source depends on attributions of trust and confidence. (See C. Hovland, I. Janis and H. Kelley, *Communication and Persuasion.* New Haven, CT: Yale University Press, 1953.) In the middle 1970s researchers Baudhin and Davis ("Scales for the Measurement of Ethos: Another Attempt. *Speech Monographs* 39, 1972, pp. 296–301.) wrote that audience members find sources credible if they are perceived as safe and possessed of personal integrity. Credibility has considerable application in the business world. Researchers have found that managers with high credibility instill a greater work ethic in employees and thus the employees work harder and feel better (See J.M. Kouzes and B.Z. Posner, *Credibility: How Leaders Gain It and Lose It, Why Some People Demand It.* San Francisco: Jossey-Bass, 1993). More recently, Gass and Seiter, (*Persuasion, Social Influence and Compliance Gaining.* Boston: Allyn and Bacon, 1999) summarized the research with a series of strategies for enhancing speaker credibility.

SELF-TEST FOR REVIEW

1. Match the following terms and definitions.

   ____ 1. Any expression of an opinion or a conclusion.

   ____ 2. Line of reasoning that connects data and claim.

   ____ 3. Reasoning that a feature or symptom suggests a state of affairs.

   ____ 4. Statements or facts used to support a knowledge claim.

   ____ 5. Degree to which a listener believes something.

   ____ 6. Reasoning that something happened because of an earlier event.

   ____ 7. Reasoning from individual cases to a conclusion.

   ____ 8. Reasoning that something is so because an expert says it is so.

   A. Warrant
   B. Inductive argument
   C. Argument from sign
   D. Argument from cause
   E. Knowledge claim
   F. Argument from authority
   G. Credibility
   H. Evidence

2. "There is ice on the lake. Winter has come early." This is an example of an argument from

   a. sign.
   b. cause.
   c. induction.
   d. example.

3. First person: "They say Tabasco sauce in raw oyster sauce kills bacteria." Second person: "Hmm. I always put Tabasco into my sauce. No wonder I never got sick from eating raw oysters." The second statement is

   a. an example of a categorical syllogism.
   b. a logically correct example of argument from sign.
   c. a logically fallacious example of causal reasoning.
   d. a correct example of inductive reasoning.

4. Match each of the testimony examples with the numbered "test" for judging the quality of testimonial evidence that could be applied to identify problems with the testimony.

   ____ a. Of course it is hot outside. In New York in January, the average daytime temperature is somewhere near 75 degrees.

   ____ b. I'm not a doctor, but I play one on TV. So I'm concerned about the common cold. Despite what they may say, one cold tablet has been shown by leading experts to cure the common cold in just seven days.

   ____ c. It's a well-known fact that the African race just isn't as smart as the Aryan race.

   1. How consistent is the testimony?

   2. Does the source have preconceived biases?

   3. Does the testimony agree with other expert opinion?

Answers: 1. 1-E, 2-A, 3-C, 4-H, 5-G, 6-D, 7-B, 8-F; 2-A, 3-C; 4. a-1, b-3, c-2.

SUGGESTED READINGS

Freely, Austin J., *Argumentation and Debate: Critical Thinking for Reasoned Decision Making.* 9th ed. Belmont, Calif.: Wadsworth, 1997. This is one of the standard works in argumentation and is essential for anyone who wants to understand the area.

Nozick, Robert. *The Nature of Rationality.* San Francisco: Laissez Faire Books, 1993. This work is sometimes difficult to read, but it is well worth the effort. The book shows clearly that rational thought is essential to civilization and human progress.

Reinard, John C., *Foundations of Argument: Effective Communication for Critical Thinking.* Dubuque, Iowa: Brown & Benchmark Publishers, 1991. This work is more difficult reading but is well worth the effort for a student who wishes to explore in greater depth the theory and methods of contemporary argumentation.

Rybacki, Karyn Charles and Donald J. Rybacki (Contributor). *Advocacy and Opposition: An Introduction to Argument, 3rd ed.* Boston: Allyn and Bacon, 1996. A basic book which provides an interesting foundation for the development and refinement of argument and tests of reasoning. It also includes emphasis on the creation of argument using the Toulmin approach.

Walton, Douglas. *Appeal to Expert Opinion: Arguments from Authority.* University Park: Pennsylvania State University Press, 1997. A brief but thorough examination of the use of authority arguments, their strengths and methods for their use. Highly recommended for persons interested in an in-depth analysis of all aspects of argument.

Warnick, Barbara, and Edward S. Inch. *Critical Thinking and Communication: The Use of Reason in Argument.* 3rd ed. Boston: Allyn and Bacon, 1997. This thorough work is clearly written and full of illustrations and examples. You will find it both interesting and easy to read.

INTERNET ACTIVITIES

1. The Federal Government has developed a lengthy and detailed web site on the rules of evidence in law. You may find parts of the site interesting. Go to the URL:
   http://www.law.cornell.edu/rules/fre/overview.html

2. Go to any search engine home page and type the words "using evidence." You will get more than half a million "hits." Try typing in these key terms from this chapter: argumentation, induction, deduction, reasoning, supporting arguments, statistics, testimony, etc. Each new search will demonstrate the overwhelming importance of developing and supporting your arguments carefully.

NOTES

1. S. Morris Engel, *With Good Reason: An Introduction to Informal Fallacies*, 3rd ed (New York: St Martin's Press, 1986), p. 9.

2. Austin Freeley, *Argumentation and Debate: Critical Thinking for Reasoned Decision Making*, 9th ed (Belmont, CA: Wadsworth Publishing Co., 1997).

3. This definition is based on the classic work of Douglas Ehninger and Wayne Brockriede, *Decision by Debate* (New York: Dodd, Mead & Company, 1963), p. 110.

4. "Workers see opportunity where others see abuse" *Mobile Register* Saturday, February 20, 1999, p. 15A, column 2.

5. Stephen Toulmin, *The Uses of Argument* (Cambridge, England: Cambridge University Press, 1964).

6. Dean C. Kazoleas, "A Comparison of the Persuasive Effectiveness of Qualitative Versus Quantitative Efficiency: A Test of Explanatory Hypotheses," *Communication Quarterly.* 41 (1993), pp. 40–50.

CHAPTER 7

HOW TO GATHER SUPPORTING MATERIALS

OBJECTIVES

1. You should be able to explain how to locate information by interviewing and corresponding with your network of friends and acquaintances.

2. You should be able to describe some of the more useful computerized database services available in libraries and on the Internet.

3. You should be able to name and use various general and specialized indexes in your library (paper-based or computer-based) and on the Internet.

4. You should be able to name and describe the departments in a college or university library and explain what those departments do, and use this information to find supporting materials in a variety of on-line libraries and resources.

5. You should be able to explain how to find, and easily and efficiently find materials in a library and on the Internet.

6. You should be able to describe how to use the holdings catalog and electronic database indices in your library (card or on-line).

7. You should be able to test the quality and sources of evidence found on the Internet.

8. You should be able to take adequate notes from library materials.

9. You should be able to develop a working bibliography for a speech.

10. You should be able to use your note card file to organize your ideas for a presentation.

OUTLINE

Objectives
Outline
Abstract
Imagine
Introduction
  A word about ethics in
    scholarship
How to Locate Information by
  Interviewing and Correspond-
  ing with Your Network of
  Friends and Acquaintances
  Information-gathering
    Interview
  Gathering Information
    Through Correspondence
How to Use the Library
  Finding Your Way Around
    the Library
  How to Use Some of the More
    Useful Computerized Data-
    bases in the Library
  How to Conduct a Key-Word
    Search
  How to Use Various General
    and Specialized Indexes in
    Your Library (Paper-based
    or Computer-based) and on
    the Internet
  How to Use Reference Works
    Atlases and Gazettes
    Biographical Aids
    Dictionaries
    Encyclopedias

How to Use the Internet
  for Research
  Search Engines
  Use the Library as a
    Metaphor for Your Research
    On Line
  Bookmark Interesting
    WebSites
  Examine Specialized
    Resources First
    Reference Sources
  Evaluate Internet and Other
    Research Documents
  Make Careful and Complete
    Notes the First Time
    Use Note Cards or Half
      Sheets
    Establish a Standard Form
      of Entry
    Use One Card Per Entry
      and One Entry Per Card
    Take Plenty of Notes
    Do Not Plagiarize, Even
      by Accident
  Develop a Working
    Bibliography
  Use Your Note Card File to
    Plan a Speech
Summary
Key Terms
Application Questions
Self-Test for Review
Suggested Readings
It's More Fun to Know
Notes

ABSTRACT

This chapter is about gathering supporting materials for discourse—an activity that lies at the heart of scholarship. Sometimes we ask questions of friends and acquaintances. Sometimes we use the library. Sometimes we go to the Internet for information.

An information-gathering interview is different from a casual conversation, even when you are interviewing a friend. The difference lies in the planning that goes into the interview and the way you organize it.

If you know you're looking for fresh fruit in a grocery store, then in Denver or Philadelphia, you know that all you have to do is locate the produce department. The departments in a library are fairly uniform from institution to institution, much as they are similar in grocery stores. Since all libraries are similar in how they are organized, once you understand the first one you will know about them all.

This chapter identifies the more useful databases in libraries and on the Internet, and shows you how to conduct a key-work search so you can use them efficiently and effectively. It also identifies and tells you how to use atlases and gazettes, biographical aids and specialized dictionaries and encyclopedias.

The Internet is the world's largest library, so you can use your college library as a model for finding materials on the Internet. But you must know how to use the tools. And so this chapter tells you how to use search engines, how to bookmark interesting and relevant websites, and how to examine and evaluate the wonderful resources you will find on the Internet.

Finally, we close with practical suggestions for such things as taking effective notes, developing a working bibliography, and using your note card file as a tool for planning discourse.

IMAGINE

When Jack Abshire,[1] a business management major, was researching the Internet for his first assigned teaching speech he stumbled across the website of the Portland, Oregon, Toastmasters' Club *<http://omhs.mhd.hr.state.or.us/tnt/>*. There he found a speech outline, complete with PowerPoint "slides" by a man named Dave Simpson titled "Building High Trust Organizations." Jack was excited because this was exactly the topic he had decided to speak about. He downloaded the outline and the PowerPoint presentation, and used these materials, with adaptations for his classroom audience and situation, to plan his own speech. After a good many practice sessions Jack went confidently to class, where he delivered a well-received speech.

Later, just as his professor was about to record an A grade for Jack, another student knocked on the professor's office door. "Jack Abshire's speech came from the Internet," he said. After locating the outline, the professor recorded an F grade for Jack's speech, and wrote to the Student Government Honor Violation Committee urging disciplinary action.

Your contacts constitute a valuable source of information. © Prentice Hall

INTRODUCTION

This chapter is about how you can most easily and effectively gather appropriate and compelling supporting material for speeches. Not only does the chapter make suggestions about how to gather information through interviews and correspondence, it also includes a thorough description of how to find materials in your library and on the Internet. The chapter tells how best to take notes, how to test the quality of the materials you find, and how to use that material. Some students find this task a struggle, while others seem to breeze through it with a smile. The difference between struggle and smile is all in the research techniques those students use. Once you know the best techniques, the task becomes both interesting and rewarding.

A Word About Ethics in Scholarship

Jack Abshire's story raises a number of ethical questions. For Jack, there is the whole matter of plagiarism. For the other student, there are questions of interpersonal loyalty and trust. For the professor, questions arise about what is in the student's best interest, and about where his responsibility to other students and his institution's plagiarism policy lies.

Ethical issues bear upon every decision a speaker makes when conducting research. For example, it seems apparent that each speaker/scholar must do everything possible to verify the accuracy of information, to verify the quality of the sources of evidence, and to present as accurate a picture of the truth as possible and practicable within the constraints of a speaking assignment.

How to Locate Information by Interviewing and Corresponding with Your Network of Friends and Acquaintances

Information-gathering Interview

Who do you know? Friends, family members, acquaintances and coworkers, colleagues and teachers all can provide valuable information if you know how to draw it out of them. An information-gathering interview is designed to do just that.[2] Such interviews usually involve five planning steps, each of which can determine whether you get the information you need or want. Exhibit 7.1 describes these steps.

Gathering Information Through Correspondence

Sometimes it's not possible to interview an information source in person. You will need writing skills and some time to get information through correspondence, but don't overlook this important means of research. Direct correspondence can often provide information not available in any other way. Moreover, with the advent of computers and email, the turn-around time between question and response could be as brief as a few minutes! The questions in Exhibit 7.1 can help you as you think about how to ask for information in a letter. But to whom should you write for information besides your immediate circle of friends and acquaintances?

The Internet includes websites for all kinds of special interest groups, and most of these websites maintain email capability. But you must be careful in using such interest groups for research—their information is always favorable to themselves.

For a thorough list of lobbyists and other interest groups[3] you can go to Internet address (URL) of the National Lobbyists Directory, *http://www.lobbyistdirectory.com/* or you can access the search engine, Dogpile, (*http://www.dogpile.com*) and type in the word "lobbyists." This "search engine" activates about 20 other search engines at once, then displays the results of this massive Internet search. A **search engine** is a tool that catalogs WWW pages and helps you

EXHIBIT 7.1

THE FIVE STEPS IN PLANNING AN INTERVIEW

Step 1. Identify whom you can go to for the information you want.

  Who knows what you want to learn?

  What background material will you need in order to ask intelligent questions?

Step 2. Identify what questions you must ask the person you interview.

  What information do you want to get from this particular person?

  How might you phrase questions to get at this information without offending the person?

Step 3. Plan how to probe into the answers you receive.

  What questions might ensure elaboration? (Examples: "Could you elaborate on that, please?" "Could you give me an example of that?")

  What questions might secure clarification? (Examples: "Could you clarify that for me, please?" "Could you give me an example of that?")

Step 4. Plan how to handle common problems in the interview.

  The reluctant respondent

  "You seem uneasy. Could you tell me why?"

  "Would you like to move somewhere else?"

  Active listening or silence may draw out a reluctant respondent.

  The emotional respondent

  "It's okay to cry. Please go on when you can."

  "We're not in a hurry. Take as much time as you want."

  "Would you rather talk at another time?"

  The hostile respondent

  "You seem angry. Would you tell me about it?"

  "Are you upset? Is anything wrong?"

  "Would you be willing to elaborate on your criticism?"

Step 5. Determine how to validate or verify what you learn in the interview.

  Seek opinions from other experts for comparison and contrast.

  Consider your source. Was the source biased? Competent? Forthcoming?

Source: Based on Gerald L. Wilson and H. Lloyd Goodall, Jr., *Interviewing in Context* (New York: McGraw-Hill, 1991), pp. 216–40.

locate them. They work by finding words on the Internet that you have commanded them to find. Exhibit 7.2 shows the screen that popped up at URL when the command "lobbyists" was typed into box. You can see that the first search engine, Thunderstone, gave links to 419 Internet documents.

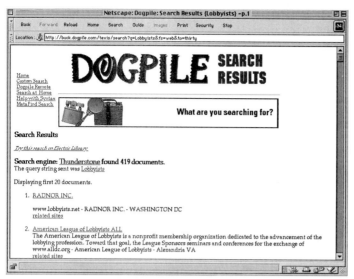

EXHIBIT **7.2** The first page of a Dogpile search results conducted in February, 1999.

HOW TO USE THE LIBRARY

You won't find a better intellectual resource than your school or public library. Plus, the library skills you learn now will be helpful to you long after you complete your course in public speaking. Libraries hold the world's knowledge—yours for the asking. But you must know what to ask for and how to ask for it.

Finding Your Way Around the Library

Think of a library as you would a department store. When you enter any large department store, you know that you will find such departments as men's clothing, housewares, electronics, cosmetics, and the like. Department stores do not all have the same floor plan, of course, but that rarely stops you from finding what you want. In general, regardless of the department store's name or location, you know what department you need to go to when you want to make a particular purchase.

Libraries resemble each other, too. Some are larger, some are smaller, and they may be organized a bit differently. Even so, most college or university libraries have the following departments: (1) reference, (2) circulation, (3) reserve readings, (4) government documents, (5) serials and periodicals, (6) microform, (7) instructional media, (8) interlibrary loan, (9) database searching, and (10) specialized collections. Exhibit 7.3 describes these library departments.

EXHIBIT 7.3

DEPARTMENTS IN A LIBRARY:	
Reference Department	The library reference department houses a broad range of reference works that usually are not circulated out of the library. Here you will find general and specialized dictionaries, general and specialized encyclopedias, almanacs, handbooks, college catalogs, directories, telephone books, and many general and specialized bibliographies, abstracts, and indexes. Students often find encyclopedias especially helpful. Encyclopedias are arranged alphabetically by subject matter and are very easy to use.
Circulation Department	Employees of the library circulation department typically maintain the library's bookshelves and check out materials that circulate. Most books, of course, circulate, as may records, tapes, CDs, portable computers, computer software, VCRs, and videotapes. The circulation department is usually located near the library's main entrance for convenient check out of materials by library patrons.
Reserve Readings Department	Many instructors place materials "on reserve" for their students. These materials may include library property and/or the instructor's personal property. Reserve materials do not usually circulate for more than an hour or two at a time. Some libraries allow overnight circulation privileges in certain cases. Materials on temporary reserve flow in and out of the department according to the institution's needs. For example, particular courses offered in a given term may require that special materials in the library be placed on temporary reserve for the students in those courses. Permanent reserve materials usually include very rare or valuable materials that the library could not replace. Libraries often house this material in an area called "Rare Books and Materials."
Government Documents Department	The government documents department in a library houses publications originating in or issued by federal, state, and local government agencies. Some of these circulate; some do not. This collection may seem daunting and difficult to access because the government has such varied interests, but it is also one of the library's most useful collections. Your library may have part of the collection on CD-ROM. If so, the task of locating materials becomes much easier. Usually, you will find a brochure in the government documents section that tells you how to use the collection.

Continued

Exhibit 7.3 *continued*

Serials and Periodicals Department	The library serials and periodicals department will help you find information in newspapers, magazines, and other serial publications. Some of these are bound volumes, while others are stored on microfilm or microfiche. The most recent issues of journals, magazines, and newspapers are stored on racks near or in a reading room. Not all libraries house these materials in one centralized location. Your library may divide the collection according to appropriate subject areas. Ask the librarian at the serials and periodicals information desk about how the department is arranged, and request help with your research if you need it.
Microform Department	The library microform department may be integrated with serials and periodicals or with print materials (especially in subject-divided libraries), or it may be a separate department. Microform materials include back issues of newspapers and magazines and such wonders as the *Library of American Civilization* and the *Library of English Literature.* These materials do not usually circulate, but you can make photocopies. Ask a librarian for help.
Instructional Media Department	The library instructional media department houses a wide variety of audio and visual materials, including records, tape recordings, foreign language lessons, plays, films, 35mm filmstrips, slides, videotapes, and photographic archives. These materials may circulate.
Interlibrary Loan Department	Even with all the materials available in a single library, serious researchers may have to borrow from more than one library. For example, a Ph.D. dissertation written by a University of Wisconsin student might hold the key to a California-based researcher's problem. Materials of all kinds move from one library to another through the interlibrary loan system. Before using this service, be sure that your own library does not have the materials you need. Interlibrary loans can be expensive. Also, although materials usually arrive within three to five days of the request, delays are not uncommon.
Database Searching Department	Your library may have a database searching department or division, while other libraries may have a database-searching unit within the reference, serials and periodicals, or interlibrary loan departments. This unit provides computer searches in specific subject areas of both the library's holdings and of materials not owned by the library. A search produces citations (with or without abstracts or summaries) of books, articles, and other documents.

Continued

Exhibit 7.3 *continued*

Specialized Collections Department	Libraries sometimes develop specialized collections that are often housed in separate facilities. For example, if you have a medical school at your institution, you will almost certainly find a medical or biomedical library. Law schools usually have a law library. Journalism schools often house a branch of the library specifically for their students. You probably will find a map library that supports your institution's programs in geography and geology. Your institution also may have a religion and theology library.
	Find out which specialized collections your library holds and where the collections are kept. Even if your special interest lies outside the medical field, you might need the books, journals, and other materials that support medical research, basic medical sciences, speech pathology, nursing, and other allied health science programs.

How to Use Some of the More Useful Computerized Databases in the Library

Most libraries now offer a vast array of electronic resources, and many have "put up" their holdings onto the Internet so users can access them from their home computers. Perhaps the most useful of all such databases is the library holdings catalog. Exhibit 7.4 displays a computer catalog entry for a book.

The key word search was "logic." The catalog produced 917 sources. Having selected the first entry on the list, this screen popped up. This entry happens to be a book, as you can see. Entries in this

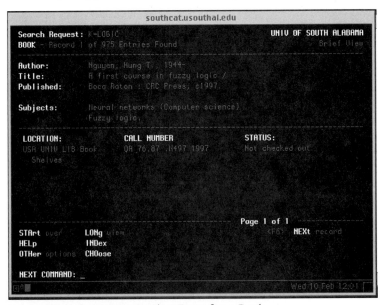

EXHIBIT 7.4 Computer Catalog Entry for a Book

catalog for periodicals also look like this screen. All the information is clearly available. Be sure to write down all the relevant data the first time you make a note! This habit will save you countless hours of doubling back on yourself. For instance, you need all of the call numbers to find a book in the stacks. The call numbers are like a street address. You would not be able to find someone's house if the only information you had was "I live on Main Street." You would need a city and state name. You would need a particular house number on Main Street.

How to Conduct a Key-Word Search

Any college student can easily conduct key-word, subject, and author searches. Exhibit 7.5 provides the Boolean syntax you will find most useful in conducting key-word searches.

EXHIBIT 7.5

HOW TO CONDUCT A KEY WORD SEARCH	
Simple Keyword Searches: And, Or, Not	K = cameras This retrieves all records that have this word. K = IBM *and* computer This retrieves all records that contain **both** of these words. K = wilson *and* organizations This retrieves records with **both** a name and another word. Most online catalogs do not use punctuation or capitalization, but yours may. K = dog *or* K9 This retrieves all items that contain **either** word. K = hamlet *not* shakespeare. This eliminates undesired records.
Qualifying Search Terms to Fields: Author, Title, Subject Headings	K = johnson.au. and president.ti This retrieves items with Johnson just in the author field and president just in the title field. Very useful for authors with common names. K = blue.ti. This retrieves items only with the word *blue* in the title. K = johnson.su. This retrieves only items with Johnson as the subject.
Qualifying Search to Format, Language, Year	K = management and s.fmt. This retrieves all records in a serial format that also have the word *management* in the record. K = fellini and f.fmt. This retrieves all films and videotapes that also have the word *Fellini* in the record.

Continued

Exhibit 7.5 *continued*

	K = opera and italian and m.fmt. This retrieves Italian operas in a music format, such as scores, records, and CDs. K = sartre and fr.la. This retrieves French language materials with the name *Sartre* in the record. K = hanna and 1999.yr. This will retrieve records with a 1999 date that have the name Hanna in the record.
Truncation of Search Terms	Some systems will let you use wild cards, such as to reduce the amount of typing necessary to access a record. Hint: Truncate only to the root word to avoid irrelevant records. K = tolst? and war.ti. This will pull up records with varied spellings for Tolstoy that also have the word *war* in the title. K = wordsworth and 197? This will produce all records that have a date in the 1970s and the name *Wordsworth*.
Stop Words	A number of short, often-used words, such as *a, an, it, no, on, the, to,* and various forms of the verb *to be,* do not work in database searching. A help screen often lists the seventy or more items that qualify as stop words in your catalog.
Qualifying by Position: *Adjacent, Near, With, Same*	Specifying the word order of a keyword search helps to eliminate unwanted records. K = child? abuse The system assumes that you mean *next to* or *on either side,* so it brings up child abuse as well as abuse of children. (*Of* is a stop word, so it is not counted.) K = home adj nursing This retrieves records with the words adjacent and in this order (that is, *home nursing*). It excludes records about nursing homes. K = writing with manual This brings up all records with the two words *writing* and *manual* in the same sentence. K = writing same editing This retrieves records that have the words *writing* and *editing* in the same set of fields. All the subject headings will be pulled up, for example.
Nested Searches	You can accomplish truly sophisticated and magical searches by using parentheses to set off different parts of the search. K = (theatre or theater) and history) and (greece or greek) This retrieves records about the theater of Greece and the history of Greece and includes records bearing the language "Greek theater" and "Greek history," no matter how you spell *theater.*
Note: The authors gratefully acknowledge the University of South Alabama Library staff for their help in providing this information.	

How to Use Various General and Specialized Indexes in Your Library (Paper-based or Computer-based) and on the Internet.

Libraries make available hundreds of general and specialized indexes, and they house them both on paper and in electronic media. An **index** is a research aid that catalogs articles from both popular and scholarly periodicals. You will have to find out what your library offers, and in what form. For example, some libraries have *Dissertation Abstracts* on paper only. Others offer the collection on CD-ROM. Others, still, subscribe to *Dissertation Abstracts* on line through the Internet. Exhibit 7.6 describes some of the most useful general indexes.

You will find a very large number of specialized indexes, too. These specialized indexes focus on nearly every subject you can imagine, so they are especially useful when you already have a clear idea of your subject matter. For example, if you knew you were interested in the topic "communication," you would find *Com Abstracts* useful. *Com Abstracts* provides access to full-text articles from EJC/REC: The Electronic Journal of Communication/La Revue Electronique de Communication. It also provides bibliographic information and abstracts for approximately 40 journals. Within the CIOS service that provides Com Abstracts you will find, also, ComWeb MegaSearch. This tool allows you to search the full text of approximately 12,000 Web pages that are related to communications topics. Links within ComWeb are only active for CIOS members. CIOS also includes a resource library with announcements of professional events, bibliographies, Communication Research and Theory Network postings, descriptions of graduate programs in communications, a research collection, a syllabus collection, and instructions to authors for submission of articles to specific journals.

Exhibit 7.7 lists just a few of the many specialized indexes available in your library. The reference librarian will be pleased to name several of interest to you, and probably will hand you a list!

Librarians want to be helpful, so they encourage students to let them help. At what point, if any, would it become unethical to rely upon a librarian's help?

How to Use Reference Works

A reference work is a tool designed to synthesize a large amount of information, and to organize that information for easy access—usually by alphabetical order. Four useful categories of reference works include: (1) Atlases and Gazettes, (2) Biographical Aids, (3) Dictionaries, and (4) Encyclopedias.

EXHIBIT 7.6

COMMONLY USED GENERAL INDEXES

Reader's Guide to Periodical Literature	Lists the articles in more than 250 of the most commonly read magazines in the United States. The chances are good that, if you know the name of a magazine, it is indexed in *Reader's Guide.*
InfoTrac	*Expand*ed Academic ASAP 1996–Feb 1999 with access to backfile (1980–1995). Use this database to find information on: Astronomy, Religion, Law, History, Psychology, Humanities, Current Events, Sociology, Communications, and the General Sciences.
	General BusinessFile ASAP 1996–Feb 1999 with access to backfile (1980–1995) Use this database to find articles on: Finance, Acquisitions & Mergers, International Trade, Money Management, New Technologies & Products, Local & Regional Business Trends, Investments and Banking.
	Health Reference Center-Academic 1995–Feb 1999. Use this database to find articles on: Fitness, Pregnancy, Medicine, Nutrition, Diseases, Public Health, Occupational Health & Safety, Alcohol and Drug abuse, HMOs, Prescription Drugs, etc.
First Search	Index to articles in many sources, and arranged in categories: Arts & Humanities, Business & Economics, Conferences & Proceedings, Consumer Affairs & People, Education, Engineering & Technology, General & Reference, General Science, Life Sciences, Medicine & Health Sciences, News & Current Events, Public Affairs & Law, and Social Sciences.
Lexis and Nexis	Provides online, full-text access to legal cases and decisions, newspapers and magazines, country profiles, law reviews, company financial information, biographical information and more.
Academic Search FullTEXT Elite	This is a general interest database offering coverage of a wide variety of topics including social sciences, business, humanities, general science, and education. Of the over 3000 journals indexed, approximately one third are full-text. TIP: When searching an education topic, Academic Search and ERIC may be searched simultaneously by checking the boxes for both databases and then choosing ENTER.
ERIC	Articles about research findings in every academic or educational area have been collected in this huge and easy-to-use database.
Public Affairs Information Service	Indexes journal articles in a wide range of areas, and includes citations for government documents. Here you will find statistical information and other works about public policy.

EXHIBIT 7.7

SOME SPECIALIZED INDEXES

AGRICOLA: indexes to books and articles on agriculture.

Dissertation Abstracts

Historical Abstracts: Index to historical materials on all countries except the United States and Canada

International DataBase (IDB): demographic and statistical data for all countries of the world.

Population Index

RISM Online: International Inventory of Musical Sources

Sociological Abstracts: Citations and abstracts for materials about the social sciences.

Statistical Abstract of the United States

WorldAlmanac

Atlases and Gazettes

An atlas contains maps, and a wealth of information about the geography of the places cited in the atlas. Two of the best known are *National Geographic Atlas of the World* and *the Rand McNally Cosmopolitan World Atlas*. A gazette is a hybrid work—something like a dictionary and something like an encyclopedia—that deals only with geography topics. They list places and give information about the places. If you want to know how many people live in France, or what agricultural products a country or a state produces, the place to go is to a gazette. Perhaps the best known is *Webster's New Geographical Dictionary*.

Biographical Aids

A **biographical aid** is a tool designed to provide information about people. Usually, but not always, the entries in these works have been prepared by the people named in the listings. So, the facts will probably be accurate, but the descriptive passages may very well be biased. When accuracy really matters, double-check the facts by cross-referencing the subject in another biographical aid if you can.

Biography Index is a good place to start, since it tells you where to find the biographical information you seek.

Among the most useful biographical aids are the *Who's Who* books. You can find a *Who's Who* book of biographies in just about any area. And there are others. For a partial list of examples:

Contemporary Black Biography
Dictionary of Hispanic Biography

The library houses a lot of material. The catalog will help you sort it out and tell you its location. But you must take careful notes or you still may not be able to find what you're looking for. © Frank Pedrick/Image Works

International Who's Who

Native American Women

Who's Who in America

Who's Who Among Asian Americans

Who's Who of American Women

Dictionaries

You probably own an excellent dictionary of the English language. You may also own a translating dictionary that will list from English to another language and from that other language into English. These books provide a wealth of information—and many are available on disk or *on line*.

But suppose you are more interested in the history of a word than in its definition. In that case you would probably go to *The Oxford English Dictionary.*

Or suppose you need a very specialized dictionary—one that will define technical terms such as you might find in law or in medicine, in electronic engineering or in computer science. The library reference room has many such technical dictionaries. Be sure to ask at the Reference Desk if your library has a specialized dictionary in your area of interest.

Encyclopedias

An **encyclopedia** is a book or a set of books that gives information on all branches of knowledge. Its entries are arranged in alphabetical order. In addition to such general encyclopedia as *Encyclopedia Americana*, or *Encyclopedia Britannica*, which are available in both paper and electronic form, and can be accessed through the Internet, you will be happy to discover a large number of highly specialized encyclopedias. Some of the best known specialized encyclopedias are:

African American Encyclopedia

Animal Life Encyclopedia

Asian Encyclopedia

Concise Encyclopedia of Western Philosophy and Philosophers

Encyclopedia of Computer Science

Encyclopedia of Education
Encyclopedia of Philosophy
Encyclopedia of Psychology
Encyclopedia of Religion and Ethics
Encyclopedia of World Art
Food and Nutrition Encyclopedia
Groves Dictionary of Music and Musicians
International Encyclopedia of the Social Sciences
Latino Encyclopedia
McGraw-Hill Encyclopedia of Science and Technology

HOW TO USE THE INTERNET FOR RESEARCH

The Internet is the richest source of information in the world. It's easy to gather information on any topic from the Internet. There are many search tools available that catalog information. Some of these show every word on a page, while others merely name the page where the information you want is located.

Search Engines

You can conduct Internet searches by category or by topic, or you can perform key word searches. To search by category, you merely click on highlighted (usually with blue, underscored type—the defacto standard WWW indicator of a hyperlink) categories provided by the search tool, or you can merely enter a topic that you want to know about. When you search by categories, the first click will take you to another list of links. You keep clicking until you find a page you want. When you search by topic you type in the topic and the search engine produces a list of pages containing the words you typed.

But the Internet has become so vast that you probably should learn how to do a key word search. Review the material above. It applies as much to on-line resources as it does to databases housed on CD-ROM in your library.

The term "search engine" means something technical to computerp specialists, but it is more commonly used by the rest of us to indicate any of a large number of Internet tools that turn the entire World Wide Web into a huge database. The most commonly used search engines include: AltaVista, Yahoo!, Lycos, Lycos' A2Z, Excite, Excite Guide, Go2.com, PlanetSearch, Thunderstone, What U Seek, Magellan, WebCrawler, Dogpile, Metafind, and InfoSeek. You can access all these by typing *http://www.**theirname**.com* and put their name after "www." and before ".com." Examples: http://www.yahoo.com and http://www.excite.com. An interesting search tool called "Savvy Search" lets you determine which of its search engines you want to use. It also knows English, Français, Deutsch, Italiano, Português, Español, Nederlands, Norsk, Hangul, Russian, Suomi, Japanese, Esperanto, Svenska, Daansk, Slovensky, Türkçe, Cesky, Slovensko, Srpsko-Hrvatski, Magyar, Polski, and Româna.

Exhibit 7.8 shows the front page of the Yahoo search engine. Tip: Notice and use the "Help" or "Tips" link for advice on how to conduct faster, more focused searches. You can also learn to use the "advanced" link on most search engines to conduct more thorough searches on a topic.

Finally, you might wish to download an add-on called "Alexa" at the URL, *www.alexa.com.* Alexa is a free advertising-supported Web navigation service. It works with your browser and watches as you surf the Internet, providing useful information about the sites you are viewing and suggesting related sites. This saves time in a general search, but it can also be distracting.

One problem with the Internet is that things change quickly. People decide they don't want to maintain their web sites. Others change their addresses. New sites are added every day. The World Wide Web is a work in progress, and this fact can seem confusing. Make careful notes about both the substance of what you find, and where you find something of interest.

Suppose you discover that a web site you have used for supporting material is no longer available on line. Would you still use the supporting material, knowing it could no longer be verified?

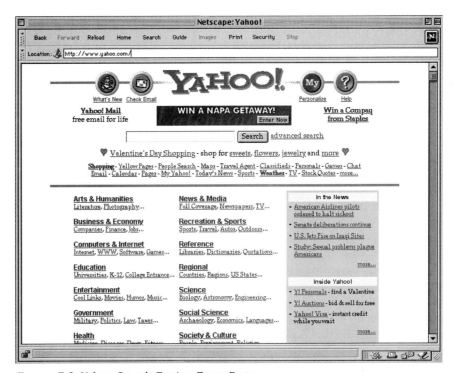

EXHIBIT 7.8 Yahoo Search Engine Front Page

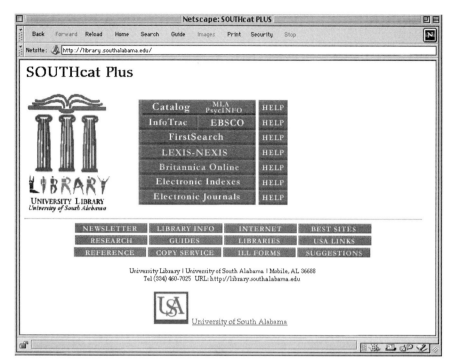

EXHIBIT 7.9 The University of South Alabama Libraries Home Page

In addition to search engines the Internet includes a variety of other means to access huge databases often sorted and organized specifically for professionals in particular fields. So if you learn to think like those professionals you will surely find their specialized databases on the WWW. Your institution's library staff has undoubtedly anticipated some of your reference needs. The library website is a good place to start. Exhibit 7.9 illustrates how one university library has organized its website to serve its faculty and students.

Moreover, many of your professors will have developed their own personal websites in an effort to help their students find materials for their classes. Ask them, then access the sites they recommend. For example, one of the authors maintains a website to support his classes at the URL *http://www.usouthal.edu/usa/communications/hanna/Ahome/MSHhome.html*

Students often "bookmark" this page so they can turn to it when they study—not only for courses in Communication, but for their other homework, as well. Exhibit 7.10 shows part of that web site.

The Internet places so much interesting and useful material at your fingertips that some people lose their focus and spend hours and hours of wasted time just browsing around. You can't afford that time when you are using the Internet for research. Here are some pointers and explanations that will help you keep your focus.

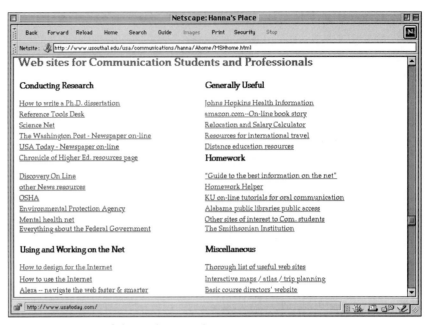

EXHIBIT 7.10 Part of the Author's Web Page

Use the Library as a Metaphor for Your Research On Line

If you have an idea where items are located in a library, then you have a fair model to help you organize your Internet research, too. Indeed, the world's largest library is on line and accessible at the URL: http://www.ipl.org/ There you will find a page organized for your convenience and modeled on the library metaphor. In fact, if you click on the "reference" collection button you go to a drawing of a reading room with the various materials and collections clearly marked.

BOOKMARK INTERESTING WEB SITES

Keep a record of the web sites you find most interesting and useful to your research project. If you don't you are liable never to find them again. This is easy to do by using your personal computer browser's Bookmarking function. However, when you access the Internet from another person's computer you will want to copy the addresses somehow. You can do it on note cards, but there's a better way. Highlight and copy the URL, then paste it to a word processing document, or save it on a floppy disk. When you do this, we recommend you include a brief annotation of what was interesting at the site. For example: "Great source of info. on termite control."

Examine Specialized Resources First

Learn to go beyond the search engines as you conduct research.

Reference Sources

The Internet provides a very broad range of reference materials. For example, on the Internet Public Library (IPL) reference section includes these sub categories of reference materials:

Almanacs (Annual publications offering lists, charts, and tables of information on various topics.)

Associations & Organizations (Directories of associations and non-profit organizations.)

Biographies (Accounts of persons' lives written by another.)

Calculation & Conversion Tools (Websites that assist with mathematical calculations, including *online* calculators and conversion dictionaries and tables.

Calendars (The organization and record of the passing of days or time.)

Census Data & Demographics (Information from official and non-official periodic enumeration of the U.S. and other populations, including related demographic data and reports.)

Dictionaries (General works containing alphabetical lists, with information given for each term.)

Encyclopedias (Comprehensive, authoritative works containing articles on a wide range of subjects.)

Genealogy (Information helpful in finding and/or interpreting records of the descent of a person, family, or group from an ancestor or ancestors.)

Geography (Information on the earth, its features, the distribution of life, and political boundaries.)

News (Information about recent events and happenings.)

Periodical Directories (Directories to periodicals, serials, journals, magazines, newspapers, newsletters, etc.)

Quotations (Resources to help identify quotations or find interesting quotations.)

Style & Writing Guides (Resources for proper grammatical usage, citation formats, or paper writing.)

Telephone (Directories on the Web listing telephone and fax numbers for people and businesses.)

The IPL includes similar lists for every imaginable category of information, including: Arts & Humanities, Business & Economics, Computers & Internet, Education, Entertainment & Leisure, Health & Medical, Sciences, Law, Government & Political Science, Sciences & Technology, Social Sciences and Associations.

All this information is available at the click of a mouse.

EVALUATE INTERNET AND OTHER RESEARCH DOCUMENTS CAREFULLY

You won't want to use all the information you find. Indeed, you could not use all the information because of its enormous volume, and because your speech class will only last one term! So you must filter through that information selecting out those pieces that are best for your use. You can apply four criteria that will simplify this task: (1) currency, (2) objectivity, (3) primary or secondary, and (4) qualifications of the source.

Currency means "the time during which anything is happening." One measure of the quality of information, then, has to do with whether it was produced at the right time. For example, technology is changing so rapidly that a resource produced in 1993 may be ancient history.

Objectivity means "without bias or prejudice." Information produced by a detached, impartial source is likely to be less biased and prejudiced than information produced by an advocate. For example, a small scandal erupted in the newspapers in early 1999 when someone discovered that the medical studies praising the potency drug, Viagra, were paid for by the company that makes Viagra.

Primary or **secondary** refers to whether materials are original and produced by the originator, or merely "picked up" by a second source and referenced there. Get as close to the primary source as possible. Errors are more likely to occur in secondary materials.

Qualifications of the source can determine the value of information. For example, a person who is not qualified to fly an airplane may or may not be able to tell you how to do it. You obviously want information from qualified sources, but this can be difficult to determine.

Look for information about the author of Internet documents—a link to his or her home page, or email address, for example. If this information is not immediately available, you may be able to locate the author through the Internet director at the IPL.

EXHIBIT 7.11

CRITERIA TO TEST THE QUALITY OF INFORMATION	
Criteria	*Explanation*
Currency	Some areas of knowledge don't change very rapidly, but others change often. The communications industry is one of the most rapidly changing areas of the world's economy. This means that what was true last week may not be true today. Thus, one measure of the *quality* of evidence is its currency. Also, the source of evidence should probably be current. Unless you are using a classic work such as reference material, or some dated source for a reason (a newspaper account written on the day of the event, for example), choose the most current sources you can find.
Objectivity	When a source of information is passionately committed to one side, the information he or she provides is likely to be biased. Look for a source of information that appears to be neutral or bipartisan, or else, try to balance one side against the other. For example, quote both a Republican and a Democrat on a policy issue, or else quote some neutral third person.
Primary vs. secondary	It is usually better to quote the original source than it is to quote someone else quoting the original source of information. This is true of print materials as well as electronic materials. Which sounds better to you? (1) "Henry James said, in his work . . . ." or (2) "The author, William Sullivan, attributes this remark to Henry James . . . ."
Qualifications of the source	You would be unlikely to accept a Doctor of Music Education's advice to have surgery. But why? Not all doctors are medical doctors, and you might believe the Doctor of Music Education is not qualified to make a medical recommendation. The qualifications of a source of information obviously bear on how much confidence you can put in the information.

Many web sites have been paid for by businesses. Others by government agencies, still others by political and other special interest groups. You must take this information into account in judging the qualifications of the source of the material (and the objectivity of the source as well.)

Make Careful and Complete Notes the First Time

Use Note Cards or Half-Sheets

The size of the cards you use for note taking depends on your personal preference. Some people prefer small note cards as a way of keeping their notes brief. Others like larger note cards so that they can later edit their notes directly on the cards. Still others prefer half-sheets of paper.

The kind of notes you take should guide your decision about note card size. Make your selection and then live with it. Make all of your notes that size.

Establish a Standard Form of Entry

Use a standard form of entry for note taking. The two most common methods of note taking are direct quotation and paraphrase. A direct quotation is an exact replication of the original, while a paraphrase is a summary of the original in your own words. Develop a system that clearly shows which method you are using. For example, put quotation marks around all quoted materials, and write "paraphrase" on any card on which you have put the author's ideas into your own words.

Use One Card Per Entry and One Entry Per Card

Note cards work well because you can shuffle them and rearrange them—but only if you follow the simple rule: one card per entry and one entry per card. The temptation, of course, is to put more than one entry from a single source on one card, thereby reducing the number of times you have to write out the complete bibliographical data. One card per entry, one entry per card also promotes better accuracy in note taking and greatly facilitates organization and outlining.

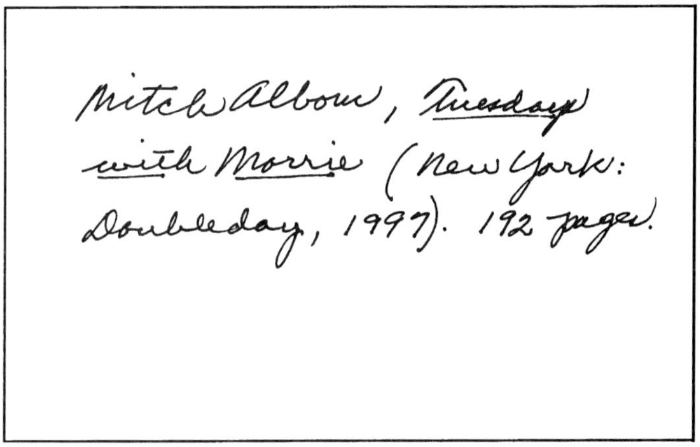

EXHIBIT 7.12 Front of a note card

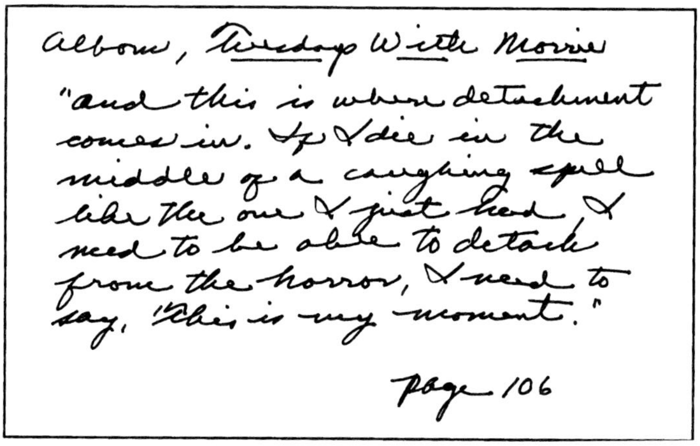
Albom, Tuesdays With Morrie

"And this is where detachment comes in. If I die in the middle of a coughing spell like the one I just had, I need to be able to detach from the horror, I need to say, 'This is my moment.'"

page 106

EXHIBIT 7.13 Back of a quote card

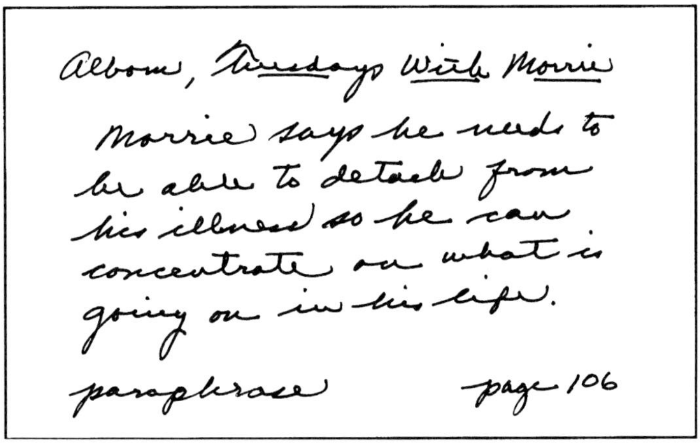
Albom, Tuesdays With Morrie

Morrie says he needs to be able to detach from his illness so he can concentrate on what is going on in his life.

paraphrase page 106

EXHIBIT 7.14 Back of a paraphrase card

Take Plenty of Notes

Every scholar learns the wisdom of taking plenty of notes. If you don't you may discover that you cannot remember the one bit of information you now need or even where you found it.

Do Not Plagiarize, Even by Accident

Plagiarism means taking another person's ideas or language and claiming them as yours. Doing this intentionally is outright stealing. Individuals who plagiarize risk ruining their careers and their lives. Most often, plagiarism occurs by accident. Honest, well-intended people use another person's ideas or language but fail to give the other person credit because they simply do not realize what they have done.

Even so, there is no excuse for plagiarism. Crediting your source is a matter of form and style, as well as of integrity. Learn and follow a correct form of entry.

Similarly, when you directly quote or paraphrase materials in your speeches, your wording must show that you are doing so. For example, you might say, "John Marshall once said . . ." or "To paraphrase John Marshall . . . ."

Develop a Working Bibliography

As you browse make notes of every book, article, or web document that seems relevant to your speech topic or that seems interesting to you. Include all the bibliographical information, as well as a brief annotation that will tell you, later, what is in the source. Include the call number if it is a library book or the exact location of an article in a journal or magazine, including where in the library you can find the article. Be sure to write out the URL if you took the note from the Internet.

Write the information down carefully—then double-check it. Slow down enough to make your notes legible. Remember the rule: one entry per card, one card per entry.

Use Your Note Card File to Plan a Speech

Your research has yielded a stack of notes. Now comes the fun part of research—pulling it all together. You have a specific purpose in mind. Suppose you have selected an organizational pattern. Your research has been guided by this organizational pattern. Prepare five note cards with the headings: (1) attention, (2) need, (3) satisfaction, (4) visualization, (5) action. Lay these heading cards out on your study table and begin to sort your notes by placing them under appropriate heading categories.

Or, suppose you have decided that a problem-solution organizational pattern might be a good way to organize. Prepare heading cards for both problem and solution areas: (1) problem, (1a) serious, (1b) inherent, (1c) relevant to listeners, (2) solution, (2a) solution solves or resolves problem, (2b) solution is practical and "doable," (2c) solution won't cause new problems, (2d) solution brings advantages not currently available. Lay these heading cards out on your table and sort your notes.

As you work with your card file you will discover new connections. If any gaps remain in your research this process will identify those gaps for you.

SUMMARY

Gathering information for a speech has become easier today than ever before. Technology has made it relatively simple for us to find the mountain of facts we want. The data bases in college libraries and the specialized indices, available both in printed copy and on the Internet, make the search for supporting material thorough and faster than it was a few years ago. A basic level of computer literacy will help you locate material on virtually any subject.

Searches for information involve exploration via a key word approach. You also have access to specialized dictionaries and encyclopedias, and magazine and newspaper articles throughout the world. Using a search engine immediately introduces you to the volume of materials available on any subject. But quantity does not equal quality. Research requires that you test the information for its quality, its objectivity, whether it is primary or secondary, and the qualifications of the source itself. Before you can integrate the information into your speech, you need to take careful notes. Careful and complete notes are a must. You also must be certain that you do not plagiarize, even by accident. Finally, make use of your note cards to plan your speech.

KEY TERMS

Ethics

Interview

Using the Library

Databases

Internet

Key-word search

Indices

Reference works

Search engines

Specialized resources

Evaluate documents

Note-taking

Working bibliography

APPLICATION QUESTIONS

1. Go to your college library and using the holdings catalog, look up the author *Sidney M. Jourard.* Does your library own anything by this author? Make a bibliography card for each work published in 1964 or 1971. Now, in the titles section, look up a book called *Word Play.* If your library owns this book, write a bibliography card. Now, in the subject catalog, see if your library owns a copy of Fred Kerlinger's book, *Foundations of Behavioral Research.* If so, write a bibliography card. Bring your bibliography cards to class. Compare your cards with those of other students. Are they exactly the same? Would you be able to find the works in the library by using other classmates' bibliography cards?

2. Some students enjoy the game of library hide-and-seek. Try to find answers to the questions that follow by researching in the library. Return to class and compare notes with other students. Where did you find the information? What questions were most difficult to answer? Why? Which ones were easiest to answer? Could you use the computer to help you? Can you draw any insights about using the library from this exercise?

Questions for Library Research:

1. When was *The Book of Mormon* first published?
2. What was in the news on June 6, 1944?
3. Who was Hetty Green?
4. What can you find out about a painting called *Les Demoiselles d'Avignon?*
5. How much money did the ransom note demand for the return of 20-month-old Charles A. Lindbergh, Jr., who was kidnapped in 1932?
6. Why did Truman fire MacArthur? When?
7. What was Marciano's knockout record?
8. For what was Margaret Sanger noted?
9. Who won the gold medal in women's high jump in the 1972 Olympics? How high did she jump? Where was she from?
10. Who was Gerald Ford's vice president?
11. Who directed *One Flew Over the Cuckoo's Nest?* Who played the leading role?
12. What was the central issue in the WhitewaterGate affair?
13. What is the current rate of exchange between U.S. dollars and French francs?

14. Where did the accident occur that killed Princess Di?

15. How fast did the last Triple Crown winner run at Belmont? How far? Which horse came in second?

IT'S MORE FUN TO KNOW

The importance of the quality of evidence has been much studied, but with mixed findings. For example, in 1953, Erwin P. Bettinghaus, Jr., wrote a master's thesis at Bradley University titled "The Relative Effect of the Use of Testimony in a Persuasive Speech upon the Attitudes of Listeners." Two years later, Robert S. Cathcart published an article in *Communication Monographs* (Vol. 22, 1955. pp. 227-233) titled "An Experimental Study of the Relative Effectiveness of Four Methods of Presenting Evidence." Both found inclusion of evidence increased attitude change.

Later, James C. McCroskey published "A Summary of Experimental Research on the Effects of Evidence in Persuasive Communication" (*QJS*, Vol. 55. 1969. p. 172) in which he concluded that initially high-credible sources don't gain much from including evidence, but initially moderate-to-low credible sources can greatly increase their credibility and the attitude change they produce by increasing evidence to support their positions.

In 1983 Rodney Reynolds and Michael Burgoon published "Belief processing, reasoning and evidence" in *Communication Yearbook* (Vol. 7, pp. 83–104), in which they supported the relationship between evidence and persuasion—especially when the credibility of the speaker was an issue. They argued that using evidence produces more attitude change than not using evidence and more than simple assertions. Citations of evidence produces more attitude change if the speaker gives the source and the source's qualifications than when the speaker does not do so. Moreover, quality evidence, well presented, actually increases the speaker's credibility.

Concern for honesty in scholarship is a universal matter. All higher education institutions have published policies which require students and faculty to maintain high standards in academic work. (See, for example, *Furman University's Faculty Handbook, File 121.4, November 1985).*

A well stocked library is a measure of the quality of an institution. The library has always been called the "heart of the university." The three things necessary for a college to function are students, faculty, and the library. Briefly stated, "Library skills . . . are essential for academic success and lifelong learning" (See *http://library.weber.edu/libinstruct/list.htm* the home page for Weber State University.)

One of the most interesting and recent pieces on basic library skills is on the Internet. Through "hot links" it provides you with a thorough tutorial on the library, its resources, and such issues as "how to cite a source" and "how to retrieve circulating books." (See *http://ollie.dcccd.edu/library/BasicSkills.htm*). Sources for information about libraries abound. The Mining Company has a site specifically for librarians, and the applications of library skills to everyday life. (See *http://librarians.miningco.com/mbody.htm?COB=home*)

The importance of carefully evaluating information secured via the Internet is just as critical as evaluating material from the printed page. (Kathleen Fulton, "Learning in a Digital Age: Insights into Issues," *T H E Journal (Technological Horizons in Education*, 25:7 (February 1998)). Failure to verify information and test information thoroughly was learned painfully by the *Arkansas Democrat-Gazette* when it was forced to retract a front page article. (See Lori Robertson, "A Source of Embarrassment," *American Journalism Review*, 19:3 (April 1997).)

SELF-TEST FOR REVIEW

1. List the five steps involved in planning for an information-gathering interview.

   a. _____

   b. _____

   c. _____

   d. _____

   e. _____

2. What information can you get from The Source?

   _____

   _____

3. Match the following library departments with their descriptions.

   a. Reference
   b. Circulation
   c. Reserve readings
   d. Government documents
   e. Serials and periodicals
   f. Microform
   g. Instructional media
   h. Interlibrary loan
   i. Database searching
   j. Specialized collections

   1. Publications originating in or issued by federal, state, and local government agencies
   2. May be part of serials and periodicals department; responsible for storing back issues of newspapers and magazines, *Library of American Civilization,* and so on
   3. Helps you borrow from more than one library
   4. Maintains the library bookshelves and checks out materials
   5. Computer searches in specific subject areas
   6. Newspapers and magazines, some of which are bound and some of which are stored in microform
   7. Biomedical collection, law collection, map collection, and so on
   8. Materials set aside for special uses or classes; do not circulate for more than an hour or two at a time
   9. Audio and visual materials, films, photographic archives, and so on
   10. Location of encyclopedias, almanacs, directories, bibliographies, abstracts, indexes, and other works of general interest

4. Suppose you go to the holdings catalog, look up a book, and find the following call number:

   DS
   774
   S59

   What should you do next?
   a. Write down everything. This is the book's address.
   b. Write down "DS 774" and go to the stacks.

c. Write down the author's name and the book title.

d. Ask a librarian for help.

5. How would you go about finding what works by George Lakoff your library owns?

6. How would you find out who wrote the book: *Women, Fire, and Dangerous Things?*

7. Suppose you would like to read something about the connection between language categories and how people think. How would you find such a work?

Answers: 1. a. Identify where you can go to discover the information necessary to conduct an interview. b. Identify the questions you must ask the person you interview. c. Plan how to probe into the answers you receive. d. Plan how to handle common problems, such as reluctance, emotion, and hostility. e. Determine how to validate or verify what you learn in the interview 2. The Source offers some twelve hundred features and programs in eight categories: communications, news and information, business, personal computing, education and careers, online shopping, computer conferencing, and fun and games. 3. a. 10. b. 4. c. 8. d. 1, e. 6. f. 2. g. 9. h. 3. i. 5. j. 7. 4. a. 5. Access the online catalog and type "a=Lakoff," or go to the card catalog and check the author index under Lakoff, George. 6. Access the online catalog and type "t=women, fire," or go to the title index in the card catalog and look it up in the W section. Or, go directly to *www.Amazon.com* and type in the title. 7. Access the online catalog and type "K=categories and thinking," and other combinations of keywords, or go to the subjects section of the card catalog and look up the keywords.

SUGGESTED READINGS

Hakala, David. *Modems Made Easy.* New York: Osborne McGraw-Hill, 1995. An excellent source for finding software libraries, how to trouble-shoot problems, bulletin board services, and much more.

Pournelle, Jerry, and Michael Banks. *Pournelle's PC Communications Bible: The Ultimate Guide to Productivity with a Modem.* Redmond, Wash.: Microsoft Press, 1992. The book title does not seem immodest when you actually hold this incredibly rich resource in your hands. It tells you more than you ever wanted to know about online services, including how to get started and a detailed discussion of the kinds of modems available, along with their strengths and weaknesses. It provides an overview of bulletin board systems and online services. It also names and provides access to all the major E-mail services, the major consumer online services, the major front-end services, and the major database and information-retrieval services.

Rathbone, Tina and Andy Rathbone. *Modems for Dummies, 3rd Edition,* Foster City, CA: IDG Books Worldwide, 1997. This is one of the most recent and basically written books on the practical use of your modem. One in a series of books designed to take the fear out the skills of technology.

NOTES

1. This name was changed to protect the student's privacy.

2. Wallace V. Schmidt and Roger Conway, *Results-Oriented Interviewing: Principles, Practices and Procedures,* (Englewood Cliffs, NJ: Prentice-Hall, 1998).

3. The Federal Regulation of Lobbyists Act of 1976 requires all lobbyists to register with the Clerk of the House and the Secretary of the Senate. The names of these registrants are then published quarterly in the *Congressional Record.*

PART 3

Organizing the Speech

CHAPTER 8

ORGANIZING THE BODY OF THE SPEECH

OBJECTIVES

After reading this chapter, you should be able to:

1. Explain why organization of a speech is important.

2. Name and define the characteristics of good organization.

3. Identify, explain, and use the following patterns for organizing a speech: (a) time, (b) space, (c) problem to solution, (d) causal order, (e) topical divisions, and (f) motivated sequence.

4. Name and describe the five steps of the motivated sequence.

5. Define and use the following organizational links: transitions, signposts, and internal summaries.

OUTLINE

Objectives
Outline
Abstract
Introduction
    Why Organization Is
      Important
    Characteristics of Good
      Organization
      Clear and Simple
      Few Main Points
      Logical Development
    Organizing the Body of
      Your Speech
      Time
      Space
      Problem to Solution
      Causal Order
      Topical Divisions

Motivated Sequence
    Attention Step
    Need Step
    Satisfaction Step
    Visualization Step
    Action Step
Organizational Links
    Transitions
    Signposts
    Internal Summaries
Summary
Key Terms
Application Questions
It's More Fun to Know
Self-Test for Review
Suggested Readings
Notes

ABSTRACT

The better organized you are in developing and presenting your speech ideas, the more effective your message will be. A well organized speech also increases the probability that listeners will pay attention to and remember your main points.

Good organization is characterized by a clear and simple format and basic language, emphasis on only a few main points, and reasonable and logical idea development. Speakers usually organize ideas by time or space; by movement from problem to solution, cause to effect, or effect to cause; according to natural topical divisions; or by following the five steps of the motivated sequence. Organizational links, such as transitions, signposts, and internal summaries, help tie together the major points of your speech.

IMAGINE

"Wow! Dr. Feldman's lecture was fantastic this morning! He's really interesting and funny, too. Trouble is, later, I'm never quite sure how to round out my notes. Once I'm out of the lecture, the whole thing seems a blur. Just look at these notes. They're a jumble, and nothing seems to connect."

"Yeah, I know," said another student. "I tried to take notes for a while, but I finally gave up. I just couldn't follow that guy. I always had to spend a lot of time figuring out what his point was."

As Dr. Feldman's two students have implied, unless a speaker can organize ideas clearly and simply so listeners can follow, audience members will give up trying.

INTRODUCTION

Every successful speech has three parts: an introduction, a body, and a conclusion. An introduction is the first part of a speech, and its purpose is to get audience attention, to state the speaker's intention, and to prepare listeners for what is coming. The body of the speech is the major portion of the speech, in which you develop and support the main ideas and arguments. The conclusion ends the speech and focuses listeners' thoughts and feelings on the speech's main ideas. We describe how to organize introductions and conclusions in Chapter 10, Introductions and Conclusions. Throughout this chapter, emphasis is on organizing the *body* of the speech.

Why Organization Is Important

Ideas and actions make more sense when they are clear and well organized. Clear speech organization is critical to a successful presentation. If ideas are in a jumble, listeners can't follow or understand them. Consider the following examples:

Poor: The major ideas about political campaigns that I want to discuss with this class are:

1. Why do we have political campaigns?
2. Bob Dole's campaign for president
3. How we should reform campaign financing

Better: The major ideas about political campaigns that I want to discuss with this class are:

1. Why do we have political campaigns?
2. How long do the campaigns last?
3. How do we pay for the campaigns?

The "poor" example has three somewhat unrelated points. "Why" we have political campaigns is a totally separate question from Bob Dole's presidential campaign. The desirability of campaign financing reform is an entirely separate issue that is not connected to the other two points.

The "better" set of major ideas is more logically and sensibly developed. Here, the speaker focuses on related issues. The sequence flows easily from why we have campaigns and their length to how they are financed. A speech this well organized is easy to follow and understand because the major ideas relate to each other and have a logical sequence.

Research indicates that an organized speaker impresses people as being well prepared and increases their own credibility.[1] When a speaker is well organized and appears to have a clearly determined destination, listeners are also more willing and more likely to pay close attention. Good organization also helps listeners identify what is important. It provides a "verbal road map." Thus a speech that contains a few, well-supported ideas, with clear and simple organization has an obvious advantage.

Characteristics of Good Organization

Characteristics of good speech organization are: (1) the organization is clear and simple, (2) only a few main points are introduced, and (3) ideas are developed in a logical sequence.

Clear and Simple

In an effectively organized speech, one idea follows simply and logically from the other so listeners are not confused. The following example is clear and simple.

I. Inflation makes your dollar worth less.

II. Nearly all items cost more when we have high inflation.

This topic has just two main ideas, and the points are clearly stated. Listeners will understand what the speaker intends to say and should be able to follow the message easily.

Another aspect of clear and simple ideas is that the language used to express those ideas should be basic and easy to understand. Here, simple language makes the point that wrestling is dangerous and that, for that reason, young children should not wrestle competitively.

Presentation Management software often includes excellent help for organizing ideas.

I. Wrestling is a dangerous sport.
  A. Many wrestlers suffer head injuries.
      B. Injuries to joints and bones are common.
    II. Children under age twelve should not wrestle competitively.

Few Main Points

Audiences listen only when it is easy for them to do so. Consider the two outlines for a five-minute speech presented in Exhibit 8.1. In the "poor" example, the idea behind the message is good, but complicated. The speaker is trying to do too much and has too many sub-ideas. The speech could be made simpler by focusing on just a few major historical events involving the American flag since the American Revolution.

Do not discuss five or six main ideas in a five-minute speech. You cannot thoroughly developed them in the available time, and the audience probably will forget the first point before the speaker reaches the fifth.

EXHIBIT 8.1

POOR AND BETTER STRUCTURES FOR A FIVE-MINUTE SPEECH

Poor   *Body*

I. Flags have an important place in our history.
  A. How the American flag was developed
  B. Betsy Ross produced the first flag.
  C. Raising the flag at Iwo Jima
II. Flags create strong personal reactions.
  A. They stand for values and attitudes.
    1. The American flag never dips.
    2. Flag destruction is legal but controversial.

Better   *Body*

I. The flag is important to the United States.
  A. We can use the flag to trace American historical developments.
    1. Betsy Ross made the first flag with thirteen stars.
    2. The number of stars has changed many times.
  B. The flag reminds us of our heritage.
    1. Fort McHenry and the flag are the heart of the national anthem.
    2. The flag raising at Iwo Jima was a sign of victory.

Logical Development

Develop main ideas in a reasonable and logical way. In the "better" outline in exhibit 8.1, there is only one main idea, and the supporting ideas contribute clearly to that single point. The subpoints flow from the following statement: "The flag is important to the United States *because*. Each subpoint provides an explanation of *why* the major point is important or true. Supporting ideas should always help to answer the question "why?" They should give listeners reasons to accept and understand the major point. Notice the use of this principle in the outline in Exhibit 8.2.

Organizing the Body of Your Speech

The structure of a speech depends, largely, on its content and purpose. There is no single "right" way to organize materials. The most common patterns for structuring speech materials are (1) time, (2) space, (3) problem-to-solution, (4) causal order, (5) topical divisions, or (6) motivated sequence. They work because they follow the listeners' habitual ways of thinking. They are, therefore, easy to identify with and easy to respond to.

Time

The **time** pattern is based on some sequence of events. Time organizes our ideas from early to late, from the past to the present. A chronology of events is something we all understand. We know that there are sixty minutes in an hour, twenty-four hours in a day, twelve months in a year, and so forth. By organizing a speech chronologically, you

EXHIBIT 8.2

LOGICAL DEVELOPMENT OF IDEAS

Specific Purpose: I want my listeners to know some of their rights as taxpayers if they are audited by the IRS.

Thesis Statement: You have important rights in an IRS audit of your tax return.

I. The IRS must conduct taxpayer interviews under specific guidelines.

  A. The agent must explain the audit process and taxpayer rights.

  B. If the taxpayer wants counsel, the interview must be halted until arrangements are made.

II. Levies may be used to collect unpaid taxes.

  A. The IRS must wait for thirty days after notification before seizing property.

  B. The sale proceeds cannot exceed the amount of tax deficiency.

provide listeners with a familiar pattern that they can follow mentally. This helps audience members to keep track of what you have already said and to anticipate where you are going. Notice how a time sequence works in this example passage from a student speech:

> The presidential primaries begin first with the caucuses in Iowa. After that, the candidates go to primaries in states such as New Hampshire. Then, after the New England primaries, they may face the "Super Tuesday" primaries in the South and Midwest. This series of primaries usually ends with the big prize in California, the biggest state in the nation. When they've finished these primaries, the candidates then go to their party convention to nominate a presidential candidate.

Exhibit 8.3 shows two examples of outlines organized in chronological order.

Legal cases are often based on timing. For example, when a person was seen leaving the scene of a crime might be the critical factor in determining her or his innocence or guilt. Would it ever be ethical to change the sequence of events in a speech organized by time? Why or why not?

EXHIBIT 8.3

TWO CHRONOLOGICALLY ORGANIZED SPEECH OUTLINES

Outline 1

Specific Purpose: I want my listeners to know the major steps in developing black and white photographic film.

Thesis Statement: You can develop your own pictures at home, without a darkroom, if you're careful and follow these steps.

Step 1. Develop the film in the canister for the time shown on the sheet of paper inside the film box.

Step 2. "Stop" the developing process by using a diluted acid bath.

Step 3. "Fix" the image on the film with liquid "fix."

Step 4. Wash the film and hang it up to dry, using a light weight to keep it from curling.

Outline 2

Specific Purpose: I want my listeners to know the basic steps in preparing a home garden.

Thesis Statement: Home gardening is easy.

I. First you must prepare the soil.
  A. Till and loosen it for planting.
  B. Rake it smooth and level.
  C. Mark the rows.
II. Next you must plant the seeds.
  A. Draw a three-inch-deep furrow.
  B. Place seeds and fertilizer in the furrow.
  C. Close the furrow.

Spatial relationships provide an effective way to organize some ideas.
© Stephen Marks/Image Bank

Space

Speeches also can be organized using **space,** a pattern that relies on geographical and spatial relationships, such as top to bottom, east to west, front to back, or side to side. The outlines in Exhibit 8.4 show the use of spatial relationship in organization.

Problem to Solution

A **problem-to-solution organizational pattern** identifies a harm or problem, then presents a solution to solve the problem. First show the nature and size of the problem. Then describe a workable solution. A sample outline for a speech using problem-to-solution organization is shown in Exhibit 8.5.

A second sample of the problem-to-solution sequence of organization is shown in Exhibit 8.6. Here, the speech outline is on the left, and the text of the speech appears on the right.

Causal Order

A **cause-to-effect organizational pattern** helps an audience to see that one set of conditions is responsible for a result. People often link conditions with outcomes. For example:

> I haven't gotten much sleep recently, and I caught a chill last night. No wonder I feel a cold coming on.

> People who invest wisely will have a large retirement "nest egg."

Cause-to-effect can be organized either forward or backward. That is, you can explain the cause first, then deal with the effect, or you can present the effect, first, then explain the cause.

Here are two sample speeches. The first, in Exhibit 8.7, shows cause-to-effect organization.

Exhibit 8.8, shows effect-to-cause organization.

EXHIBIT 8.4

OUTLINES ORGANIZED BY THEIR SPATIAL RELATIONSHIPS

Outline 1

Specific Purpose: I want my listeners to know how an architect plans academic buildings.

Thesis Statement: Architects plan the most utilitarian classroom buildings with you in mind.

I. The main function of a building gets first consideration.

    A. Classrooms and workspaces must accommodate the teaching/learning activities that will go on inside them.

    B. Food service and recreational space are placed as far away as possible from the work space.

II. Space for supporting functions must be convenient to the main functional spaces.

    A. Utility space and restrooms must be adjacent to both work space and recreational space.

    B. Storage space must be convenient to other spaces.

    C. Everything must be accessible from a central entry space.

Outline 2

Specific Purpose: I want my listeners to know which is America's most scenic highway.

Thesis Statement: You can take America's most scenic drive without ever leaving U.S. Highway 89.

I.   In the north, you see Glacier National Park, Yellowstone National Park, and the Grand Tetons National Park.

II. About midway, you drive into the great canyon lands of America, including Bryce Canyon, Zion Canyon, Lake Powell, and the Grand Canyon.

III. Toward the south, you drive into the Painted Desert, through Oak Creek Canyon and Sedona, and onto the vast Sonoran Desert.

EXHIBIT 8.5

SPEECH OUTLINE WITH PROBLEM-TO-SOLUTION ORGANIZATION

Specific Purpose: I want each of my listeners to contribute fifteen dollars to the student scholarship fund.

Thesis Statement: Many students are unable to continue their education because of the high cost of college.

I. College tuition costs are rising at approximately twice the rate of inflation.

II. Increased scholarship money would help to solve the financial problem of tuition for many worthy students.

EXHIBIT 8.6

OUTLINE AND SPEECH USING PROBLEM-TO-SOLUTION ORGANIZATION

Outline:

Specific Purpose: I want my listeners to write their congressional representatives and ask for an immediate improvement in the equipment for air-traffic control.

Thesis Statement: Solving the air-traffic control equipment problem will increase public safety in the air and on the ground.

I. Air traffic congestion is a serious problem in skies throughout America.

II. The best solution to this problem is the immediate installation of new equipment already ordered by Congress.

Brief Sample Speech

Aircraft collision "near-misses" are one of the most serious problems in our transportation system. Air traffic controllers themselves report there are at least six "incidents" each day in which passenger aircraft fly too close to each other. The air in the U.S. is literally "jammed" with planes.

One result of increased commercial flights is the inadequacy of 1970's equipment to manage such a traffic load. It is frightening to realize that the control system actually "lost" Air Force One three times last year. Think how likely it is that the ordinary commercial flight might not be tracked by the now obsolete technology.

Air travel is vital to business and for the leisure traveler also. We consider the US to be at the "cutting edge" of technology, but our air traffic system is still operating on a system that uses vacuum tubes and not transistors. Congress has mandated that the system be upgraded before the mid-1990's, but the Federal Aviation Administration has, to date, only improved the control equipment at three major airports. The appropriations have been made, but the money has not been spent. Every day that is wasted offers additional opportunities for that inevitable mid-air crash of two commercial jet liners.

This is a problem that must be solved because it affects the lives of every family in the country. We must insist that our legislators require that the FAA install the technologically advanced air traffic equipment so that lives can be saved, traffic will move more rapidly, and people will be less concerned.

EXHIBIT 8.7

SAMPLE OUTLINE AND SPEECH USING CAUSE-TO EFFECT ORGANIZATON

Outline

Specific Purpose: I want my listeners to get a flu shot before winter begins.

Thesis Statement: Go to the school clinic or to your family doctor and get a flu shot.

I. Each winter, millions of people contract viruses through coughs, sneezes, or by breathing the exhaled breath of others.

II. These viruses can cause the flu unless these people have received a shot that makes them resistant to the "bug."

Body of a Brief Sample Speech

Millions of people across the country and many in this room will get the flu this winter. You'll get it from the sneezes of others or by breathing in the germs from their coughs. Just by being in a closed area, like a theater or a meeting room, you breathe the air these "sick" people exhale. You then are "at risk" of catching the flu.

Ever wonder why so many people catch the flu in the winter? It's because people are indoors and the temperature outside is so low that the viruses creep inside and thrive. The most casual contact passes the virus from one person to another.

It doesn't have to be this way. You can still have contact with others, but take a simple precaution. Go to the health clinic or your family physician and ask for a flu shot. It's simple and inexpensive. In most cases, people who get flu shots either won't get influenza or they'll have only a mild case. Even a mild case is better than spending a week in bed with a pounding headache and a body that feels like it's under a steamroller.

So go to the clinic or your doctor today. You'll be glad you did when you see the sunken, dark eyes of your friends who didn't bother to get their shots.

Topical Divisions

The natural, or **topical divisions** of a subject suggest a method for dividing the topic into manageable units. For example, a speech about the human body might be organized around the various body systems: skeletal, circulatory, respiratory, muscular, nervous, and so on. If you wanted to talk about the effects that running a marathon has on the body, your topical divisions organization might resemble the outline in Exhibit 8.9.

Exhibit 8.10 shows another example of topical division. A student first drew the pattern, or "scatter diagram," and then worked from that diagram to create the outline. While neither the diagram nor the outline are perfect, they clearly illustrate organization by topical division.

EXHIBIT 8.8

SAMPLE OUTLINE AND SPEECH
USING EFFECT-TO-CAUSE ORGANIZATION

Outline

Specific Purpose: I want my listeners to know the effect that technology has on our society.

Thesis Statement: Advances in technology are seriously damaging the humanity of the world.

I. Television, computers, airplanes, satellites , and the Internet have destroyed many of the close relationships between people.

II. Impersonal technology reduces the amount of direct contact people have with friends, relatives, neighbors, and business associates.

Brief Sample Speech

We've become so technologically oriented that, sometimes, we forget we're people. We sit in front of a TV set and just watch. We turn on our radios and "soak up some tunes." People retreat to their computers. The great reliance we have on technology makes us become more impersonal. We don't need others because we have our computers for entertainment, our TV for news, and our radios to listen to others talk. But we aren't a talking society much anymore.

It's not so necessary for us to talk with our neighbors when we can get the news from television, radio, or on the computer. Why, people ask, should I ask my insurance salesperson about my auto policy when I can get information from my home computer or watch an "infomercial" on TV about buying insurance and saving money?

Let me ask you one question: When you have to have personal attention, how well will that "infomercial" serve you? It can't answer your Sunday call, contact the claims department, or counsel you about any possible rate increase. Consider the kinds of bonds we create when we talk with people. They understand us, and we appreciate them. Think about that the next time you decide to kill time by watching TV or turning on the radio. Make a friend. Talk to someone.

EXHIBIT 8.9

SPEECH OUTLINE SHOWING
ORGANIZATION BY TOPICAL DIVISIONS

Specific Purpose: I want my listeners to understand the effects that running a marathon has on some key parts of the body.

Thesis Statement: When you run a marathon, certain parts of your body have abnormal needs.

I: Your respiratory system must operate efficiently to provide enough oxygen for your blood and your heart.

II: Your cardiovascular system must pump nearly twice the normal amount of blood to all portions of your body.

III: The muscles of your body burn most of the stored glycogen and require regular liquid replenishment during the race.

EXHIBIT 8.10

A PATTERN, LATER DEVELOPED INTO AN OUTLINE, ORGANIZED BY TOPICAL DIVISION

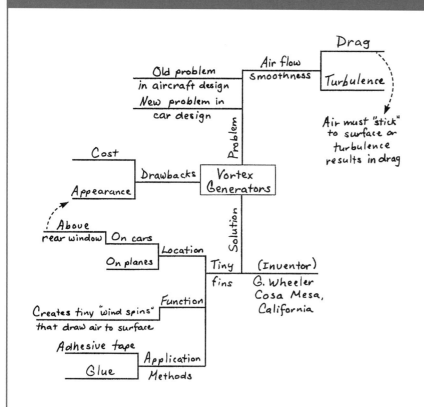

Vortex Generators

I. The problem we must solve is called "drag."

   A. Air must "stick" to the surface of a car, or else the turbulence results in "drag."

   B. Drag is an old problem in aircraft design.

   C. Drag is a new problem in automobile design.

II. The solution to drag is called "vortex generators."

   A. Vortex generators were invented by G. Wheeler of Cosa Mesa, California.

   B. Vortex generators are tiny fins that create tiny "wind spins."

   C. Vortex generators are placed above the rear window on a car.

   D. Vortex generators are glued or taped on.

III. Vortex generators do have two important drawbacks.

   A. One drawback is the added cost of the car.

   B. Another drawback is the appearance of the vortex generator.

Motivated Sequence

Alan H. Monroe developed the **motivated sequence,** a pattern for organizing persuasive during the mid-1930s.[2] The motivated sequence has five sequential steps, as shown in Exhibit 8.11.

Attention Step

The attention step is designed to gain the attention of listeners. One speaker got listeners' attention with the following:

> *Most of you probably are still watching movies on video tape. That's an old technology. Try the DVD technology that is available on many new recorders and on computers as well. Watch the movie in sparkling color with brilliant resolution. Choose from a host of titles and bring the theatre into your living room with DVD technology.*

Need Step

The need step describes or defines a problem or shows that the audience has a need for the speech you are about to give. One way to develop a need in listeners is to tie your topic to issues that directly affect all of your listeners. For example:

> *We live in a global economy. The United States is tied to the economies of China, Japan, the rest of the nations of the Pacific rim, all of Europe including Russia and, certainly, the Middle East. When the Brazilian currency catches a cold, Wall Street sneezes. Our imports exceed our exports by many billions of dollars each month. When the Russian currency collapsed in September 1998, our own stock market fell. Our corporations such as Coca-Cola, Caterpillar, General Electric, Microsoft, Philip Morris, and hundreds of others, earn much of their profits from overseas operations.*

EXHIBIT 8.11

STEPS IN THE MOTIVATED SEQUENCE	
Attention Step	Gets the attention of the audience for the speaker and the subject
Need Step	Provides listeners with a reason to listen; may identify and prove that a problem exists
Satisfaction Step	Gives the audience information and solves any proven problems
Visualization Step	Helps listeners to "see" themselves in the situation—solving the problem or performing the action
Action Step	Asks listeners to take the action outlined in the satisfaction and visualization steps

And we are the largest export market for countries such as China and Japan. With the arrival of the Euro dollar in 2002, world economies will change again.

You and I must be prepared to understand and appreciate that buying foreign goods is not bad; it's part of the international economy. The best slogan of the late 1990's may have been "Think and act internationally!"

When the goal of your speech is to convince an audience of a problem, only the first two steps of the motivated sequence, attention and need, are involved. A speaker who intends to show how the problem can be solved will present the third step: satisfaction.

Satisfaction Step

The purpose of the satisfaction step is to show how the problem described in the need step can be solved. In solving the problem (or satisfying the need), explain that the solution is desirable, fits the problem, and will not create new difficulties. For example:

One of the reasons many people avoid investing in individual securities is the cost of the transaction. With a traditional stock broker, it costs a minimum of $70 to buy and, later, sell shares of, for example Apple Computer or General Electric. With the arrival of the Internet, it's now possible to "bypass" the broker if you are willing to do your own research. And if you trade stocks on the Internet, it's possible to reduce the cost of buying that Apple or GE stock to just $7 from $35. If you do much trading, it can add up to considerable money.

You may have seen the TV advertisement for one of the Internet Brokerage operations. It shows a physician in an operating room with the voice saying, "This is Dr._____. He saves lives by day and makes a killing trading his own stocks at night. Shouldn't you consider making your next trade with ZQR Brokers for just $7 a trade?"

Visualization Step

The purpose of the visualization step is to get listeners to "see" in their mind's eye the consequences of their choices. For example, see yourself slipping the disk into your new DVD player and then sitting back to enjoy some of the most lifelike photography you've ever experienced. And, with the purchase of a unit, most manufacturers will give you several DVD movies to view as an introduction.

What ethical issues can you find embedded in the visualization step? Refer to page 10 as you think through this question.

Action Step

After you have attracted listeners' attention, created and satisfied need, and encouraged listeners to visualize themselves in the situation you describe, you use the action step of the motivated sequence to get listeners to agree with you or to perform the action suggested. Get the audience to say, "Yes, I'll do what you suggest," or "I believe you." For example:

Dr. Jack Kevorkian has focused public attention on "mercy killings, assisted suicide, and euthenasia." His actions were intended to challenge state laws on ending the lives of

> *terminally ill patients. He was so determined to press his case that he permitted the CBS program "60 Minutes" to televise a scene in which he administered a deadly injection to a man who died while the cameras recorded the episode. We must stop this charade!*
>
> *Join me in calling for the punishment of anyone who purposely takes the life of another. You and I cannot play God. Since murder is prohibited by law, then these acts are crimes and should be punished according to the law.*

During the action step, you should also clarify the action you want listeners to take:

> *So, plan to go to Augusta, Georgia, in the spring. See the azaleas, the dogwood, the redbud. See the greatest golfers in the world playing in a tournament with the most prestige possible. If you take just one day from your schedule to go to Georgia, you'll walk the Augusta National Golf Club with such legends as Jack Nicklaus, Ben Hogan, Arnold Palmer, and Sam Snead. You can walk the fifteenth hole, where Gene Sarazen scored his incredible double eagle on his way to victory in the Masters.*
>
> *It's a trip through history. It's a treat to the eye. No one plays here except by invitation. You have that once in a lifetime chance. Yes, tickets cost a hundred dollars, but how much is it worth to see the best in the world? Save two dollars a week for a year, and treat yourself to the greatest tournament in golf in nature's most magnificent setting next April.*
>
> *I urge you to go to the Masters next year. For anyone remotely interested in golf, this is the ultimate fantasy: "seeing the Masters live." Winning the Masters is so important to pro golfers that the prize money is incidental. It's the pride.*
>
> *Share the pride. See the Masters.*

In this example, there is little question about the desired action. If you develop and organize your speech clearly and help listeners to understand what you want them to do, they will be more likely to act on your words.

Organizational Links

The parts of a message need to be tied together in a coherent way. A speech may have only two main points, but the movement from the first to the second must be smooth. The relationship of one point to the other also must be clear. Similarly, the speech introduction must have an obvious relationship to the body of the speech, and the speaker must tie the conclusion to the speech's main ideas.

Organizational links tie a speech together and keep listeners headed in the right direction. Use transitions, signposts, and internal summaries.

Transitions

Transitions are verbal bridges designed to move listeners from consideration of one idea to consideration of the next. They tie major ideas together, focus attention, and keep the speech interesting. Indeed, the best speeches are characterized as much by effective transitions as they are by strong arguments or emotional appeals. Here are examples of different types of transitions:

> *Besides* being slow-moving, cricket *also* is a very complicated sport.

> *Although some people would argue that history is boring,* let me show you how it helps us to understand what the future holds.

> *Meanwhile,* people ignore the slaughter on our highways.

> Those are the two main problems. *Now, let's see how they can be solved.*

> *Finally,* look at the three simple techniques you can use in writing a letter of application.

> *To summarize,* we have the three elements for violence in all our major cities.

Signposts

A **signpost** is a unit of speech that announces or points to some new or important idea. Sometimes, a signpost is merely a number. At other times, it takes the form of a direct question, or it may highlight a key idea. Here are some examples of each type:

> Hold onto this idea.
> The thing to remember is . . .
> The first major objection . . .
> The third and final problem . . .
> Try to remember this!

In a speech with three major points, you might say, for example, *"The first reason we should be interested in ozone depletion is . . ."* As the speech progresses, you could introduce the next points by saying: *"The second problem associated with ozone loss is . . ."* and *"Third, and finally, ozone loss affects us because . . ."* This approach announces the introduction of new ideas and keeps audience members aware of the idea sequence. Signposts make speeches easier to follow and help listeners to identify and remember major ideas.

Internal Summaries

Internal summaries, sometimes called mini-summaries, are an effective way to remind listeners of the ideas you have discussed. Internal summaries often occur at the conclusion of a major point in a speech. A speaker might say:

> *As I said, there are several ways to stop groundwater pollution. First, . . .*

> So you can see, worker attrition isn't an easy way to slow the growth of government.

> For this reason alone, televised football games provide a large source of revenue for athletic departments.

> Fire can spread through a house very rapidly. You need to remember that smoke detectors will warn you. Next, . . .

SUMMARY

Effective organization of ideas is critical to successful public speaking. When you are well organized and appear to have a clearly determined destination, listeners are more willing and more likely to pay close attention. In addition, listeners who can follow your message easily will also be able to recall and act upon your major ideas.

A well-organized speech is clear and simple; only a few main points are introduced, and ideas are developed in a logical sequence. The best-known and most frequently used organizational patterns are time, space, problem to solution, causal order, and topical divisions. A sixth organizational pattern—motivated sequence—works primarily for persuasive speeches and has five steps: (1) attention, (2) need, (3) satisfaction, (4) visualization, and (5) action.

Organizational links, such as transitions, signposts, and internal summaries, offer bridges between ideas, tie a speech together, and point out significant ideas.

KEY TERMS

Causal order Cause-to-effect
Effect-to-cause
Internal summaries
Motivated sequence

Organizational links
Problem-to-solution
Signposts
Space pattern

Time pattern
Topical divisions
Transitions

APPLICATION QUESTIONS

1. Describe to a group of friends how to get from home to work. What organizational pattern did you use in your description? Ask your friends to tell you how successful your description seemed. How could you have provided better directions?

2. With a group or the class, identify a course and a professor you particularly enjoy. What are the characteristic elements of organization this professor uses for the course materials? What did you learn from this exercise that you can use in your own speaking?

3. Working with a classmate, select a television commercial that you find attractive. If possible, audiotape or videotape the commercial. Then try to identify how the commercial was organized. That is, does the commercial follow any of the organizational patterns and strategies described in this chapter? If so, which? Why do you think so? If not, how was the commercial organized? What inferences can you draw from this study? Be prepared to discuss this exercise with your class.

IT'S MORE FUN TO KNOW

It is not difficult to realize that ideas which are easy to follow are better remembered and more easily understood than those which are confusing or difficult to recall.

We know that it is easier to listen to a well organized message (James A. Gilchrist and Shirley A. Van Hoeven, "Listening as an Organizational Construct," *International Journal of Listening*, (1994) 8: 6-30) than one poorly structured. In fact, one scholar argues that communication is, itself, an organizing phenomenon (representing much of our intellectual activity) (see Francois Cooren and James R. Taylor, "Organization as an Effect of Mediation: Redefining the Link Between Organization and Communication," *Communication Theory*, (August 1997) 7: 3, 219).

Structure has, in fact, been the concern of both teachers of writing and speaking for many years. Writers tend to think of structure as a hierarchical tree (as in the chapters of a book), and encourage people to remember that approach as they compose (see *http://www.w3.org/Provider/Style/Structure.html* as an example).

Organization has been at the center of effective public speaking for so long that one admonition given to students has been "if you are disorganized you are lost." More recently, the technology revolution has moved into this area to make organization simpler and more easily learnable. (See Dave Axon, *Public Speaking Process: Computer Assistance for Speech Organization and Development*, (New York: Harcourt Brace, 1993).

SELF-TEST FOR REVIEW

1. A *signpost* is
   a. a major subject heading in an outline.
   b. a unit of speech that announces a new or important idea.
   c. a transition.
   d. a main idea and its subordinate points.
   e. *a* and *d*

2. A *transition* is
   a. a main idea.
   b. a verbalized pause between key ideas.
   c. a signpost.
   d. a bridge between key ideas.

3. List the names of the six major organizational patterns discussed in this chapter.
   a. _____
   b. _____
   c. _____
   d. _____
   e. _____
   f. _____

4. Which organizational patterns are most appropriate for speeches to persuade?

5. "Drive to the second light. Turn left on Wilson Boulevard and go five blocks. You'll come to . . ." is an example of which organizational pattern?

6. Suppose the following problem: You think that things are satisfactory the way they are, but you would like to see a change to create a benefit that is not possible at present. What would be the best way to organize your speech?

Answers: 1. b. 2. d. 3. a. time, b. space, c. problem to solution, d. causal order, e. topical divisions, f. motivated sequence. 4. problem-to-solution pattern and motivated sequence. 5. space. 6. problem-to-solution pattern.

SUGGESTED READINGS

Structure of a speech makes a difference. See Regina M. Hoffman, "Temporal Organization As A Rhetorical Resource," *Southern Communication Journal*, 57 (1992), 194-204. The author addresses the effect of structure in both speeches and other public communications.

Welch, Natalie. *"Inspiration* Lets Users Organize, Show Off Their Bright Ideas Faster: Version 4.0 Improves Outlining, Charting." *Macweek,* 9 November 1992, 8. Computer programs to assist speakers in organizing and refining their ideas are now available to the general public. As more sophisticated approaches to the development of ideas spread in the software community, a flow of programs that will assist both the novice and experienced speaker are likely.

NOTES

1. Noelle C. Nelson, *Winning! Using Courtroom Techniques To Get Your Way in Everyday Situations*, (Paramus, NJ: Prentice-Hall, 1997), p. 16.

2. Alan H. Monroe, *Principles and Types of Speech*, (Chicago: Scott, Foresman, 1935).

CHAPTER 9

OUTLINING THE SPEECH

OBJECTIVES

After reading this chapter, you should be able to:

1. Compare and contrast planning outlines and speaking outlines.

2. Describe the steps in developing a planning outline.

3. Develop a planning outline.

4. Describe the steps in developing a speaking outline.

5. Develop a speaking outline.

OUTLINE

Objectives
Outline
Abstract
Imagine
Introduction
  How to Develop a Planning
    Outline
    Label the Major Parts of
      the Outline
      The Introduction
      The Body
      The Conclusion
    Use a Standard Outline
      Format
    Write the General Pur-
      pose, the Specific Pur-
      pose, and the Thesis
      Statement
    Support the Thesis State-
      ment with Main Ideas
      and Subpoints

Consistently Follow an
    Organizational Pattern
  Write Simple Sentences
    with Action Verbs
  Plan Organizational Links
  Include Appropriate
    Documentation
  How to Develop a Speaking
    Outline
Summary
Key Terms
Application Questions
It's More Fun to Know
Self-Test for Review
Suggested Reading
Internet Activities
Notes
Sample Outlines

ABSTRACT

Chapter 8, "Organizing the Body of the Speech," examined the types of organizational patterns used in most public speaking situations. This chapter tells how to develop and use: (1) planning outlines and (2) speaking outlines.

Any outline provides a framework for idea development. A planning outline helps in determining the most appropriate organizational sequence for a given audience. It is therefore more detailed than the speaking outline, which is made to be used as notes. Its only purpose is to help you to stay on track during the presentation.

IMAGINE

When Connie Gonzalez graduated from college she landed a job that requires her to travel all over the United States, and often to Europe and Asia. As a representative of her company, she makes lots of presentations to physicians, executives from pharmaceutical companies, hospital administrators, and other professionals in the medical industry. Early in her career she realized she needed help. "All my life I have been writing speeches and essays, and thinking they're good," she said. "Now I'm getting feedback that says my ideas don't hang together and my speeches are hard to follow." She asked her professor, "What can I do?"

The professor asked one question: "Are you outlining carefully?" Connie admitted she by-passed writing out an outline.

"You're in the major leagues, now, Connie," said the professor. "It's time you start acting like a pro. What you need to do is outline carefully, and on paper."

Some years later Connie thanked her professor for the advice. "You were right," she said. "Outlining has made a lot of difference to me. In fact, I can listen to someone else's presentation, or I can read someone else's article, and know almost immediately whether or not they did an outline first. I once thought making an outline was a waste of time. Now I know outlining saves time and makes my speeches more credible and interesting. Plus, I think they're easier to follow."

Connie's statement speaks for itself and provides the strongest justification for learning how to outline. Outlining saves time and makes speeches and essays more credible and easier to follow.

INTRODUCTION

It may be difficult to persuade you that outlining is important. For years, many highschool and undergraduate college students have been doing as Connie did. They write an essay, then attempt to impose an outline upon what they have written. Or they plan out a speech, then attempt to make an outline that "fits" what they have planned. They take this approach in the naïve hope they will save time and effort. We hope you are not one of these students. To make an outline is to speed up the writing and planning process.

Is the behavior described here—first writing, then imposing an outline upon what you have written—ethical, unethical, or merely unwise?

There are two kinds of outlines: (1) a planning outline and (2) a speaking outline. A planning outline develops the structure and relationships among these parts. It also helps you examine how the evidence that supports those ideas fit together. A speaking outline is very brief. It is derived from a planning outline. Its purpose is to provide you with notes you can refer to as you speak.

How to Develop a Planning Outline

Since a planning outline requires much more time, research, and critical thinking to prepare than a speaking outline, most of this chapter focuses on how to develop a planning outline. In this chapter, most of the discussion focuses on guidelines for outlining the body of the speech. You can read more about introductions and conclusions in Chapter 10, "Introductions and Conclusions." Exhibit 9.1 shows the steps in developing a planning outline.

The Internet includes a good deal of help on outlining. For example, you can type the URL: *http://users.arn.net/~ngsapper/rules.html* and the computer will take you to a page of rules and suggestions for sentence and topic outlines. At *http://parallel.park.uga.edu/ ~sigalas/ENG101/Handouts/retro-outlining.html* you will find an interesting description by Joseph Sigalas of how to do a retro-outline on material you may have prepared without benefit of an outline.

Exhibit 9.2 shows a partial planning outline. Supporting materials have been dropped from the outline to highlight the relationships among ideas, but the words *Supporting evidence* indicate where this material was placed in the original outline.

Label the Major Parts of the Outline

Each part label should appear prominently in your outline. Some instructors want them in the center of the page. Others prefer that they be aligned on the left-hand margin. This chapter assumes a preference for centered part labels. Find out what your teacher prefers and follow that preference consistently.

Be sure to plan frequent transitional materials and other organizing links such as signposts and internal summaries. © PhotoDisc

The Introduction

Under the centered label *Introduction,* include such subtitles as *Opening, Thesis statement, Preview,* and *Transition.* Other possible subtitles are *Importance, Definition,* and *Name,* as you will see in some of the examples in this chapter. Which of these labels you include will depend entirely on your speech.

The opening should be designed to draw listeners' attention. A startling statement of opinion, a reference to one of the audience members or to the common experience of the audience, or even the simple greeting: "Good morning, ladies and gentlemen. My name is ____" will gather listeners' attention.

The thesis statement tells listeners what you want from them or what you plan to discuss.

The preview—a brief description of your analysis, a hint at the main ideas—is sometimes included to provide a quick overview your listeners will find helpful.

A transition is a sentence or two designed to move listeners smoothly from the introduction to the body of the speech. It might be as simple as, "So, let's consider the first part of the problem we are facing."

Exhibit 9.3 shows two sample introduction outlines. The assignment was to give a persuasive speech

EXHIBIT 9.1

STEPS IN DEVELOPING A PLANNING OUTLINE

Label the major parts.	The major parts are "Introduction," "Body," and "Conclusion." Label these major parts to guarantee you will include each part in your speech.
Use a standard outline format.	Identify the main points of your speech with Roman numerals, the subpoints with capital letters, the sub-subpoints with Arabic numerals, and the supporting evidence with lowercase letters. Indent each level consistently to prevent confusion as you flesh out your ideas. No absolute rule limits the number of subpoints and sub-subpoints you can have, but common sense suggests not going beyond three or four indentations.
Write the general purpose, the specific purpose and the thesis statement.	The general purpose may be either self-expression, to inform, to entertain, or to persuade. The specific purpose is what you want to accomplish with your speech—the action goal or the particular response you want from listeners. The thesis statement is the sentence in the speech introduction that states your most important point or purpose. Write these out before you begin to outline the body of the speech. Double-check that the thesis statement does not carry more than one idea and that it implies an action. Refer back to Chapter 4 for additional guidelines for developing your general purpose, specific purpose, and thesis statements.
Support the thesis statement with main ideas and support the main ideas with subpoints. Support the subpoints with evidence.	Use the *because* test to determine all your main ideas support the thesis statement and all your subpoints support the main ideas. The *because* test works like this: *Thesis: Someone should do something.* (How do you know?) *Because this main idea argues the point.* (How do you know that?) *Because these subpoints make it clear.* (How do you know you can believe the subpoints?) *Because this evidence proves them.*
Follow an organizational pattern. And follow it consistently.	Organize by time, space, cause to effect, effect to cause, problem to solution, or follow the motivated sequence. (See Chapter 8, "Organizing the Body of the Speech," for a thorough review.)
Make outline entries complete, simple sentences with action verbs.	Sentence fragments present only idea fragments. Outline entries should be complete sentences. In addition, use action verbs whenever possible.
Plan organizational links.	Transitions, signposts, and internal summaries help listeners follow and remember your line of thinking.
Include appropriate documentation.	Standard practice is to include appropriate documentation of all citations and references in speech outlines, just as you would in a formal term paper. Give credit where the credit is due. Supply complete bibliographical data.

EXHIBIT 9.2

A PLANNING OUTLINE

Women Serve Effectively as Combat Pilots

INTRODUCTION

Opening: Good afternoon. I'm Joan Britz and I'm a naval fighter pilot. I may not look like it, but I am a professional aviator who has attacked hostile targets overseas.

Thesis Statement: Women can serve as effectively as men in air combat missions.

Preview: People who have opposed women serving in combat have used these arguments. They say women pilots are not as good aviators as men, that they can't take the stress of bloody warfare, and that women shouldn't be exposed to the possibility of capture if their planes landed in hostile territory.

Transition: Please consider their arguments.

BODY

I. **Main Idea:** The notion that women are not as good aviators as men has been disproved. *(because)*

   A. Women pilots undergo the same training as men. (Supporting evidence)

   B. Women pilots must pass the same physical and intellectual tests as men. (Supporting evidence)

   C. Both female and male pilots must have excellent fitness ratings. (Supporting evidence)

Transition: Since women must meet the same fitness and training requirements as men, it's strange that we should still hear the second argument.

II. **Main Idea:** The argument that women can't take the stress of bloody battle is nonsense. *(because)*

   A. Women pilots used air-to-ground missiles in flights against Iraq in late 1998. (Supporting evidence)

   B. Women generally manage stress better than men. (Supporting evidence)

Transition: It's clear, then, that women fly as well as men and they manage stress and danger well. But there's still another groundless argument.

III. **Main Idea:** Women should not be exposed to the dangers of capture if their planes land in enemy territory. *(because)*

   A. Any pilot faces the dangers of capture if their planes are shot down in enemy territory. (Supporting evidence)

   B. Women can make these types of choices as well as men.

CONCLUSION

Summary: It's clear that women can fly effectively in combat missions. Already, women have undertaken combat missions, used their weapons, and performed successfully in flights from aircraft carriers in the Mid-East. Our performance was just as outstanding as our male counterparts. This type of experience puts to the rest the long-held belief that women should not or could not handle the rigors of combat, especially air battle.

Closing: Let's tell those people who argue against women fighting for their country that it's already happened and that they performed admirably. Tell them that women, like men, can and do risk their lives and perform in an equally outstanding way in the defense of liberty.

EXHIBIT 9.3

TWO SAMPLE INTRODUCTION OUTLINES

INTRODUCTION

Opening: As I drove here today, I was struck by the evidence of wealth that surrounds us just before Christmas. People were rushing around, doing their last minute shopping, arms filled with packages. The Downtown Merchants' Association tells us that this is going to be nearly a record-breaking year in retail sales. But not everyone in this country is so lucky.

Thesis statement: Today, within just a few miles of where we sit, there are people who desperately need our help if they are going to have any Christmas at all.

Preview: I am going to ask you to make a Christmas gift before you leave this room—a gift of caring that will do more good than all of those presents you will place under your own Christmas tree.

Transition: But first, I would like to tell you a true story.

INTRODUCTION

Opening: Good morning, class. As you know, my name is Tomas Elshani.

Topic: This morning I want to talk about an endangered species right here in Cooper County that's probably going to go extinct in the name of progress.

Thesis statement: We will all lose something that can never be replaced if we don't act now to stop the loss.

Preview: Today I am going to ask you to become a political activist. Today I want you to think like an environmentalist. Today I need for you to take a positive action to save the only habitat left for Cooper County's Creel Snail. To do that, we'll have to persuade casino builders to move their location several miles to the east.

Transition: First, I'd like you to think about what happens when an animal species goes extinct.

that calls for audience involvement in some social problem. Notice how each of the parts has been labeled.

The Body

The body of the speech includes all the main lines of analysis and all the supporting evidence and arguments. Once you have a clear idea of the thesis statement, develop the body outline first. Outline the body before the introduction and the conclusion. From the body you will be able to draw ideas for the introduction. Certainly, you will need the body outline before you can outline the conclusion. Exhibit 9.4 shows how the two students outlined the bodies of their persuasive speech assignment.

The Conclusion

Under the centered label *Conclusion* put such subtitles as Summary and Closing. The summary is a brief recapitulation of the main ideas that you developed in the speech. The closing is a statement designed to focus listeners' thinking and feelings on what was said or what you wanted from the listeners. Exhibit 9.5 shows the conclusion outlines produced for the persuasive speaking assignment.

Exhibit 9.4

Two Sample Body Outlines

BODY

I. **Main Idea: Nearly** one-fifth of the people in Cedar Ridge are living at or near the poverty level. *(because)*
  A. The poverty level in our country, for a family of four, is $16,450.
  B. Of the 2014 total population in Cedar Ridge, 463 earn incomes below $16,000.

Transition: When income is sufficient only for food and shelter, people can't afford to buy special gifts and decorations. This claim seems self-evident. Yet,

II. **Main Idea:** Some people living near us lack the finances to celebrate one of our traditional holidays. They can't afford a gift exchange or even a tree. *(because)*
  A. Jackie Bur's mother can't afford to purchase gifts.
  B. According to the County Welfare Officer, Mrs. Bur will probably not ever get out of poverty on her own.
  C. This means Jackie Bur may never enjoy a gift exchange in his childhood.

Transition: Apparently, because of bureaucratic rules and regulations, as things stand now, no government agency is set up to help this particular family.

III. **Main Idea:** But you can help. *(because)*
  A. You can give money.
  B. You can volunteer your time and energy.

BODY

I. **Main Idea:** When a species goes extinct the entire ecology suffers. *(because)*
  A. The food chain system is affected.
  B. The natural system of checks and balances is affected.
  C. In the end, no one can say for sure how much damage can result.

II. **Main Idea:** The Cooper County Creel Snail is about to go extinct. *(because)*
  A. The Cooper County Creel Snail lives only on the Missouri River banks in Cooper County.
  B. Now the Missouri Gaming Commission has approved placing casinos in the Cooper Country Creel Snail habitat.
  C. This action will wipe out the Cooper County Creel Snails

Transition: You might ask, What difference does this little snail make to me?

III. **Main Idea:** We students can do something to prevent another life form from going extinct by becoming politically active environmentalists. *(because)*
  A. Casino operations are sensitive to public opinion.
  B. We can have a powerful effect on public opinion.
  C. We can participate in the public forum.

Transition: I guess you can tell what I'm leading up to.

IV. **Main Idea:** Now I'm asking you to sign this petition. *(because)*
  A. The media will only respond to a large number of signatures.
  B. To sign your name is to act for an important cause

EXHIBIT 9.5

TWO SAMPLE CONCLUSION OUTLINES

CONCLUSION

Summary: In summary, not everyone will be able to enjoy Christmas this year. But you can help.

Nearly one-fifth of the people in Cedar Ridge are living at or near the poverty level.

Most of us are not aware that some people living near us lack the finances to celebrate one of our traditional holidays. They can't afford a gift exchange or even a tree.

Closing: So now I'm asking you for your help. Jackie Bur needs your money. His mother needs your help.

CONCLUSION

Summary: This morning I've argued that we're all about to lose something very valuable. The Cooper County Creel Snail is about to go extinct because its habitat is about to be destroyed so a gambling casino can be built.

I. But we—you and I—can do something about it. We can become environmentalists—political activists.

II. The media and the EPA are sensitive to public opinion—your opinion.

III. We can express ourselves by writing our names on this petition. I've already signed it.

Closing: While I'm passing it around I'd like you to think. Is it too much to ask that a gambling casino be built a little way down river—only two miles? Wouldn't that change of plans be worth the payoff of saving a species from extinction?

Use A Standard Outline Format

Follow a standard outlining format, like the one used in the examples in this chapter. Separate the body from the introduction and conclusion. Exhibit 9.6 shows a standard outline symbol and indentation pattern. Notice how indentations suggest the relative importance of particular ideas. Do not indent main ideas. Clarifying and supporting materials are indented according to their significance: The less significant the idea, the greater the indentation. Consistent use of the same outline pattern will eliminate a good deal of confusion.

Write the General Purpose, the Specific Purpose, and the Thesis Statement

You may wish to review Chapter 4, "Selecting and Narrowing Your Topic." Exhibit 9.7 highlights some relevant material from that chapter.

EXHIBIT 9.6

A STANDARD OUTLINE SYMBOL AND INDENTION PATTERN

INTRODUCTION

Thesis statement
Transition

BODY

I. Main idea:
  A. First subpoint
    1. First sub-subpoint
      a. Supporting evidence
      b. Supporting evidence
    2. Second sub-subpoint
  B. Second subpoint
Transition
II. Main idea:
  A. First subpoint
    1. First sub-subpoint
      a. Supporting evidence
      b. Supporting evidence
    2. Second sub-subpoint
  B. Second subpoint
Transition

CONCLUSION

Summary
Closing

EXHIBIT 9.7

REVIEW OF GENERAL PURPOSE, AND SPECIFIC PURPOSE, AND THESIS STATEMENT

The general purpose	TO INFORM	TO PERSUADE	TO ENTERTAIN
The specific purpose	To know	To believe	To amuse
	To understand	To value	To delight
	To discriminate	To want	To charm
	To comprehend	To hope	To please
	To discern	To request	To laugh
	To perceive	To urge	To smile
	To conclude	To demand	
The thesis statement	Is the statement expressed in one, simple, declarative sentence? (It should not be a question.)		
	Does the statement summarize the purpose and main ideas of the speech?		
	Does the statement specify or at least clearly imply what you want listeners to remember after the speech?		
	Is the statement free of judgmental and figurative language?		

Support the Thesis Statement With Main Ideas and Subpoints

Every thesis statement needs support. To illustrate, suppose you decide to give a speech comparing commercial television to public television. Your thesis is: "Public television is far superior in quality to commercial television." How do you know? Clearly, your argument needs the support of other arguments and evidence. This sample outline shows how you might support the thesis statement with main ideas and subpoints. Notice the parenthetical expression, *(because)*. It makes clear that the next item in the outline answers the *How do you know* question.

> **Thesis statement:** Public television programming is far superior to commercial television. *(because)*
>
> **I. Main idea:** Commercial television panders to the lowest common denominator. *(because)*
>
> **A.** Commercial television program producers seek the largest viewing audience possible. *(because)*
>
>   **1.** The larger the television audience, the higher the ratings. *(because)*
>
>   **a.** evidence
>
>   **b.** evidence
>
>   **2.** The larger the television audience, the more valuable the commercial time. *(because)*
>
>   **a.** evidence
>
>   **b.** evidence
>
> **B.** Commercial television advertisers seek the largest possible audiences. *(because)*
>
>   **1.** The larger the television audience the more likely that advertisers will sell products.
>
>   **a.** evidence
>
>   **b.** evidence

Consistently Follow an Organizational Pattern

Decide what type of organizational pattern would work best for your topic (time, space, cause-effect, problem-solution, motivated sequence). (See Chapter 8, "Organizing the Body of the Speech.") You are ready to outline the body of your speech. Your outline should follow the organizational pattern you select consistently. Otherwise you may confuse your listeners, not to mention yourself.

For example, one student decided to organize her talk about her summer study trip to Paris chronologically. Exhibit 9.8 shows a portion of her planning outline.

EXHIBIT 9.8

PARTIAL PLANNING OUTLINE
ORGANIZED CHRONOLOGICALLY

Thesis statement: My study-abroad trip to Paris was wonderful.
Body

I. **Main idea:** Getting to Paris wasn't easy. *(because)*
   A. Jet lag created a problem.
   B. Jet Jazzercise helped.

II. **Main idea:** The six days in France were very busy. *(because)*
   A. The monuments of Paris could take a month.
   B. We traveled to Chartres and Versailles.
   C. We walked our socks off.
   D. The Latin Quarter was a highlight.

III. **Main idea:** The return home was an important part of the trip. *(because)*
   A. Saying good-by to Paris wasn't easy.
   B. Meeting Mr. and Mrs. Harris helped.
   C. Mom and Dad had a surprise "Welcome Home" party for me.

The student knew that she could not possibly develop her entire outline in the six minutes she was allowed for her speech. To focus her topic, she decided that she could only talk about her idea that six days in France were very busy. She turned this idea into her thesis statement. Exhibit 9.9 shows how she did this.

EXHIBIT 9.9

REVISION OF EXHIBIT 9.8 PLANNING OUTLINE

Thesis statement: My study-abroad trip to Paris was wonderful.
Body

I. ~~**Main idea:** Getting to Paris wasn't easy. *(because)*~~
   ~~A. Jet lag created a problem.~~
   ~~B. Jet Jazzercise helped.~~

II. **Main idea:** The six days in France were very busy. *(because)*
   A. The monuments of Paris could take a month.
   B. We traveled to Chartres and Versailles.
   C. We walked our socks off.
   D. The Latin Quarter was a highlight.

III. ~~**Main idea:** The return home was an important part of the trip. *(because)*~~
   ~~A. Saying good-by to Paris wasn't easy.~~
   ~~B. Meeting Mr. and Mrs. Harris helped.~~
   ~~C. Mom and Dad had a surprise "Welcome Home" party for me.~~

The student's work and final planning outline appear in Exhibit 9.10.

EXHIBIT 9.10

FINAL PLANNING OUTLINE

(Used with Permission of Michelle Rampulla.)

INTRODUCTION

Opening: Good morning. My name is Michelle Rampulla. Last summer, I spent six days in France as part of my summer study program.

Thesis statement: I can tell you for sure that six days in France aren't enough!

Importance: I've never been to a place where it's possible to learn so much so fast.

Transition: Each day was absolutely full of activities and excitement. I only have time to tell you about a few of the highlights.

Body

I. **Main idea:** The monuments of Paris came first. *(because)*

    A. We saw a dozen beautiful churches.

        1. Notre Dame was the most famous and the biggest.

        2. Saint Germaine was the oldest.

        3. Sacre Cour had the best view of the city.

        4. Sainte Chapelle was the most beautiful.

    B. We saw many civic monuments.

        1. The Arc de Triomphe was a highlight.

        2. The Eiffel Tower provided the best view of the city.

        3. The Hôtel des Invalides is the world's first military hospital.

        4. The Louvre is more than an art museum.

Transition: We loved the monuments of Paris, but I had always wanted to visit Chartres Cathedral and Versailles Palace.

II. **Main idea:** We traveled to Chartres and Versailles in one day. *(because)*

    A. We spent only three hours at Chartres.

        1. The cathedral is the highest example of medieval Gothic architecture.

        2. Part of the old village is still evident.

    B. We spent four hours at Versailles.

        1. The building is immense.

        2. Ten thousand acres of grounds were designed as a setting for the palace.

Conclusion

Summary: Six days won't begin to give you enough time to see France. The museums, the restaurants, the walks, and the river were all beautiful. But for me, the monuments of Paris and a day at Chartres and Versailles were the highlights of the trip.

Closing: I fell in love with France. I'll go back some day, and it won't be long.

You can develop a planning outline for any organizational strategy you choose. Exhibit 9.11 shows a planning outline that uses space as an organizational pattern, while Exhibit 9.12 shows how you might plan to follow a problem-to-solution sequence. Exhibit 9.13 shows a partial planning outline using an effect-to-cause organizational strategy. All of these organizational strategies are discussed in detail in Chapter 8, "Organizing the Body of the Speech."

EXHIBIT 9.11

PLANNING OUTLINE USING SPACE AS AN ORGANIZATIONAL PATTERN

(After an outline developed by Baptist Glenos. Used with permission.)

INTRODUCTION

Opening: Good afternoon. You know me by now.

Name: My name is Baptist Glenos. My family and I moved here just three years ago. Dad retired from the Air Force and bought a farm. When we first came to the farm, I didn't have any idea about farming. I thought all those buildings were just a display of my father's wealth.

Thesis statement: Every building on the property is a working structure.

Transition: I'd like to tell you about three of the most interesting ones to me.

BODY

I. **Main idea:** The barn sits farthest from the house. *(because)*

    A. The barn has two levels.

        1. The loft serves two functions. [Supporting evidence]

        2. The main level has three areas. [Supporting evidence]

    B. The barn is the heart of the farm. [Supporting evidence]

Transition: Having looked at the barn, you might be just as interested in the shop.

II. **Main idea:** The shop lies between the barn and the garage, nearer to the house. *(because)*

    A. Tool repair and maintenance are done in the shop. [Supporting evidence]

    B. Metal and wood parts and equipment are built in the shop. [Supporting evidence]

Transition: The shop is busy all the time at our farm. So is the garage.

III. **Main idea:** The garage is closest to our house. *(because)*

    A. The garage houses cars, trucks, and tractors. [Supporting evidence]

    B. Rolling stock is maintained and repaired in the shop. [Supporting evidence]

Transition: So what have I said so far about our farm?

CONCLUSION

Summary: Of all the working buildings on the farm, the garage, the shop, and the barn seem the most important. Three years ago, I was surprised how important these buildings are to the farm.

Closing: Now I can hardly wait to go home.

EXHIBIT 9.12

PARTIAL PLANNING OUTLINE USING A PROBLEM-TO-SOLUTION ORGANIZATIONAL PATTERN

(After course materials submitted by Tony Divilbis. Used with Permission.)

INTRODUCTION

Opening: Hello, again. I'm Tony Divilbis. I'm a junior student majoring in sociology. This morning, I want to talk about the biggest government rip-off in America.

Thesis statement: I think the federal government should drastically change the welfare system.

Definition: By welfare, I mean all federal entitlement programs and give-away programs except Social Security and Medicare.

Importance: The welfare system is costing taxpayers more than it should, and it's doing more harm than good.

Transition: So what are the problems I'm talking about?

BODY

I. **Main idea:** The problems with the current welfare programs seem insurmountable. *(because)*

    A. The economic costs are staggering. [Supporting evidence]

    B. The human costs are unsupportable. [Supporting evidence]

    C. The programs are impossible to administer fairly. [Supporting evidence]

Transition: It's easy to see that the current welfare system presents staggering problems. But what can be done about them?

I. **Main idea:** The solution will require a complete redesign of government's ways of helping people who can't help themselves. *(because)*

    A. The government should abolish all federal entitlement programs and give-aways except Social Security and Medicare.

    B. The government should institute a guaranteed minimum annual cash income for everyone. [Explanation and definitions]

    C. The government should establish the requirement that there are no free lunches by making indigence a crime. [Explanation and definitions]

    D. The government should administer and enforce the new program through the Internal Revenue Service. [Explanation]

CONCLUSION

Summary: In summary, I have argued that the problems with federal welfare programs can no longer be supported. I have urged your support for a plan in which the federal government would abolish those programs and implement a new plan. I have shown you that a guaranteed minimum annual cash income program, carefully designed and carefully administered, would solve the problems and would be a far more effective way to take care of the nation's poor.

Closing: There aren't any free lunches. Someone has to pay for them. If you pay taxes, raise your hand and look around. You folks with your hands up, the federal government wastes your tax dollars by the millions and millions every day.

EXHIBIT 9.13

PARTIAL PLANNING OUTLINE USING AN EFFECT-TO-CAUSE ORGANIZATIONAL PATTERN

INTRODUCTION

Opening:

Thesis statement: Our public schools are a mess because of serious underfunding.

Preview:

Transition:

BODY

I. **Main idea:** Our public schools just aren't doing the job. *(because)*

   A. In four critical areas, our city has the highest illiteracy rate in this state.

      1. The students can't read. [Supporting evidence]

      2. The students can't do math. [Supporting evidence]

      3. The students don't know geography. [Supporting evidence]

      4. The students can't run computers. [Supporting evidence]

   B. Our schools produced the lowest SAT and ACT scores in a five-state region. [Supporting evidence]

Transition:

II. **Main idea:** Five factors—all the result of serious underfunding—combine to cause this sorry state of affairs. *(because)*

   A. Poor teaching is a factor. [Supporting evidence]

   B. Overcrowded classes play a part. [Supporting evidence]

   C. Obsolete or nonexistent technology characterizes our schools. [Supporting evidence]

   D. School buildings are antiquated and in disrepair. [Supporting evidence]

   E. The problems are so big that people think nothing can be done. [Supporting evidence]

Transition:

CONCLUSION

Summary:

Closing:

The planning outline in Exhibit 9.14 illustrates the motivated sequence organizational strategy originally developed by Alan H. Monroe in the mid-1930s.[1] Speakers use the motivated sequence to organize many different kinds of persuasive speeches. It works because it conforms to the way people think. Rather than the usual introduction, body, and conclusion, this sequence has five steps: (1) attention, (2) need, (3) satisfaction, (4) visualization, and (5) action. Refer to Chapter 8, "Organizing the Body of the Speech," for a more complete discussion of the motivated sequence.

Exhibit 9.14

Planning Outline Following the Motivated Sequence

(Used with permission of Debra Campbell.)

Foreign Language Competence: A Key to Employment in the New Millennium

General purpose: To persuade

Specific purpose: I want to persuade my listeners to learn a foreign language as a way to help them get jobs when they graduate.

I. Attention step

Greeting: Wouldn't it be great to walk into a job interview after you graduate, knowing that you have a skill your prospective employer desperately needs—a skill most other applicants don't have?

Preview: Today, I want to tell you about a skill that you can develop here at South that will give you an edge over the competition no matter what your field is. The skill is being able to speak a foreign language.

Thesis statement: Learning a foreign language can mean the difference between landing a job or not.

Transition: Let's look at some of the reasons that speaking a foreign language can help you get into corporate America.

II. Need step

  A. U.S. corporations must look outward, not inward.

    1. Senator Paul Simon stated in 1990 that "Cultural isolation is a luxury the United States can no longer afford."

    2. As businesses continue to expand in Europe, Latin America, China, and Russia, they will have to communicate in their clients' native languages.

    3. Abby Joseph Cohen, strategist for Goldman, Sachs emphasized the nature of the global economy in the September 14, 1998 issue of *Newsweek.*

    4. Americans can't rely on speaking English slower and louder to make deals.

  B. U.S. companies are looking for employees who can speak foreign languages.

    1. Dr. Carol Fixman, in "The Foreign Language Needs of U.S.-Based Corporations," says they are.

    2. The 1998 issues of *The Wall Street Journal* say employers give special weight to people with language skills.

    3. Companies need foreign language capabilities even in the United States.

      a. QMS provides an example of one such company.

      b. Omni International of Mobile provides another example.

      c. Degussa Chemical provides a personal example.

Transition: Well, we've seen that corporations need to look beyond the English-speaking world, and they need people who can help them do that. Where does that leave you?

Continued

Exhibit 9.14 *continued*

III. Satisfaction step

A. You can learn a foreign language here at South while you finish your degree.

1. All Arts and Sciences majors must complete a three-quarter cluster.

2. You can take two or more intermediate language classes to fulfill the Humanities requirement.

3. Just eight hours beyond the intermediate sequence will give you a minor in a language.

B. The most difficult part is deciding which language to study.

1. To help you decide, consider which languages are most sought after by employers.

  a. Spanish (44%)

  b. Japanese (33%)

  c. French (8%)

  d. German (5%)

  e. Russian (1%)

2. All of these languages, plus Greek and Arabic, are offered at South.

3. All of the sources I consulted advised job seekers to learn the language that most interests them.

IV. Visualization step

A. Picture yourself as you walk into your first interview.

1. You are confident because you speak the language this employer needs.

2. When the interviewer asks, "Do you speak /ru/ ?" you smile with confidence.

3. The interviewer makes a note and nods her head.

B. You know you've got the advantage because you made the effort to meet the company's needs.

V. Action step

Summary: It's all up to you. I've told you about foreign language needs that globalization of business has caused, and I've told you how to prepare yourself to meet those needs. To quote the July 1991 *Forbes Magazine,* "Knowledge of a language usually means money to someone's career."

Closing: Act now. Registration for summer quarter begins in a week. Get yourself into a foreign language class. Your future might depend on it.

Write Simple Sentences with Action Verbs

Planning outlines help you to crystallize your thinking. Sentence fragments are merely idea fragments. Thus, your outline entries should be complete sentences. In addition, use action verbs whenever possible, since forms of the verb *to be* often seem weak and lifeless. The following outline entries demonstrate these guidelines:

> ***Wrong:*** The problems in higher education
>
> ***Better:*** State colleges and universities are in financial trouble.
>
> ***Best:*** State colleges and universities face increasing financial trouble.

Plan Organizational Links

Organizational links are transitions, signposts, and internal summaries that help listeners to follow and remember your line of thinking. To review, a transition is a unit of speech designed to move listeners from consideration of one idea to consideration of the next. A transition serves as a bridge between ideas. A signpost announces or points to some new or important idea. Signposts can be numbers ("The first issue is . . ."), direct questions ("What is the solution to this problem?"), or highlights of key ideas ("If you forget everything else, remember this . . ."). Internal summaries are short reviews or recapitulations of some part of your message ("To summarize, I've talked about three key areas . . .").

Label organizational links without numbers or letters, at the outline's left-hand margin. To illustrate for transitions, suppose your argument includes the following three lines of analysis:

> **Thesis statement:** The budget committee should increase the library budget by 25 percent. *(because)*
>
> I. **Main idea:** Periodical holdings do not support undergraduate major programs in three colleges.
>
> II. **Main idea:** A 25 percent increase in budget would bring the holdings up to the standard needed.
>
> III. **Main idea:** The money is available in existing university budgets.

This complex argument would require a good deal of development. To help listeners follow your analysis, you would want to develop a transition between each of the main ideas. Between the first and second main ideas, you could say:

> **Transition:** We have seen, then, that the periodical holdings don't support the undergraduate majors in Arts and Sciences, in Allied Health, or in Business Administration. Will the proposed 25 percent increase in library budget be enough to solve this problem? I think so.

Between the second and third main ideas, you might say:

> **Transition:** Well, the periodical holdings don't support undergraduate majors in three colleges and we've seen that that a 25 percent increase in the library's acquisitions budget would be enough to cover the costs. The next question we have to consider is whether the money is available.

Put it all together and you have the outline in Exhibit 9.15.

EXHIBIT 9.15

OUTLINE OF MAIN IDEAS AND TRANSITIONS

Thesis statement: The budget committee should increase the library budget by 25 percent. *(because)*

I. Main idea: Periodical holdings do not support undergraduate major programs in three colleges.

Transition: We have seen, then, that the periodical holdings don't support the undergraduate majors in Arts and Sciences, in Allied Health, or in Business Administration. Will the proposed 25 percent increase in library budget be enough to solve this problem? I think so.

II. Main idea: A 25 percent increase in budget would bring the holdings up to the standard needed.

Transition: We have seen, then, that the periodical holdings don't support undergraduate majors in three colleges and that a 25 percent increase in the library's acquisitions budget would be enough to cover the costs. The next question we have to consider is whether the money is available.

III. Main idea: The money is available in existing university budgets.

Include Appropriate Documentation

Standard practice is to document an outline just as you would for a term paper, placing full bibliographical data either at the foot of the relevant page or at the end of the outline. Documentation styles vary, depending on which style manual you are following.[2] Learn a standard style, and use it consistently. It would be a good idea to ask your professor about which style to follow.

Exhibit 9.16 presents a planning outline checklist. Use this table to double-check that your planning outline includes all of the necessary information, logically organized, and in an appropriate format. Exhibit 9.17 at the end of the chapter is a complete, annotated, full-sentence planning outline developed in preparation for a six-minute argumentative speech. Although not perfect, the outline shows most of the outlining features described in this chapter.

How to Develop a Speaking Outline

Once you are satisfied with your planning outline, you can begin to develop the speaking outline. Much briefer than the planning outline, a speaking outline becomes notes to use while giving your speech. Include only the topics you will discuss. The pointers in Exhibit 9.17 will help you to develop your speaking outline.

Exhibit 9.18 shows a Planning Outline for a speech by Cheryl Cope about women in the work force.

EXHIBIT 9.16

PLANNING OUTLINE CHECKLIST

1. Have I labeled the introduction, body, and conclusion as separate parts? Are the labels centered?

2. Have I included the appropriate side-headings in the introduction and conclusion?

3. Have I written out the general and specific purpose and the thesis statement? Do I know clearly what response I want from my listeners?

4. Have I identified and consistently followed an organizational strategy (time, space, problem to solution, motivated sequence, etc.)?

5. Have I followed a standard outline symbol system to indicate superior and subordinate relationships among ideas?

6. Have I used complete, simple sentences and action words?

7. Have I double-checked that the main ideas support the thesis statement and that subpoints support the main ideas? (Have I used the *because* test?)

8. Have I planned and included transitions, signposts, and internal summaries?

9. Have I included supporting and bibliographical material?

EXHIBIT 9.17

POINTERS FOR DEVELOPING A SPEAKING OUTLINE

1. Follow the planning outline.	Use the same standard set of symbols and indentation pattern that you used in your planning outline. If you alter the pattern, you run the risk of confusing yourself during the speech.
2. Be brief.	Because the purpose of a speaking outline is to jog your memory, there is no need for more than a few words. If your outline is too detailed, you may spend too much time studying the outline and not enough time looking at the audience. Keep your speaking outline as brief as possible.
3. Make the speaking outline a working tool.	The speaking outline is a good place to make marginal notes about things you want to remember. For example, you may have just met a member of the audience and want to mention her name during the speech. Print her name in the margin of the speaking outline at the appropriate place. Similarly, you may wish to remind yourself of any visual aids you plan to use. A marginal note or sketch at the appropriate place in your speaking outline will help you to remember when to use the visual aids

EXHIBIT 9.18

PLANNING OUTLINE

(Used with permission of Cheryl Cope)

WOMEN IN THE WORK FORCE: ARE THEY BETTER OFF?

It is a good idea to state the purpose of a speech in writing before you begin to outline. This helps you test the accuracy and completeness of the outline.

General purpose: To change belief.

Specific purpose: To persuade my audience that the Family Medical Leave Act has made the problem worse (too few women are promoted to upper executive ranks).

Label each part separately, in the center of the page.

INTRODUCTION

Gathers audience attention.

Opener: Good morning, class. My name is Cheryl Cope. I'm working on my degree in business. And I'm worried.

Note how this thesis statement flows from the specific purpose

Thesis statement: I'm worried because, despite what they tell you on television, things are getting worse for women executives, not better.

Note how this transition builds the importance and relevance of the topic. It also previews the main ideas and alerts listeners to what is coming.

Transition: I think I can show you at least three reasons why, whether you're a man or a woman, you should be concerned, too. The number of women employees is growing rapidly, but the number of women executives is not. And now, the Family Medical Leave Act has made things worse, not better.

Centered label shows this is a separate, distinct part of the speech.

BODY

Main idea stated in full sentence. Note reference to source and use of the because test.

I. **Main idea:** Very few women gain entry into upper executive ranks.[1] *(because)*

Subpoints directly support the main idea, and the sub-subpoints provide evidence to support the subpoints.

  A. Yet, women make up the majority of new entrants into the work force each year. *(because)*

    1. The number of women in the work force has grown from 20 million to 50 million in the years from 1960 to 1990.

    2. The percent of women in the work force grew from 33 percent in 1960 to 45 percent in 1990.

  B. At every level of employment, women earn less than men.[2]

  C. Less than 10 per cent of the country's largest employers have women on the Board of Directors.[3]

  D. Ninety-five percent of the senior managers in Fortune 1500 companies are men.[4]

Continued

Exhibit 9.18 *continued*

See how the transition ties the first main idea to the second. Write out and label transitions.	**Transition:** You have to conclude from these figures that there aren't many women executives and that, even though the number of women employees is growing rapidly, the number of women executives isn't keeping pace. But why? How can this be true when we hear all the time about how conditions are getting better for women?
Helps listeners remember, and serves as transition to help them follow from one idea to the next.	**Internal summary:** Sex-role stereotypes may have something to do with the problem. It may be that sex-role stereotyping keeps women out of the executive suite. And things aren't likely to get better.
Full sentences force you to think clearly.	**II. Main idea:** The Family Medical Leave Act that became effective in 1993, makes it more difficult for women to break through into senior management positions. *(because)*
Here the speaker pulled out of the act only those provisions that support her arguments. When asked about other provisions Cheryl was able to respond knowledgeably.	A. The Family Medical Leave Act makes sweeping changes.[5] 1. Any organization that employs fifty or more people within a seventy-five-mile radius must offer workers as much as twelve weeks of unpaid leave for certain qualified medical reasons. 2. Employers must continue health-care coverage during the leave. 3. Employers must guarantee that their employees will return to either the same job or a comparable one.

The student extended this part of the speech with illustrations of three women she knew personally.	B. Women are more likely to take more leaves than men.
	
	 1. Women remain the primary caregivers (mothers, wives, etc.).
	
	 2. Women have babies.
	
	 C. The costs associated with the FMLA continue to decrease the number of women hired for executive positions.
	
	 1. The costs of benefits inhibit employers from promoting women.
	
	   a. Benefits continue for the person taking leave.
	
	   b. Benefits must be paid for the replacement person.

Continued

Exhibit 9.18 *continued*

Speaker could have provided an example or two here to illustrate her ideas. She might have found the information by calling personnel officers.	2. The costs of replacing women who take the leave inhibit employers from promoting and hiring women executives.
	a. Although the women taking leave will not be paid salaries, the employer must still recruit new people to replace them.
	b. Replacement employees have to be trained at employer expense.
It would have been extremely difficult to develop direct testimony as evidence for these arguments, but something is needed to support them.	3. The costs of reinstating women employees also inhibits employers from hiring and promoting women executives.
	a. An employee who has been away for an extended period of time has to be retrained.
	b. An employee who elects to distribute leave creates a different problem.
An illustration using a hypothetical case.	**Example:** Employee says to boss, "Beginning next month, I will be gone every Monday and Friday."
	CONCLUSION
Restatement helps listeners remember main ideas.	**Summary:** So, things aren't as good for women in business as you hear. The problem of sex-role stereotyping was keeping women out of the executive suite before the Family Medical Leave Act.
Speaker ends on an optimistic note, then doubles back on her introductory idea.	**Closing:** I don't know what can be done about this situation. Perhaps nothing. As for me, I'm going to do the best I can to make it when I'm finally out there. But I'm going to have to work harder and sacrifice more than men will, and I'm mad about that.
Standard practice is to include footnotes in an outline. Give complete bibliographical data and be sure to follow your teacher's preferred style manual carefully.	1. "Women in Corporate Management," *Miami Herald,* 27 July 1993.
	2. U.S. Department of Commerce. *Statistical Abstract of the United States, 1996* (Washington, D.C.: Bureau of the Census, 1996), p. 399.
	3. "Glass Ceiling Commission Fact Finding Report and Recommendations," *Government Printing Office*, 1997.
	4. Ibid.
	5. "Family Medical Leave Act" *Minnesota Department of Labor and Industry*, 1998.

Exhibit 9.19 is the annotated speaking outline that corresponds Cheryl's planning outline. Notice how the speaking outline follows the same outline format as the planning outline. Yet, the speaking outline has only key words and phrases. Notice also the "meta-notes"—notes Cheryl made as reminders to herself. (See Exhibit 13.5 for more information in meta-notes.)

EXHIBIT 9.19

SPEAKING OUTLINE WITH ANNOTATIONS

(Used with Permission of Cheryl Cope.)

WOMEN IN THE WORK FORCE: ARE THEY BETTER OFF?

INTRODUCTION

Speaker used these meta-notes to remind herself to remain calm.

Opener: Greeting. I'm worried.

Trans: Three reasons to be concerned.

BODY *Pause Breathe*

Note how the speaker reminds herself to pause, and to work with the members of her audience.

I. Few gain entry (*Miami Herald,* 27 July 1993)

   A. Majority of new entrants

      1. 20-M to 50-M, 1960 to 1990

      2. 33% to 45%, 1960 to 1990

   B. Women earn less than men

   C. Less than 10 percent of largest employers women on Bd of Directors (Glass Ceiling Commission Report)

   D. 95% of senior managers in Fortune 1500 companies are men.

Trans: Not many women executives and number not keeping pace. WHY? *Pause Move*

II. FMLA (Aug. 4) made it more difficult.

   A. Sweeping changes

Useful reminders in the margins

The names remind Cheryl to tell the women's stories for supporting material.

      1. 50 + people w/in 75 miles = 12 weeks unpaid leave

      2. Employers must cont. health care . . .

      3. and guarantee same or comparable job

   B. Women more likely to take leave

      1. Primary caregivers *Ex. Mrs. Wilson*

      2. Women have babies. *Ex. Jeannie Donna*

   C. FMLA costs = decrease number of women executives.

      1. Benefits = inhibit employers

      2. Recruitment and training = inhibit employers

      3. Guaranteed return to job = inhibit employers

Example: "Beginning next month . . ."

CONCLUSION *Pause Move*

One word reminds speaker to summarize key ideas.

Summary:

Key ideas of planned closing

Closing: Do best—work harder—sacrifice more.

I'm mad!

SUMMARY

Double check to assure your speaking outline is brief and that you can actually use it as a working tool. You can include useful meta-notes in the margins. © Tony Stone Images

Planning outlines and speaking outlines simplify the task of organizing a speech. A planning outline helps you to study the relationships among ideas and to determine the amount and kinds of evidence needed to support your thesis statement. A speaking outline provides you with notes you can refer to while giving your speech.

Label the introduction, the body, and the conclusion. The introduction usually includes an opening statement or greeting, the thesis statement, a preview of what you are going to discuss, and a transition to your first main idea. The body includes all the main lines of analysis and all of your supporting evidence and arguments. The conclusion often consists of a short summary and a closing statement. Learn and follow a standard outlining format to indicate the various parts of the speech and the relationships among those parts.

A good outline depends on a clear, limited focus for the speech. Write out the general purpose, specific purpose, and thesis statement. Once you have a thesis statement, everything else in the outline must support it. Use the *because* test to determine that all of your main ideas support the thesis statement and that all of your subpoints support the main ideas. Outlines should follow an organizational strategy—for example, cause-to-effect or problem-to-solution.

Outline entries should be strong, active, simple sentences. Incorporate and label organizational links, such as transitions, signposts, and internal summaries. Also include specific supporting evidence and documentation.

Develop a speaking outline after you are satisfied with your planning outline. Brevity is the key. Include only enough information to help you remember your key ideas. Make notes to yourself that will make the speaking outline a working tool for your speech presentation.

KEY TERMS

Because test	Outline	Summary
Closing	Planning Outline	Thesis Statement
Meta-notes	Preview	Transition
Opening	Speaking Outline	

APPLICATION QUESTIONS

1. Do you outline before you write? How do your classmates approach the problem? Often, people pattern their ideas in their minds, write the essay, and then make the outline. What are the advantages and disadvantages of this approach?

2. Agree with your classmates to write a letter to someone—a local politician, for example, or a favorite teacher. Agree, also, on a thesis statement for the letter. Working alone, select an organizational pattern and develop a planning outline for this letter. Then sit down with your classmate to compare and contrast your work. Notice, especially, the main arguments and supporting materials each of you used to develop the thesis. What did you learn from this exercise? Would you want to send your letter? Why or why not?

3. See if you can develop a full-sentence outline from one of the sample speeches found in Appendix A at the end of this book. Bring it to class and be prepared to discuss the following questions:

   1. Do you think the writer developed an outline before writing the speech? Why or why not?

   2. Did you find any gaps or thin spots in the logic or supporting materials?

4. Select an editorial from *USA Today* or from your local newspaper. See if you can develop a full-sentence outline from it. Then bring the outline to class and be prepared to discuss the following questions:

   1. Do you think the writer developed an outline before writing the editorial? Why or why not?

   2. Did you find any gaps or thin spots in the logic or supporting materials?

IT'S MORE FUN TO KNOW

Outlining, coupled with organization, have been major concerns of scholars interested in oral communication from the beginning of the study of speech. Cicero spoke directly about this matter in *De Oratore, Part III, Book II*, Translated by H. Rackman (Cambridge, MA: Harvard University Press, 1948, p. 317). Much of the scholarship in this area has stemmed from the use of "written outlines" to assist in the preparation of oral materials, while most students have only been introduced to outlining in an early phase of their writing education in primary and secondary school.

More recently, outlining has been emphasized as part of preparation structure (See Sharon Kane, "The View from the Discourse Level: Teaching Relationships and Text Structure, *The Reading Teacher*, 52:2 (October 1998). Applications in business fields have emerged, also, as an effective means of improving business through specific and careful outlining of major directions (Michelle Robidoux, *Folio: The Magazine for Magazine Management*, 27:8 (June 1998). Interestingly, professional organizations encourage their members to present their ideas in outline form as an effective means of avoiding apprehensions and mistrust during presentations (see Brian J. Lewis, "You May Not Think So, But You Are A Salesman," *Journal of Management in Engineering*, 14:3 (May-June 1998).

Recently, institutions have made curricular and on-line commitments to improving outlining skills. For example, "The Virtual Presentation Assistant" at *http://strategis.ic.gc.ca/SSG/mi04462e.htmp* helps you to both plan and organize an effective presentation. "Outlining Reports" by Michael E. Newman at *http://www.ais.msstate.edu/aee/3203/ppslides/Outlining/index.htm* is an especially useful, contemporary site to consult. The most comprehensive information available from the many on-line sites is "Outlining" at *http://www.ceap.wcu.edu/Houghton/EDELCompEduc/Themes/Outlining/outlining.html*.

SELF-TEST FOR REVIEW

Identify items 1–5 as either A (describing a planning outline) or B (describing a speaking outline):

_____ 1. Full sentences

_____ 2. Includes supporting material and documentation

_____ 3. Key words and phrases

_____ 4. Notes in the margins

_____ 5. Superior and subordinate relationships tested with the *because* test

_____ 6. Which of the following best describes the *because* test?

    a. A technique for identifying subordination

    b. A technique for identifying a planning outline

    c. A technique used in speaking outlines for argumentation

    d. None of the above describes the *because* test

_____ 7. A transition is

    a. a bridge between ideas.

    b. a simple word or phrase that points to an important idea.

    c. a speech unit designed to move listeners from one point to another.

    d. both a and c.

_____ 8. A signpost is

    a. a statement that serves as a bridge from one idea to another.

    b. a statement that points to an important idea.

    c. a 4-inch-by-4-inch post stuck in the ground.

    d. Both b and c.

—— 9. Record from memory a standard set of symbols for use in planning outlines.

Answers: 1A. 2A. 3B. 4B. 5A. 6a. 7d. 8d. 9. 1-A-1-a

SUGGESTED READING

Brigance, William Norwood. *Speech: Its Techniques and Disciplines in a Free Society.* New York: Appleton-Century-Crofts, 1952. This old chestnut set the standard for outlining for American speech teachers. It is still the best source available, but it is out of print. Check to see if your library owns it.

Reid, Loren. *Speaking Well, Fourth Edition.* New York: McGraw-Hill Companies, 1982. This book is also out of print, but its instruction on outlining is especially useful. Check to see if your library owns a copy.

Price, Jonathan. *Outlining Goes Electronic* Stamford: Ablex Publishing Corporation, 1999. A modern work that will help you use available technology in your outlining efforts.

INTERNET ACTIVITIES

1. Go to the URL *http://www.altavista.net* and type the words "outlining for speech" into the search box. AltaVista will locate about a million web pages for you. Follow the first few hyperlinks, making notes along the way. Can you find any advice in these links that is significantly different from the advice in this chapter? How do you account for the similarities and differences you find? Prepare to discuss your ideas with your classmates.

2. Go to the URL *http://www.mindmapper.com* There you will find an offer of free software you can use to organize your thinking. Explore what you find there and prepare to discuss it with our classmates. Would you download the free software? How might you use it in speech preparation?

SAMPLE OUTLINES

Model Speaking Outline

WHY SHOULD YOU PAY SOMEONE ELSE TO HELP YOU PAY YOUR TAXES?

INTRODUCTION

Opening: Good evening. I'm Charles Davidson and I work as an income tax preparer for a large national firm.

Thesis Statement: You can prepare your own taxes as accurately as I can at one-fifth the cost.

Preview: Most people believe since taxes are complicated they need to hire a professional to complete their federal tax returns. They say the government regulations are so complicated they have to rely on a preparer to avoid being audited.

Transition: Let's look briefly at the income tax and see how its complications can be overcome by today's technology.

BODY

Main idea: I. The federal tax code is enormously complicated and frightens the average person *(because):*

    A. The tax code is so bewildering that most people do not understand it.

Slide of one page of Tax Code Regulations

        1. Cancelled checks are not proof of contributing to charitable organizations. You must have a written statement from the charity.

        2. Cancelled checks are adequate proof for payment of loans, business expenses, etc.

    B. Congress has required the Internal Revenue Service to become more "user friendly."

Congressional directive to IRS to assist rather than confront taxpayers

        1. Director of IRS violated the directive by ruling that anyone catching McGwire's 63rd home run ball must pay taxes on its value.

Visual showing headline from St. Louis Post-Dispatch, September 1998

        2. IRS has increased the number of employees who give telephone assistance. If you are misinformed by them, you are still are responsible for obeying the law. (meta-note Slide showing public statement by IRS that employee advice is only a suggestion.)

Transition: With such confusion, where can we turn for low-cost, accurate advice and direction in completing our tax filing?

Main Idea II. Today's low-cost technology offers an inexpensive solution to the problem *(because)*

    A. The personal computer is a highly accurate processor of information

Slide of personal computer costs

    1. By 2001 over half the homes in America will have a personal computer

Show current issue of PC Magazine

    2. Nearly all college graduates are proficient in the use of the computer

Slide from the Chronicle of Higher Education

    3. Since computers are being used by students in virtually every elementary school in the country, the technology is no longer frightening

Slide from Journal of Elementary Education

  B. We should put the computer to work doing the simple, computational tasks it does so well.

    1. The personal computer makes no errors in addition, subtraction, or multiplication.

    2. Over half the errors on income tax filings are the result of errors in addition or subtraction

Slide—Report from the IRS Commissioner

Transition: So, our challenge is to harness the strength of the computer to prepare the personal tax return.

Main Idea III. Well written tax preparation programs for the personal computer are the best answer *(because)*

  A. A carefully written program can provide answers to all tax questions while helping you prepare your return

Slide on tax programs from The Wall Street Journal

    1. A good program will make it easy to complete your return by asking you all the necessary questions.

Mention "Personal Finance" column in The Wall Street Journal.

    2. The same program will enter your answers in the correct location on your return.

  B. The information you need to complete your taxes is the same information you would need if you paid someone to complete your taxes

Kiplinger Magazine on tax programs

    1. You only need to collect the information and answer questions in an interview with the computer program.

    2. The programs have a "review" section which compares your return to the tax law and to the "typical limits" for each category.

From Intuit Corporation promotional material

    3. You can file by mail or if you file electronically your refund will be deposited in your bank account.

IRS e-filing letter sent to taxpayers

4. Programs such as *Tax Cut* and *Turbo Tax* are available at any software outlet and cost only about $20-35, far less than the cost of a tax preparer.

Transition: So what is the conclusion that I think most of you should follow?

Conclusion

Summary: Don't hire me. Use your computer to prepare your taxes. You should not waste $100-$300 per year to have your taxes professionally prepared. You can do it yourself with the same programs that tax preparers use and prepare your own return without fear of the IRS.

Closing: Why should you pay someone else to help you pay your taxes?

Model Speaking Outline with Annotations

GOVERNMENT BY ATTEMPTED SECRECY

The speaker used these notes to keep calm, and look at the audience

INTRODUCTION

Look   Breathe

Opener: Hi. This is interesting.
Trans: We may have a problem.

Pause   Move

See the inclusion of source materials. They helped the speaker build credibility and stay calm.

BODY

I. Secrecy is growing
   A. Overestimated information (Newsweek)
      1. Soviet economic size greatly exaggerated
      2. Military had crumbling buildings, runways with grass growing.
   B. Number of classification officers decreased by 75%.
   C. Classification up over 300% (Security Oversight Office)
      1. Fewer people classifying more info.
      2. Even insignificant often class.

Trans: Info even kept from President

Pause   Move

Useful reminder

It was easy for the speaker to follow these notes during the speech.

II. Denial of information affects national policy.
   A. The ASA withheld information from Truman. (Archives of the FBI)
   B. Lack of information had major impact on spending and national security.

III. Classified information easily available today

A. Present in the public domain (read New York Times) Published on the Internet.

Useful reminders

Ex. Washington Post

Ex. Drudge Report

Pause   Move In

CONCLUSION

A single word reminds the speaker to summarize

Summary:

Closing: Urge audience to be attentive to the problem.

Speaker uses key portion of planned closing

NOTES

1. Alan H. Monroe, *Principles and Types of Speech*, (Chicago: Scott Foresman, 1935)

2. Ask, for example, if they would prefer you use the *American Psychological Association Publication Manual* format, the *MLA Style Sheet*, or *The University of Chicago Manual of Style*.

CHAPTER 10

INTRODUCTIONS AND CONCLUSIONS

OBJECTIVES

After reading this chapter, you should be able to:

1. Name and describe the functions of a speech introduction.

2. List and provide examples of eight different strategies for speech introductions.

3. Name and describe the functions of a speech conclusion.

4. List and provide examples of five different strategies for speech conclusions.

OUTLINE

Objectives
Outline
Abstract
Imagine
Introduction
   The Introduction
     Purposes of the
      Introduction
     Strategies for Introductions
       Quotation
       Startling Statement
       Illustration
       Story
       Preview of Main Ideas
       Simple Greeting
       Humor
       Rhetorical Question
   The Conclusion

Purposes of the Conclusion
   Strategies for
     Conclusions
     Summary
     Quotation
     Reference to the
      Introduction
     Call for Action
     Combinations
Summary
Key Terms
Application Questions
It's More Fun to Know
Self-Test for Review
Suggested Reading
Internet Activities
Notes

ABSTRACT

This chapter discusses the most effective techniques for beginning and ending a speech. Strong introductions and conclusions ensure listeners will pay attention to the message and remember the main ideas. A speech introduction should secure attention and interest, establish a positive relationship between speaker and listeners, prepare listeners for the message, and set the tone for the speech. Quotations, startling statements, illustrations, stories, previews of the main ideas, and simple greetings are effective at the beginning of a speech. Introductions that use humor and rhetorical questions are more difficult for inexperienced speakers but can be used successfully.

A conclusion should review the main ideas of the speech and focus the thoughts and feelings of listeners on what has been said. The conclusion should also lend a sense of completeness or finality to the speech. Summaries, quotations, references to the introduction, calls to action, or a combination of these often work effectively to clarify what you want from listeners.

IMAGINE

When the highly rated television program "60 Minutes" first comes on the air, one of the reporters previews the feature stories of that evening's program by saying something like:

> Tonight, on "60 Minutes," we'll examine the real story behind the Scandinavian Air catastrophe in Nova Scotia and see how it paralleled the TWA 800 disaster. [Cut to videotape for 10 seconds.] We'll go to Los Angeles and visit with Kelsey Grammer and see how he's adjusted to life after "Cheers," and the success of "Frazier." [Cut to videotape for 12 seconds.] Ed Bradley will show you our investigation of migrant farm workers in Wisconsin, Ohio, Indiana, and Illinois. [Cut to videotape for 15 seconds.] And Andy Rooney wonders why a large size really is the smallest we can buy at the grocery store. That, and much more, tonight on "60 Minutes."

INTRODUCTION

Every communication event, written or oral, through whatever communications medium, must have a beginning, a middle and an end. Just as a television program or a movie or a book must have an effective introduction and conclusion, so must a well-developed speech. A speaker needs to get off to a fast start because the first few moments of a speech can determine whether or not the speech is successful. The end of the speech is just as important.

The purpose of this chapter is to describe how you can most easily and most effectively produce introductions and conclusions for your speeches.

The Introduction

Purposes of the Introduction

In general, an introduction should call attention to the subject matter and establish the relationship among you, your listeners, and your speech. In particular, its purposes are to gain attention and interest, to establish rapport with the audience, to orient audience members to what they are about to hear, and to set the tone for the speech.

Strategies for Introductions

Eight different introduction strategies work effectively to secure listeners' attention (see Exhibit 10.1). The sections that follow discuss these in more detail and provide examples.

EXHIBIT 10.1

	STRATEGIES FOR INTRODUCTIONS	
Strategy	*Definition*	*Examples*
1. Quotations	Statement of another (often famous) individual to focus attention	The famous American poet, Robert Frost, wrote in "The Death of the Hired Man," "Home is the place where, when you have to go there, they have to take you in." For most of us, that piece of writing is very true. Home is a warm, loving place. It's a place where we keep our fond memories and where we always feel wanted. They "have" to take us in because they love us. But for many people in their teens and twenties, home is a place where they feel rejected. They may have been abused or ignored, shamed by their parents, and severely punished for what you and I would call "no good reason."
2. Startling statement	Arresting, interesting fact or incident that arouses attention	"It might surprise you to learn that trucks and suburban utility vehicles are more popular than cars in the U.S. In late 1998 they captured 51 per cent of what is called the 'light vehicle market.'[1] Owners claim they are more versatile and durable with ample seating, comfortable interiors, and a good ride. So, if you want to keep up with the neighbors, maybe you should purchase a Ford Explorer or a Chevy Silverado."
3. Illustration	Example or case that helps involve listeners	There's a group of tumbledown shacks just outside Las Cruces, New Mexico, that might astound you. Just a mile from the city limits, families of migrant farm workers are living in the pits of poverty. Up to six men, women, and children sleep together in the same hot room. There's a single cold-water pipe that the families share, but there's no bathroom. Instead, they use the old-fashioned outhouse on the property. These families are from Mexico. They were brought here by American businessmen to harvest melons, peppers, and tomatoes. Though their living conditions in that New Mexico city are better than they had in Mexico's slums, they are awful.
4. Story	Extended, interesting narrative about the subject to involve listeners	Most of you have heard, time and again, about how important it is to wear a seat belt. Let me tell you about my experience last week. My friend Hal and I were returning from a business dinner. He was driving his Miata, and we were talking about some business matters. The street was fairly narrow . . . .

Exhibit 10.1 *continued*

5. Preview of main ideas	Outline of the main points of the speech	We've all heard about the problems people have with credit cards. They forget the charges they make really cost money, that interest is charged each month when they don't pay the entire balance. Let me give you a different angle. Today I'd like to show how a credit cared can be used to pay your expenses and to manage your money. Most importantly, it's the best proof you have of payment, and it's accepted almost everywhere. I'll explain to you why each of these reasons should be enough for you to use your credit card instead of your checkbook or cash.
6. Simple greeting	Welcoming statement to establish rapport with audience	Good afternoon, members of the Chamber of Commerce. I'm Rosa Ketner, Executive Secretary of the United Way. Thanks so much for being here. It's an honor to be with you today. I'd like to discuss with you the issue of . . . .
7. Humor	Amusing story, anecdote, or situation that creates a favorable climate for the speaker	At a highschool basketball game, Oklahoma City police officer Eldridge Wyatt became dissatisfied that no fouls were being called on No. 21, and walked onto the court to point out the player's elbowing to the referees. When referee Stan Guffey told Wyatt to leave the officiating to him, Wyatt arrested Guffey. Guffey was un-arrested a few minutes later so that the game could continue, but when a reporter asked Wyatt after the game what had happened, Wyatt tried to arrest him too.
8. Rhetorical question	A question that implies its own answer and leads audience to interest in the subject	Most of us know there are many things in life that can cause harm. Sometimes, the damage is immediate. Sometimes it's long term. How much do you think the cost of failing to fund Social Security adequately now will affect you when it comes time to retire?

Quotation

Many introductions incorporate quotations from a recognized, public figure. You do not always have to quote famous people to use this strategy, but the people you quote should be perceived as credible.

One student presented a speech that dealt with the elements of leadership and the characteristics that many people in prominent positions should possess. She used a slogan originated by a past U.S. president to suggest the quality of leadership that society needs:

> *"The buck stops here." This sign, which rested on the desk of President Harry S. Truman, told the world how he felt about responsibility. Mr. Truman made many difficult decisions during his presidency, but he always maintained that, once he made up his mind, he was willing to take the criticism of his choice. He liked to say, "If you can't stand the heat, get out*

Students have sometimes complained that it is unethical to manipulate listener behavior as Exhibit 10.1 suggests. What do you think, and why?

of the kitchen" as a way of showing that leadership meant a willingness to stand up for your decisions and not to pass the ball to a subordinate to handle.

Another student speaker wanted to support the idea that values should be taught in the home, and not as part of the high school curriculum. In her introduction, she said:

My mother told me three things that have had the greatest influence on my life. She said, "Work hard, love your family, and be honest with everyone." Those words of guidance have helped me shape my actions, and they've governed how I react to people and situations in my life. They can be a guide to you in dealing with life and the people you encounter.

Startling Statement

You can introduce a speech with a startling statement of fact or opinion, but be sure your attempt to startle listeners is appropriate to both situation and topic. The statement should be related to listeners' interests and in keeping with their expectations. Exhibit 10.2 presents examples of startling statements for several topics. In each of these introductions, the objective is to give listeners information that is surprising to them in an effort to arouse interest in the subject.

Illustration

An introduction can illustrate the issue you plan to discuss. This strategy works best when you want to involve listeners emotionally in some problem. Make the illustration rich in detail. Exhibit 10.3 shows an example illustration.

An introductory illustration such as this stimulates and emotionally involves listeners and also gives them a way of identifying with the situation.

Story

Most people like a good story, especially one that is amusing or provocative. Choose a story you know well and that applies to the subject you

Speeches often succeed or fail during the introduction. An effective introduction sets the tone for the speech and the relationship between the speaker and the listeners. © Tom McCarthy/Stock Market

EXHIBIT 10.2

EXAMPLES OF STARTLING STATEMENTS
USED IN SPEECH INTRODUCTIONS

1. *"Most of us think we realize that we are in a 'world economy.' It might surprise you to learn that 72 per cent of the American people believe we should not increase immigration to this country, and 58 per cent believe that foreign trade is bad for the U.S. economy because it hurts wages and jobs.[2] Doesn't this seem inconsistent with the global dependency we have? We're happy to find inexpensive TV's, cameras, and VCR's, but a majority of the people who buy these products say they don't believe we should have the form of trade that creates those low prices."*

2. *"The ABC program 'Nightline' is a well-established hit. One night, guest host Cokie Roberts put the show ahead of dinner with the president of the United States. Because she was substituting for Ted Koppel that evening, she had to leave the dinner table at the White House while seated next to President Clinton. Not many of us would walk out on the president, but for this reporter, the news came first."*

3. *"Most of us think we pay too much of what we earn in taxes. But here's some information that might get your attention. We know that California, New York, and Texas are our most populous states. You'd guess, then, that people who live there probably pay the most taxes. Not true. Residents of the District of Columbia pay 41 per cent of their income in taxes while residents of New Hampshire pay only 31 per cent of their income to state, federal and local governments. Shouldn't we do something about equalizing that burden, especially since the residents of the District of Columbia do not even have voting rights?"*

EXHIBIT 10.3

EXAMPLE ILLUSTRATION

Good morning ladies and gentlemen. For a little while I want to take you down memory lane.

Most of you have a fond memories of your childhood. You probably remember a trip to the zoo, swimming at the pool, your first train ride, or the joy you experienced when school was dismissed for weather reasons.

But, there's a group of children in this country who don't have fond memories of their childhood and their number is increasing dramatically. I'm talking about the 45 per cent of our children who live in poverty or near-poverty households. They're the ones whose fond memories are of a few full meals, a warm house, and perhaps, new clothes instead of "hand-me-downs." Let me discuss with you the problem of child poverty in this country and what is causing it to increase so rapidly.

intend to discuss. Include many relevant details so listeners can imagine being personally involved. One student used the following narrative for an effective introduction.

EXHIBIT 10.4

SAMPLE STORY

Most of you have heard, time and time again, about how important it is to wear a seat belt. Let me tell you about my experience last week.

My friend Hal and I were returning from a business dinner. He was driving his Miata, and we were talking about some business matters. The street was fairly narrow, with cars parked on the driver's side of the street. We were laughing about some incident of the past week, and I looked off to my right. Hal turned his head toward me, but when he and I looked back at the street, we were about to hit one of the parked cars.

I braced myself for the impact. We struck the Mazda RX7 at the driver's side headlight. The Miata ran up the hood, onto the roof, and then rolled off onto the pavement. A thousand things went through my mind as we skidded and scraped for what seemed like hours. Suddenly, there was silence.

I shook my head, reached up to see how much blood there was. Surprise! I wasn't bleeding. I unfastened my seat belt and slid out of the car. Hal was trapped on the crushed driver's side of the car. I helped him get loose and crawl across and come out on the passenger's side. His face was covered with blood, but no sooner was he out of the car than we could hear an ambulance. Someone had called 911.

They took Hal and me to the hospital. Hal required seventeen stitches to close the cut in his head. I had four small cuts on my hands and a bruised arm. The Miata will cost $6,000 to repair. But the important thing to Hal and me is that we're alive. We're alive because, with the top down in a convertible, we had only our seat belts to keep us from being crushed. Scary experience? Yes, the worst of my life. But believe me, I'll never ride without a seat belt, even on the way to the store.

A story like this sets the mood for the message. It arouses emotions and helps the audience focus attention on the major theme.

Preview of Main Ideas

Provide listeners with a clear sense of what you want. Show how your ideas relate to them. Exhibit 10.5 shows how Darius Lanier used this technique.

Simple Greeting

Another way to start your speech is with a simple greeting. For example, try the direct approach Thelma O'Cain used in one of her informative speeches.

> *Hello, again, class. You know me. I'm Thelma O'Cain. You may not know that I've just changed my major to the Communications Technology track.*

Humor

Humor is a powerful tool for arousing audience, but use it *carefully*. What is amusing to one person may be offensive to another. Jay Leno

EXHIBIT 10.5

EXAMPLE PREVIEW OF MAIN IDEAS
By Darius Lanier, and used by permission
This morning I will argue that discrimination is still prevalent all over the United States, and especially here in the South. Lots of evidence exists to support this claim. The Equal Employment Opportunity Commission is backlogged with complaints of discrimination. Minorities consistently suffer higher unemployment rates than do white people. The courts are full of cases about discriminatory treatment by such huge corporations as Avis and Texaco. The Glass Ceiling Commission has documented many cases of discrimination against women. No, ladies and gentlemen, discrimination is not a thing of the past. It is, right now, in 1998, an ugly blot on our society that costs each one of us both our dollars and our dignity.

provided the following general guidelines about the kind of humor to avoid:

> *AIDS isn't funny. Child molestation isn't funny. Vietnam isn't funny. Jokes that belittle other cultures aren't funny. A subject that's always in the news—a plane crash—isn't funny.*[3]

In addition, off-color jokes and racial and ethnic jokes are neither funny nor appropriate. Humor requires a subtle touch. Exhibit 10.6 lists several categories of humor that could be used effectively.

The types of humor presented in Exhibit 10.6 do not cover all possible categories. Rather, the list includes the most commonly used and most effective types of humor for inexperienced speakers. Other types of humor are sometimes used by professional comedians and persons skilled in entertainment. Among these are such techniques as slapstick, defiance, and violence, but these are difficult for beginning speakers to present effectively.

It is unlikely anyone would find any of the Exhibit 10.6 examples offensive. They set a lighthearted mood and help to relax the audience for the rest of the speech. The best advice for using humor in your introduction is to be as certain as you can that the humor is appropriate for the subject, the audience, and the occasion.

Rhetorical Question

A rhetorical question is asked to arouse curiosity rather than to seek information. The strategy is sometimes used in a speech introduction as an attention-getting device. The answer to the question is either implied by the question or is part of a strategy designed to get listeners involved in your topic.

Rhetorical questions can sound trite and can detract from a speech unless you prepare carefully. A question can draw the wrong answer from the audience! For example, a student asked the following question to introduce a speech to change beliefs: "Don't you agree that

EXHIBIT 10.6

	SEVERAL CATEGORIES OF HUMOR	
Category	*Definition*	*Example*
Absurdity	Using materials that are illogical in thinking or in language	*Dr. Roland Cross of Loyola Medical, Chicago, got a bill from the hospital. The **doctor** got a bill—$309 for anesthesia during Cesarean delivery. Dr. Cross notified hospital auditors that he had not been hospitalized for any reason. And certainly a seventy-year-old male would not be having a C-section. The hospital blamed its computer. But guess what? Now Dr. Cross has been notified by Blue Cross that his hospital bill has been paid. Three hundred nine dollars for anesthesia—during Cesarean delivery—and Blue Cross further offers its congratulations on the birth of TWINS.[4]*
Confusion	Misunderstandings or contradictions that are potentially amusing	*Sometimes, it does all get lost in the translation. "Please leave your values at the front desk," says the sign at a Paris hotel. Hungry? From a Polish menu, select "roasted duck let loose" or perhaps "beef rashers beaten up in the country people's fashion." A Swiss eatery proudly warns, "Our wines leave you nothing to hope for." A Budapest zoo puts people first: "Please do not feed the animals. If you have any suitable food, give it to the guard on duty." A Rhodes tailor wants early orders for summer suits "because in big rush we will execute customers in strict rotation."[5]*
Human problems	Situations in which a person appears foolish or is overcome by events; includes situations where the speaker or the activity of the speaker appears laughable	*A commuter lost his temper in 90-degree heat at Waterloo station when he asked a British Rail supervisor to explain why his train was delayed and was told that there was no such word as explanation in the British Rail rule book. . . . Malcolm Stuart's delayed train was still listed on the information board, but after waiting 20 minutes without announcement of a delay, he approached a station supervisor and asked about the train. . . . The supervisor, who was described as "obese" and with heavily tattooed arms, told him: "Look, cloth ears, there's been a points failure. There will be a train when there's a train." . . . Mr. Stuart took out his black (pen) and started writing the word explanation on the front of the supervisor's white shirt. Stuart was found guilty of criminal damage and threatening behavior and was fined 250 pounds, 100 pounds court costs, and ordered to pay 50 pounds compensation for the shirt.*
Exaggeration	Overstatement related to persons, places, sizes, the way people feel or act, and personal experiences	*Mendoza's Law of Purchasing says: (1) When shopping, never look for something specific, you won't find it. (2) Always shop for nothing, you'll always come back with something. (3) After a heavy day's shopping, the perfect purchase is in either the first or the last place you've looked.[6]*
Playful ridicule	A sympathetic teasing and acceptance of human faults	*A twenty-dollar bill and a one-dollar bill were on their way to final destruction. During the trip, they struck up a conversation. The twenty-dollar bill said, "I've had a good life. I've gone to glamorous places like San Francisco, Montreal, New York, New Orleans, and Las Vegas. It's been a lot of fun, and I've always been excited. How about you?" he asked the one-dollar bill. The dollar bill answered, "Boring, boring. Go to church, go to church, go to church."*
Surprise	Making use of unexpected or unusual feelings, events, or facts	*I told my husband I wanted to be surprised for dinner, so he soaked the labels off the cans.* *The nice things about dictating letters is that you can use a lot of words you don't know how to spell.* *He'd be great in the Olympics. He can hang his chin over a bar for hours.* *Behind every successful person stands a devoted spouse—and a surprised mother-in-law.*

drinking ought to be a matter of choice for everyone who has reached the age of eighteen?" The students in the audience lived in a state where the legal drinking age was twenty-one. How do you think listeners reacted? Some listeners were about eighteen, but some were much older. One person was nearly sixty. A few audience members opposed drinking because of their religious beliefs. One woman was a member of MADD (Mothers Against Drunk Driving). Clearly, the speaker's opinion was not shared by many audience members. In this case, the rhetorical question was detrimental to the speaker's goal.

THE CONCLUSION

Purposes of the Conclusion

A conclusion should (1) focus audience attention on what you have said, (2) signal listeners that you have finished, and (3) give some final thrust to the speech. A carefully planned conclusion provides listeners with a sense of closure and puts them in a mood either to do as you have asked or to think about your thesis statement. The conclusion should unify the ideas and the tone developed in the body. Listeners need a concise reminder of the ideas or themes you developed plus an indication that you have finished speaking. The conclusion is the final impression you leave with the listeners. Decide what feelings, attitudes, actions, or information you want listeners to take away from the speech. Then craft your conclusion around that decision, using the techniques outlined here.

Strategies for Conclusions

As shown in Exhibit 10.7, there are five main strategies for "wrapping up" your speech. Consider how each of them relates to your thesis, and then choose the strategy most appropriate for your speech. More detailed discussion and examples of each of these strategies follow.

Strong speakers often finish with a strong, rousing appeal. © Image Bank

EXHIBIT 10.7

	STRATEGIES FOR CONCLUSIONS	
Strategy	*Explanation*	*Example*
Summary	Restates the main ideas of the speech.	*So, what have I said to you this morning? I've shown you that capital punishment is not an effective deterrent to crime. I've argued that deliberately taking another person's life to punish them is nothing more than legalized murder. And I've shown you an alternative that is more humane than capital punishment. At best, imprisonment without chance of parole, along with intelligent use of the prisoner's lifetime, can do something positive for society.*
		But the law won't be changed unless you act. It's up to you and to other Americans. It's the right thing to do.
Quotation	Uses a statement by another person to focus audience attention on the theme of the speech.	*So, in the words of Franklin Delano Roosevelt, "Never before have we had so little time in which to do so much." We must get moving. If we're going to be successful, we must begin today. Time is running out on this project, and our funding will disappear if we don't show considerable movement. Pitch in. Sign up. Become part of the team that will restore the beauty of this truly American campus.*
Reference to the introduction	May restate the words or reinforce the mood set in the opening remarks.	*I hope that you won't have to be as terrified as I felt when I bumped my head along the pavement. It's not only convertibles that "flip." Remember that most of the fatal accidents happen within five minutes of your residence. Think of that when you jump in the car to drive to the store next week.*
Call for action	Asks listeners to do something described clearly in the body of the speech.	*Most of you know that the Special Olympics is one of the greatest experiences for the mentally and physically disadvantaged kids in this community. You've heard how rewarding this event is to the participants. It's just as rewarding to you when you see the 10- to 20-year-old straining with joy in their opportunity for competition. They don't care so much if they win. They love the chance just to compete. We want your help.*
		Skip sleeping in next Saturday. Come to the Red Springs track and give us a hand to help your friends. Sign up on the sheet I'm passing around now. I guarantee you'll find it one of the most rewarding experiences you've ever had. Come on—give these kids a hand. You'd want them to help you, wouldn't you?
Combinations	May combine a quotation with a call for action, ask for action and restate the introduction, or any of the other possible combinations.	So, as I mentioned to you at the beginning, remember the Biblical admonition because it applies to each of us in our daily lives: "Let him among us who is without sin cast the first stone." Tomorrow, when you are tempted to question the motives of another person, ask yourself when you yourself have been selfish, mean, or spread gossip. It's difficult to change our mode of behavior but we all know we have shortcomings. From now on, let's try to recognize our own faults, be our own critics, and stop being judgmental about others.

Summarizing your main ideas is an effective way to conclude. Here is how another student restated the major idea of his speech on addi-

Summary

Summarizing your main ideas is an effective way to conclude. Here is how another student restated the major idea of his speech on additional funds needed for instructional programs:

> *A truly good university consists of an ample library, well stocked with books and periodicals. We must have money for scholarships which will attract the best and most diverse student body. And our faculty must be the best teachers available because teaching is the primary mission of this school.*

A summary, however brief, can be an important part of any conclusion. It helps listeners to remember the main ideas and serves to justify any final appeal you make.

Quotation

A quotation helps to focus audience attention. Often, speakers prefer to repeat a quotation that was part of their introduction. Sometimes, a different quote is more effective. The quotation you select, however, whether used previously in the introduction or new, should reinforce the basic theme of your speech.

In the conclusion to a speech about how important it is for people to find the fun in their lives and to learn to let go of their troubles from time to time, a student speaker effectively quoted G. K. Chesterton:

> *I think G. K. Chesterton had a profound message for all of us when he wrote: "Angels can fly because they take themselves lightly." If you want to succeed, you sometimes have to take yourself lightly. Find the fun in your life, or learn how to put fun into your life. Fly.*

Reference to the Introduction

A theme that you explored in the introduction can be reused in your conclusion with very powerful effect.

> *We may not want to face the fact that "binge drinking" on campus is a pervasive problem. I mentioned in the introduction that college officials and student leaders want to control alcohol. The recent highly publicized deaths at several prominent schools have gotten the attention of nearly everyone. It's one case where peer pressure can be extremely strong. As one student who subsequently died from an alcohol overdose from "binge drinking" said, "You just have to do it. It's part of being accepted. Don't worry! Nothing bad will happen to me."*

Call for Action

Your speech will often have a goal of asking listeners to do something. The actions you seek may range from volunteering to work in a food bank to helping with voter registration. When you have goals like these, a straightforward call for action is often best.

> *When people between 18 and 21 demanded that they be given the right to vote, one of their slogans was "old enough to fight, old enough to vote." But what's been the result of giving them the vote? Their turnout has been the lowest of any age group (in the mid-20's) of any part of the US population. So, you have a duty and a right to go to the polls this week and cast your vote. If you don't like the candidates, write in someone you want. But, remember, many people have died just so you could have the right to register your opinion at the ballot box. It only takes a few minutes, so walk, run, or ride to the polls tomorrow and exercise your right. You can't complain if you don't participate. So vote early, but above all, cast your ballot.*

Combinations

You probably have already realized that it is possible to combine several conclusion strategies into a single conclusion. A combined approach may provide you with the strongest possible conclusion. Since your closing words may be the ones most clearly remembered by your audience, make them memorable.

SUMMARY

How a speech begins and ends is just as important as what comes in the middle. The aims of a speech introduction are to secure the attention and interest of listeners, establish a good relationship between speaker and listeners, and orient listeners to what they are about to hear. An effective introduction sets the tone for the speech.

Eight different introduction strategies can be used to secure listeners' attention. Many introductions incorporate a quotation, a startling statement, an illustration that emotionally involves listeners, a story that makes a point, a preview of the main ideas, or a simple greeting. Humor can be effective in an introduction, but it must be used carefully. Types of humor that inexperienced speakers might want to consider using include absurdity, confusion, human problems, exaggeration, playful ridicule, and surprise. A rhetorical question is also a useful strategy for an introduction but requires thoughtful preparation.

The conclusion of a speech should focus the thoughts and feelings of listeners on the speech's central ideas, signal to listeners that the speaker is finished, and offer some final motivating thrust for the speech. Listeners want closure, with the speech brought to an orderly end that is consistent with the ideas or actions the speaker suggested. Five effective conclusion strategies are: (1) summarizing your main ideas, (2) using a quotation to focus audience attention, (3) referring back to something stated in the introduction, (4) calling for action, and (5) combining several of the previous four conclusion strategies into a single conclusion.

KEY TERMS

Absurdity
Call for action
Confusion
Exaggeration
Humor
Human problem

Illustration
Playful ridicule
Preview of main ideas
Quotation
Reference to the introduction
Rhetorical question

Simple Greeting
Startling statement
Story
Surprise
Summary

APPLICATION QUESTIONS

1. Working with one or two of your classmates, decide how you might develop an introduction and a conclusion that would relate each of the following topics to your classroom audience. Be prepared to explain your choices.
    A. Automobile repair
    B. Mountain climbing
    C. Money management
    D. Defense spending
    E. Capital punishment
    F. Chocolate mousse
2. Pay attention to the opening moments of your favorite television show. *How* did the show open? What features, if any, could you describe using the ideas in this chapter? Bring your notes to class, and be prepared to discuss your findings.
3. As a small group, select one of the topics in Application Question 1. Working individually, develop the best introduction for your classroom audience that you can imagine, using the suggestions in this chapter. Make notes about the reasoning behind your decisions. Compare and contrast your ideas with those of other group members. What insights can you draw from this experience? How do you account for any differences in approach?
4. When will a new quote confuse the audience? Have students consider the strategic implications of using a new quote at the end of their speech. The key to new information is that it must be coordinated with the overall message and purpose. If it stimulates new thinking in another direction, speakers risk making their point. Providing an answer to a quote used in the beginning of the speech might be better than introducing totally new information at the end.

IT'S MORE FUN TO KNOW

From the early days of public speaking, people have considered the beginning and ending of the speech to be critical. The famous Roman orator Quintilian discussed, in considerable detail, the major purposes of the introduction in *The Institutio Oratoria of Quintilian*, (H. E. Butler, trans.).

Cambridge, MA: Harvard University Press: The Loeb Classical Library, (1920). Cicero wrote about the major divisions of a speech and provided examples of the types of introductions and conclusions that are most appropriate in his classic work *De Oratore, Book III* (H. Rackman, trans.) Cambridge: The Loeb Classical Library), 1948.

More recently, Jean Hibben has written several useful articles in *The Speech Communication Teacher* from 1991-1994 which focuses on the sources of useful materials for beginning a speech. They are built around the classical models which apply still today.

SELF-TEST FOR REVIEW

1. Name and describe the functions of a speech introduction.

_____

_____

_____

_____

2. Match the following introduction strategies to their definitions.

___ a. Humor
___ b. Illustration
___ c. Preview of main ideas
___ d. Quotation
___ e. Rhetorical question
___ f. Simple greeting
___ g. Startling statement
___ h. Story

1. Statement of another individual used to focus attention
2. Arresting, interesting fact or incident
3. Example or case that helps to involve listeners
4. Extended, interesting narrative about a subject
5. Outline of main points of a speech
6. Welcoming statement to establish rapport with audience
7. Amusing story, anecdote, or situation used to create a favorable climate
8. Question that implies its own answer and leads audience to interest in the topic

3. Name and describe the functions of a speech conclusion.

4. Match the following conclusion strategies to their definitions.

___ a. Call for action
___ b. Combination
___ c. Quotation
___ d. Reference to the Introduction
___ e. Summary

1. Restates main ideas
2. Combines quotation with call for action
3. Asks listener to do something described in body of speech
4. Uses statement by another person to focus audience attention
5. Restates mood or words of opening remarks

Answers: 1. An introduction calls attention to subject matter and establishes relationships among the speaker, the subject of the speech, and the listeners. The goals are to gain attention, establish rapport with the audience, orient listeners to what is coming, and set the tone for the speech. 2. 1-d; 2.-g; 3- b; 4-h; 5-c; 6-f; 7-a; 8-e. 3. A conclusion should focus audience attention on what has been said, signal that the speech is over, and provide a final thrust to the speech. 4. 4-a; 3, b.; 2, c., 4.; 5, d.; e., 1.

SUGGESTED READINGS

Aristotle. *Rhetoric.* Translated by W. Rhys Roberts. New York: Modern Library, 1954. This book is suggested to make the point that speech teachers and rhetoricians have been giving the advice in this chapter for a very long time. *Rhetoric* was written about 340 years B.C. See Book III, chapters 13 and 19, especially. The W. Rhys Roberts translation is probably the best.

Reid, Ronald F. *Three Centuries of American Rhetorical Discourse,* Prospect Heights, IL: Waveland Press, 1988. An historical examination of the best in American public discourse that is tied more to the cultural orientation of Americans than Aristotle's universal guides. The same principles apply in American public communication.

INTERNET ACTIVITIES

1. Go to several standard search engines (For example, *http://www.zebra.net/search.html)* and type, including the quotation marks: "Introductions and Conclusions." Follow two or three of the links. What do you find there? You should have found advice about both written and oral communication. Further, you should have found differences among the "hits" generated by different search engines. Prepare to discuss what you found with a group of your classmates.

2. Go to the Altavista search engine (*www.altavista.com*) and type the language, including quotation marks: "Introduction, Body, Conclusion." What do you find there? Follow three of these links and prepare to report to the class on what you found.

3. Most university libraries offer lots of help to student scholars. The library at University of South Alabama offers excellent support for student research. Go to the URL: *http://www.usouthal.edu/sauer/index.html* What did you find there? How might this site be useful in planning a speech introduction or a speech conclusion?

NOTES

1. "U.S. Trucks Reach Major Milestone," *The Wall Street Journal* (December 3, 1998), p. A2
2. "Despite Buoyant Economic Times American's Don't Buy Free Trade," *The Wall Street Journal* (December 10, 1998), p. A10
3. Jay Leno, "Laughing At Our Fears," *USA Weekend,* March 22-24, 1991
4. Paul Harvey, Jr. ed., *Paul Harvey's For What It's Worth,* (New York: Bantam Books, 1991), 87
5. Charles Goldsmith, "Look See! Anyone Do Read This And It Will Make You Laughable," *Wall Street Journal,* November 19, 1992, B1
6. Paul Dickson, *The Official Explanations,* (New York: Delacorte Press, 1980) 141.

PART 4

Delivering The Speech

© Tony Stone Images

CHAPTER 11

LANGUAGE:
THE KEY TO SUCCESSFUL SPEAKING

OBJECTIVES

After reading this chapter, you should be able to:

1. Define the term language, and explain two reasons why it is important to use language wisely and carefully.

2. Explain the relationship between language and cognition.[1]

3. Illustrate how language creates emotional affect.

4. Define, compare and contrast, and illustrate denotative and connotative meaning.

5. Define relational meaning and explain how it affects the speaker-audience relationship.

6. Specify and explain the characteristics of appropriate language.

7. Illustrate the importance of keeping language simple and clear.

8. Explain various ways to make language vivid for listeners.

9. Explain how language ambiguity creates problems.

OUTLINE

Outline
Objectives
Abstract
Imagine
Introduction
    Language: Sharing Reality
      and Meaning
      Language Creates Reality
        Language and Cognition
        Language and Affect
      Language Carries
        Meaning
        Denotative Meaning
        Connotative Meaning
        Relational Meaning
    Using Language Well
      Use Appropriate
        Language
        Avoid Offensive
          Language

Avoid Insensitive and
    Sexist Language
    Avoid Trite Expressions
Use Simple Language
Use Clear Language
Use Vivid Language
    Be Specific
    Use Action Language
    Use Comparison and
      Contrast
    Use Illustrations
Use Accurate and
    Unambiguous Language
Summary
Key Terms
Application Questions
It's More Fun to Know
Self-Test for Review
Suggested Readings
Internet Activities
Notes

ABSTRACT

This chapter explores the magical human tool of language. Language creates reality. It controls what we think and feel. Language also allows us to share three kinds of meaning: (1) denotative, (2) connotative, and (3) relational. Thus, your success in achieving the effect that you want from a speech depends, more than anything else, on how skillfully you select and use language.

This chapter explains how to choose appropriate, simple, clear, vivid, and accurate language. Offensive, insensitive, or sexist language always damages a speech, as do trite expressions, big words, and technical jargon.

IMAGINE

Good communication gets the effect you want. If communication does not achieve the desired effect something is wrong. Often the problem lies in awkward or inept language usage. To illustrate, consider the statements in Exhibit 11.1, which were taken from actual insurance company accident-report forms. Although these statements were written, not oral, they illustrate the most important point of this chapter. The images and impressions you derive from statements result from language choice and usage. In these examples, language usage has obscured the intended message.

INTRODUCTION

If you found humor in the statements, the humor was a result of your surprise at the unexpected and unconventional use of language, not because it was what the writer intended. Moreover, any judgments you may have made about the principals involved are based on language usage.

Language: Sharing Reality and Meaning

Language can be defined as a system of signs and symbols used by a **speech community** (all of those who use the same language system) to share meaning and experience. The words and phrases you choose create reality, both in your head and in the heads of listeners. Because

EXHIBIT 11.1

STATEMENTS TAKEN FROM ACTUAL INSURANCE COMPANY ACCIDENT-REPORT FORMS

1. I thought my window was down, but found it was up when I put my hand through it.
2. I pulled away from the side of the road, glanced at my mother-in-law, and headed for the embankment.
3. To avoid hitting the bumper of the car in front, I struck the pedestrian.
4. The pedestrian had no idea which direction to run; so I ran over him.
5. I saw a slow-moving, sad-faced old gentleman as he bounced off the hood of my car.
6. I had been driving for forty years, when I fell asleep at the wheel and had an accident.
7. In my attempt to hit a fly, I drove into a telephone pole.
8. That guy was all over the road. I had to swerve a number of times before I hit him.
9. The indirect cause of the accident was a little guy in a small car with a big mouth.
10. I told the police that I was not injured, but on removing my hat, I found that I had a fractured skull.

they carry three kinds of meaning: (1) denotative, (2) connotative, and (3) relational. Word choice defines the relationship that exists between you and listeners.

Language Creates Reality

Truth and reality are always personal. What you believe in, trust in, have confidence in, and feel right about constitute your truth, your reality. Your ideas may not coincide with someone else's notion of truth and reality.

For example, one of your friends may be convinced that the President's domestic policies are right, while another friend disagrees. One of your friends may take a strong position on the issue of abortion, while you may disagree. One of your friends may be a devout church-goer, absolutely committed to the ideology of the church, while another may be a militant atheist. Where lies the truth? What is real?[1]

When we want to learn from, believe, or be persuaded by others, we rely on language. If you want others to share understanding or experience with you, you use language. In this way we use language to create reality.[1] As explained in the next two sections, in the process of creating reality, language works through cognition and affect.

Language and Cognition[2]

Cognition is the act, power, or faculty of apprehending, knowing, or perceiving. According to Dean Hewes and Sally Planalp, cognition requires (1) information or knowledge structures and (2) cognitive processes.[2] An **information structure** is how you have organized information in your mind. More simply, it is what you know—the body of knowledge you have gathered and assimilated. A **cognitive process** is a mechanism used to handle information in the mind. Cognition is primarily a language activity.

Language and Affect

Affect is a combination of physical experience plus the language we use, either consciously or unconsciously, to describe the experience. An affective state is a subjective experience. When people are moved to do things,

The language we hear and use deterines the reality we experience.
© Bob Daemmrich/Image Works

they always have feelings to accompany their motives. Indeed, sometimes, our emotions provide all the motivation we need—for example, if your excitement and pleasure at seeing your team make a winning touchdown causes you to jump to your feet and cheer.

Human emotional experience requires two factors: (1) we must be aroused or stimulated in some way and (2) we must make something of that arousal. We have to label our arousal as an emotion. Both are necessary. A word is not emotion without arousal. Arousal is not emotion without a word.

What does all this mean as you consider how to use language in speech making? It means that what listeners comprehend, know, or perceive of your messages and intentions depends entirely upon your skill in choosing language. It means language is intimately tied to what we think and feel. Without language to process it, the reality outside our skins would seem no more significant to us than the air in the living room seems to your house cat or the water in the pond seems to the fish living there. Without language, our feelings would resemble mere physical experience, devoid of human passion. Clearly then, if you want to have an impact on the thoughts and feelings of your audience, you need to know how to use language.

Is the advice in this paragraph—learn to use language well—mere sophistry?

Language Carries Meaning

Language carries three kinds of meaning: denotative, connotative, and relational. Exhibit 11.2 compares and contrasts these three kinds of meaning.

EXHIBIT 11.2

THE THREE KINDS OF MEANING CARRIED IN LANGUAGE		
Denotative meaning	*Connotative meaning*	*Relational meaning*
The literal dictionary definition of a word. Refers to associations usually called up by a word among members of a speech community. Native speakers of a language share denotative meanings. E.g.: *chair* refers to something people sit on.	The affective value or meaning of a word. Connotation is the emotional association individuals bring to or impose on a word. E.g.: *chair* may cause you to think of a specific favorite chair—perhaps one you have inherited from your grandparent.	Refers to the speaker's definition of the relationship between self and listener or reader. May imply "one up" or "one down" positioning. E.g.: *sit in that chair* may be a command, implying a one-up definition of the relationship in the speaker's mind.

Denotative Meaning

All words carry denotative meanings, or we could not exchange messages with each other. But since not everyone always knows the dictionary definitions, you should use simple, clear language when communicating. To illustrate, if a professor started tossing around highly technical terms without first providing definitions of those terms, you probably would feel confused. You might even stop listening. Similarly, if you as a public speaker start using words that your listeners do not commonly use, your listeners may tune you out.

Connotative Meaning

Connotation is the emotional association an individual brings to or imposes on a word. You can get an idea about connotation by playing with the classic exercise in Exhibit 11.3, which is based on Charles Osgood's idea of semantic space.[3]

Compare your responses to those of a classmate who chose the same word to see how you two rated the word differently. The differences lie in connotative truth.

EXHIBIT 11.3

AN EXERCISE TO STUDY CONNOTATION

Directions: Write a word in the space provided below. For example, you might write the word *Mother.* Then place a check mark ✔ along each continuum according to how you experience the word.

Write the word here: _____

Good								Bad
Soft								Hard
Active								Passive
Cruel								Kind
Heavy								Light
Slow								Fast
Honest								Dishonest
Weak								Strong
Hot								Cold

Osgood's idea was that words stimulate meaning inside people along three "dimensions" that he intuitively described and named: (1) evaluative dimension, (2) potency dimension, and (3) activity dimension. You can use this idea to make your speeches more compelling. These are the very features of words that cause people to identify emotionally with your ideas. It is not a digression, then, to go into each of these dimensions a little as a means of learning to strengthen the emotional impact of your speeches.

According to Osgood, the **evaluative dimension** involves overall positive and negative determinations stimulated by a word. Such words as *good-bad, kind-cruel,* and *honest-dishonest* characterize the evaluative dimension. This idea was illustrated by a young mother-to-be, who when asked, "Do you know what you are going to name the baby?" replied:

> *If it's a boy, we'll name him Sam. My husband wants to name*
> *the baby Sylvia if it's a girl, but I hate that name. When I was*
> *in high school, I knew a Sylvia that I didn't like at all. I sure-*
> *ly wouldn't want to saddle my baby with that name.*

Clearly the name "Sylvia" stimulated powerful negative evaluations in the young woman.

Osgood defines the **potency dimension** as a power dimension, involving such judgments as *strong-weak, hard-soft,* and *heavy-light* that people apply to words. The same young mother-to-be also provided a good example of the potency dimension. When asked, "Why the name Sam?" she replied:

> *It's a strong name, an American name. It's got a simple, unas-*
> *suming power to it. A baby grows up to his name.*

The **activity dimension,** according to Osgood, is a movement dimension and relates to a word's dynamics—to what a word does. *Hot-cold, fast-slow,* and *active-passive* fill this dimension. When you write or speak the name of someone who has influenced your life, you experience an aspect of this dimension.

Once again, let the young mother-to-be's struggle to find a name for her baby provide the illustration. When asked, "What girl names are you thinking about?" she replied:

> *I really like the name April. It sounds like springtime and joy*
> *and new grass to me. It's got a touch of sunshine in it.*

The point of all this is that people respond to language not only intellectually (the denotative meaning) but also emotionally (the connotative meaning). It is important, then, to choose language that elicits both the cognitive and emotional responses you want. Exhibit 11.4 gives pointers on using language effectively.

EXHIBIT 11.4

POINTERS ON USING LANGAUGE WELL

The Pointer	Explanation	Example	
1. Use appropriate language.	Avoid offensive language.	Language that attacks, insults, slurs or slights others in any way. Words that affront a listener's sensibilities.	
	Avoid insensitive and sexist language.	Language that focuses on some irrelevant feature of a person. Language that implies something negative, such as pity, or (with disabled people) inability to function. Insulting euphemisms.	
	Avoid trite expressions.	Expressions that have been overused. Avoid these "like the plague." They may seem "worth their weight in gold," but in the "dog-eat-dog" world of public speaking, a speech full of trite expressions will get your message "signed, sealed, and delivered"—to no one.	
2. Use simple language.	Prefer small words to big words. As a general rule, the larger your audience the simpler the language ought to be. Use language your audience analysis suggests the listeners can handle.	**Don't say:** Accompany Accordingly At the present time Cognizant Enumerate Parameters	**When you mean:** Go with So Now Aware Count Limits
3. Use clear language.	English is full of words that say nothing. You can't use them if you want to be clear.	**Some "Say nothing" words** A lot Kind of Sort of Perhaps	You know It seems like I hope very
4. Use vivid language.	Be specific.	If you want listeners to form an image you must provide specific materials for them to use. Use real names. (Say "My sister Judy" rather than "my sister.") Include real numbers (Don't say "a lot" when you mean eighty-five.") Mention colors.	
	Use action language.	**Passive voice doesn't show action.** The new bill *was passed* by Congress. The poem *is liked* by Mary. The play *was seen* by the critic. The ball game *was delayed* by a rainstorm.	**Active voice shows action, and is usually more vivid.** Congress *passed* the new bill. Mary *likes* the poem. The critic *saw* the play. A rainstorm *delayed* the ball game.
	Use comparison and contrast.	Especially useful when you talk about something new or unknown to the listeners. Compare the thing they know to the thing you're trying to explain.	
5. Use illustrations.	An example, story, analogy, etc. used to make something clear.	"'The fleece are beginning to guy,' said Bob Meadows today. He meant, 'The geese are beginning to fly.' This common slip of the tongue is a spoonerism, or technically, a metathesis-a deliberate or inadvertent transposition of consonant between words. It is named after W. A. Spooner, dean and later warden of New College, Oxford, who by repute was responsible for such skewings of sound and sense as 'roaring pain' for 'pouring rain,' 'tons of soil' for 'sons of toil,' and 'I'll sew you a sheet' for 'I'll show you a seat.'"[4]	
6. Use accurate and unambiguous language.	Recognize that words often swing more than one way. Work hard to control the direction your sentences take.	**Sentences that can have more than one meaning** This is an *acceptable* alternative. He *admits* he was home by 10:00 p.m. He *claims* he was home by 10:00 p.m. She's a *clever* person. She's a *fair* woman. Her file is *virtually* complete.	

Relational Meaning

The **relational meaning** in language tells people how speakers define their relationship with listeners. If a person talks down to you, you know it and probably also resent it. If someone builds you up, you know that, too.

Relational meanings are completely subjective. Listeners observe the speaker and then guess (based on what they observe) how the speaker has defined their relationship and whether the definition seems appropriate. For example, suppose that you and your friend decide to treat yourselves to a nice dinner in an upscale local restaurant but the waiter treats you with disdain and puts on a haughty "you're not good enough to eat in this restaurant" attitude. The waiter's messages clearly indicate what he thinks of the relationship between you. The definition seems inappropriate to you, so you take offense, and rightly so.

As another example, if you decide that a speaker is racist, you probably have assigned relational meanings to the speaker's language choices. If a speaker seems sexist, that also probably results from the language choices the speaker has made. If a speaker seems prejudiced against old people, or people with disabilities, or gay people, these perceptions and interpretations involve relational meanings.

You can see this phenomenon at work in you classes. Most professors are very careful about how they relate to students, although they may or may not be consciously aware of what they do. They manage the relationship to produce an effect they want from the classes they teach. Most professors approach their classes with respect. They treat students as fully matured adults. Unfortunately, occasional teachers feel superior to their students and make their feelings clear to their classes.

Whose classes would you rather take? Which teachers would you rather know? Which teachers are more likely to succeed in the teaching and learning process? Your answers, here, suggest why this matter of relational meaning is important to you as a speaker. Listeners will monitor your speeches to see how you define your relationship with them and whether or not that definition seems appropriate. When it does seem appropriate, listeners will give you a hearing. When it does not seem appropriate, your audience may give you less than rapt attention.

Using Language Well

You have already seen in this chapter that language can create problems. When language is used well, however, it can create many special effects of imagery and mood. What can you do to use language more effectively as you speak? Exhibit 11.4 gives six pointers on using language well.

Use Appropriate Language

Avoid Offensive Language

A good rule of thumb about choosing language is: "If you're in doubt about the appropriateness of a word or expression, don't use it." This injunction extends to impertinence, any kind of inappropriate innuendo, making a joke at another person's expense, and attempting to diminish someone on the basis of religion, race, gender, or disability. Dirty jokes, sexual innuendoes, profanity, and indecency of any kind have no place in public speaking. You never have to do it.

Avoid Insensitive Language

Avoiding insensitive and sexist language is as important as avoiding offensive language, and for the same reasons. Exhibits 11.5 and 11.6 offer some alternatives for insensitive or sexist expressions.

The idea of gender-neutral language has sometimes been ridiculed as politically correct, or "PC" language. What do you think about the matter? How far, if at all, should people go to use gender-neutral language in speech and writing?

Sexist language adversely affects both men and women. When women are taught language use that diminishes their gender, they, too, must learn to use language in gender-neutral, nonevaluative ways. For a theoretical discussion on this issue, see Karlyn Kohrs Campbell, "Hearing Women's Voices," *Communication Education* 40 (January 1991): 33–48.

Avoid Trite Expressions

Trite words and phrases give the impression your ideas are second-hand. They call such powerful attention to themselves listeners may focus on the expression and miss what you are trying to communicate. Exhibit 11.7 lists two dozen clichés and you can probably think of several dozen more.

EXHIBIT 11.5

INSENSITIVE EXPRESSIONS AND ALTERNATIVES	
Instead of saying	*Try*
The deaf person	The person
The woman doctor	The doctor
The blind man	The man
The amputee	The person
The mentally retarded child	The child
Ellen is confined to a wheelchair.	Ellen uses a wheelchair.
Ellen is burdened with a grossly disfiguring disease.	Ellen has acne.
Ellen is a victim of cancer.	Ellen has cancer.
Ellen, an exceptional child, . . .	Ellen . . .
Ellen is suffering from . . .	Ellen has . . .

EXHIBIT 11.6

SEXIST WORDS AND ALTERNATIVES			
Sexist	*Alternative*	*Sexist*	*Alternative*
Businessman	Executive, manager, leader, person	Foreman	Supervisor
Cameraman	Photographer, camera operator	Man and wife	Husband and wife
Chairman	Leader, presiding officer	Manmade	Artificial, manufactured
Cleaning lady	Custodian	Manpower	Workers, work force, labor
Congressman	Representative	Policeman	Police Officer
Fireman	Fire fighter	Salesman	Salesperson, representative

EXHIBIT 11.7

EXAMPLE TRITE EXPRESSIONS		
Worth its weight in gold	Cool as a cucumber	Mother Nature
Over the hill	Crying over spilled milk	Father Time
Fresh as a daisy	Greased lightning	Dog-eat-dog
Hard as nails	Pretty as a picture	Crack of dawn
Make a long story short	Flat as a pancake	Spring chicken
Sick as a dog	Dumb as an ox	Signed, sealed, delivered
Sly as a fox	Red as a rose	Open-and-shut case
Rate race	Black as pitch	Armed to the teeth

Use Simple Language

Prefer the nickel words to the eighty-five cent words and avoid twelve-dollar words altogether.

This does not mean you cannot create vivid images or be powerful in language choice. Match your choice of language to the level you believe your least skillful listener is capable of understanding.

Clear language says something. It avoids the modifiers that weaken its impact and spoil its style. Eliminate as much meaningless language as you can. Such words lack power and directness. Prove it to yourself by comparing the weaker and more powerful sentences in Exhibit 11.8.

EXHIBIT 11.8

WEAK SENTENCES MADE MORE POWERFUL BY ELIMINATING MEANINGLESS LANGUAGE	
Weak examples	*More powerful examples*
What we need is a lot of money.	What we need is $300,000.
This is kind of a difficult problem.	This is a difficult problem.
This idea is sort of problematic.	This idea is problematic.
Perhaps this will solve the problem.	This will solve the problem.
We should act now, you know?	We should act now.
It seems like you are hesitating on this.	You're hesitating on this.
I hope I can get this done by Wednesday.	I'll have this done by Wednesday.
I think that this will solve your problem.	This will solve the problem.
This engine is very powerful.	This engine is powerful.
Well, the next main idea is . . .	The next main idea is . . .
The solution is definitely the best.	This is the best solution.

Use Clear Language

Sometimes, a speaker gets wrapped up in fancy language. Do not talk like a bureaucrat who has spent a lifetime hiding behind language excess. The more you complicate your sentences, the more you are likely to confuse listeners. For example, read the following notice about an upcoming workshop:

> *The computer tool seminar and workshop, which will be presented on September 15 in the Small Engineering Conference Room, may be of special interest to process engineers, but all interested personnel are invited to attend. Please advise Technical Training of your group's attendance plans before September 8.*

Now read the following edited version of the workshop notice. Which is clearer?

> *If you're a Process Engineer, you will find the computer tool seminar especially interesting. The workshop will be held on September 15 in the Small Engineering Conference Room. If you want to attend, please let us know before September 8.*

Use Vivid Language

Eliminate language that does not promote your message, but add language that does. Four pieces of advice will help you to use language more vigorously and more vividly: (1) be specific, (2) use action language, (3) use comparison and contrast, and (4) use illustrations.

Be specific

Listeners must take what you give them. If you want them to form an image you must provide the specific materials they need to form it. Generalizations do not provide sufficient material.

Dan McDonald, Professor Emeritus of English, uses what he calls the "Ginger Principle" to emphasize the importance of being specific. The "Ginger Principle" involves three concrete details: (1) proper nouns, (2) real numbers, and (3) color. These specific details help listeners form images in their heads. Don't say "my sister," when you mean "my sister, Ellen." Don't say "a lot" when you mean "eighty-eight." Don't say "pretty" when you mean "The bottoms of those white clouds had turned gold and mauve against an intense azure sky."

Use Action Language

Action language includes action verbs, and also short sentences, time words, and interrupted rhythms. Compare the passages that follow from a student's speech. The student's "after" version was written following a lecture on short sentences, time words, and interrupted rhythms.

Keep your language consistent with your topic. If your topic is very active, your language should be active, too. © PhotoDisc

> **Before:** *We are now in the midst of a new era—the communications age. But our American schools aren't preparing our students to cope with the new age. Technology is changing so very rapidly that yesterday's advances are already obsolete. But the schools aren't changing, and perhaps they can't. They don't have the technology and they don't have the know-how to change. But clearly, something has to be done, and it must be done now.*

> **After:** *We are all affected. We can't escape the problems of the communications era. But we're not ready, and the schools are not ready. Technology has changed the educational calendar, but it hasn't changed the educational system. Each day is but a single tick of the giant clock of history. And the hands of the clock move relentlessly toward a new day. They move at a real-world speed that leaves us breathless. It's seventeen minutes before midnight on that clock. We'd better do something, and do it now.*

Use Comparison and Contrast

Comparison and contrast add vividness and accuracy to a speech. They help you to clarify your ideas by placing one concept next to another and showing similarities and differences. Different forms of comparison and contrast include analogy and metaphor. **Analogy** explains a particular subject by pointing out its similarities to another subject, usually one that is better known or more easily understood. **Metaphor** is an implied comparison between two unlike things that is used to show some unexpected likeness between the two.

The analogy of the clock in the "After" example in the previous section gives the passage a sense of urgency and force it would not otherwise have had. The power comes from comparing something listeners know to something they do not know. Thus, comparison and contrast help people to comprehend and understand.

Here is how one speaker used comparison and contrast to argue against building an elevated interstate highway spur through downtown Mobile, Alabama. Partly because of powerful speaking like this, that elevated highway spur was never built.

> We have lots of evidence that putting an elevated interstate highway through a downtown area creates a slum in the area under the highway. This certainly has been the case in Kansas City, Chicago, Detroit, Denver, Los Angeles, and New York. And it will be true of Mobile, as well.
>
> If you want to see what your support for the elevated highway will bring to Mobile, take a drive to New Orleans on Interstate 10. When you get there, follow along the interstate, but underneath it. You will find empty buildings with broken windows. You will find abandoned cars. You will find winos sleeping in the doorways of abandoned businesses. But be sure to lock your car and close the windows, because you will also find a criminal element on that trip ready and willing to knock you on the head and steal your car and your money.
>
> I can't believe that anyone here wants that to happen in Mobile. But it most certainly will happen to Mobile if this highway is built. It has happened in every metropolitan downtown area where an elevated highway has been built. So the question is not whether we ought to have an interstate highway extension through our city. The question is whether we want to create a slum in our beautiful downtown area.

Use Illustrations

People think about concepts by trying to visualize a concrete image that makes sense to them. They seek an illustration. Knowing this, you can help listeners to understand your idea by illustrating it. Use lots of examples and illustrations to provide audience members a common ground on which to come to grips with your ideas.

Use Accurate and Unambiguous Language

Finally, language is nothing if it is not ambiguous. No direct relationship exists between a referent and the word that represents it. When you say *car,* or *rock,* or *tree,* listeners have to process the words and make their own meanings. That is easy when the word refers to something concrete. For example, when you hear the word *tree,* you get a picture in your mind of something you have experienced. You see a tree. But, because your experience is unlike anyone else's, you create an image in your mind unlike any other. This is why we have emphasized using language well. Try to use language that accurately reflects your ideas—language that leaves no doubt about your point of view. Language provides the raw material from which people make images, attach emotions, and create identification. When you increase your skill in using language you increase your power to inform and persuade.

Politicians and advertisers sometimes use highly ambiguous language because they do not wish to be clear. Can you find ethical fault with this strategy?

SUMMARY

More than anything else, your language skills will determine whether you succeed in getting the effect you want from your speeches. Language is the system of signs and symbols used by a speech community (a group of individuals who use the same language system) to share meaning and experience.

Language creates reality because it is intimately tied to what we think and feel. Language carries three kinds of meaning: (1) denotative (a word's literal definition), (2) connotative (a word's emotional associations), and (3) relational (the speaker's relationship with listeners). Thus, language allows us to share meaning with others and to understand our relationships with them.

To use language well, speakers should concentrate on making their words appropriate, simple, clear, vivid, and accurate. Appropriate language does not offend, is not insensitive or sexist, and does not consist of trite expressions or clichés. Simple language requires the use of nickel words over eighty-five-cent words so that your least skillful listener is capable of understanding. Clear language is language that says something without getting tangled in meaningless modifiers or technical jargon. Vivid language requires providing specific information, using action language, comparing and contrasting, and incorporating numerous illustrations. The accuracy of your language will determine whether you are actually able to communicate your message to listeners.

Learn to use language wisely and well. The quality and success of your speeches depend on it.

KEY TERMS

Activity dimension of language
Affect
Analogy
Cognition
Cognitive process
Connotations
Denotation

Evaluative dimension of language
Information structure
Language
Metaphor
Potency dimension of language
Relational meaning
Speech community

APPLICATION QUESTIONS

1. Ask five of your friends who have not studied public speaking or communication: What is language? Notice how their responses compare and contrast. How do you account for the similarities and differences?

2. Pay close attention to a televised commercial. If possible, videotape the commercial and then write out the exact spoken and written language used. Do you notice any relationship between the language choices and the commercial's intended goal? In terms of this chapter, what are those relationships?

3. Make a list of car names (Camry, Mirage, Crown Victoria, Sable, and so on). Do you find any relationship between the kind of car the name represents, the car's name, and the intended market? Make a similar list of truck names (Bronco, Blazer, Trooper), and perform a similar analysis. How might you use your insights to improve your speech making?

4. Does using simple language mean that speakers should condescend to their audiences? By addressing the "lowest common denominator," do speakers imply that they consider themselves superior? Doesn't this practice insult audience members with greater experience, education, or ability? In discussing these issues, remind students of the goals of public speaking. Further, nothing precludes speakers from trying to increase the skill level of their audience. For example, explaining something to someone does not require condescension.

IT'S MORE FUN TO KNOW

Language plays a crucial role in the ways we relate to each other. Language is sometimes described as "power" although research by Lindsey Grob, Renee A. Meyers, and Renee Schuh "Powerful/Powerless Language Use in Group Interactions," *Communication Quarterly*, 45:3 (Summer 1997) finds little support for the notion that men use more powerful language than women. And recent research explains that language is now not nearly as sexist as once had been believed (Ann Weatherall, "Women, and Men in Language," *Human Communication Research*, 25:2 (December 1998), 275–292). Perhaps some of this belief may come from the essential abstract nature of language, a function that often creates confusion and generalizations (Judee K. Burgoon and Ellen J. Langer, "Language, Fallacies, and Mindlessness-Mindfulness in Social Interaction," *Communication Yearbook*, 18 (1995), 105–132). These abstractions lead to unintended meanings and often create ironic situations. (Raymond W. Gibbs, Jr., Jennifer E. O'Brien, and Shelly Doolittle, "Inferring Meanings That Are Not Intended," *Discourse Processes*, 20:2 (September-October 1995), pp. 187–203. These findings confirm many who have suspicions about political talk.

The results of one study of language in this area claims that politicians use indirectness strategies to be more polite and gain the upper hand. (See Samuel Gyasi Obeng, "Language and Politics: Indirectness in Political Discourse," *Discourse and Society*, 8:1 (January 1997) pp. 49–83.

Language becomes a nationalistic symbol as well. In countries where there is a choice in the use of language, the native language is now chosen more often than is the previously most commonly chosen English language. (See Louisa Ha, "Changes in Language Use and Value Appeals Under Political Transition Hong Kong Advertising 1991-95," *Asian Journal of Communication*, 8:1 (1998), pp. 53–72).

SELF-TEST FOR REVIEW

1. Which of the following *best* defines the term *language?*
   a. A system of signs and symbols used by a speech community to share meaning and experience
   b. A phonetic sound system used in speech behavior to isolate morphemes
   c. A system of words, plus rules for their use, that allows people to correspond
   d. A complete set of signs and sounds that allows speaking and writing among people in the same community

2. Which of the following is accurate regarding the statement that language creates reality?
   a. This statement is true because language controls what we think.
   b. This statement is true because language controls what we feel.
   c. This statement is true because language both controls what we think and how we feel.
   d. This statement is false. Language does not create reality.

Mark the following items: R = relational, C = connotation, D = denotation.

____ 3. Refers to associations usually called up by a word in a speech community

____ 4. Refers to the affective value of a word

____ 5. Evaluative, potency, and activity dimensions

____ 6. The dictionary definition of a word

____ 7. Charles Osgood's semantic space

____ 8. A speaker's attitude toward listeners

9. What is *relational meaning?*

   a. The relationship between denotation and connotation

   b. The similarities between connotation and denotation

   c. The message that speakers send about how they understand their relationships to listeners

   d. The phenomenon of interpersonal attraction that operates in a public speaking situation

Correct the following statements by striking through meaningless modifiers.

10. Ladies and gentlemen, may I present the charming and beautiful Miss Judy Jackson.

11. Thank you for your kind hospitality so generously extended to me during this visit.

12. Open your wonderful textbook to page 344.

Rewrite these sentences, using the active voice.

13. The new bill was passed by Congress.

14. The play was seen by the critic.

15. The plane was delayed by the weather.

Answers: 1. a. 2. c. 3. D. 4. C. 5. C. 6. D. 7. C. 8. R. 9. c. 10. Ladies and gentlemen, may I present the ~~charming and beautiful~~ Miss Judy Jackson. 11. Thank you for your ~~kind~~ hospitality ~~so generously extended to me during this visit~~. 12. Open your ~~wonderful~~ textbook to page 344. 13. Congress passed the new bill. 14. The critic saw the play. 15. The weather delayed the plane.

SUGGESTED READINGS

Eschholz, Paul, Alfred Rosa, and Virginia Clark, eds. *Language Awareness.* 6th ed. New York: St. Martin's Press, 1994. This reader includes some of the most interesting and provocative excerpts about language available in any one source. Contributors include George Orwell, Jeffrey Schrank, Edwin Newman, Hugh Rank, Gordon Allport, S. I. Hayakawa, Neil Postman, and Stephen King.

Fromkin, Victoria, and Robert Rodman. *An Introduction to Language.* 5th ed. New York: Holt, Rinehart and Winston, 1993. This is a comprehensive but easy-to-read introductory text about language. This book should be on the desk of anyone who cares about understanding and using language.

INTERNET ACTIVITIES

Go to the URL of the International House International Language Centre Group h*ttp://www.ilcgroup.com/interactive/* and find their excellent and fun Interactive English Language Exercises. Try these, then report your experience to the class.

Go to the Comenius Language Center at the URL *http://www.comenius.com/index.html* to see what they are up to. Come to class prepared to discuss the question, "What drives people to develop a web site like this?" And "How might this web site be useful to students in Public Speaking?"

Purdue University maintains an on-line writing center at the URL *http://owl.english.purdue.edu/*. Does it offer anything useful for public speaking students?

Allyn and Bacon offers a series of modules which assist the beginning speaker plus there are links to numerous other helpful web sites at *http://www.abacon.com/pubspeak/index.html*.

NOTES

1. One of the good recent works is John R. Searle, *The Construction of Social Reality*, (New York: Free Press, 1995).

2. See C. Douglas McCann and E. Tory Higgins, "Personal and Contextual Factors in Communication: A review of the 'Communication Game'" in Klaus Fiedler, *Language, Interaction and Social Cognition* (Newbury Park, CA: Sage Publications, 1992), 144–172.

3. Charles E. Osgood, "The Nature and Measurement of Meaning," *Psychological Bulletin,* 49 (1952), 197–237.

CHAPTER 12

SUPPORTING IDEAS VISUALLY

OBJECTIVES

After reading this chapter, you should be able to:

1. Specify when to use visual aids.

2. Name what you should support with visual aids and explain why.

3. Describe the steps in developing a visual aid program.

4. Explain how to apply three criteria for choosing the right visual medium for a visual aid program.

5. Explain why overhead projectors are popular speaking tools, and list several tips for using overhead projectors in your visuals program.

6. Describe and use the principles of layout and design including (a) the rule of thirds, (b) straight lines and curved lines, (c) the balance of triangles, (d) eye movement and negative space, (e) sketches and illustrations, and (f) language and lettering.

7. Demonstrate correctly how to introduce, present, explain, and put away visual aids.

OUTLINE

Objectives
Outline
Abstract
Imagine
Introduction
  Why Don't People Use
    Visual Aids?
  Why Should You Use
    Visual Aids?
  When to Use Visual Aids
    To Simplify Complexity
    To Help Listeners Organize
      Your Ideas
    To Control Audience
      Attention
    To Help Listeners Under-
      stand Abstract Ideas
    To Help Listeners Remember
    To Help You Remain
      Organized While Speaking
  What to Support with Visual
    Materials
  Steps in Developing a Visual
    Aid Program
    Think About Key Ideas
    Develop a Rough Plan for the
      Visual Program
    Design Thumbnail Sketches
      of Each Visual Aid
  Choose the Visual Media for
    the Program

Convenience of Use
Costs Versus Benefits
Communication Power
Produce Rough Visual Aids
  for Practice
Produce the Finished Visual
  Aids for the Program
How to Make a Two-
  Dimensional Visual Aid
  The Rule of Thirds
  Straight Lines and Curved
    Lines
  The Balance of Triangles
  Eye Movement and
    Negative Space
  Sketches and Illustrations
  Language and Lettering
Review and Revise the
  Final Program
How to Use Visual Materials:
  Matters of Delivery
Summary
Key Terms
Application Questions
It's More Fun to Know
Self-Test for Review
Suggested Readings
Internet Activities
Notes

ABSTRACT

Well-made visual supporting materials enhance most public speeches, but only if they contribute something to the speech. In this chapter, you learn when to use visual aids, what to show on them, how to develop visual materials, and how to use them.

Use visual aids to simplify complexity, to help listeners organize your ideas, to control audience attention, and to help listeners understand your ideas and remember them. In addition, a well-designed visual aid program helps you organize your thoughts and stay on track during a speech. Visuals are especially helpful for showing problems, solutions and benefits, processes, procedures, and steps in a sequence.

Developing a visual aid program involves a number of steps: (1) identifying the key ideas that need support, (2) designing thumbnail sketches, (3) practicing with "rough" visuals, and (4) reviewing and revising the final visuals program. You should also consider the convenience, cost, and communication power of each visual medium. The principles of effective layout and design presented in the chapter will aid you when producing a visual aids program. The chapter concludes with a description of a simple, four-step procedure for using your visual aids: (1) Introduce the visual aid before you present it. (2) Present the visual aid with a minimum of talk so that listeners can concentrate on looking instead of listening. (3) Explain the idea you are trying to illustrate. (4) Then put the visual aid away.

IMAGINE

Charlie Swan never could understand why people sang the praises of front-wheel drive cars. There didn't seem, to him, to be much difference. Then he heard a speech in a beginning engineering class about the operation of front-wheel drive. The speaker used several visual aids which showed how the weight of the engine was placed over the front wheels. One diagram showed how, in snowy weather, the weight of the engine helped create more traction in the front wheels.

Another diagram, depicting a rear-wheel drive vehicle, showed how the weight of the engine was over the front wheels. But the power was delivered to the rear wheels, which spun on the snow because they couldn't get traction. Charlie now understood why the rear tires of his car always spun on snow and why it was hard to get traction. The engine weight in his vehicle was not over the wheels that propelled the car.

A third diagram showed how a front-wheel drive vehicle "pulled" the car through turns while the rear-wheel drive pushed the vehicle when it was turning. The speaker made the point that it was easier and safer to steer if you are pulled rather than pushed. And, with the weight in the front, according to the speaker, there would be fewer chances to slide when making a turn.

Charlie bought a front-wheel drive car when he made his next auto purchase.

INTRODUCTION

The term *visual* implies looking. The term *aid* implies support. A **visual aid** is any object, photograph, chart, graph, sketch, or lettered image that supports a speech or the speaker. Visual aids can be three-dimensional, but as a rule, two-dimensional visual materials work better to support a speech. A three-dimensional object small enough to manipulate easily is *probably* too small to be an effective visual aid, although there are exceptions, of course.

With the help of a computer and the right software, visual aids are easy and fun to make. Moreover, you can render very sophisticated 2-dimensional images including wonderful clip art, animated lettering, photographs, full-motion video, recorded voices and music, and the like. Each of these capabilities has an appropriate place in speech making. However, these sophisticated effects can also damage the impact of a presentation. Just because you *can* do it doesn't mean you should do it!

Effective visual aids help listeners to understand or identify with a speech, or they help the speaker. If visual material fails to make a positive contribution, it is not an aid. In fact, some visual materials may even detract from the speaker's goals.

Why Don't People Use Visual Aids?

Given the value of visual materials to speech making, you might wonder why so many speakers either don't use them at all, or design and use them so badly as to make them counterproductive. The reasons lie in misunderstanding the communication process, and in attitudes that just don't apply to today's reality.

We are taught to treat visual materials as less valuable and less important than words. In written materials, especially, visuals are developed after the text is written. You can verify this claim for yourself: Most textbooks you've seen place graphic materials in some separate, secondary part of the book, or away from the related portions of the text material. Often, graphics are distorted in order to "fit" into the margins of text material, and they merely reproduce what has already been said in the text.

Watch carefully to see how many times student speakers and professors omit visual materials and try to explain everything with words. This especially happens when a speech or lecture is coming up and the student or professor has not planned far enough ahead.

Too often, you will find graphic materials used merely as decoration next to text materials. This happens in overhead projections, and on the pages of many textbooks you have read. This phenomenon probably comes straight from our early training. We insist our children study language (reading, writing, speaking), but we don't insist they study visual codes (graphic design, nonverbal communication).

Finally, we don't have any "rules" or standards we can apply to visual materials. In contrast, we study grammar, syntax, spelling from our earliest school experiences. Is it any wonder speaking students seem reluctant to spend the time necessary to develop an effective visual aids program for their work?

Why Should You Use Visual Aids?

Because vision is our dominant sense mechanism, visual materials make it much easier for listeners to follow a speech. Exhibit 12.1 lists seven reasons why visual materials make speeches work better.

EXHIBIT 12.1

WHY VISUAL MATERIALS MAKE SPEECHES WORK BETTER	
Visual aids transcend language barriers	There are about 5000 languages spoken in the world. Business is conducted in about 100 of these languages. Mergers create multinational corporations in which native speakers of one language must communicate with listeners in another. Visual materials make it easy to cross language barriers.
Visual aids help people who can't read	Many speakers use blocks of type as visual aids. These help readers. But many people cannot read! UNESCO has reported that 885 million of the world's people cannot read.[1] Graphic presentations do not require literacy.
Visual aids are compelling	Educators have found that (visual) images are more effective than words in teaching higher level thinking.[2] Additionally, others have discovered that using visuals in the curriculum enhances learning.[3]
Visual aids increase credibility	People really do believe that "seeing is believing." Research findings are unequivocal on this point.[4]
Visual aids help people think better	Problem solving is largely a visual process. Graphic designs help people process more information more rapidly and effectively than they would be able to without graphical information. Moreover, the solutions they come up with tend to be simpler and more efficient and effective!
Visual aids explain when words do not	Images work much better than words when you want to show relationships between colors or textures, how things look, how they compare in size, etc.
Visual aids are remembered	People recall graphics better than words. They recall graphics almost perfectly. Visual images tend to last.[5]

When to Use Visual Aids

Full and frequent use of visual materials will help you succeed in almost every kind of speech. Probable exceptions would be speeches in which you introduce another speaker or acceptance speeches for receiving an award or nomination. For these types of speeches, visual aids probably would not be necessary. But in most other speeches, visual aids can contribute to your speech goals. Exhibit 12.2 tells when to use words, when to use graphics, and when a balance of words and graphics is needed. Exhibit 12.3 lists six important uses of visual supporting materials.

Exhibit 12.2

WHEN TO USE WORDS, GRAPHICS, AND COMBINATIONS		
Use words alone	*Use graphics alone*	*Use a combination*
To explain abstract concepts, or describe emotions. When you need the subtle nuances of language.	To show how something looks.	To aid understanding.
To describe the sensory experiences of touch, smell and taste.	To clarify ideas that may be confusing.	To show or explain complex ideas or tasks.
When it is inappropriate to show something visually—for example, certain body parts.	To show objects that must be recognized or remembered.	When words by themselves are too vague.
		When the listening audience is broadly diverse.

Exhibit 12.3

SIX USES OF VISUAL SUPPORTING MATERIAL
• To simplify complexity
• To help listeners organize your ideas
• To control audience attention
• To help listeners understand abstract ideas
• To help listeners remember
• To help you remain organized while speaking

To Simplify Complexity

Try to present ideas as simply as possible. However, sometimes, you must discuss complex material that listeners may have trouble following. For example, engineers and financial people often need to present very technical information to managers or other decision-makers who do not have technical training. In these situations, listeners may need visual materials to understand the speaker's ideas. Charts, graphs, tables, models, drawings and flowcharts will make complex information easier for listeners to understand. Exhibit 12.4 shows how data can be more effectively presented as visual material. Here are data for four salespersons.

Imagine trying to present this information without any visual material at all. It would be very nearly impossible.

To Help Listeners Organize Your Ideas

Suppose you want to discuss two or three main ideas, each of which you want to break down into two or three subpoints. Or perhaps you want to describe both a problem and a solution to the problem, each part of which has two or three main ideas. Visual supporting materials will help listeners follow your organization. Exhibit 12.5 shows how a college debater might construct three visual aids to help listeners follow a complex ten-minute speech.

EXHIBIT 12.4

THE DATA SHOWN IN DIFFERENT FORMATS

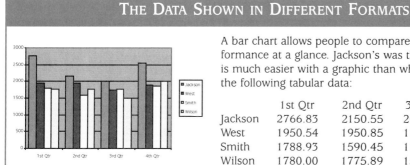

A bar chart allows people to compare individual performance at a glance. Jackson's was the best. This task is much easier with a graphic than when trying to read the following tabular data:

	1st Qtr	2nd Qtr	3rd Qtr	4th Qtr
Jackson	2766.83	2150.55	2000.00	2540.75
West	1950.54	1950.85	1735.88	1895.50
Smith	1788.93	1590.45	1758.98	1845.90
Wilson	1780.00	1775.89	1500.89	2022.45

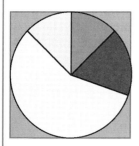

A pie chart shows relative proportion. In this case the first quarter performance was clearly more than half the year's performance.

In general, do not divide a pie chart into more than four or five divisions. The idea is to keep the visual information easy to get at a glance.

```
┌─────────────────────────────┐   ┌─────────────────────────────┐   ┌─────────────────────────────┐
│ The Problem                 │   │ Action Plan                 │   │ Advantages                  │
│                             │   │                             │   │                             │
│  I. The Problem is Real     │   │  I. Abolish the _____ │   │   I. The first advantage    │
│     (because)               │   │     A. (Reason) _____ │   │      is _____          │
│     A. (Reason) _____  │   │     B. (Reason) _____ │   │  II. The second advantage   │
│     B. (Reason) _____  │   │                             │   │      is _____            │
│ II. The Problem is Serious  │   │ II. Repair the _____  │   │ III. The third advantage    │
│     (because)               │   │     A. (Reason) _____ │   │      is _____          │
│     A. (Reason) _____  │   │     B. (Reason) _____ │   │                             │
│     B. (Reason) _____  │   │     C. (Reason) _____ │   │                             │
│ III. The Problem is Inherent│   │                             │   │                             │
│     (because)               │   │ III. Adopt the _____  │   │                             │
│     A. (Reason) _____  │   │     A. (Reason) _____ │   │                             │
│     B. (Reason) _____  │   │     B. (Reason) _____ │   │                             │
└─────────────────────────────┘   └─────────────────────────────┘   └─────────────────────────────┘
```

EXHIBIT 12.5   Visual aids help listeners follow speech organization.

To Control Audience Attention

Listeners must pay attention before they can learn or be persuaded by what you say. As a speaker, your job includes controlling listener attention. Visual aids can help.

Television advertisers know how to use visual material to hold viewer attention. To see how they do it, watch your television set for any two-minute period. Turn the sound off, and count the number of times the picture changes. Examine the movement on the screen. Those changes, that movement, hold viewer attention so well that some people cannot focus on anything else. In fact, the television viewing habits of American show that their sets are on for seven hours and forty minutes per day.[6]

You can use visual materials with much the same effect during a speech or presentation. When you present an idea, refer to a visual aid, then put the visual away, you move the audience's attention from yourself to the visual and then back to yourself again. This psychological movement helps you control listener attention because it asks listeners to participate with you in creating the communication event.

To Help Listeners Understand Abstract Ideas

Abstract concepts presented without visual materials can overwhelm your audience. One student addressed this problem in a speech comparing and contrasting asteroids and comets. She wanted to compare these celestial objects by size, origin, and composition. Plus, she wanted to explain what would happen if one of these objects would strike earth. Exhibit 12.6 shows what she said and how she visualized her ideas. Her speech had some problems, but her visual materials really helped her audience follow the difficult ideas she was presenting.

EXHIBIT 12.6

HOW ONE STUDENT VISUALIZED DIFFICULT IDEAS

Good afternoon, class. As you know, I'm Joycelena Slate. I've been taking astronomy this semester, and I learned something you'll be interested in—the differences between asteroids and comets. An asteroid is a huge rock—like a small planet, really—in orbit in our solar system, hopefully between Mars and Jupiter. A comet is made of ice and dirt. They orbit our sun, too.

There are three main differences, but it wouldn't matter if either one of them would strike the Earth (because any of them would cause an immense amount of damage).

One main difference is size. The biggest asteroid we know of is called Ceres. It is an irregular rock-shape and about 620 miles in diameter. In contrast, the Hale-Bopp comet is probably no more than 24 miles in diameter at the nucleus. But of course, the tail goes out thousands and thousands of miles.

The second main difference between asteroids and comets is what they're made of. All asteroids are solid. Usually they are stone or metal—mostly iron. On the other hand, comets are made of ice crystals at the nucleus, and the tails are made of gasses and space dust.

Where do they come from? That's the third main difference between asteroids and comets. Asteroids originate from the main asteroid belt between Jupiter and Mars, whereas comets come either from a huge cloud beyond the planets, and very close to the sun. Or from a cloudy belt that's on the other side of Neptune and Pluto.

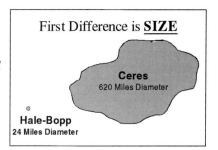

First Difference is **SIZE**

Ceres
620 Miles Diameter

Hale-Bopp
24 Miles Diameter

Second Difference is **CONTENT**

ASTEROIDS made of rock and iron.

COMETS made of ice crystals and gas.

Third Difference is **ORIGINS**

ASTEROIDS come from the asteroid belt between Jupiter and Mars

COMETS come from a space cloud beyond the planets

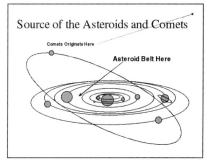

Source of the Asteroids and Comets

Comets Originate Here

Asteroid Belt Here

To Help Listeners Remember

Good visual aids not only teach—they help listeners remember. Both functions are critical.

To illustrate, a student lawyer told her audience of student court members they needed to understand and remember the answers to three questions if they were going to reach a fair decision about her client. The student on trial was accused of damaging university property through malicious mischief. Apparently, he had broken up with his steady girlfriend, drunk too much beer, and then smashed a lamp by throwing it across his dormitory room. The student court had the authority to expel the defendant if court members thought he was guilty and if the situation warranted such a response.

"You must remember these three questions," said the defendant's representative, while displaying an overhead transparency like that in Exhibit 12.7. "Did Tom Johnston do malicious mischief?" She pointed to the first question on the visual aid. "Were there any extenuating circumstances?" She pointed to the second question. "Was what he did really serious enough to warrant expulsion from this university?" She pointed to the third question on the poster and then explained her position:

Malicious Mischief?

Extenuating Circumstances?

How Serious?

Exhibit 12.7

Tom surely did break the lamp. He surely did throw it across the room. He did smash university property, and he has since bought a new one. Those are the facts, and the facts are not in question.

But did Tom do malicious mischief? He didn't just tear up the lamp in his room for the fun of it. He didn't do an act of common vandalism. He didn't set out in advance to trash his dorm room. What he did was thoughtless, unpremeditated. It wasn't malicious mischief, and that is what he is being tried for. The answer to the first question is "no."

And clearly, there were extenuating circumstances. Tom's behavior can't be condoned, but it can be understood. Wouldn't you also feel like throwing something if you had just broken up with someone special to you?

But let's suppose he had set out, in advance, to trash his room. And suppose, also, that Tom had not just broken up with his steady. We deny these things, but suppose them anyway. You still have to consider the third question. Was what he did serious enough to merit throwing him out of college?

Certainly not. A broken-up lamp is not worth a broken-up education. A smashed light fixture is not worth smashing a man's college program.

So, as you consider what you will do about Tom Johnston, please keep these three questions in mind. They make the difference in this case.

After concluding her speech, the student walked to her chair, leaving the transparency and its three questions shining on the screen in front of the student court. It was a dramatic use of visual material to help listeners remember the purpose of her speech.

To Help You Remain Organized While Speaking

Your visual aid program can also serve as "notes" you can use during your speech to keep yourself on track. This use of visual materials works so well that the market for "presentation software" has grown into a multi-million-dollar industry in the United States. Exhibit 12.8 illustrates how one student used Microsoft's PowerPoint presentation software to support a speech about the NASDAQ.

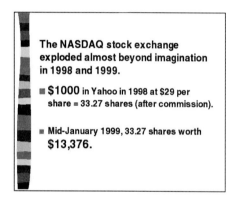

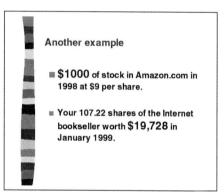

EXHIBIT 12.8

Here is the text of the student's speech.

The price of Internet related stocks on the NASDAQ stock exchange exploded almost beyond imagination in 1998 and 1999. If you had a strong stomach, modest knowledge, and a little bit of cash, you could make yourself a great deal of money.

I don't want to talk about whether or not the prices were at all related to the value of the companies. During this period, most of the companies were not even making a penny! People were wagering that they would make money in the future.

Here's what you could have done with your money. If you had invested $1000 in Yahoo in 1998 when it was at its low of approximately $29 per share you would have owned 33.27 shares (after commission). In mid-January 1999, your 33.27 shares would have been worth $13,376. Nice pocket change!

Here's another example. Let's suppose you purchased $1000 of stock in Amazon.com in 1998 at $9 per share.

Because of the explosion in this stock during 1998 and early 1999, your 107.22 shares of the Internet bookseller would have been worth $19,728 in January 1999.

People who study the stock market say this is "speculative froth." But the people who have become instant millionaires are smiling all the way to the bank.

What audience members may not realize is that these transparencies serve the speaker as much as they serve audience members. The same visuals that help listeners follow your ideas also help you follow your speech plan.

What to Support with Visual Materials

A student speaker complained: "I just don't think I need any visual aids in this speech." By now you probably know that the student was emphasizing the wrong thing: *You* may not need any visual aids, but listeners almost certainly will need them. Keep your focus on the audience as you consider what to support with visual materials. Exhibit 12.9 suggests especially helpful uses of visual supporting materials.

Steps in Developing a Visual Aid Program

So far, you have studied what to support with visual materials and when, but developing the actual visual materials is another matter. The remainder of the chapter focuses on steps in developing a visual aid program, choosing the right medium for visual supporting materials, designing and making your own visual materials when your circumstances require it, and using those materials to maximum effect.

If you have a clear notion of what you want to say in your speech, the steps involved in developing a visual aid program should fall neatly into place. Exhibit 12.10 shows the steps in developing a visual aid program for a speech.

Think About the Key Ideas

Which of your ideas seem complex? Which ones stand on their own? Which ones require visual support? Review the discussion of how to use note cards to help you plan the main ideas of your speech (see Chapter 7, "How to Gather Supporting Materials"). Those note cards can help you with this part of speech preparation, too. Lay them out again, or look closely at your planning outline (Chapter 9, "Outlining the Speech").

EXHIBIT 12.9

WHAT TO SUPPORT WITH VISUAL MATERIALS		
What To Show	*Explanation*	*Example*
Show problems.	People must "see" to understand and care about a problem.	An engineer shows photographs of corrosion damage to cabinet-rank officials because she cannot take the officials to the damage.
Show how to do something.	People must visualize a task before they can do it.	**How to hold a divider.**
Show steps in a sequence.	People follow along better when they see the steps.	A student uses presentation management software to explain enumerated steps, one by one.
Show processes and procedures.	People often have to see and do before they can learn.	A trainer projects a copy of a form that must be filled out correctly, then distributes a paper copy to each trainee. Together they fill out the form—the trainer using the projected image, and the trainees using the paper copies.
Show solutions and benefits.	Many people cannot visualize easily.	The Mayor shows the city council and the press corps architectural renderings of a proposed convention center, plus a series of carefully planned charts and graphs to explain the potential financial impact of the center on the city's economy.
Show organization.	People must see how ideas are related and how parts fit together in order to understand these relationships.	The CEO shows his cabinet-ranked officers a chart of his proposed reorganization plan. A teacher shows her class a table of relationships among species. A lawyer shows a time-line of events to a jury. An architect shows the client and the contractor blueprints of a floor plan.
Show what things look like.	People often have to locate, recognize or imagine things that are not actually present.	A supervisor tells, shows, and provides a drawing of the control panel to a new employee. An interior designer shows the decision-making group renderings of the restaurant dining room planned for their building. A cop distributes a forensic artist's drawing of a suspect to people in the neighborhood.
Show comparison and contrast.	Things that are similar often look different, and things that are different often look similar.	A scout leader teaches the troop members how to discriminate between Virginia Creeper and Poison Ivy. A sales representative contrasts the computers in her proposal from the machines in her competitor's proposal.

EXHIBIT 12.10

STEPS IN DEVELOPING A VISUAL AID PROGRAM FOR A SPEECH

1. Think about key ideas.
2. Develop a rough plan for the visual program.
3. Design thumbnail sketches of each visual aid.
4. Choose the visual media for the program.
5. Produce rough visual aids for practice.
6. Evaluate each visual aid and the whole visual aids program.
7. Produce the finished visual aids for the program.
8. Review and revise the final program.

Develop a Rough Plan for the Visual Program

From the listener's point of view, what kinds of visual materials would be most useful to understanding your ideas? Which of your key ideas seem most difficult, most important, most memorable? Decide what kinds of visual materials you intend to use and what ideas these materials will illustrate or support. Exhibit 12.11 may help you make these important decisions.

EXHIBIT 12.11

A CHECKLIST FOR DEVELOPING VISUAL SUPPORTING MATERIAL

Who will see the visual aid?	Rely on your audience analysis. How well do the listeners understand the materials represented in the visual aid? Can you assume they know anything? Or must you include everything they need to know in the visual aid?
	The less knowledgeable the viewer the less technical the information on the visual aid. The amount of detail you include can rise with the level of sophistication of your listeners—but not very far.
Is the purpose of the visual aid clear?	Setting objectives for visual supporting materials is much like setting objectives for the speech they support. What do you want the viewer to do as a result of seeing the visual aid? Buy something? Perform an action? Carry out some procedure? Make a particular decision? Experience some emotion?
What kind of information must the visual aid carry?	If you want to convey factual information, then write out the most important question the visual aid must answer. If the information is to be emotionally charged, then write out what emotion you want the visual aid to call up in the listeners.

Design Thumbnail Sketches of Each Visual Aid

Lay out a series of thumbnail sketches of planned visual aids. Do you need to add any? Delete any? Exhibit 12.12 shows an outline developed in PowerPoint and a series of thumbnail sketches for visual program developed by a public speaking student. The layout includes six separate visuals for a six-minute speech. What do you think? Are there too few? Too many? Only practicing your speech with your visual aids will tell you if your visual aids program is too ambitious or incomplete.

All of us have three jobs.

- The work we do for a living
- The work we do for ourselves
- Housework and care giving.

The work we do for a living is increasing rapidly.

- In two decades, average time spent at job has risen from 43.6 to 47.1 hours per week.
- The line between work life and private life is vanishing.
  - The work place is a more predictable "home" than their own homes.
  - We must keep up by using e-mail and voice mail and reading at home.
  - Work is a means of self-fulfillment (not a means to an end.)

Working life has changed for four reasons:

- Vietnam overheated the economy at the same time the oil crisis was happening.
  - (This combination led to very high inflation. People's money didn't go as far. So they had to work harder.)
- The baby boom meant cheaper help.
  - (The relative earnings of college graduates declined. Baby boomers felt they had to work harder.)

Why working life has changed, continued.

- The feminist movement happened just when the average family needed more money.
  - Women entered the workforce in large numbers, so men had to share household chores. The result was less leisure and family time for either adult.
- Technology—especially computers—has changed the nature of work.
  - (Many jobs eliminated by computers.New jobs require training. Decision making has shifted downward, so people must work longer and harder.)

What can we do to prepare for these changes?

- Keep on studying, even after you graduate.
  - Stay in school. Some employers will pay, but if not, take courses anyway.
- Offer to work odd hours if you can.
  - You set yourself apart. reate a more flexible schedule for things like classes. Put yourself in a position to negotiate.
- Find out what your employer needs and learn to provide it.

Summary.

- American work loads are increasing.
- This change is changing American lives, both at home and at work.
- American workers will have to work smarter.
- You can prepare to meet these changes.

EXHIBIT 12.12

Choose the Visual Media for the Program

Consider the advantages and disadvantages of the various media available to you. Remember that you can use more than one medium—for example, OHP transparencies plus a chalkboard—on condition that your selection is motivated by the needs of the listeners. Exhibit 12.13 will help you make these choices.

Choosing the right visual medium for your visual aids program requires thoughtful analysis. Three criteria should guide your thinking: (1) convenience of use, (2) costs versus benefits, and (3) communication power.

Convenience of Use

Convenience of use should be one of your first considerations in choosing a visual medium. You want visual aids to assist you, not hinder you. For a classroom speech, the time you take to make an elaborate visual aid, such as 35-millimeter slides, would be better spent in practicing and improving your speech. Add the troubles of securing a projector and screen, plus determining who will run the equipment, and you may find the visual aid's potential value is not worth its inconvenience.

On the other hand, if you have access to a computer and presentation management software, you will find it easy and very convenient to develop strong visual supporting material.

Costs Versus Benefits

The cost of producing certain visual materials can far outweigh their usefulness as supporting materials for a speech. For example, professionally made videotape can cost more than $10,000 per minute. Professionally made photography also can break a small budget.

On the other hand, very sophisticated visual supporting materials can be made with a computer very cheaply. If you don't have to buy the computer, and if you have access to the right software, you can draw free clip art and photography from the Internet for insertion into the visual aids you generate with your computer, and the entire process will cost you nothing.

However, there may be indirect and hidden costs involved in the decision to use a certain visual medium. What is your time worth? Must you pay a fee for use of equipment and materials? Will you end up paying someone for her or his help? And are these costs justified by the overall purpose and objective of your speech?

Exhibit 12.13

COMMUNICATION POWER OF VARIOUS VISUAL MEDIA			
Equipment	Reasons for Using Equipment	Audience Size	Image Area Size
Flip Chart	Short lead-time. Inexpensive. Drawback: not everyone can print legibly or draw.	Ten or under	27" to 34" maximum
Chalkboard	Informal, in-house or classroom communications. No development time. Same drawbacks as for flip charts.	Approximately 16–20	Limited only by size of chalkboard.
Velcro Board, Felt Board	Informal, but professional presentation to valued audience. Fairly long lead time required.	Up to 24	48" x 36" 48" x 72"
Overhead Projector	Complex materials requiring extensive discussion. Cheap after initial investment in equipment and software.	48 maximum. More with excellent equipment.	60" x 60" screen. More with larger screen.
Computer Projector	Complex materials requiring extensive discussion. Easy to develop and inexpensive after initial equipment investment.	48 maximum. More with excellent equipment.	60" x 60" screen. More with larger screen.
35mm Slides and Projector	Important audience and message; professional tone wanted. Professional photographer may be required for high quality images. Room lights must be turned off.	Usually limited only by room size.	6-feet or more
Videotape and Monitor	Important audience, credibility needed. Cheaper than film but still expensive to produce. Low resolution means details lost in photographs. Use simple graphics and large type.	One person per 1 inch of monitor size. Thus, a 24" monitor can serve 24 people.	Rear-projection screens can be as large as 5-feet (diagonal), but are very expensive.
Videotape and Projector	Important audience, credibility needed. Cheaper than film. Use simple graphics and photos that do not require great detail.	Depends on quality of projector and size of screen. Image quality is an issue on large screens.	Any size for large screen projection.

Communication Power

Advertisers have known for a long time that camera angle, relative image size, colors, and composition of an image can all influence receiver behavior. Can you list ways that visual supporting materials might be used unethically?

The term **communication power** refers to the degree of potency and memorability of visual or other symbolic material. Communication power has to do with the impact a particular communication strategy has on listeners. An enormous industry exists to serve the demands for more and more communication power in presentational speaking. To illustrate, the *Directory of Video, Computer & Audio-Visual Products* (published each year by the International Communications Industries Association) lists and illustrates more than 1500 different hardware and software products. Each entry describes computer compatibility, gives technical specifications, provides size, power and weight information, and lists optional accessories. You can visit the International Communications Industries Association web site at *www.icia.org.*

Produce Rough Visual Aids for Practice

The task of producing roughs for a visual support program has been greatly simplified for people who are lucky enough to own or have access to a computer and presentation management software. However, you do not have to own a computer to plan an effective visual aids program. You can use colored markers to produce rough mock-ups of your visuals on 8-1/2" by 11" sheets. The artwork does not have to be fancy. As you practice your speech with these mock-ups, you will get an idea of whether or not the visuals you have chosen are needed or require any design changes.

We recommend using a computer if you have access to the hardware and software. The outline function in PowerPoint serves a very useful organizing function. And if you are lucky enough to have access to a 1998 or later version of this software, you can take advantage of the PowerPoint *Wizard* function. This highly useful innovation in presentation software takes you through a series of questions, including questions that will help you identify what you want to accomplish with your presentation. The software then organizes the presentation for you! In the outline view you can see and edit the text of each "slide." Finally, the software designs each slide automatically.

Produce the Finished Visual Aids for the Program

If you have access to a computer with a good word processor or presentation manager, producing the finished visual aids for your speech is easy. But even without these tools, you do not have to spend a lot of money to produce good visual aids. Also, using a computer probably will not teach you any more about visual aids than if you choose paper as your medium. Regardless of the medium you use, however, think about your visual aids from the listener's point of view. Exhibit 12.14

EXHIBIT 12.14

CHECKLIST FOR THINKING ABOUT
VISUAL AIDS FROM THE LISTENER'S POINT OF VIEW

1. Is the main point of the visual aid immediately accessible and obvious?
2. Is each element of the visual aid (symbol, word, line, color, shape) needed?
3. Does the visual aid conform in "look" and "feel" to the rest of the visual aids program?
4. Does the visual aid look good to you? Will it look good to your listeners?
5. Can any element (symbol, word, line, color, shape) be eliminated without obscuring the point?
6. Do the elements stand out from the background?
7. Are the graphic elements clear and obvious?
8. Is the visual aid easy to see from the distance of the farthest target listener?
9. Does the visual aid conform to the listener's expectations and habits?
10. Can any component part (symbol, word, line, color, shape) be changed to improve the over all visual aid?

is a checklist designed to help you think about visual aids from the listener's point of view.

One question comes up frequently in public speaking classes. Which is better for a visual aid—photographs or drawings? In general, the answer to this question depends on what you are trying to accomplish. If you need to show a lot of detail and can project the visual aid onto a large enough screen, use a photograph. Otherwise, and much more often, use drawings to reduce the amount of information and detail in a visual aid, and to show very select details. Exhibit 12.15 answers this question in greater detail, and can serve as a guideline when you are planning a visual supporting materials program.

How to Make a Two-Dimensional Visual Aid

Because they apply to every visual aid you will ever make, two criteria should guide your thinking about two-dimensional design: simplicity and accessibility. With regard to visual aids, **simplicity** means plain, immediately obvious, easy to see from a distance, unmistakable even to a person who is not familiar with the subject, while **accessibility** means that the audience must be able to understand the visual material. Mere numbers or lists of statistics, for example, may confound audience members, even if they know how to work with figures.

Good visual materials result when you consider listeners and their possible reactions to your message. Then tie this consideration to your layout and design. You do not have to be an artist to make intelligent choices, but neither should you leave the selection and design of visual materials to chance or take them for granted.

EXHIBIT 12.15

PHOTOGRAPHS VS. DRAWINGS	
Use photographs	*Use drawings*
When you want to show exactly what something looks like.	When you want to show very small detail, or some detail internal to a structure—for example, a cut-away view of a machine housing.
When you want to show the details precisely.	
When you want to show the exact relative locations of items close to each other—for example, two switches on a machine.	When you want to show something that doesn't exist or has not occurred—for example, a rendering of a concept car before a model is built.
To prove something happened or exists—for example, someone's signature on a document, or the crumpled fender resulting from a car crash.	When you want to reduce detail in order to draw attention to something—for example, a tracing of a photograph in order to show how two parts of a machine relate to each other.
When you need visual proof and you don't have time or skill to draw it out.	

A complete course in two-dimensional layout and design cannot be presented in a public speaking textbook. However, a few basic principles will make it easier for you to develop your own visual supporting materials and to judge the quality of visual aids that others may develop for you.

The Rule of Thirds

Two-dimensional visual aids are more pleasing when design elements conform to what people expect. The **rule of thirds** is based on the idea that the center of interest in your visual aids should fall on (or close to) imaginary intersections that divide the plane into thirds, both horizontally and vertically.

Exhibit 12.16 shows how those imaginary lines have guided the composition of three photographs. Exhibit 12.17 shows how a student applied the rule to a visual aid with text only.

EXHIBIT 12.16

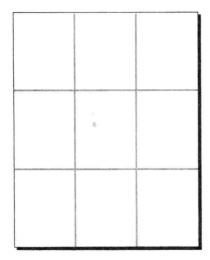

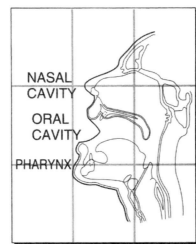

EXHIBIT 12.17

Straight Lines and Curved Lines

Straight lines suggest strength and purpose, while curved lines suggest calm and delicacy (Exhibit 12.18). If you want to suggest vitality, energy, and action, incorporate angles and straight lines in your visual aid. If you want to suggest tranquility or peace, use curved lines.

Lines can also suggest movement. If you draw the eye from right to left along a line, you pull viewers into the image. When eye movement is from right to left, viewers feel compelled to follow the line of movement. An image that draws the eye from left to right suggests movement toward the viewer. Exhibit 12.19 illustrates this principle.

The Balance of Triangles

Triangular compositions typify most Western painting and drawing. Use this idea when you design visual material and the layout will look fine. Exhibit 12.20 illustrates the balance of triangles.

Eye Movement and Negative Space

In a visual aid, blank space can be more important than the filled area. Graphic designers use white space to control eye movement. Leave a lot of white space around the text and any drawings or pictures. Make it easy for the receiver. Also, don't crowd very much language onto a single visual aid. Listeners must be able to read and register the text at a glance.

Exhibit 12.21 illustrates the power of white space in controlling eye movement. Notice that one of the illustrations is so full of material that negative space is virtually nonexistent. Consequently, the eye does not know where to focus. In the other illustration, the eye immediately comes to rest on the important feature of the visual aid.

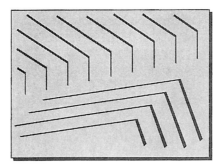 

EXHIBIT 12.18

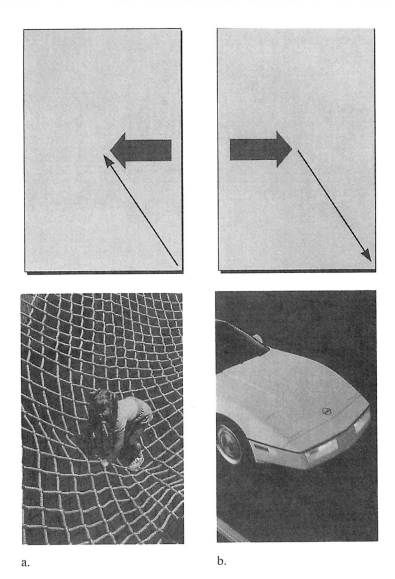

a.   b.

EXHIBIT 12.19

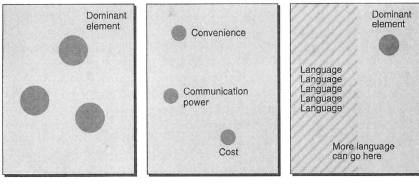

EXHIBIT 12.20

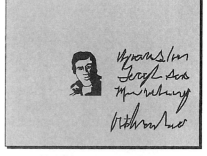

Too full: no negative space.　　　　　Negative space moves the eye.

EXHIBIT 12.21

Sketches and Illustrations

Carefully rendered drawings, paintings, or other art illustrations are usually more trouble than they are worth for visual supporting material. With the wealth of clip art available—much of it free for the taking on the Internet—you will have little trouble finding appropriate sketches and illustrations to support most of your ideas. Still, developing a simplified sketch is sometimes necessary to illustrate your idea. A detailed, carefully labeled technical illustration will not be helpful. *Keep your sketch or illustration as simple as possible.* A freehand cartoon often works better than a carefully rendered drawing.

Compare the three drawings in Exhibit 12.22. Each drawing illustrates the same technical idea. Which one do you think carries the idea more forcefully? Notice that lack of labeling in the visual aid diagram does not inhibit the visual aid's ability to communicate the speaker's goal.

Student speakers occasionally try to reproduce the kind of illustrative materials they find in their textbooks. A speaking situation, however, presents different kinds of receiving problems for listeners than reading situations present for readers. Readers have time to study illustrations in a textbook. Indeed, students often study the illustrative materials without reading the text. So, authors tend to present more information in textbook illustrations than listeners could possibly understanding a public speaking situation. Listeners do not have time to study a visual aid. They must assimilate information at the speaker's speed.

Exhibit 12.23 reproduces a visual aid used to support a student's speech on rock climbing. The student had just returned from a two-week camping experience in the mountains. She wanted to show how climbers can hang from the surface of sheer rock and to describe the devices that make this feat possible.

The label "Mountaineering" does not contribute anything special to this visual aid. Without it, however, the visual aid would be incomprehensible. If you look carefully, you can make out the silhouette of an individual hanging from the face of the rock. The two objects to the right show the anchoring devices the student planned to describe.

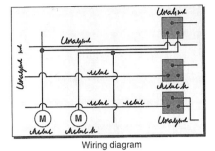
Wiring diagram

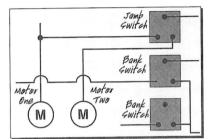
Simplified wiring diagram

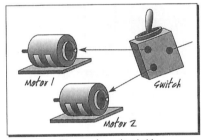
Diagram for a visual aid

EXHIBIT 12.22

These items are not immediately obvious or recognizable. Since the student's purpose was to show how rock climbers anchor themselves to the surface of sheer rock, she should have developed a separate drawing for each of the anchoring devices (see Exhibit 12.24).

Language and Lettering

Do not clutter a visual aid with extraneous language. Rather, include only enough information to guarantee that the visual aid will be immediately understandable. Compare the two drawings in Exhibit 12.25. One drawing is cluttered with labels. In the other, all extraneous language has been removed, with the result that the visual aid seems cleaner, simpler, and easier to grasp.

Most speech visual aids consist entirely of language—for example: outlines and other word-only visual aids that help listeners to follow your ideas. These can powerfully support your speech. They also have

EXHIBIT 12.23

the potential for confusing listeners if they are overcomplicated. Let simplicity guide your design choices.

You do not need elaborate computer programs to make serviceable OHP transparencies. You can make an effective transparency by laying a piece of clear plastic over tablet paper and using the lines to guide you as you letter the plastic with a felt-tip pen. Or you can mount a visual aid on 8-by-11-inch paper and then use a copy machine to convert it into an OHP transparency.

Piton

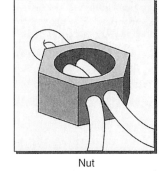

Nut

EXHIBIT 12.24

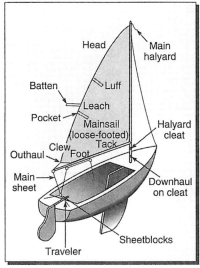

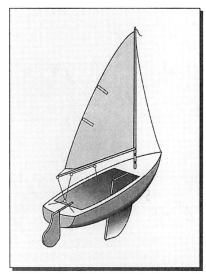

Too much language   Language removed

EXHIBIT 12.25

Flip charts, chalkboards, and marker boards are commonly found in classrooms and conference rooms. Some speakers elect to use these to generate visual aids "on the fly"—that is, they write down key ideas or terms on these media while delivering their speeches. You also may occasionally use these media, but beware. Your hands may shake when you are under pressure and working in front of an audience. You also risk turning your back on your audience for long periods.

When the nature of the speech requires quality lettering and you do not feel adept enough to tackle it, find someone to help you do it right. In most situations however, your own lettering will be adequate if you remember the following pointers:

1. Print, don't write.
2. Print big.
3. Use block letters.
4. Use the simplest words you can.
5. Eliminate every word you can.

Review and Revise the Final Program

Practice your speech using the final visual aid program. If your visual aids are on a flip-chart easel, practice with the easel. If you are using overhead transparencies, turn on the projector and use the visuals as you practice your speech. You may still discover ways of enhancing the visual aids or of making them more useful to listeners.

EXHIBIT 12.26

QUESTIONS ABOUT COMPUTER-GENERATED PRESENTATIONS	
Question	*Answer*
What about using color?	Use color when the overall "look" is very important or when the color is an important part of the message. Color makes things appear more interesting and it focuses attention. In addition, color adds emotional impact to an image and it helps a viewer to find key areas of focus.
	But be very careful. Color can overwhelm a presentation. And color can be very expensive and difficult to reproduce in a fixed medium such as an overhead projection transparency. You don't have to use color photographs and graphics. Don't do it when your budget won't support it, or when the color might distract the viewer. Be sure all text contrasts with the background.
OHP or computer projection equipment?	Nearly every classroom and boardroom in America has an overhead projector (OHP). Not all have computer projection equipment. <u>You must know what is available in the location where you will make your presentation.</u> And you must know how to use the equipment. You are fortunate if you have access to projection equipment. With it you can animate your presentation, dim points you have already discussed, and move seamlessly from one visual aid to another merely by clicking a button.
What about using animations?	This question assumes you will have available the equipment necessary to display animations. Remember to keep the listeners in mind. Don't use animations just because the equipment lets you. Use animations only when they lend something to the overall impact of the presentation.

If you are using presentation software to produce the visual aids program, then you must answer several additional questions. Exhibit 12.26 asks and answers three of those questions.

Exhibit 12.27 presents tips for using overhead projectors wisely.

How to Use Visual Materials: Matters of Delivery

The skills involved in handling and using visual aids come easily if you think about what your audience needs. Unfortunately, many speakers fail in this regard. Your visuals do not deliver your speech—you do. If you do not have a reason for a visual aid, don't use one. Focusing audience attention on yourself and your ideas seems far better than presenting a visual which is not motivated by the need to explain or reinforce your key points.

EXHIBIT 12.27

TIPS FOR USING OVERHEAD PROJECTORS

1. Keep your transparencies simple. Resist using all the fancy fonts, borders, colors, and illustrations that you may have available on a computer program.
2. Prefer horizontal to vertical layout. This makes better use of the usual OHP image and screen size.
3. Use large type. People must read your visual aids easily from the back of the room. Generally, do not go much smaller than 24-point bold-faced type unless you know that your farthest audience member will be close enough to read the smaller type easily.
4. Use heads and subheads. These help listeners to focus on content and to understand your ideas.
5. Use less, not more. Limit yourself to two or three key ideas, each expressed in no more than three or four words. If your visual has to be more complex than this for listeners to understand your explanation, consider giving listeners a handout.
6. Do not let background "wallpaper" and other patterns overpower your visual aids. Just because your machine can generate them does not mean you have to use them. Use color instead.
7. Plan the room layout if you can. Work to ensure maximum visibility, both for yourself and your visual program (see Exhibit 12.11).
8. Choose a screen large enough to guarantee people in the back seats will be able to see easily. Raise the screen high enough so that people in the back can see the bottom of the screen. Get an OHP whose lenses will throw the images to the screen without too much distortion.
9. Think about sight lines, and do not put seats in the corners near the front.
10. Ask for a projector stand on wheels so you can move the OHP out of the way when you want to. If the stand has a recessed area for the projector, and a space where you can put your transparencies, so much the better. If possible, set the stand where the projector's lenshead will not be in anyone's sight line.
11. Try to dim the lights immediately above the screen. You can use an OHP in full light, but listeners will see the image better if the lights immediately above the screen are dimmed. One experienced speaker removes the fluorescent tubes from the panel immediately over the screen.

Effective public speakers generally follow a predictable four-step sequence when presenting a visual aid: (1) Introduce the visual, (2) present it, (3) explain it, and then (4) put it away. Exhibit 12.28 presents additional "Dos" and "Don'ts" regarding visual aid use.

SUMMARY

Visual supporting materials can enhance most public speeches, but only if they actually contribute something to the speech. A visual aid is any object, photograph, chart, graph, sketch, or lettered poster that supports a speech or the speaker. Visual aids simplify complexity, con-

EXHIBIT 12.28

HOW TO USE VISUAL AIDS	
Do	*Don't*
Simplify visual materials as much as possible.	Stand between your visual aid and the audience.
Prefer 2-dimensional visual aids. Print big, block letters.	Leave a visual aid on display when it is not in use—unless you have a sound rhetorical reason for doing so.
Use simple words—as few as possible.	
Err on the side of too many visuals rather than too few.	Develop elaborate visual aids.[7]
	Write longhand on a visual aid.
Think about the convenience of using a visual aid.	Assume all necessary equipment will be available.
Design visual aids using the rule of thirds.	Assume everyone in the back row will be able to see a visual aid clearly.
Triangulate the design of visual aids. Use lots of negative space.	Use the chalkboard unless you have a sound rhetorical reason for using it.
Follow this sequence when using a visual aid: (1) introduce it, (2) display it, (3) discuss it, then (4) put it away.	Pass items around for your audience to study while you talk. They will study them, and ignore you.
Place a pencil on the OHP to cast a shadow for a pointer.	Gesture at an OHP with your finger.

trol audience attention, and help you to remain organized while delivering your speech. They also help listeners to organize your ideas, understand abstract concepts, and remember your main points. Visual materials are especially helpful for showing problems, solutions and benefits, processes, procedures, and steps in a sequence.

Before developing a visual aid program, you should think about your key ideas and decide what kinds of visual materials you intend to use and what ideas these materials will illustrate or support. Design thumbnail sketches of each visual aid and make rough visual aids for practice. When you feel satisfied with your visual aids program, produce the finished visual aids and then review and revise your presentation if necessary.

Convenience of use, costs versus benefits, and communication power are the three C's that help you select the right visual medium for your particular situation. Overhead projectors (OHP), coupled with computers and software, may be the ultimate speaking tool. When using OHPs however, resist the temptation to make your transparencies fancy—simple visual aids work best. Also, work to ensure maximum visibility, both for yourself and your OHP visual program.

The best visual materials are simple and accessible. They conform to certain principles of two-dimensional design, such as applying the rule of thirds and using straight and curved lines to create moods.

Experiment with triangulation to produce a pleasing composition, controlling eye movement with negative space, and develop effective sketches, illustrations, and lettering.

When using a visual aid, introduce it, present or display the visual smoothly and quietly, explain it, and then remove the visual from view so that listeners can concentrate on your next point.

KEY TERMS

Accessibility
Communication power
Overhead projector (OHP)

Rule of thirds
Simplicity
Visual aid

APPLICATION QUESTIONS

1. Agree with a group of your classmates to spend some time watching television with the sound off. Count the number of times the picture changes during a two-minute period. Include every camera change, each time the camera angle changes by panning or zooming, and each time language is superimposed on the picture. Notice how these changes are used to focus viewer attention. Now turn the sound on and pay attention to the sounds. How do the sounds and the sights work together? Return to your group and compare notes. Can any of this information be applied to public speaking?

2. This chapter is filled with illustrative materials. Even so, it is not as visually rich as a magazine. Bring a magazine to class. With a group of classmates, go through the magazine looking for examples of curved and straight lines, triangulation, and the use of blank space to control eye movement. Are the examples easy to find? What can you learn from this exercise about developing visual supporting materials for a speech?

IT'S MORE FUN TO KNOW

Vision is the dominant sense mechanism in human beings. All human beings think visually. This is so universal that we humans would be unable to perform even the simplest tasks—such as going from one room to another—without thinking visually.[2] But we do not all think visually in the same ways or with the same level of skill. We have to learn how, and of course, people learn differently. The result is that human beings are different in their ability to locate part of a whole image, and to hold an image in mind. Some find it very difficult to create an image in their minds, while others seem to do it without difficulty. And some people's images are quite sharp while others' images are fuzzy.[3]

These facts demand that oral communication be supported visually.[4] They also demand that you learn to think visually if you wish to develop useful, effective visual supporting materials. You have to observe and practice. Indeed, you may even have to learn to see things more effectively and accurately.[5]

The good news is that you can train yourself. Get a copy of Henning Nelms' *Thinking with a Pencil* (Berkeley, CA: Ten Speed Press, 1981) or Betty Edwards' *Drawing on the Right Side of the Brain: A Course in Enhancing Creativity and Artistic Confidence* (Los Angeles, CA: J. P. Tarcher, 1979). Work through some of the exercises and you will discover you have more talent than you may have thought.

SELF-TEST FOR REVIEW

Mark the following statements: A = Good advice about using visual aids or B = Bad advice about using visual aids.

_____ 1. "Try to present ideas as simply as possible."

_____ 2. "Visual aids can help to simplify complex information."

_____ 3. "A visual aid should not be just words. You ought to use some kind of graphic on every one."

_____ 4. "Remember, visual materials help you control audience attention, so use them often."

_____ 5. "The first and most important criterion for selecting a visual medium is *consistency*."

6. List what you should support with visual aids.

   a. _____

   b. _____

   c. _____

   d. _____

   e. _____

7. Which of the following are **not** recommended steps in developing a visual aid program?

   a. Think about key ideas.

   b. Think about the available communications media.

   c. Develop a rough plan for the visual program.

   d. Develop an outline of visual materials you will produce.

   e. Design thumbnail sketches of each visual aid.

   f. Make "dummy" visual aids full-size, on newsprint sheets.

   g. Produce the finished visual aids in the media you selected.

8. Which of the following is the *best* definition of the rule of thirds?

   a. Divide topics into three main ideas.

   b. Divide a plane into thirds, both horizontally and vertically.

   c. Use one third of your preparation time for audience analysis, one third for speech preparation, and one-third for practice.

   d. People think in threes—therefore, they will best remember what is divided into thirds.

9. What are the two characteristic features of all well-designed visual supporting materials?

   a. Simplicity and accessibility

   b. Convenience and communication power

   c. Creativity and clarity

   d. Low cost and convenience of use

Mark the following true or false.

____ 10. The amount of language on a visual should be limited as much as possible.

____ 11. Eye movement can be best controlled by filling blank space with design elements.

____ 12. Straight lines and angles suggest calm.

____ 13. The virtual standard of Western visual design is a plane divided into fourths.

____ 14. A distributor cap—a small plastic part about the size of half a grapefruit—would be a good visual aid for a speech about the electrical system of a car.

____ 15. Leave a complex visual aid before audience members throughout the speech so they will have plenty of opportunity to understand it.

____ 16. A visual aid is any object, photo, chart, or lettered poster that supports a speech.

Answers: 1. A. 2. A. 3. B. 4. A. 5. B. 6. a. problems, b. solutions and benefits, c. processes, d. procedures, e. steps in a sequence. 7. d, 8. b, 9. a. 10. T. 11. F. 12. F. 13. F. 14. F. 15. F. 16. T.

SUGGESTED READINGS

The following two periodicals constitute the best resources for information on visual aids anywhere. Dozens of other similar periodicals may be found at your local newsstand.

AVC Presentation for the Visual Communicator (Melville, N.Y.: PTN Publishing).

Publish: The Art and Technology of Graphic Design (San Francisco, Calif.: Integrated Media).

INTERNET ACTIVITIES

1. Go to the AltaVista search engine *(http://www.altavista.com/)* and type the words, including quote marks, "free clip art". AltaVista will find more than 5,000 web sites from which you can "download" images. Play with several of these sites, then report your findings to the class.

2. Find the Principles of Design URL of the University of Houston on Line at: *http://www.coe.uh.edu/courses/cuin7317/design.html* Click on several of the principles from the *Language of Art* page. Share anything you have learned your classmates.

3. For a good list of links about computer graphics on the World Wide Web, go to the URL: *http://ls7-www.informatik.uni-dortmund.de/html/englisch/servers.html* After clicking on several of the links, return to class prepared to discuss what you have found there, and how the information might be useful to your classmates in public speaking.

NOTES

1. "UNESCO And The Elimination of Illiteracy: Fifty Years of Fight (1946–1998)." *See http://unesco.uneb. edu/educprog/literacy/lit_eng.html*

2. See, for example, D. Hyerle, *Visual Tools for Constructing Knowledge* (Alexandria, VA: Association for Supervision and Curriculum Development, 1996), and, C. Cave, *The Mind MapBook, http://www. ozemail.com.au/~caveman/Creative/Mindmap/Radiant.html* (1996)

3. G. C. Rakes, T. A. Rakes, and L. J. Smith, "Visuals to Enhance Secondary Students' Reading Comprehension of Expository Tests, *Journal of Adolescent and Adult Literacy*, 39:1 (1995) 46–54.

4. William Wright, "Business Visualization Adds Value," *IEEE Computer Graphics and Applications,* 18:4 (July-August, 1998), p. 39, and, Donald T. Hawkins, "Information Visualization: Don't Tell Me, Show Me!", *Online*, 23:1 (Jan. 1999), p. 88.

5. Michael E. Patterson, Donald F. Danscreau, and Dianna Newbern, "Effects of Communication Aids on Cooperative Teaching," *Journal of Educational Psychology*, 84, (1992) 453–461.

6. *The New York Times Almanac 1999*, (New York: The New York Times Company, 1998), p. 395.

7. An example of the over-elaborate use of visual aids appeared in the presentations by members of House of Representatives Committee of Managers in the impeachment trial of President Clinton. C-Span Television, January 14, 1999.

CHAPTER 13

DELIVERY

OBJECTIVES

After reading this chapter, you should be able to:

1. Compare and contrast four different methods of delivery (manuscript delivery, memorized delivery, extemporaneous delivery, and impromptu delivery), and explain what is meant by "invisible" delivery.

2. Differentiate between written and oral styles of speaking.

3. List characteristics of your speaking voice that you can control or change.

4. Explain how nonverbal elements, such as gestures, eye contact, and personal appearance, contribute to effective public speaking.

5. Specify four procedures for making your speech practice more effective.

OUTLINE

Objectives
Outline
Abstract
Imagine
Introduction
  Choosing a Method of
    Delivery
    Manuscript Delivery
    Memorized Delivery
    Extemporaneous Delivery
    Impromptu Delivery
  Differences Between Written
    and Oral Styles
  The Speaking Voice
    Rate
    Pitch
    Volume
  Nonverbal Messages
    Gestures

Gestures Related to the
  Speaker's Words
Gestures for Visual
  Punctuation
Gestures That Suggest a
  Speaker's Feelings
  Eye Contact
  Personal Appearance
  and Behavior
  Practicing Your Speech
Summary
Key Terms
Application Questions
It's More Fun to Know
Self-Test for Review
Suggested Readings
Internet Activities
Notes

ABSTRACT

Speakers must choose a method of delivery from four separate approaches: (1) manuscript, (2) memorized, (3) extemporaneous, and (4) impromptu. Although there are times when a speaker may wish to use manuscript or memorized delivery styles, you would be smart to stay with the extemporaneous style in most cases. The extemporaneous style gives you most of the advantages of memorized and manuscript speaking, but none of the disadvantages. In addition, extemporaneous speaking provides certain advantages you cannot have from the other two. If you must speak impromptu or off the cuff, take a moment to organize your thoughts.

The speaking voice can be used to increase awareness and heighten suspense or tension with variations in rate, pitch and volume. Plus, it is possible to learn how to gesture more effectively, and to make and use eye contact. Personal appearance and behavior are part of the whole matter of delivery and these matters are entirely a matter of choice.

Finally, there is no substitute for practice. The more you practice, the more successful your speeches are likely to be.

IMAGINE

When Angela Maes decided to explain the latest fashion trends in swimming suits, she thought wearing the suit while speaking would be the best way to present her ideas. However, when she entered the room fully clothed and then removed clothing as she talked, audience attention focused more on her actions than on her message. In the discussion that followed her speech, it was clear the class wanted to talk about her clothing and the appropriateness of her presentation style instead of the message.

INTRODUCTION

Delivery is the vehicle speakers use to transmit ideas to listeners. This chapter focuses on both the verbal and nonverbal aspects of effective delivery. The setting and the audience often suggest different methods of delivery, such as reading directly from a manuscript, memorizing your speech, preparing an extemporaneous presentation, and delivering impromptu remarks. Language occurs in at least two styles, written and oral. Written style sounds formal and stilted when it is spoken. Oral style sounds more like conversation.

Your speaking voice—in particular, the rate, pitch, and volume of your voice—and your nonverbal messages, such as your gestures, eye contact, and personal appearance and behavior, affect how listeners perceive you and your message. In this chapter, you will learn how to use your speaking voice and gestures to compliment your speech rather than contradict it.

Practicing your speech will help you to polish your methods, style of delivery, your speaking voice, and your nonverbal messages so that all of these elements work together to deliver your message in the most effective way possible.

Delivery refers to using the voice and the body to convey ideas to listeners. Effective delivery concentrates the audience's attention on the message instead of the speaker. Thus, effective delivery should be invisible to the listeners. To illustrate, if a member of your audience would say: "That speaker had a wonderful voice. It was loud and nicely pitched." Or if she said: "I liked the speaker's gestures. They seemed so spontaneous and smooth," you would know your voice or body called listener attention away from your ideas.

In contrast if an audience member said: "That was a dynamite speech. You had a clear idea and your enthusiasm for the subject is contagious," or "I hadn't thought about foreign languages in the way you talked about them," you would know your delivery seemed invisible to the listener—your body and voice did not call attention to themselves and away from your ideas.

Good communication gets the effect you want. Any aspect of your delivery that interferes with reaching that goal is a distraction and should be eliminated. With practice you can go a long way toward making improvements in these matters of delivery. But it takes practice.

Choosing a Method of Delivery

Every speaker must choose the method of delivery for every speech. Should you recite from a manuscript, deliver your speech from memory, speak extemporaneously, or try an impromptu style? There are reasons why you might make any of these choices. But you must choose carefully because your decision will directly affect the likelihood your speech will succeed.

The setting or the audience may suggest the most appropriate method of delivery. Consider what is expected of you in a particular speaking situation, then choose a delivery method consistent with the occasion, your listeners, and your message. As you read about the methods of delivery—manuscript, memorized, extemporaneous, and impromptu—decide which concerns about setting and audiences apply to you and the speech you plan to deliver. Exhibit 13.1 compares and contrasts the four methods of speech delivery.

Manuscript Delivery

You may feel tempted to write out your speech and then read it from the manuscript. **Manuscript delivery** is a style of delivery in which

EXHIBIT 13.1

COMPARISONS OF FOUR METHODS OF DELIVERY			
Manuscript	*Memorized*	*Extemporaneous*	*Impromptu*
The text of a speech is written out, then read from the paper on which it is written, or projected onto a "teleprompter" or other speaker aid.	The text is written out and committed to memory.	There is no prepared text. Rather, the speaker follows a carefully prepared outline and notes, but concentrates most attention on the listeners to assure their attention.	No prepared text nor outline. Speaker works on the "spur of the moment" using a standardized organizational pattern to pull the speech ideas together.

the speaker reads from a written document. Manuscript delivery has a number of disadvantages. Nevertheless, delivering a speech from a manuscript may be appropriate when:

1. You must weigh your language carefully.
2. You must present your material in a specific sequence.
3. You need to use technical assistants for cueing (television, lighting, and so on).

Delivery from a manuscript requires great skill. This speaker has lost contact with the audience. © James L. Shaffer

Important business and government speeches are frequently read from a manuscript. In class situations, however, teachers often discourage manuscript delivery. Exhibit 13.2 describes three major problems that flow from speaking from a manuscript.

If you decide on a manuscript delivery, read the manuscript aloud many times before the actual speech. Be familiar with every word, and be certain of the correct pronunciation. Have at least one dress rehearsal during which you flip every switch, show every visual, and turn each page. Try to make the speech sound spontaneous—as though it is occurring to you for the first time. If you have a problem, go through the speech again as many times as necessary.

EXHIBIT 13.2

THREE MAJOR PROBLEMS OF MANUSCRIPT DELIVERY

Problem	Reason
Eye contact tends to be restricted to the manuscript.	You concentrate on the manuscript and not on the audience because you want to be certain you say everything you have written.
The speech sounds stilted.	There are substantial differences between written and spoken language. (See the section "Differences between Written and Oral Styles" later in this chapter.)
You may appear "wooden."	You are "tied" to the manuscript and cannot deviate from the written material.

An extemporaneous speech is carefully prepared, but it is not memorized and it is not read from a manuscript. © David Turnley/ Black Star/PNI

Memorized Delivery

Memorized delivery is a style of delivery in which the speaker commits the speech to memory and delivers a word-for-word progression of ideas. The advantages of memorized delivery lie in the advance planning the method allows. However, the disadvantages of memorization outweigh the advantages (see Exhibit 13.3). Unless your speaking situation requires a memorized address, you should probably avoid this style of delivery.

Students sometimes resort to memorization so they won't forget what they wanted to say. But memorized speeches create considerable fear because the students then have to worry about memory lapses. Few situations are more agonizing for a speaker and more uncomfortable for an audience than the silence where a forgotten line should have been. Nearly as worrisome is the half-remembered argument, which leaves listeners with an incomplete jigsaw puzzle instead of an idea.

Another problem is that a memorized speech tends to *sound* memorized. Speakers who are preoccupied with remembering every word

EXHIBIT 13.3

ADVANTAGES AND DISADVANTAGES OF MEMORIZED DELIVERY	
Advantages of Memorization	*Disadvantages of Memorization*
You can choose the exact wording.	You can easily forget a sentence or phrase, which can lead to an embarrassing silence.
The timing will be exact.	
You know exactly what you want to say.	Your speech may sound memorized because of a lack of vocal variety, emphasis, and changes in rate.
The sequence of ideas will be precise.	
The subtle implications can be prepared and worded carefully.	It discourages audience response.
	It may increase listeners' apprehension about the speech.
	You cannot be flexible in idea development or change.

tend to speak in either a monotone or singsong pattern that advertises memorization. They lose the vocal emphasis and variety needed to sound interesting or enthusiastic.

Finally, a memorized speech does not give you the opportunity for any audience feedback. When you have decided in advance exactly what you are going to say, there is little built-in incentive to look at the audience since feedback will not change your speech. You tend to be less sensitive to audience reaction. Your speech lacks flexibility, which makes it difficult for you to adapt.

So, although there is occasionally a place for them, manuscript and memorized speech making probably don't have much place in a public speaking classroom. They are really separate skills from basic public speaking. They both have very specialized advantages and difficulties. In learning the elements and practices of good public speaking, you probably have enough to do without trying to master these special forms.

Extemporaneous Delivery

Extemporaneous delivery is planned carefully, but the speaker has minimal notes. It is different from impromptu delivery, which is a no-notes, "off-the-cuff" type of presentation.

Your concern in an extemporaneous speech is presenting ideas and supporting proofs in a logical sequence. Your goal is not a word-for-word progression of ideas. Because you have prepared carefully using an outline, all you typically need are a few notes or your visual aids to remind you of your key ideas in the order in which you plan to present them (see Chapter 9, "Outlining the Speech").

Exhibit 13.4 shows an example note card that helps you to remember your main ideas and the order in which you want to present them. Meta-notes are notes about your notes. Use them to remind yourself of such things as preplanned movement or where and when to use visual materials (see Exhibit 13.5).

Practice with your notes to increase confidence and give yourself a better command of your ideas. Each time you go over the speech, you develop and refine your language.

Extemporaneous speaking has most of the advantages of memorized speaking and manuscript speaking, but few of the disadvantages. Plus it seems more direct and spontaneous to the listeners than either memorization or manuscript reading. You are free to interact with audience members and listeners are more likely to view you and your speech as an interpersonal event that involves them as individuals.

Students sometimes worry that the extemporaneous method does not afford them any help in remembering what they are going to say next. However, notes, visual aids, and practice provide all the basic tools you need to be successful. Exhibit 13.6 lists characteristics of extemporaneous delivery and potential advantages of these characteristics.

EXHIBIT 13.4

EXAMPLE NOTE CARD

```
        HEART ATTACKS
   I. CAUSES
      A. Smoking
      B. Poor Diet
      C. Heredity
  II. RECOMMENDATIONS
      A. Don't Smoke
      B. Rest and Relax
      C. Diet
```

An example note card. A few handheld notes will help you remember your main ideas and their sequence while not bogging you down and taking your attention away from the audience.

EXHIBIT 13.5

META-NOTES ON A NOTE CARD

```
  II.  King had prosperous family life.    Slide 6
       A. Rev. King, Sr., was pastor.
       B. Nice Atlanta house             Slide 7

                      Slides 8, 9, 10
  III. King was good student.
       A. Atlanta U Lab. School      Slide 11
       B. Booker T. Wash. H. S. (grad. at 15)   Slide 12
       C. Morehouse College (grad. at 19)
                  Read: p. 43, as marked
```

Meta-notes serve as reminders to attend to other aspects of the speech, such as when to display visual aids or read quotations.

EXHIBIT 13.6

CHARACTERISTICS OF EXTEMPORANEOUS DELIVERY

Characteristic	Advantages of the Characteristic
Speaker engages in extra preparation and practice.	Increases speaker's confidence and spontaneity.
Speaker uses minimal notes.	Allows speaker to have more audience contact and feedback.
Speaker talks directly to listeners.	
Speaker uses visuals as notes (see Chapter 12, "Supporting Ideas Visually.")	Greater "conversational tone" in the speaker's voice.
	Visuals beneficial for both audience and speaker.

Impromptu Delivery

Impromptu delivery is speaking without preparation or advance planning. It is "spur-of-the-moment" speaking with no notes. Speech teachers generally do not assign impromptu speeches. If however, you know enough about a subject and have been asked to share your ideas without notice, the following techniques for impromptu speaking may be helpful:

1. Take a moment to organize your thoughts. Ask for this time. No one will be offended by the momentary delay, and your speech and your credibility will benefit.

2. Make a few notes. Just a word or two can stimulate a complete idea. Begin by identifying the point you want to make or the position you want to take. Then quickly sketch out the subpoints.

3. Organize around a simple, repetitive pattern. Many speakers who find themselves in this kind of situation rely on a familiar approach. They "tell them what they're going to tell them, tell them, and then tell them what they've told them." That technique makes it easy for both the speaker and the audience to remember the main ideas.

Differences Between Written and Oral Styles

Written style refers to a style of language usage that may be fairly complex, rather abstract, and formal in expression. These may be desirable characteristics for written material. However, when read aloud, these same characteristics may seem confusing to listeners, and hard to understand.

In the same way, speakers who use a written style of speaking, sound like they are reading from books or prepared papers. They seem to lack spontaneity or real enthusiasm. The following passage from a student speech is a good example of the written style:

> We need to do more to encourage people to live in rural areas. At an increasing rate, the population is moving from rural to urban living. Most striking is the fact that the urban population increased by nearly 2 percent from 1980 to 1990.[1] If the flight from rural America continues, in the early part of the 21st century there will be literally no one living on farms. Now, the percentage is at an all-time low of less than 25 percent of our people. We cannot permit this flight to the cities to continue. It will mean the end of the American way of life as we have known it. It is our duty to preserve the family farm and do all we can to encourage our youth to remain in rural areas so our heritage can be retained.

This is not the way people talk in normal conversation. It is much more stilted and formal, uses long words, and does not have the repetition listeners need. Here is another version of the same message—presented in oral style. **Oral style** refers to a style of language usage characterized by short words, repetition of ideas, and use of contractions.

> We're living in a technology age. One commentator said recently that the move to technology in the US is like the Industrial Revolution. It's changing the entire way that we do business, correspond with other people (via e-mail), do our banking, and keep our records. For many of us, if our computers fail it seems to be a real problem to write a letter by

hand. Can you imagine a world without credit cards, television, or CD's? Well, all of that is technology and it's in the middle of our lives.

This passage sounds more like talk. So, although there is occasionally a place for them, manuscripts probably don't have much place in a public speaking. Both memorized delivery and manuscript reading encourage written style. When speakers talk as if they are reading from books or prepared papers audience members often do not feel compelled to listen. They may even wonder why you have not just sent them a document to read for themselves. Extemporaneous delivery, on the other hand, relies on oral style, which tends to free you from your notes and allow you to act more spontaneously. This in itself tends to attract listeners' attention.

Exhibit 13.7 compares and contrasts the oral and written styles. classroom. It is obvious why the oral style is more appealing to listeners. Simple, informal language and lots of repetition make listening easy.

The Speaking Voice

Would you recognize your own voice if you heard it played back on a tape recorder? Some people do not recognize their own voices because the sound inside their heads is different from the sounds others hear when they speak. Many elements contribute to the unique sound of a voice, including the different size of our vocal chords, the size and shape of our heads, our sinus cavities, and the size and shape of our mouths. These are not characteristics you can change.

You do have some control over several characteristics of your speaking voice however, and you can alter these to your speaking advantage. These characteristics are rate, pitch, and volume. To understand and to manage these characteristics is to have control of the transmission system for your speech.

Exhibit 13.7

Comparison of Oral and Written Styles	
Oral Style	*Written Style*
Short words	Polysyllabic words
Short sentences	Long sentences
Much repetition	Little repetition
Contractions	Few contractions
Concrete terms	Abstract language

Rate

The term **rate** describes the speed at which a person speaks. A typical rate of speech is approximately 140 to 160 words per minute. People speak at a variety of rates. For example, President John F. Kennedy spoke at about 180 words per minute, with bursts up to 200 words per minute. President Franklin Delano Roosevelt spoke much more slowly, in a smooth, melodious voice, at about 120 words a minute.

Many famous speakers change their rate of speaking within their speech. Exhibit 13.8 shows how rate changes affect the message.

The rate at which we speak bears greatly on how audiences perceive us. There is the stereotype of the "fast talker" who is trying to put something over on us. If someone is in a hurry, it often suggests they don't want us to take time to evaluate carefully what they have to say. However, a measured, deliberate rate of delivery hints at a thoughtful consideration of ideas.

The pressure of the public speaking situation often causes beginning speakers to rush through a presentation. The result of this rush is that their listeners not only have trouble understanding them, but also, the listeners are less likely to believe what the speaker says.

All of us can learn from the business world. Increase your ethical perception by speaking in a slow, measured rate. Act interested in what you have to say by facial expression and gestures. Stand still, except when movement is appropriate. You are much more likely to be perceived as an ethical, credible communicator if you follow these guidelines.

You send many message to your audience by the rate of your speech. You signal listeners that you are uneasy. The faster you speak, the more likely the listeners will sense your anxiety. Listen to yourself and if necessary, attempt to speak slowly. You can monitor your rate by tape-recording a practice run-through of your speech.

You tell listeners if ideas are important. Speakers do not rush through material that they think is important for others to understand.

Your rate tells listeners how important they are to you. When you are concerned with people, you take your time talking to them. A frantic rate of delivery suggests you only want to be finished with the

EXHIBIT 13.8

HOW RATE CHANGES AFFECT THE MESSAGE	
Fast Rate	*Slow Rate*
Conveys a sense of urgency	Stresses the idea
Can show anger and surprise	Can show sadness or concern
Is less persuasive	Is more persuasive

Source: George B. Ray, "Vocally Cued Personality Prototypes: An Implicit Personality Theory Approach," in *Communication Monographs, 53,* 1986: 266–76.

speech, that you are not vitally interested in your listeners and in getting the ideas across to them.

Also remember that the larger the audience, the slower you have to speak. Most of us get into a rhythm that is appropriate for talking to a small group and forget that floor noise, distance, poor lighting, and other distractions require a much slower delivery. Unlike the conversational setting, your listeners cannot see you easily in public address, hear each nuance of your voice and its inflection, pick up on micro-momentary changes in muscle tone, or read your lips. You can help to compensate for these disadvantages by taking your time and slowing down.

Could learning to control your voice ever introduce an ethical problem? For example, is it sincere if you practice, then control rate, pitch and volume so that you "sound" sincere?

Pitch

Pitch is the level of the vocal sound at which your voice mechanism works with maximum efficiency and ease. Your natural pitch is the level at which you usually carry on conversation. Singing voices are also classified by pitch into groups of sopranos, altos, tenors, baritones, and basses. You can learn to control and vary your pitch for rhetorical effect.

A higher than normal pitch shows emotion or excitement. Listen to the excited voices at an athletic contest or the vocal pitch of your close friend who tells you about an "A" on a final exam. A lower than normal pitch suggests that a person is intense or quite serious. When an event requires us to express ourselves carefully and seriously (such as giving testimony in court or giving an order to another worker), we attempt to lower our pitch to demonstrate intensity and feeling.

Changes in pitch reflect our feelings. Sometimes, we are not even conscious of our pitch changes, but listeners hear the difference. People in public speaking classes often speak at a higher than normal pitch. Their voices reflect the tension and excitement of appearing in front of a group. Usually, speakers' vocal pitch and rate return to normal after they become convinced that they can succeed.

A short-term change up or down in pitch within a sentence or short passage is called **inflection.** For example, rising inflection (pitch) at the end of a sentence suggests a question, while a downward inflection is associated with the completeness of a thought and gives emphasis to an idea. In the middle of sentences, the rising and falling of our voices emphasize certain points and minimize others. In the following sample sentences, give rising inflection to the word or words that are underlined:

> Fred *did* understand the assignment for tomorrow.
>
> Did *Marie* buy that new Mercedes?
>
> Is a vacation in New Hampshire is a *special event?*
>
> Without a *ticket* to the concert, you have *no chance* of getting in.

I refuse to spend *another cent* on food from that lousy restaurant.

Now experiment with changing the meaning of these sentences by moving the inflection to other words. The message can change drastically.

Thus, rising or falling inflections within sentences emphasize different words and ideas. Voices without inflections are called "flat." Individuals with "flat" voices do not introduce any vocal variety into what they say, and for that reason, their voices are uninteresting. Their lack of inflection also suggests that all of their words are equally important.

Your knowledge of pitch and inflection gives you important tools to improve the effectiveness of your delivery. Vary your pitch and use changes in inflection to emphasize ideas or words within statements. Pitch and pitch changes within sentences can alter much of what you say.

Volume

The **volume** or loudness of your voice determines whether or not people can hear you. You have adequate vocal volume if the people seated farthest from you do not have to strain to hear your words. Listening should be easy for them. And you don't have to strain to accomplish this goal. Ask if they can hear you, and if necessary, adjust your volume accordingly.

Outside the classroom, the setting for a speech may be noisy or large. You may need to use a microphone to enhance your volume so that everyone can hear you. Do not hesitate to ask audience members if they can hear you. Then make whatever adjustments are necessary to assure that they can.

Embrace the attitude that your message is worthwhile, that you will speak out and speak up. People are lazy listeners. Make it easy for them to listen to you by speaking at a volume level that keeps their attention.

Nonverbal Messages

You have often heard the statement, "What you do speaks louder than what you say." This statement shows that nonverbal cues are important in communication. The field of nonverbal communication is too complex for a complete exploration in a single chapter. However, if you wish to study further, thorough materials on the subject can be found in some of the "Suggested Readings" at the end of this chapter.

This discussion focuses on those nonverbal elements that play a significant role in effective public speaking: (1) gestures, (2) eye contact, and (3) personal appearance and behavior.

Use gestures and body movements to complement your words, but be sure they appear natural, and that they are consistent with the language and tone of your speech. © Bob Daemmrich/Image Works

Gestures

The word **gesture** refers to movements of the body or parts of the body to express ideas or emotions. When you move your hands or body to help communicate an idea or feeling, you are using gestures to complement your words, to help you emphasize what you say. Gestures are vital to the flow of a speech.[2] Without them, speakers would have to pause more, and listeners would have more difficulty remembering parts of the message. But most of us, most of the time, are unaware of your gestures, facial expressions, body movements, and the like.

If they are going to be credible, movements and gestures must appear natural, be emphatic enough to be noticed, and be consistent with your words. These characteristics are easy to accomplish in a conversation with your best friend—the situation makes it possible for your friend to see and respond to tiny movements and very slight changes in facial expression. In a public speaking situation however, very tiny movements are lost. So gestures must grow larger and more dramatic if audience members are to see and respond to them. At first such gestures may well feel and seem "studied" both to you and to your listeners. You can only learn how to gesture and move effectively in a public speaking situation with practice.

After you have given a speech, ask your speech teacher or one or two of your classmates if your gestures and movements seemed studied and unnatural. Listen carefully to the response. And celebrate if the response is something like: "I didn't notice." In that case gestures and movements were probably invisible to the respondent. If so, they also probably contributed to your speech.

In public speaking especially, three categories of gestures can work with the speaker's words to effectively communicate a message: (1) gestures that relate to the speaker's words—descriptive or abstract, (2) gestures that operate like visual punctuation, and (3) gestures that suggest a speaker's feelings.[3]

Gestures Related to the Speaker's Words

The category **illustrators** refers to gestures that relate to the speaker's words. If the words are concrete, the speaker can use very descriptive gestures. If the message is abstract, the gestures may be less specific, such as when a speaker raises both hands when talking about "Heaven." Exhibit 13.9 describes descriptive and abstract gestures.

President Harry S. Truman was famous for his frequent use of a hand-chopping gesture to emphasize important ideas. The next time you see Al Gore on TV, watch how he motions to indicate feelings about ideas. Some critics have accused Mr. Gore of being dull, not realizing they are responding to his relative lack of gestures. In contrast, critics still name Presidents John F. Kennedy and Ronald Reagan "great communicators." Almost certainly, part of this image came from their use of gestures to reinforce their speeches. Kennedy in particular, used a stabbing index finger motion to indicate strong feelings about ideas.

Gestures can also be used to show divisions or parts of a speech. For example, in talking about two important parts of an idea, when you discuss the first point you show the first part by holding two hands in front of yourself, palms facing each other. Then when you discuss a second part you move your hands slightly, keeping the same space between them, to show that there is another, equally important segment to your discussion. For a second example of punctuation, you can indicate first, second, and third parts by first showing your index finger, then by showing both index and middle fingers, then showing index, middle, and ring fingers at the same time.

Gestures That Suggest a Speaker's Feelings

Speakers who convey feelings about their topic often show these feelings in gestures that do not fit into either of the gesture categories already discussed. Physical action is so important to speaking—especially speaking with feeling—that if people consciously refrained from using gestures while talking, it would damage their train of thought. They would pay less attention to what they were saying and focus more on what they were doing. Thus, gestures that suggest a speaker's

Are planned movements and gestures "phony?" Do they constitute an ethical problem?

EXHIBIT 13.9

DESCRIPTIVE GESTURES AND ABSTRACT GESTURES	
Descriptive Gestures	*Abstract Gestures*
Pointing (to indicate person or object)	Sketching the air with a hand (to show movement of an idea)
Drawing (to show a shape or movement)	Expansion and contraction gesture (to show the scope of the subject)
Waving (to indicate hello or goodbye)	Circular hand movements (to show you mean more than the words)

Source: Mark L. Knapp and Judith A. Hall, *Nonverbal Communication in Human Interaction,* 3d ed. (Orlando, Fla.: Harcourt Brace Jovanovich, 1992), 199–203.

feeling, while not neatly categorized or identified, nevertheless are critical to receiving the speaker's entire message.

To illustrate this idea, imagine a supervisor in a warehouse who is speaking to the warehouse crew. He has discovered they have stacked the barrels much too high for safety and he is afraid for them, so he has called them together. "Come on, you guys," he says, "think about your safety. You don't need to stack those barrels clear up to the ceiling!" His voice conveys his emotion, but so does his gesture. He waves his arm emphatically over his head, pointing to the ceiling.

There is no effective way to plan such gestures. Rather, the best advice is just to let them happen. When you learn to trust your natural tendencies, gestures that convey emotion will come automatically.

Eye Contact

Eye contact refers to the rhetorical act of touching or meeting someone else's eyes—looking at the person to establish a sense of relationship. Because our eyes indicate the object of our attention, eye contact with listeners suggests concern and interest in the listeners. Since vision is the dominant sense mechanism, regular eye contact carries an important part of the overall effectiveness of a speech. In addition to helping audience members feel "connected" to you, eye contact provides you with audience feedback. You see listeners' reactions and notice their interest, or lack of it, and are able to make any necessary adjustments.

Speakers who are interested in their listeners look at them. While that sounds simple, it may seem hard to do. Standing in front of a group of people often makes speakers feel vulnerable. Some students try to feel less threatened by looking at the floor, gazing at note cards for the entire presentation, staring out the window, focusing on a spot slightly above listeners' heads, or looking at the lectern or desk. These avoidance behaviors can ruin an otherwise fine speech. You can "pretend" there is no one else in the room, but whether your pretend or not, the listeners don't go away.

Listeners want—and need—you to make eye contact with them. They use eye contact to decide if you are sincere and if they should believe what you are saying. The eye contact does not have to be long. Most visual attention, even in conversation, lasts only about 3 to 4 seconds. Then we generally look somewhere else before once again looking at the person.

The same approach works in a public setting. Try looking at each person for a few seconds before moving on to another member of your audience. You will find the listeners looking back at you and pleased you care enough about them to make eye contact.

Avoid staring at one person or one part of your audience. Just as you may feel threatened under the constant scrutiny of audience members, a listener may feel threatened if you stare at her or him.

Regular and effective eye contact takes work and practice. During your early speeches concentrate on "sweeping" the room with your eyes.

Personal Appearance and Behavior

Your personal appearance and behavior can help present your message. How you look and what you do speak just as loudly as what you say. If you are confident and well poised, listeners will view you and your message as more believable and interesting. Exhibit 13.10 compares positive and negative speaking behaviors.

Practice Your Speech

Success in speaking is a direct function of the amount and quality of planning and practice. Do not wait until the night before your presentation to begin working with your ideas. You must determine your purpose, analyze the audience, select and narrow the subject, gather materials, and make an outline before you can even begin to practice. And nothing substitutes for practice.

Speech practice sessions will be more effective if you follow certain procedures:

1. **Keep your practice sessions brief and flexible.** In your early practice, go over the speech two or three times each session. Do not worry about the exact language or about forgetting some parts. *Avoid memorizing any part of the speech.*

EXHIBIT 13.10

SPEAKING BEHAVIOR DO'S AND DON'TS	
What to Do	*What to Avoid*
Stand quietly or have a reason for moving.	Don't fidget or play with your hair or clothes.
Smile and appear interested in the listeners.	Don't stand on one leg or wrap our legs around each other.
Approach the front of the room with apparent confidence and interest—even if you don't feel confident and you'd rather be anywhere else.	Don't shuffle to the front of the room and keep your head down.
Return to your seat with apparent confidence, acting satisfied with your presentation.	Don't shake your head and act disgusted with your presentation.

Experiment with your notes and with the way you have organized your ideas. The best time to make changes always comes during practice sessions.

2. **Practice in different settings.** You do not have to wait until you are alone or in a vacant classroom to practice your speech. You can run through it while driving to work or walking your dog. Try to present your speech to at least one of your close friends. That will give you another practice opportunity and the chance to receive some honest suggestions from someone you trust.

3. **Practice with your visual aids and mechanical equipment.** If you plan to use visual materials, prepare them before you speak. Then practice using them. Flip charts do not flip themselves, and overhead projectors must be aimed and focused carefully. Experience in using pointers, placing transparencies in the proper direction, and leaving slides projected long enough for the audience to understand them is important.

4. **Practice until you are comfortable.** As you first practice your speech, you make changes until the ideas and general language seem right. When you are comfortable with your ideas and language, stop practicing. With good planning, you should reach this stage a day or two before you speak. Then you can relax and just add any "finishing touches" you think are appropriate.

Summary

Delivery is the verbal and nonverbal expression of ideas, feelings, and impressions, and involves using the voice and the body to convey a message to listeners. Good delivery is invisible; that is, delivery is effective when listeners do not "see" or pay attention to any aspects of the delivery but instead concentrate on your message.

The setting and the audience may suggest the most appropriate method of delivery. Manuscript delivery and memorized delivery are usually avoided because they discourage audience responses, sound stilted, and do not allow speakers to be flexible. Impromptu delivery also tends to be avoided because it involves speaking without preparation or advance planning. Extemporaneous delivery, on the other hand, increases speakers' confidence and spontaneity, allows for more audience contact and feedback, and helps to make the speech an interpersonal event.

The language you use in presenting your ideas is part of the impression you convey to your audience. Oral style is characterized by short words and sentences, much repetition, concrete terms, and contractions, while with written style, statements are longer, language is more complicated, and there is less repetition.

During a speech you communicate with your voice and through nonverbal messages. The effective speaker talks at a rate all people can understand, varies pitch and inflection to emphasize ideas or words, and speaks loud enough that all listeners can hear. Nonverbal elements that play a significant role in effective public speaking are gestures, eye contact, and personal appearance and behavior. These should all visually compliment your message, appear spontaneous, and not call attention to themselves. Practice your speech in brief sessions and different settings. Practice with your visual aids and equipment in advance.

KEY TERMS

Delivery
Extemporaneous delivery
Eye contact
Gesture

Impromptu delivery
Manuscript delivery
Memorized delivery
Oral style

Pitch
Rate
Volume
Written style

APPLICATION QUESTIONS

1. Think of a speech you heard recently. What speaker behaviors do you remember most clearly? Did they add to or detract from the message? Were these behaviors verbal or nonverbal? Which type seemed most important in the speech?
2. Of the prominent speakers you have heard, who is the most effective? What method of delivery does this person use? Why do you think that the speaker has chosen that method? Identify the individual's speaking strengths and weaknesses.
3. What are the most common nonverbal behaviors you see exhibited in classroom presentations? How do they contribute to or detract from speaker effectiveness?

IT'S MORE FUN TO KNOW

From the time of the ancients, we have known that effectiveness in communication involved "the good person speaking well." Effective delivery was an important element from the very beginning. More recently, Erving Goffman emphasized that the way we behave in public is similar to the performance of an actor on stage, creating impressions and sending messages.[4] We also know that delivery suggests to listeners the underlying intent of the speaker.[5] If there was any doubt about the role that our personal activity plays in public communication, the study of Levy and McNeill documents the high relationship between speech and gestures.[6] The effective integration of physical behavior and the way that we present ourselves to listeners is crucial to successful message sending and receiving.

SELF-TEST FOR REVIEW

Mark each of the following as either true (T) or false (F).

1. It is possible to determine a person's feelings by the sound of his or her voice.   T   F
2. When you are speaking to a large audience, you should increase your rate slightly.   T   F

3. When you present an impromptu speech, you talk from a few notes on a topic you prepared in advance.   T   F

4. Eye contact with the audience is an important component of nonverbal delivery.   T   F

5. Oral style makes use of slightly longer and more complex sentences than written style.   T   F

6. Extemporaneous delivery refers to a style of presentation that is carefully prepared but that has a conversational, direct approach.   T   F

7. Audiences tend to discount a speaker's physical appearance.   T   F

8. An important principle of speech practice is to know the material word for word so you won't forget anything.   T   F

9. Using effective delivery to make the correct impression at the beginning of a speech can have a major effect on the rest of the speech.   T   F

Answers: 1. T, 2. F, 3. F, 4. T, 5. F, 6. T, 7. F, 8. F, 9. T.

SUGGESTED READINGS

Brigance, William Norwood. *Speech Composition.* New York: Appleton-Century Crofts, 1937, 1953. This is one of the classic works on preparing and delivering a speech. Its principles have been adopted in various forms by virtually all public speaking teachers. For an interesting and comprehensive study of public communication and the constancy of its presentation, this book is the prime source.

Hickson, Mark L., III, and Don W. Stacks. *NVC—Nonverbal Communication: Studies and Applications.* 3d ed. Dubuque, Iowa: Brown & Benchmark, 1993. This work is a veritable annotated bibliography of the research literature on nonverbal communication, but it also includes lucid explanations of scholars' theoretical and practical approaches to nonverbal communication.

Knapp, Mark L., and Judith A. Hall. *Nonverbal Communication in Human Interaction.* 4th ed. New York: Harcourt Brace ,1996. This latest revision of a standard work offers a wealth of illustrative and scholarly information on the communicative effect of physical and vocal cues. The references and the array of investigations into this area of communication make this a valuable reference source for anyone interested in nonverbal messages.

Joseph A. DeVito, Michael L. Hecht, and Laura K. Guerrero (ed) *Nonverbal Communication Reader.* Chicago: Waveland Press, 1998. This is a solid, easy to read contribution to the literature.

INTERNET ACTIVITIES

1. Go to the URL: *http://www.speakdyn.com/index2.htm* and study the photographs of Dr. Bennie E. Bough, a professional speaker. Decide if you think the photographs of Dr. Bough suggest an effective speaker, then bring your notes to share with your classmates.

2. Go to the URL: *http://www.goto.com/* and type the words "speech gestures" (without the quotation marks). Click on "find it." Browse through some of the essays and articles you find there, then bring your notes to share with your classmates.

3. Are you surprised by the extent of interested shown at the Carnegie Mellon Interactive Systems Laboratory interest in the relationship between speech and gestures? Check it out at: *http://www.is.cs.cmu.edu/ISL.research.html*

4. Who would think to own a domain name "speakers.com?" Try the URL: *http://www.speaking. com/* browse through their web site, then share with the class not only what you found there, but also what you think about what you found.

5. Go to the URL *http://www.metafind.com/* and enter terms such as speech delivery or gestures. This is one of the most powerful yet discrete "search engines" available. Look carefully at the interesting "sorted" results it provides you and then click on the ones that appear most useful. This will be a most productive and interesting activity.

6. An interesting site, with an historical perspective on the issue of delivery is *http:humanities. byu.edu/rhetoric/delivery.htm,* a site maintained by Brigham Young University. It will provide you with the background for rhetoric in addition to excellent contemporary applications.

7. The Virtual Presentation Assistant from the University of Kansas-Communication Department can be found at *http://strategis.ic.gc.ca/SSG/mi04464e.html.* In the words of the site, it "offers guidelines and links to help you present your speech effectively." Especially helpful are materials on Guidelines for Effective Delivery and Format of Delivery.

8. Do you think the National Speakers Association is concerned about effective speech delivery? Check out their WWW web site at *http://www.nsaspeaker.org/* and come to class prepared to discuss your findings.

NOTES

1. *The New York Times Almanac* (New York: Penguin Putnam, Inc. 1999), p. 264.

2. Jurgen Streeck, "Gesture as Communication I: Its Coordination with Gaze and Speech," *Communication Monographs,* 60:4 (December 1993), 275–299.

3. *Ibid.*

4. Erving Goffman, *The Presentation of Self in Everyday Life* (Garden City, NY: Doubleday/Anchor Books, 1959).

5. Valerie Manusov, "Perceiving Nonverbal Messages: Effects of Immediacy and Encoded Intent on Receiver Judgments," *Western Journal of Communication,* 55:3 (Summer 1991), 235–253.

6. Elena T. Levy and David McNeill, "Speech, Gesture, and Discourse," *Discourse Processes*, 15:3 (July-September 1992), 277–301.

PART 5

Common Types of Speeches

© Bob Scott/Archive Photos/PNI

CHAPTER 14

INFORMATIVE SPEAKING

OBJECTIVES

After reading this chapter, you should be able to:

1. Explain why listeners must know your speaking goal is to inform.

2. Name, define, and explain three ways of characterizing informative speaking.

3. Name, define, and choose appropriately among the four kinds of informative speeches.

4. Describe how to develop each of the four kinds of informative speeches.

5. Name and explain four guidelines for informative speaking.

6. List seven techniques for generating attention and interest.

7. Explain how to keep an informative speech simple.

8. List ways of making an informative speech credible.

9. Describe techniques for making informative speeches memorable.

OUTLINE

Objectives
Outline
Abstract
Imagine
Introduction
   Ways of Characterizing
     Informative Speeches
    The Speaker's Intention
    Function of the Information
    Listeners' Perception
    Types of Informative
     Speeches
     Demonstration
     Description
     Explanation
   Guidelines for Informative
    Speaking
    How to Generate Attention
     and Interest
     Provide Specific Details
      (Concretion)

Build Suspense
Show Action
Introduce Conflict
Hook Ideas to the Things
   Listeners Already Know
Associate Derived Interest
Tie Ideas to Listeners'
   Self-Interests
Keep It Simple
Make It Credible
Make It Memorable
Summary
Key Terms
Application Questions
It's More Fun to Know
Self-Test for Review
Suggested Readings
Internet Activities
Notes

ABSTRACT

In informative speaking, ideas are passed from a speaker to an audience. The message can be as simple as explaining how a pump pulls water from a well or as complex as a discussion of how intelligence is tested.

A speech to inform differs from a speech to persuade in three ways. (1) The speaker's intention is to inform rather than persuade. (2) The information contained in the speech works to inform rather than to persuade. (3) Listeners perceive the speech either as informative or persuasive.

Informative speeches define, demonstrate, describe, or explain something. To accomplish any of these goals, speakers must generate listener attention and interest, keep the language and organizational structure simple, build credibility for themselves and their ideas, and make the message easy for listeners to understand, retain, and recall.

IMAGINE

Every Wednesday morning at nine the management group at a local chemical plant meets to review the progress they are making toward their goals and to make adjustments in their planning where necessary. From time to time they invite employees to give progress reports and proposals at this meeting.

Joe Munos had that assignment recently. His immediate supervisor assigned him the task to "tell the management group how we're doing on installing the new rail car unloading equipment. They'll want to know where we stand, how long it'll take to finish, and how we're doing on the budget." The assignment, in essence, was for Joe to give a simple speech to inform—a scenario that happens every day in almost every organization in the land.

INTRODUCTION

The essence of informative speaking is transmitting ideas from one person's mind to another person's mind. For example, one of an instructor's primary function is to convey information. So in all your formal education you have been exposed to various forms and styles of informative speaking.

Exhibit 14.1 describes the steps effective public speakers follow when preparing to inform. This checklist will be helpful as you plan for and prepare your informative speaking assignments.

Ways of Characterizing Informative Speeches

Speeches to inform differ from speeches to persuade on the basis of three characteristics. The first is the speaker's intention—how does the speaker categorize the speech? Second, what is the function of the information in the speech—does it teach or explain, or does it support some argument? Third, how do listeners perceive the speech? The comparison of the three characteristics that follows will give a better understanding of both informative and persuasive speaking and also will help you know what you must do to get the desired response from listeners.

EXHIBIT 14.1

STEPS IN PREPARING AN INFORMATIVE SPEECH	
What to do	*Pointers*
Select your topic and do research.	See Chapter 4, "Selecting and Narrowing Your Topic." Go with what you find interesting. Stay with what you know.
Analyze your audience.	See Chapter 5, "Audience Analysis." Be as realistic as you can. Do not imagine listeners know more than they do. Look for ways to tie your subject matter to their interests and to their worlds.
Decide on a single, observable goal.	See Chapter 4, "Selecting and Narrowing Your Topic." What do you want listeners to do or to be able to do after they have heard your speech?
Identify the main ideas.	What do you have to do to bring listeners to the goal you have in mind for them? Consider writing out each main idea as a single sentence.
Organize the main ideas.	See Chapter 8, "Organizing the Body of the Speech." Given what you want from listeners, which idea should come first? Next?
Develop the supporting materials.	What evidence do you need? What explanations, stories, examples, illustrations, and so on, do you need? See Chapter 6, "The Process of Proving, Discovering and Developming Ideas for Speech," and Chapter 7, "How to Gather Supporting Materials."
Plan the introduction and the conclusion.	See Chapter 10, "Introductions and Conclusions." Remember that an introduction is supposed to get attention and prepare listeners for what is coming. Try to develop their curiosity. Build their desire for your information. State your thesis clearly. Remember the purposes of a conclusion: to summarize the key ideas and to focus listeners' thinking and feelings on your key point.
Develop your visual aids program.	See Chapter 12, "Supporting Ideas Visually." Thumbnail sketches will help. For each main idea, and for each supporting idea, try to imagine how you might use visual materials to strengthen the speech. Keep your specific purpose in mind. After you have a good idea of the overall visuals program, develop a "dummy" of each visual aid.
Practice the speech.	Use the "dummy" visual aid program as you go through the speech. Keeping your specific purpose in mind, do you think anything needs to be changed? Would it be better to rearrange the ideas? Strengthen the support? Eliminate irrelevant materials? Drop one or more of the visual aids? Do you need to add any visual aids?
Complete the final visual aids program.	Develop and number each visual aid in the overall program.
Practice the speech again—and again.	See Chapter 13, "Delivery." Think about your impact on listeners. You will know you are ready to give the speech when you feel confident your ideas make sense, that you know what you are talking about, and that your message "fits" the audience and the occasion. *Do not memorize the speech.*

The Speaker's Intention

The speaker's intention boils down to a simple question: What does the speaker want from listeners? In other words, what does the speaker want listeners to do or be able to do after hearing the speech? Chapter 4, "Selecting and Narrowing Your Topic," revolves around this central question.

Your credibility rests on listeners being sure of your intentions. If they become skeptical about what you are trying to do, they may begin to criticize your ideas or doubt your honesty. Make sure listeners understand what you are trying to accomplish with your speech.

The most important goal of an informative speech is to transmit information. © Miro Vintoniv/Stock Boston

In an informative speech, the speaker wants listeners to know and understand something. For example, a speaker who says, "I want you to know three things before you leave here today" leaves no doubt about an intention to inform. The same would be true of a speaker who began a speech with: "In the late 1990s scientists studied ocean currents by tracking a spilled cargo of Nike sneakers. I'd like to tell you how this worked."

In contrast, a persuasive speaker wants belief or action. Listeners hear something like: "We've just got to take a stand, right now, to protect our environment from industrial pollution." Listeners know immediately from this sentence that the speaker intends to persuade. A call to action in the next sentence ("Won't you please help? Won't you please sign this petition . . . ?") confirms the speaker's persuasive intention.

Function of the Information

Suppose you hear a lecture about technological advances in the housing industry. The speaker says the new technology saves energy, protects the environment, and even helps people with disabilities live more comfortably and more conveniently than previously. How would you classify this speech —to inform or to persuade? The answer lies partly in how the information *functions*. What does the information do? When information explains or clarifies an idea, it informs. But, when information supports or proves an argument, it persuades. If the speaker's goal in this example is to inform, you might expect to hear: "This is how the new technology improves housing." But you would know the speaker has a persuasive goal if you hear: "We must incorporate these desirable advances into the city building code."

Listeners' Perception

Listeners also *perceive* whether a speech is informative or persuasive, and their perception strongly influences how they respond to the speech. For example, some students might think a classroom lecture on the Roman Catholic idea of the Holy Trinity is informative, while others might believe the lecture has a persuasive goal. Any differences in perception flow from what listeners *think* the speaker is up to ("What's this guy doing? Is he trying to convert me?"). It is a speech to inform if the listener thinks the speaker is trying to teach or is giving authoritative information regardless of motive. It is a speech to persuade if the listener thinks the speaker is trying to persuade or has an ulterior motive.

Listeners' perceptions can affect your credibility as a speaker, with powerful influence on the overall effectiveness of the speech. For example, suppose you decide to give a speech that compares and contrasts several brands of sport utility vehicles. You might increase your knowledge of this popular type of vehicle by referring to the magazine *Car and Driver*. And by quoting from a recent issue which compared the Lincoln SUV and the Lexus, you could provide basic information about the comparative strength of the chassis, the handling of the vehicle, and gas mileage (12-14 in the city, 16 on the highway). *Car and Driver* concluded that, although the Lexus was $10,000 more expensive at $46,000, it was still a better buy.

By citing a credible source and the detailed information it provided, you are able to inform your audience of the basic elements of the vehicles in a highly believable way.

Types of Informative Speeches

Although there is some overlap, most informative speeches fall primarily into one of four categories: definition, demonstration, description, and explanation. Because these categories serve distinctly separate informative functions, an effective speaker will learn how to design presentations to accomplish all four.

Definition

Definition refers to the formal statement of the meaning or significance of a word or phrase. You use definition when you want to teach listeners what something means. Exhibit 14.2 illustrates this idea by presenting several titles of successful definition speeches.

Most speakers use one or more of the following techniques when they give definitional speeches:

Comparison and contrast work as definition when you show how something is similar to or different from what listeners already

EXHIBIT 14.2

POSSIBLE TITLES FOR A DEFINITION SPEECH	
What is euthanasia?	What does it mean to pull yourself up by your bootstraps?
What is a bit, and what is a byte?	What is behaviorism?
What is the national debt?	What is a fact?
What is baroque art?	What is artificial intelligence?
What does pro-choice mean to me?	What does post-metaphysical thinking mean?
What are the limits of personal freedom?	What is presentational painting?
What does the grade "C" mean?	What means success?
What does foreign policy mean?	Discipline or child abuse?
What is laser light?	Some call it terrorism.
What does it mean to argue?	
What is friendship?	

know. For example, one student speaker compared his first experience with "virtual reality" to "being inside a living video game."

Synonyms are words that have the same, or nearly the same, meanings as other words. For example, a thesaurus might list the following six synonyms for the abstract word *loyalty:* devotion, allegiance, homage, faithfulness, fidelity, and fealty. **Antonyms** are words that have the opposite meanings from other words. For example, *short* is the antonym of *tall*. Both synonyms and antonyms work well to define some concept or term.

Etymology means study of the history of change in the meaning of a word. Using etymology to define a term, then, involves talking about the word's origins and history. For example, the English word *democracy* comes from the Greek *demos,* meaning "people," and *karetin,* meaning "rule." So *democracy* means "rule by the people." The *Etymological Dictionary of Modern English* and the *Oxford English Dictionary* are two interesting and useful resources.

Differentiation involves defining by separating or distinguishing something from other members of its class. One student speaker wanted his listeners to be able to identify how a swallow is different from other birds. He used a number of drawings to differentiate the swallow from other types. A transcript of part of his speech follows:

> *Swallows have slender bodies and long wings. You can tell a swallow mainly by its tail, however. The tail is deeply forked, and the male's outer tail feathers form long streamers. You can also tell a swallow by watching it fly. The swallow can go as high as ten thousand feet or more. It beats its wings evenly and gracefully, and it makes sudden changes in direction, up or down, side to side, without apparently changing this rhythm, and without any apparent loss of speed.*

Swallows love company. When they migrate, the flocks can have hundreds, even thousands of individuals. When they nest, they usually prefer rural areas and farms. They build their nests in rafters, on beams in sheds, or in open chimneys. Sometimes, you can find swallow nests in the understructures of bridges. In fact, the bridge over the Chickasabogue River in Saraland has a community of swallows that return every year on the same day every year, and within about a hour of the same time they did last year. The nests are built of mud mixed with saliva. They are open at the top and are lined with grass and feathers.

Operational definition means defining something by describing what it does. A student speaker used this approach when she talked about what she, as a physical therapist, does:

I help people get well. For example, one of my patients had a bad automobile accident and was laid up in a cast that held his arms in place for eleven weeks. In that time, the muscles had atrophied. I mean they had gotten weak from not being used. So my job was to help the patient learn to use those muscles again. I started by actually holding his arms and moving them, making the muscles move. Then we added some weight training, and my job was to develop the weight training program. As the patient got stronger and stronger, I increased the weights until he was able to recover most of the strength he originally had.

Demonstration

Is this visual aid easily seen from all parts of the audience? Is it easy to manage? © James L. Shaffer

To **demonstrate** means to describe, explain, or illustrate by examples, specimens, experiments, and the like. When you demonstrate, you exhibit something. Thus, in a demonstration speech, more than in any other kind, you try to show how something works, how it is made, how it is done, or how it happens. If you wanted to show your audience how to judge the difference between a good-quality touring bicycle and a poor-quality bicycle, you would probably have to give a demonstration speech. Most demonstration speeches rely heavily on visual aids, so you may wish to review Chapter 12, "Supporting Ideas Visually." Exhibit 14.3 lists possible titles for a demonstration speech.

One glance at the list of possible titles in Exhibit 14.3 shows that the perceived value of a demonstration speech rests entirely with the listeners. If you already know how to change a car tire, you might perceive a speech on this task to be irrelevant, trite, boring, useless, and redundant. If you do not know how to change a tire and plan to accompany your aged grandmother on a long car trip, that same speech might seem highly relevant and useful.

Exhibit 14.3

Possible Titles for a Demonstration Speech

How an internal combustion engine works

How a cello is made

How to remove water marks from furniture finishes

How to make chicken curry

How to make a mortise and tenon joint the old-fashioned way

How to change an electrical switch

How to encourage wildlife into your garden

How to use your nine-iron

How a sailboat moves upwind

How a laser printer works

How to clean out a pea trap

How to hook your television to your stereo system

How to draw the human form

How to change a car tire

So as you plan a demonstration speech, you must understand and adapt to listeners' needs and interests. If listeners have no interest in the differences between good-quality and poor-quality bicycles, a speech on that subject will likely bore them. Find a way for listeners to identify with your ideas. Then focus and narrow the speech, paring it down to manageable limits.

It takes a long time to demonstrate something. One student decided to teach listeners how to build a router table. Given the time limits of the assignment (6 minutes) and the diversity of the listening audience (twenty-four men and women, ranging in age from nineteen to forty-seven), the student did not have a chance of completing the speech adequately. To demonstrate the particulars, the speaker would have had to show listeners:

* How to select the appropriate building materials
* How to calculate the angles of the various cuts
* How to measure and mark the materials for cutting
* How to set up and use a saw to make the cuts
* How to select and use wood fasteners

Each of these items would take a good deal of time to learn. In addition, the student would have needed a variety of equipment—saws, measuring tapes, and the like. The guidelines in Exhibit 14.4 will help you to succeed when you have to demonstrate something.

Description

Description means using language to picture some object, phenomenon, or event. Descriptive speeches require precise, concrete, and colorful language. As shown in Exhibit 14.5, which lists some possible titles for descriptive speeches, many of the lectures you hear take the form of descriptions.

EXHIBIT 14.4

GUIDELINES FOR DEMONSTRATION SPEECHES

1. Do I know enough about this subject to demonstrate it clearly? To focus it and narrow it down?
2. Can this subject be demonstrated in the time limit?
3. Will the location of the speech support or allow the speech?
4. Can I relate this subject to the interests and needs of my listeners? Do they have a reason to care about this subject? Is this subject appropriate for this audience?
5. Will the necessary visual aids be visible? Easy to manage? Convenient? Readily available?

EXHIBIT 14.5

POSSIBLE TITLES FOR A DESCRIPTIVE SPEECH

Terrorism in America: What's next?

What to look for in a news magazine

Choosing the right watch

How the brain controls emotions

Do you need a spread sheet?

What computer should you buy?

The rape crisis center volunteer

Karate is for everyone

Indo-European origins of English

Cajun country: The Atchafalaya Basin

Coming out: The problems of a homosexual in the U.S. military

AIDS in the new millennium

Descriptive speeches succeed when student speakers take the time to polish their language skills. You may wish to review Chapter 11, "Language: The Key to Successful Speaking," which examines how to use language wisely.

The following is part of a transcript from a student's descriptive speech about what it means to be a stepparent. The student had married a man with two small children. Notice how vividly she uses language:

> *I've had to learn a lot about kids. I've also had to learn a lot I didn't anticipate, and didn't want to know, about myself. For me, step parenting offered the challenge to create a close-knit family in which everyone is happy and contented. This meant I had to love both my stepchildren equally and instantly and to receive love from them instantly.*
>
> *But they didn't want me. One was quiet about it; the other was openly hostile. This came out the first time at one of our evening meals. After their mother died, my husband and his kids lived on his cooking. That meant macaroni and cheese*

dinners. I decided the way to those kids' hearts was through their stomachs, so I spent the better part of that day planning and cooking a gourmet meal. I had veal picatta, with all the trimmings, and a lovely dessert. I set a beautiful table, including cut flowers. I had candles. I served wine for us, milk in stemware for the children. I put classical music on the CD. When everything was ready, I called my new family to dinner.

It was a disaster. The kids hated every minute of it. Ken was trying to make the children appreciate my efforts. "Mind your manners," he'd say. "Sit up straight, and be careful not to break the stemware." I was trying to act as though the meal was no big deal. The kids wanted macaroni and cheese, wouldn't eat the "funny stuff," spit out the veal, and turned up their noses at the bread pudding I'd spent two hours making.

Finally I couldn't stand it. I think I must have proved to those kids I was the wicked stepmother they thought I was.

The checklist of questions in Exhibit 14.6 may help you describe things more vividly.

EXHIBIT 14.6

A CHECKLIST OF QUESTIONS TO HELP YOU DESCRIBE

1. What *size* is the thing you are describing? How does that size compare to something the listeners are likely to know?

2. What is the thing's *weight?* You can say something is "heavy," or you can say something weighs 2,000 pounds. Either way (subjective or objective), you clarify a description of weight by comparing it to something with which listeners are already familiar. For example, you might say something like: "That cat weighed 17 pounds—about twice the weight of a normal tabby."

3. *Shape* can produce difficult description problems. What shape is the thing you want to describe? Square? Round? Triangular? Spherical? Cylindrical? Some objects in nature are irregularly shaped, so you will have to approximate to a geometric form. An example of a shape description is: "The dome house is a hemisphere. It looks something like half of a huge basketball with doors and windows cut in."

4. What *color* describes the thing? The human eye is capable of perceiving more than a million different values and hues, so merely to say a thing is red does not describe it very well. Try comparing the colors to things listeners are likely to know. Say: "blood red," or "dark green, like grass under an oak tree on a sunny afternoon in June."

5. What *material* is the thing you want to describe made of? If you tell listeners what something is made of, they can see it better. Listeners can see a "snowball," but they have to guess what a "ball" looks like. Is it leather? Aluminum? Rubber?

6. How old is the thing? *Age* changes things. They get used, dog-eared, weatherbeaten, worn out.

7. In what *condition* is the thing you want to describe? Age alone may not tell the story. For example, a 1957 Chevy can be a pile of junk or a collector's item in pristine condition.

Explanation

Explanation means making clear by describing or interpreting how something works, how to evaluate it, or why it occurred. Every social, political, or economic issue, every historical event, every process, principle, theory, or hypothesis, every piece of music, artistic movement, novel, movie, or drama bears explanation. Exhibit 14.7 lists titles for possible explanation speeches.

When you explain something, you expose its essence to listeners. The following questions will help you find that essence:

1. What is really important here?
2. How does it work?
3. Why does it work?
4. What difference does it make to me?
5. What difference does it make to my listeners?
6. Can I show my listeners how this subject makes a difference to them?

Guidelines for Informative Speaking

Successful informative speakers (1) generate attention and interest, (2) keep it simple, (3) make it credible, and (4) make it memorable.

How to Generate Attention and Interest

Two skills generate listener attention and interest.[1] First, to get and hold interest, you have to keep your ideas moving, and listeners have to feel the ideas are going somewhere. Second, your ideas must seem relevant to listeners so they have a motive to keep on listening. They must believe your ideas bear directly on them—their hopes, wants, customs, needs, and lives. It is up to you to show and tell the listeners how your ideas are relevant to them.

EXHIBIT 14.7

POSSIBLE TITLES FOR AN EXPLANATION SPEECH	
The national debt	*Gone With the Wind*
Truman's 1948 whistle-stop tour	The defeat of the Spanish Armada
Pro-choice is pro-life	Africanized killer bees
The theory of generative grammar	Evolution
Cubism	How to make home brew
Compost heap	How snow fences work
Madame Butterfly	Backyard boat building

About the worst thing a beginning speaker can do to listeners is leave them wondering: "So what?" Anticipate the "So what?" question and respond to it before it occurs to the listeners and they will lean forward in their chairs with interest. If you do not, listeners will decide there is no reason to keep on listening. Boredom dooms a speech faster than any other audience response.

Exhibit 14.8 describes seven techniques you can use to generate attention and interest.

EXHIBIT 14.8

TECHNIQUES FOR GENERATING ATTENTION AND INTEREST		
Technique	*Don't say*	*When you mean*
Provide specific details.	"It cost a lot"	"The price was eighty-three dollars."
	"You insulted me recently."	"You accused me of cheating last Wednesday afternoon."
	"Last night the weather was lousy."	"It rained four inches between 10 PM and 1 AM."
Build suspense from the questions *who, what,* and *how.*	"John Strange did it."	"John Strange proposed a computer solution to registration that saves all of us time in line and hours of preparing schedules."
	"Sue's solution will solve the shoplifting problem."	"Sue suggests we require that everyone leave their backpacks and cases in free rental lockers outside the entrance. Their property will be safe and so will ours."
	"Melanie was driving over the speed limit."	"Melanie was going 45 MPH in a 20 MPH speed zone. She couldn't see the people in the crosswalk and nearly struck them."
Show action by choosing action words and by using the active voice.	"He knows what should be done."	"He can describe all the events in the homecoming activity in detail."
	"She believes in charity."	"She made a commitment of 50 hours of her time to work at the soup kitchen."
	"The committee agreed to support this cause."	"The committee authorized a $400,000 capital improvement budget for sidewalk repair."
Introduce conflict between opposing interests or principles.	"You only have one choice."	"Either you believe in the sanctity of human life or you support the death penalty for capital crimes."
Hook new ideas to things the listeners already know.	"Centrifugal force is easy to understand."	"You all have ridden on a carnival ride that spun you around at a high speed. You were forced to the outside of the seat. That was centrifugal force."
Associate ideas with things the listeners already find interesting.	"You will like the idea you can win money at a sport."	Teacher to a plane geometry class: "I won $20.00 from Jackson last night playing pool. I won because I understand the geometry of the pool table."
Tie ideas to the listeners' self-interest.	"You should buy this car."	"This car will make you feel powerful. Imagine how proud you will when you drive it."

So, the seven techniques for generating attention and interest—for keeping your ideas moving and making your ideas relevant to listeners—are: (1) Provide specific details (concretion), (2) build suspense, (3) show action, (4) introduce conflict, (5) hook ideas to the familiar, (6) associate derived interest, and (7) tie ideas to listeners' self-interests. Some of these may bear further explanation.

Provide Specific Details (Concretion)

The term **concretion** refers to the act or process of making something real, tangible, or particular. You make something concrete when you ground it in specific facts, actual circumstances, and conditions. For example:

> Horace Greeley was correct when he said "Go West, young man, Go West." That statement certainly is accurate if we apply it to jobs in the future. Nearly two thirds of the job growth from 1998-2025 will be in cities west of the Mississippi.[1]
>
> We all have an idea how defeat feels, but sometimes it's difficult to describe. Former President Jimmy Carter, who both won and then lost a campaign for president, summed up how it felt to lose: "Show me a good loser, and I'll show you a loser."[2] Or, as Adlai Stevenson, a two time loser in his candidacy to be president said, quoting Abraham Lincoln " . . . He said he felt like a little boy who stubbed his toe in the dark. He said he was too old to cry, but it hurt too much to laugh."[3]

Build Suspense

Suspense means mental uncertainty and excitement. When listeners cannot anticipate how something will turn out, or when they know how it will turn out, but they don't know when or how, they pay attention. Knowing this, all the great speakers of history learned to be great storytellers. They used narratives—stories, accounts, tales, and parables—to drive their ideas home.

Steven Spielberg certainly has been a contemporary master of this art via the movies. Consider the stories he has told in Raiders of the Lost Ark, E.T., and Schindler's List. The latter was one of the great message films about World War II and the Jews.

Show Action

Here is how Don Wright, a runner, used the principle of showing action to help his listeners pay attention. Don did not say merely, "He ran a marathon." His listeners could not have seen that. Rather, because he knew the subject from personal experience, Don compelled his student audience to listen with this narrative:

> For the first few miles he was part of the pack, running easily at a pace that covered a mile every seven minutes. By the eighth mile, the pack had thinned to sprinkles—four runners here, two more there, a group of three up ahead. Gradually, the distance between runners and between groupings

increased, but not the pace. A mile every seven minutes. Mile after mile, through the heat, through the pain in the thighs, through the shortness of breath, through the stitch in the side, the runner thinks only of the pace. Go up the hill. Round the turn. Pound out the pace—seven minutes per mile, a mile every seven minutes.

Introduce Conflict

Conflict means antagonism or opposition between interests or principles or to be at variance. Conflict—whether between people on a collision course or between ideas—holds attention and stimulates interest. Here is an example speech using conflict to build attention and interest.

> *It was an interesting experience. I had just stopped by the supermarket to pick up some milk and cereal for breakfast tomorrow. When I checked out, I handed the cashier a $10 bill, took the change, and put it in my pocket without looking. I was in a hurry so I rushed to my car and drove straight home. A little later, after dinner, I was sitting on the sofa and reached into my pocket. Imagine my surprise when I found a $50 bill and some change.*
>
> *I thought back and remembered giving the cashier a $10 bill for payment. He must have just reached into his drawer and mistakenly pulled out a $50 instead of a $5.*
>
> *What should I do? I had never been in that store before so no one knew me. I was $45 richer but the clerk also was "short" $45 in the cash drawer. My conscience told me I should drive back to the store and return the money I'd mistakenly received. But, another little voice inside said, "Finders keepers, losers weepers." I had been short of cash for about a week and I didn't know how I would pay all the rent this month. But that clerk didn't deserve to be cheated.*
>
> *What decision would you make?*

Hook Ideas to Things the Listeners Already Know

People pay attention to the familiar—what they know and have seen before. To illustrate, suppose you buy a two-year-old Toyota Camry. Before you bought the car, you never paid much attention to the Toyota Camrys on the road. Now, you always notice how many Camrys you pass because Camrys are now a part of your experience—they are familiar to you. Or suppose you are reading about how democracy works in the United States in the election of a President. You may be unusually interested in the topic because you grew up not far from the home of Rutherford Hayes, a U.S. President who was elected although he received 250,000 votes fewer than his opponent. Here is how Billy le Cleede used the principle.

> *Most of you probably know a great deal about "the birds and the bees." But let me tell you about one application of reproduction in nature that's unfamiliar to most of you. When I*

was in high school, I worked during the summers "detassel-ing" corn. That doesn't sound very glamorous. But it's vital if we're going to have hybrid seed corn, one our most important farm crops. Here's how it works:

The corn is planted in spring. Six rows of female seed and then two rows of male corn. Alternate this order across the field. Then when the corn reaches about half of its growth, ears begin to sprout from the stalk. A few weeks later, small shoots called tassels emerge from the top of the stalk. It's the job of the detassler to walk down each "female" row of corn and remove the tassels from the stalk. The tassels in the "male" rows are left, and they will later pollinate the silk on the female ears of corn.

If the tassels were not pulled, the corn would be contami-nated and the grower would feed it to livestock. But because it is properly pollinated, it is sold as seed corn and com-mands a premium price. Sometimes it is necessary to use rather basic science to grow the food we all love.

Associate Derived Interest

Derived interest means interest flows from associating a new sub-ject with something listeners already care about. Ask yourself: Can I arouse interest in the familiar—a story, a book, a recent news event, an on-campus event, a basketball game, and so on—and then tie it to my subject matter? Marcus Young built interest in his subject by hooking it to the class' concerns for appropriate use of their tuition money.

"I'm sure all of you saw the article in the newspaper today about the Athletic Department's plans to enlarge the press box at Farout Field. Their reason, they said, was to make more "sky-boxes" available and build corporate suites. Add to that the intention to actually increase the space for the work-ing press. They admitted the expansion would reduce the number of seats available to the general public.

What they failed to tell you though, was that this move is just another step in the big money game that is college sports. Sky boxes, corporate suites, donations to the athletic depart-ment which qualify the donor for a fine seat are all symptoms of a money sickness. Once, long ago, the game was played for the students. They had the best seats and the alumni sat nearer the end zone. Now, the students at some schools have to participate in a lottery to get a seat for more than one game per season.

What has happened to the students? Do they forget we pay fees and the game is supposed to be for our entertainment. Has big money gotten in the way? Is the game part of a mas-sive public relations tool for the school? How much longer shall we wait before we take back sport which is just as much a part of the university as History, Spanish, Journalism, Communication, Microbiology, or Mathematics? Money talks, but our fees and tuition are money—big money. Let's make them talk for us! We pay for fair treatment each semester when the bills for tuition and fees arrive. Shouldn't we get preferential treatment since we are the student body?"

Tie Ideas to Listeners' Self-Interests

Exhibit 14.9 lists fourteen things listeners really want, without including the obvious like money, goods, and services. You can undoubtedly add to the list. Here is how Regina May Johnson tied her idea about her job experience to her listeners' self-interests.

> *"I'd like to tell you about a rewarding experience I had last week. I believe it's the sort of experience we all wish we would have, but sometimes employers and other workers don't let it happen.*
>
> *For the last three years, I've been working as a teller at First Regional Bank. In the middle of the afternoon, my boss asked me to go with her to the conference room. There she told me she was promoting me to 'Senior Teller' because of the quality of work I had done and because of my being recognized as 'Employee of the Month' six times.*
>
> *This new job pays much more than my previous assignment, and I will work with new tellers and provide in-service training for new hires in three branches. It isn't the money that is so important: it's the feeling I have succeeded and that my interest in my customers means something to the bank. Mrs. Andrews usually forgets to add her deposit slip correctly, but I should be happy to help her with it. And when she tries to give me a tip during the holidays, I always tell her being courteous to my customers is my way of saying 'thanks' for giving us their business. And Mr. Sappington often con-*

Are the techniques for generating attention and interest ethical? Why or why not? Would it be possible to manipulate listeners unethically with any of these techniques? If you think so, how might a speaker safeguard against such unethical manipulation?

EXHIBIT 14.9

FOURTEEN THINGS LISTENERS WANT

1. Power
2. To feel good about who they are
3. To be recognized in a positive way—as having good sense, good judgment, etc.
4. To find or keep a job, and to be promoted
5. To meet personal goals without sacrificing their moral principles
6. To believe what they are doing really matters
7. To be listened to—and heard
8. To be liked, respected, valued, included
9. To be treated with respect
10. Excitement, travel, adventure, good food, fun
11. The truth
12. To avoid getting trapped, boxed in, caught
13. To avoid trouble, risk, put-downs, hassles, insecurity that comes from surprises and changes
14. To avoid betrayal—by you or anyone else

fuses a five dollar bill with a ten, but we're there to help them avoid mistakes or to correct the ones they make. That's what keeps customers coming back and, above all, it's just being treated the way you would want to be treated yourself.

I know this new job is another challenge, but I want to try to help my fellow workers understand their customers do have a choice. But they will do business with us if we treat them properly as we help them manage their money."

So far, you have seen how to gather, build and maintain listener attention and interest. Remember, you can only use these techniques if you understand your audience. You may wish to review Chapter 5, "Audience Analysis."

The next sections present additional guidelines for making your informative speech successful: keep it simple, make it credible, and make it memorable.

Keep It Simple

Simple means basic, uncomplicated, not complex, readily understood, without superfluous materials, fundamental, and easy to follow. A speech to inform should be simple. An excellent example of simplicity came in an informative speech by Yolanda Jameson. Notice that the speech is characterized by: (1) a clear thesis statement, (2) a few main ideas clearly expressed, and (3) materials that support and explain the main ideas

Good afternoon. Most of you are familiar with the climate on the Pacific Coast, but today I would like to discuss with you three reasons why San Diego is such an attractive city for both visitors and natives.

First, the weather is almost always ideal. In the cold of the winter, rarely does the temperature ever fall below thirty degrees. That's one of the reasons they are able to be one of the most productive orange growing areas in the United States. Combine warm temperature with the breeze that blows directly from the Pacific Ocean and the Japanese current and you have a very moderate climate, one that is great for living, vacationing, and farming.

Second, the transportation system of San Diego is very progressive and inexpensive. For example, the Trolley System can take you from Mission San Diego, about 15 miles north and east of the city, all the way to the border with Mexico. And the cost for this trip is only $1.75. All of the cars are freshly painted and new, travel quietly on rails, and pass through the heart of the downtown area. When you coordinate the trolley with the highly efficient bus system, it's not essential to have a car to travel throughout the city. Public transportation can carry you easily from Qualcomm Stadium in the north to the world-famous San Diego Zoo in the east. It's safe, fast, and inexpensive.

My final reason for you to look carefully at San Diego is the beauty of the city itself. In recent years, the city has followed thematic development in the building of skyscrapers

which dot the skyline. Most of them are designed to resemble hand tools. One building uses the top ten floors or so to represent a Phillips screwdriver. Another looks like a hand socket set. Still another, the Hyatt Hotel, resembles a simple slot screwdriver. It's striking to look at the skyline and see the marvelous diversity of the architecture, all pulled together with this common theme. I know of no other city in this country that has developed its downtown design around a theme such as this one.

You also must look at the waterfront, Coronado Island, the view from the bay at sundown, and the pastel colors of the homes. They help create a warm, and inviting atmosphere and compliment the cleanliness of this Southern California city on the water. Is it any wonder San Diego is one of the most rapidly growing cities in this country?

You do not have to sell out an idea to keep it simple. Indeed, the simple speech is often the strongest speech.

Make It Credible

Credible means believable. Audience members invest credibility in you as a speaker, and they do not take this investment lightly. You have to earn it. Exhibit 14.10 suggests four key principles in making a speech credible.

EXHIBIT 14.10

FOUR WAYS TO MAKE A SPEECH CREDIBLE	
Principle	*Explanation*
Be prepared.	When you have planned and practiced carefully, you speak with greater confidence, you seem knowledgeable, and your fluency and command compel audience members to listen.
Be audience-centered.	When listeners sense a speaker's focus on them, they pay attention, get interested, and believe in the speaker's credibility.
Be enthusiastic.	A listening audience cannot stay with a speaker who is not enthusiastic. Enthusiasm starts with having a positive attitude about your topic and then showing you really want listeners to get the information. Lack of enthusiasm is evident in poorly made or sloppy visual aids, as well as in lackluster body language and subdued or boring voice dynamics. Take the time to plan and prepare carefully.
Be on time.	Listeners observe your behavior and then draw inferences about you on the basis of what they have observed. Your punctuality can reflect on your credibility. It says, "I care enough about these listeners not to waste their time."

Make It Memorable

Memorable means worthy of being remembered—easily retained and recalled. If you want your informative speech to have an impact on listeners, you must make it memorable. Exhibit 14.11 lists techniques you can use to make your informative speeches memorable.

SUMMARY

Because speeches to inform and speeches to persuade overlap, listeners often become confused about what speakers are trying to accomplish. If listeners misconstrue your intention—if they think you are trying to persuade when you are trying to teach—they might never give you what you want. Such confusion damages both your credibility and the impact of your speech.

Informative speeches differ from persuasive speeches on the basis of three characteristics: (1) the speaker's intention, (2) how the information in the speech, and (3) how listeners perceive the speech. Listeners have to be sure about the purpose of a speech or they cannot and will not respond the way you want them to.

Most informative speeches aim at definition, demonstration, description, or explanation. Definition speeches teach listeners what something means through comparison and contrast, synonyms, antonyms, etymology, differentiation, and operational definition. Demonstration speeches show how something works, how it is made, how it is done, or how it happens. Description speeches use precise, concrete, and colorful language to picture some object, phenomenon, or event. Explanation speeches describe or interpret how something works, how to evaluate it, or why it occurred.

Whichever type of informative speech is your goal, you can generate attention and interest by providing specific details, building suspense, filling the speech with action, introducing conflict, hooking ideas to the familiar, associating derived interest, and tying ideas to listeners' self-interests. Keep your language and organization of ideas simple, direct, and straightforward. You can increase your credibility with listeners by being prepared, audience-centered, enthusiastic, and on time. And your informative speech will be memorable if you repeat the key ideas, tell how the ideas relate to listeners, suggest memory aids, polish transitions, use appropriate humor, and present visual aids.

Exhibit 14.11

TECHNIQUES FOR MAKING INFORMATIVE SPEECHES MEMORABLE		
What to Do	*Why*	*Example*
Repeat the key ideas.	Repetition places emphasis on an idea. Thus, repetition makes it more likely that listeners will remember the idea you repeat.[4]	"One fourth of all Americans will have cancer by the time they reach fifty. Think of it—one out of every four men and women."
Tell how the ideas relate to listeners.	People pay attention to things that bear on their own lives.	"What does this mean to you? Well, let's try something. Look at the person to your left. Now look at the person to your right. Now touch the person in front of you. If one of those people doesn't get cancer by age fifty, you will."
Suggest memory aids.	People need help. Just as you determine ways to remember important information for yourself, you can point out ways to help listeners remember.	"When you find yourself trying to compensate for an alcoholic's behavior in your life, remember the three C's. You didn't *cause* it, you can't *cure* it, and you can't *control* it."
Polish transitions.	Listeners need your help in following you from one idea to another. Allow transitions to make this movement clear.	"So you see the problem. Secondhand smoke is as dangerous as smoking directly. Now we come to the hard part. What are we going to do about it? Ladies and gentlemen, I want to argue smoking must be banned from all public places in our city."
Use appropriate humor.	Listeners usually remember the point of a story that takes the light approach and they are likely to associate their pleasure in the humor with the idea you want them to remember. (Stay with what you know and with what is relevant to the audience and the occasion.)[5]	In a speech about the problems facing the Mobile County Schools: "I'm not kidding—some of the schools in Mobile County are so old-fashioned, the kids have to raise their hands and get permission before they punch the kid at the next desk."
Use visual aids.	Listeners are more likely to remember what they *see* as well as *hear*.	See Chapter 12, "Supporting Ideas Visually."

KEY TERMS

Antonyms

Comparison and contrast

Concretion

Definition speech

Demonstration speech

Derived interest

Descriptive speech

Differentiation

Etymology

Explanation speech

Operational definition

Synonyms

APPLICATION QUESTIONS

1. In your experience as a listener, what kinds of topics have made the most interesting informative speeches? Why do you think so?

2. Select the professor who in your experience, gives the best (most interesting, most informative) lectures. Attend one of the lectures, and pay particular attention to the professor's speaking strategies. Try to consider all of the techniques that apply—generating attention and interest, keeping it simple, and making it credible and memorable. Make careful notes to share with your classmates in public speaking class. Does the professor's style of speaking agree with suggestions in this chapter? If not, in what ways? What can you learn from this that will help you to give better informative speeches?

3. Effective teachers try to build new ideas on information you already have. Attend an informative speech (classrooms are full of such speaking) with this idea in mind. Do you think the speaker was successful in introducing and building new ideas on the foundations of information you already had? If so, how was that accomplished? If not, what suggestions could you make to help the speaker do it better?

IT'S MORE FUN TO KNOW

For many years, we have known speaker believability has a strong effect on the message. Audiences listen to and believe speakers they think are credible. Starting with Aristotle who said the speaker should be "the good man speaking well" (what we call today *ethos*), we have been guided to the importance of a positive reputation.

The importance of "trustworthiness" in presenting information was highlighted by Applebaum and Anatol in 1973.[6] Additionally, the more information audiences have about the speaker's training, education, and amount of experience creates more believability for both the message and the speaker.[7] These studies help us realize that both perceived and real competence by the speaker make information much more credible.

Credibility does not come just from what is said. Burgoon, Birk, and Pfau in 1990 found that facial and vocal expressiveness enhanced speaker believability.[8] So, not only is it important that you be well informed and believable, you must speak like a credible source. It is so important to be believable, that credibility has come to be a more important factor than liking the speaker.[9] It's clear then, if you are perceived as well informed and honest, that is even more important than being liked by your listeners. Add to this the importance of "dynamism" or enthusiasm about your subject. Berlo and others in early research identified this element as one of the three factors most frequently used by listeners in evaluating speakers.[10]

Any effective informative speech begins with a believable source and good information. If the information and source are credible and the message follows the suggestions we have offered earlier in this chapter, an effective message and the desired result should occur.

SELF-TEST FOR REVIEW

What is the best choice for completing the following statement?

1. For an informative speech to be successful, audience members must believe the speaking goal is *to inform* because
   a. listeners can respond to a speech even if they do not understand the goal.
   b. audiences always project themselves into the speech situation.
   c. a confused listener always stops listening.
   d. listeners who think the speaker may be trying to persuade may resist the persuasion they think they are being subjected to.

2. The three characteristics of informative speaking are
   a. definition, description, and explanation.
   b. intention, function, and perception.
   c. inclusion, control, direction.
   d. illustration, example, and anecdote.

3. Match each of the following speech characteristics with the type of informative speech in the right-hand column to which it applies.

   ____ a. Formal statement of the meaning or significance of a word

   ____ b. To explain or illustrate by examples, specimens, experiments

   ____ c. Using language to picture a phenomenon or event

   ____ d. Interpreting how something works or how to evaluate it

   ____ e. The defeat of the Spanish Armada (speech title)

   ____ f. How to use your nine-iron (speech title)

   ____ g. What is "baroque" art? (speech title)

   ____ h. The rape crisis center volunteer (speech title)

   1. explanation
   2. description
   3. definition
   4. demonstration

Evaluate each of the following statements for you personally by checking one of the three alternatives.

4. I understand and can name six ways to develop a speech of definition.   ____ Yes ____ Needs work ____ No

5. I know how to develop a demonstration speech.   ____ Yes ____ Needs work ____ No

6. I can use differentiation as a technique for defining a term. ____ Yes ____ Needs work ____ No

7. I know how—and why—to use specific details in a descriptive speech. ____ Yes ____ Needs work ____ No

8. I know how to bring an explanation into focus for an audience. ____ Yes ____ Needs work ____ No

9. I can specify two general speaking skills that generate listener attention and interest. ____ Yes ____ Needs work ____ No

10. I can describe two techniques for building suspense. ____ Yes ____ Needs work ____ No

11. I can name seven techniques for gaining listener attention. ____ Yes ____ Needs work ____ No

12. I know how to use derived and self-interest to establish an idea as relevant to my listeners. ____ Yes ____ Needs work ____ No

13. I can name and explain four techniques for building credibility. ____ Yes ____ Needs work ____ No

Answers: 1. d. 2. b. 3. a. 4. c. 2. d. 1. e. 1. f. 4. g. 3. h. 2. Only the reader can judge the accuracy of items 4 through 13.

SUGGESTED READINGS

Freeley, Austin J. *Argumentation and Debate: Critical Thinking for Reasoned Decision-Making.* 9th ed. Belmont, Calif.: Wadsworth, 1997. This old chestnut (first edition appeared in 1961) is still one of the best resources available to public speakers. For example, Chapter 4, "Analyzing the Controversy," includes a lucid and thorough explanation of how to define terms.

Goss, Blaine. *The Psychology of Human Communication, Second Edition.* Prospect Heights, IL: Waveland Press, 1995. This little text (142 pages, plus end matter) may be the clearest presentation of how people process information to be found anywhere between two covers. The prose is lively and clear, and the materials are directly relevant to the task of adapting informative speeches to listeners.

Edward S. Inch, ed., and Barbara Warnick. *Critical Thinking and Communication: The Use of Reason in Argument, Third Edition* (Boston: Allyn and Bacon, 1997). This is a thorough and clearly written work that is right up to date and very useful.

INTERNET ACTIVITIES

1. If you open the AltaVista search engine (*www.altavista.com*) and type the two words "informative speaking" into the search window, AltaVista will return more than 750,000 "hits." To refine the search—and to get it focused to manageable limits—click on the link "Refine your search" and follow instructions. Make some notes to share with your classmates about what you did and what you found.

2. The writing center at Colorado State University maintains a very helpful web site at the URL: *http://www.colostate.edu/Depts/WritingCenter/index.html* Go to that site and explore it in detail. Especially click on the Index button and see what they offer that might help you and your classmates. Click on the button for "references" and follow the links and helpers to "informative speaking." Bring your notes to class so you can share your findings.

3. Professors often put transparencies of their lectures on line. For example, Dr. Frank Flauto has put his lecture notes on line at the URL: *http://www.finearts.swt.edu/speechcomm/Flauto/Lecture_Notes1310.html* Go to that address to see if he is still maintaining his web site. If he is, compare his thinking about informative speaking to the advice we offer in this chapter. Are there any differences? If there are differences, in what way, if any, are those differences important to Dr. Flauto's students?

NOTES

1. "Your Next Job," *Newsweek*, February 1, 1999, p. 44.

2. Jimmy Carter quoted in Bob Dole, *Great Political Wit* (New York: Doubleday, 1998), p.52.

3. *Ibid*, p. 50.

4. J. T. Cacioppo, R. E. Petty, and C. D. Stolenberg, "Processes of Social Influence: The Elaboration Likelihood Model of Persuasion," in P. C. Kendall, *Advances in Cognitive-Behavioral Research and Therapy*, Volume IV, (New York: Academic Press, 1985), 215–274.

5. For example see Elizabeth E. Graham, "The Involvement of Sense of Humor in the Development in Social Relationships," *Communication Reports* 8:2 (Summer 1995), 158–169, and, John C. Meyer, "Humor in Member Narratives: Uniting and Dividing At Work," *Western Journal of Communication, 61* (Spring 1997), 188–208.

6. R. L. Applebaum and K. W. E. Anatol, "Dimensions of Source Credibility: A Test for Reproducibility," *Speech Monographs*, 39, 216–222.

7. R. A. Swenson, D. L. Nash, and D. C. Roos, "Source Credibility and Perceived Expertness of Testimony in a Simulated Child-Custody Case," *Professional Psychology*, 15, 891–898.

8. Judee K. Burgoon, Thomas Birk, and Michael Pfau, "Nonverbal Behaviors, Persuasion, and Credibility, *Human Communication Research*, 17:1 (Fall 1990), 140–169.

9. H. W. Simons, N. N. Berkowitz, and R. J. Moyer, "Similarity, Credibility and Attitude Change: A Review and a Theory," *Psychological Bulletin*, 73, 1–6.

10. David K. Berlo, James B. Lemert and Robert J. Mertz, "Dimensions for Evaluating the Acceptability of Messages Sources," *Public Opinion Quarterly*, 33:4 (Winter 1970), 563–576.

CHAPTER 15

PERSUASIVE SPEAKING

OBJECTIVES

After reading this chapter, you should be able to:

1. Cite several ethical guidelines for persuasive speakers.

2. Present a brief history of the study of persuasion, discussing Aristotle's artistic proofs, the intensification/downplay and evoked recall models of persuasion, and Rokeach's hierarchy of beliefs.

3. Describe how values can be differentiated from beliefs and why speakers should appeal to both values and beliefs of listeners.

4. Describe the three elements of the effective persuasive speech.

5. List and explain four credibility components of the persuasive speaker.

6. Explain the concept of logical completeness and how it relates to message credibility and propositions of fact, value, and policy.

7. Describe and give examples of four kinds of persuasive message strategies: (1) one-sided versus two-sided arguments, (2) explicit versus implicit conclusions, (3) evoked recall appeals, and (4) organizing in a motivated sequence.

8. Cite the eight primary needs that underlie the use of evoked recall appeals as a persuasive message strategy.

9. Discuss two research-supported principles with regard to the use of fear appeals as a persuasive message strategy.

10. Explain why the five steps of the motivated sequence—attention, need, satisfaction, visualization, and action—comprise an effective organizational strategy for persuasive speeches.

OUTLINE

Outline
Objectives
Abstract
Imagine
Introduction
Ethical Considerations
Theories of Persuasion
    Aristotle and Artistic Proofs
    Intensification/Downplay
      Model of Persuasion
    Evoked Recall Model of
      Persuasion
    Beliefs and Values
      Beliefs
        Primitive Beliefs
        Shared Beliefs
        Derived Beliefs
        Matters of Taste
      Changing Beliefs
      Values
Characteristics of Effective
  Persuasive Speech

Speaker Credibility
Message Credibility
    Fact
    Value
    Policy
Message Strategies
    One-Sided Versus Two-
      Sided Arguments
    Explicit versus
      Implicit Conclusions
    Evoked Recall Appeals
    Organizing in a Motivated
      Sequence
Summary
Key Terms
Application Questions
It's More Fun to Know
Self-Test for Review
Suggested Readings
Internet Activities
Notes

ABSTRACT

Persuasive speaking aims at influencing the attitudes, beliefs, and behaviors of listeners. For that reason, persuasive speakers must be ethically responsible and accountable for what they say. This chapter examines four theories and models of persuasion that have developed over time and then explores the characteristics of effective persuasive speeches. For a persuasive speech to be effective, the speaker must have high credibility with listeners, the persuasive message itself must be credible, and the speaker must use message strategies that appeal to listeners' rational and emotional needs.

IMAGINE

Joe Hendricks felt that he had to tell his class audience about the high cost of being sick. But most of them just went to the Medical Center and settled for the free or low cost care of the resident physicians. Joe approached his professor and told him about his dilemma. "I just don't know how to get the rest of the people really involved in this subject."

Professor Bening replied, "Well, Joe, you have to appeal to their needs. Make them see what will happen when they're no longer students and have to pay for medical care like the general population. That's the first step. After you make them aware there's a serious problem, you have to find a way to make them believe it will affect them."

Joe did a little research and discovered that health care costs are among the fastest growing expenses in the American economy. To make himself more believable to his colleagues, he collected even more information about prescription drugs, hospital costs, and physician office visits. "This is going to be complicated, but I believe everyone is going to feel this is a problem they can't ignore," Joe said.

Then, after consulting his text, Joe realized he must decide how much fear he wanted to build into his speech. Did he want to risk frightening his audience greatly or might that "turn them off"? Did he have an specific answer to the large problem of exploding health care costs and how did he want to present it?

The conclusion Joe drew was that an effective persuasive speech is a complicated matter. It may be easy to generalize about changing people's minds, but putting together a message that is appealing, establishing yourself as an authority figure, and marshalling the facts and appeals in a sensible way, is one of a speaker's greatest challenges. "Tough job, but if I follow the guidelines, even with this topic, I think I'll be successful," Joe decided.

INTRODUCTION

We often attempt to influence the thoughts, beliefs, or actions of others. For example, we might say:

> "Hey, I've had enough studying for one night. Let's go get a pizza."

> "You know the concert tickets go on sale today, and the good seats will go first. Do you want me to pick up a ticket for you when I get mine tonight?"

> "You certainly look nice, but I've got to tell you that I like the first shirt better with those slacks. Maybe you should . . ."

Statements like these are common in our daily lives, but most of the time, we do not perceive them as persuasion. They seem instead, to be merely part of the conversational climate we live in. However, these statements are rather rhetorically sophisticated in the variety of persuasive appeals they use.

Gass and Seiter define persuasion as involving ". . . one or more persons who are engaged in the activity of creating, reinforcing, modifying, or extinguishing beliefs, attitudes, intentions, motivations, and/or behaviors within the constraints of a given communication context."[1]When we try to persuade others we choose and implement strategies we hope will produce some *observable* change in others. If we do it right, the change occurs. This chapter describes persuasive strategies that are at once effective and ethical. Plus, they are easy to learn and fun to use. But they do raise certain ethical considerations.

ETHICAL CONSIDERATIONS

When you understand how to persuade others, you also understand how you can exercise power. The exercise of power implies certain ethical considerations. Exhibit 15.1 summarizes and reviews the ethical system described in Chapter 1. They seem worth repeating here.

EXHIBIT 15.1

TENETS OF AN ETHICAL SYSTEM FOR PUBLIC SPEAKING	
In General	*In Particular*
1. Tell the truth.	• Strive to benefit your listeners as well as yourself.
2. Do no harm.	• Respect your listeners by valuing their diversity.
3. Treat people justly.	• Be candid as you reveal your thoughts and feelings.
	• Do not make arguments you cannot support.
	• Do not support arguments with misleading evidence.
	• Do not oversimplify complex matters.
	• Do not use emotional appeals you cannot support with evidence and reasoning.
	• Do not pretend to be sure of something when you are not.
	• Do not coerce or mislead listeners. Let them make up their own minds.
	• Do not misuse the power of language to create reality in the heads of other people.

THEORIES OF PERSUASION

People have studied how persuasion works since well before Aristotle wrote his *Rhetoric* about 350 BC. That effort has produced a large number of theories. Four theories especially help beginning persuasive speaking students: (1) Aristotle's artistic proofs, (2) the intensification/downplay model, (3) the evoked recall model, and (4) beliefs and values. Exhibit 15.2 summarizes these four theories.

Aristotle and Artistic Proofs

Aristotle's work on persuasion, *Rhetoric*, was so influential that most of the study of modern persuasion in the western world builds upon his principles. Aristotle described what he called artistic proofs. The artistic proofs included **ethos** (the kind of person you are, including your education, honesty, reputation, and skill in delivering a speech), **logos** (appeals to the rational intellect), and **pathos** (appeals to the passions or to the will—the so-called emotional proofs). These were described, explained and illustrated in Chapter 6.

EXHIBIT 15.2

SUMMARY OF FOUR USEFUL THEORIES OF PERSUASION	
Aristotle's Artistic Proofs	The persuader can create, control and use proofs in three areas: (1) ethos—the kind of person you are, (2) logos—appeals to the rational intellect, and (3) pathos—appeals to the passions or to the will.
Rank's Intensification/Downplay Model	Persuaders can play up their own strong points and play down their competitors' strong points, or they can play down their own weak points and play up their competitors' weak points. In practice, persuaders typically do all these things.
Evoked Recall	People must persuade themselves. The rhetor attempts to stimulate a set of memories, attitudes, beliefs, and values in the receiver with which the receiver will associate the persuader's messages and appeals.
Beliefs and Values	Beliefs and values control what people accept as true and important. Persuasive messages must either be consistent with a receiver's beliefs and values, or designed to change those beliefs and values.

Intensification/Downplay Model of Persuasion

In the 1970s, Hugh Rank first developed the **intensification/ downplay model of persuasion** which remains applicable today.[2] He discovered people tend to use two persuasive tactics: (1) play up their own strong points and their competitors' weak points or (2) they play down their weak points and their competitors' strong points. The idea is for the persuader to help listeners reframe their views of a thing—to come to see or experience the thing differently. Ford Motor Company used the first strategy when it showed pictures of a Ford Tempo beside a Honda Civic, along with a narrative similar to the following:

> *A Honda Civic with radio, automatic transmission, and air conditioning costs $1,500 more than a comparably equipped Ford? What are you spending your money for? See your local Ford dealer.*

Persuaders also play down their own weaknesses and their competitors' strengths. For example, the American Plastics Council showed a picture of a picnic table with the caption: "How to Save the Planet and the Picnic at the Same Time." Plastic wrap covered the hot dogs, salad, and watermelon. The message claimed that plastic saves energy but neglected to mention that plastic comes from petroleum, a nonrenewable fossil fuel. The council also neglected to mention its competitors' strengths, which in many cases would be reusability or renewability.

Evoked Recall Model of Persuasion

Does a speaker have to let audience members know when she or he is attempting to use evoked recall to persuade? Is it okay to trigger evoked responses without fair warning?

The **evoked recall model of persuasion** established a method of message presentation that remains effective today.[3] It argues that pulling a persuasive message out of a receiver is easier than putting one in. Evoked recall relies on a set of memories, experiences, attitudes, and opinions people already hold. For example, Proctor and Gamble advertised using a full-page photograph of a smiling young woman hugging a package of its Charmin toilet tissue. The only part of the package that shows between the arms of the young woman is imprinted with the picture of a cute baby and the product name, Charmin. The legend is: "So much squeezable softness, you gotta hug it." Clearly, the advertiser is attempting to evoke a recall—that is, the advertiser wants viewers to make a connection between the images on the screen and something inside themselves. This process called **identification,** is the most important part of persuasion in the evoked recall model. All of us carry images from the past that can influence our perceptions in the present.

Beliefs and Values

In addition to carrying images from the past, we all have developed a set of beliefs and values out of the training and experience of a lifetime. Beliefs and values control what people accept as true and important. Your position on any issue depends on your values and beliefs. You accept or reject what people tell you about a controversy according to what seems consistent or inconsistent with your values and beliefs.

To illustrate using a case of long-standing controversy, suppose you believe that life begins at conception—that the moment the two cells combine they constitute a living human being. You feel that only self-defense or national defense justifies taking the life of another human being. Given these beliefs and values, you probably would disagree with a proposal that the government make abortion available to women on demand.

Important issues are rarely that simple, however. You may hold related opinions. For example, you may feel any baby should have some chance of happiness, including parents who want the baby and can support it. You may also think a conception resulting from rape or incest would be repugnant. You can hold all of these opinions at the same time. They are not necessarily inconsistent and they do not seem inconsistent to the people who hold them. But they do confound the question of whether to support or oppose using federal funds to pay for abortions. How a person sorts through these issues remains a function of her or his beliefs and values. This explains why so many people have so much controversy. There is no objective "right" answer. Any statement of value essentially rests on a fundamental, subjective belief that cannot be proved or disproved objectively. Both sides of an argument can and usually do, offer compelling "good reasons" for their arguments.

Beliefs

A **belief** is a statement that something *is*. Milton Rokeach felt some beliefs are more significant than others and that this explains why people can hold conflicting beliefs at the same time without discomfort. Rokeach developed a structure of beliefs and placed them in a hierarchy (see Exhibit 15.3).

Primitive Beliefs

According to Rokeach, **primitive beliefs** are beliefs we have about ourselves, about existence, and about our personal identities. These primitive beliefs are more central to our lives than other beliefs. Typical belief statements in this category might be:

1. "I'm an honest person."
2. "I always have bad luck."

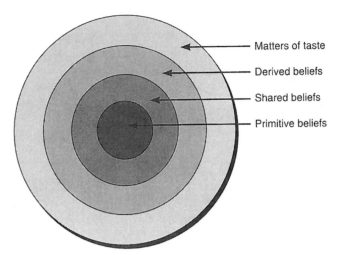

EXHIBIT 15.3 Rokeach's Structural Hierarchy of Beliefs

   3. "Life is never fair to me."

   4. "Darkness frightens me."

   5. "I think I'm a good-looking person."

   6. "I can't do anything athletic."

   7. "I'm very affectionate."

   8. "I can do anything if I set my mind to it."

We rarely express primitive beliefs aloud, but they substantially influence our communication behavior.

Shared Beliefs

Shared beliefs result from experiences we are willing to discuss with others. They are the basis for our talk with other people and are less central to the hierarchy than are primitive beliefs. We express a belief, others confirm or deny it, and we accept or reject their confirmation or denial. Because we share this level of belief with other people, shared beliefs become a common ground of understanding. Examples of shared beliefs include:

> "It seems to me people should be willing to tell where they stand on an issue. We can agree to disagree!"

> "Hopefully, you will agree with me that we can't afford to cut our defense budget any more."

Primitive, or core, beliefs are difficult to change. If they change at all, they tend to change slowly. Knowing this, advertising aims at modifying shared beliefs. This lesson from marketing research bears upon your speech making as well. You are unlikely to be able to change core beliefs with a single speech or even several speeches. For example, you probably cannot hope to convert someone in your class to your religion across the course of a semester. Focus your attention on shared and more peripheral beliefs instead.

Derived Beliefs

Derived beliefs usually emerge from a combination of other beliefs and, as shown in Exhibit 15.3 of Rokeach's belief hierarchy, are less central than either shared or primitive beliefs. To illustrate, suppose you discover that someone changed your schedule for the winter term and enrolled you in Philosophy 101. You say to your friends: "I don't know why they changed my schedule and put me in a course that'll be boring." Amy says, "Last year I took the same course and felt just like you. But it was great. I learned more about myself in that course than anything else I took for the entire year." Henry agrees: "You're going to thank the Registrar for changing your schedule. I'll bet you a pizza that you'll end up saying that was the best course you ever had. The teachers in that department are great, too." After this conversation with your friends you decide to give the course a chance, especially because the people who share your ideas also enjoyed it. If so, then on the information gleaned from conversations with others, you will have derived a belief about the new course.

Matters of Taste

Matters of taste lie at the outer rim of the Rokeach model (see Exhibit 15.3). They are arbitrary and rather insignificant beliefs about the world, such as:

> "I like country music better than soft rock."
>
> "The flowers at Bellingrath Gardens seemed more beautiful than usual today."
>
> "I love the view in the Napa Valley."
>
> "If you ask me, Helen Hayes was one of the finest performers in the entire 20th century."

Changing Beliefs

The closer a belief is to the outside of the ring in Exhibit 15.3, the easier it is to change. Thus, matters of taste are easier to modify than shared beliefs or derived beliefs. If you make a statement that appears inconsistent with someone's core primitive beliefs, the listener may think that your position is not credible—even if you support your statement with compelling evidence and argument.

People hold beliefs whether or not their beliefs can be verified. Sometimes they just seem self-evident, and so they don't seem to need support. For example, each of the following claims seemed self-evident to the people who made them, but the truth of these statements may not seem evident to you.

> "The violence in Northern Ireland is primarily a religious conflict."
>
> "If given a chance, American farmers could feed the world."

"Racism is the fundamental source of social problems in America's large cities."

"Nationalism is the principal cause of conflict in Eastern Europe and the Middle East."

"Controlling hospital costs will reduce most of the health care crisis."

To change beliefs a persuader must gather enough information, evidence, and, arguments to support her ideas and to give listeners an opportunity to modify their beliefs.

To illustrate the importance of using adequate supporting material, suppose you have decided to give a speech about cleaning up the waterways in your area. To be effective, you have to present information and use appeals that seem consistent with listeners' beliefs. Your argument goes:

The stream is polluted.

The chemical plant upstream polluted the water.

The managers of that chemical plant bear responsibility for the pollution.

For an audience to accept these statements, you need to provide proof. A listener might ask:

How do you know that the stream is polluted? How do you know that the chemical plant is the source of the pollution? How do you know that the managers of the chemical plant are responsible? Are they directly responsible or indirectly responsible? How do you know that?

For listeners to accept your statements they must hear evidence and arguments they can agree with. Some listeners may be skeptical because their belief systems differ from yours. What seems important to them may be quite different from what is important to you. For example, they may think: "Well maybe there is some pollution, but because we need the jobs that the chemical plant brings, we should tolerate some pollution to keep the plant operating." If your arguments are to seem credible, they may have to overcome the effects of listeners' belief systems to the contrary.

Values

A **value** is a statement containing the words *should* or *ought,* or such subjective terms as *good, beautiful, correct,* or *important.* The following value statements provide examples:

"Driving seventy-five miles per hour was a dumb thing to do. You ought to drive that car a lot slower. So much speed isn't safe. And besides, you ought to obey the law."

"That is a very interesting and informative course. And the information is so important. In fact, the course probably ought to be required. Maybe we should require it some time during the sophomore year."

Each of these statements implies the existence of a set of rules or standards—a value system—that justifies the words *should* and *ought*. When you use such terms as *dumb, interesting,* or *important,* you are also applying a value system. Values are internal—they are inside you and inside your listeners. People tend to base their thinking on their value systems—on what *ought* to be. As a persuasive speaker, you have to think of ways to adapt to or overcome resistance from listeners' value systems. To illustrate, suppose you have decided to make the following arguments:

Listeners view speakers as highly credible and more likely to be persuaded by them if the speakers' values and judgments seem close to their own. © Bob Daemmrich/Stock Boston/ PNI

1. Most people are responsible.
2. Therefore, most people will act responsibly given the choice.
3. In any case, people should be given the freedom to choose the responsible option.
4. The speed limit law in the United States does not permit individual drivers freedom to choose a responsible option.
5. A deliberate choice to exceed the speed limit might be the most sensible choice.
   For example, you might break the speed limit to move freight more quickly or because your car operates safely at high speeds.
6. Thus, the law that limits speed should be replaced with a general law that gives people a choice about what speed is safe and reasonable.

These are controversial claims. If you want to persuade listeners to accept them, you will have to choose evidence and arguments that are consistent with *listeners'* ideas about what they should and ought to do.

These, then, are four of the many theories of persuasion. We have selected them because they are easy to understand and apply. Once you understand them you will begin to develop more and more effective persuasive speeches.

CHARACTERISTICS OF THE EFFECTIVE PERSUASIVE SPEECH

An effective persuasive speech, one that achieves the desired audience response, is generally characterized by three elements. First, the speaker must have established a high level of credibility with listeners. Second, the message must be credible. Third, the speaker's chosen message strategies should appeal to both the rational and emotional needs of listeners. Including these three elements in a single speech requires hard work and concentrated effort. Exhibit 15.4 explores how you can develop and include these characteristics in your persuasive speeches.

Speaker Credibility

Speaker credibility is the degree to which listeners believe in you as a source. It is not just the message and your presentation of ideas that makes a persuasive speech effective. The audience also judges your believability and intellectual and physical attractiveness in deciding whether or not to accept your arguments. Exhibit 15.5 offers additional pointers you can use to enhance your credibility.

Message Credibility

Appearance boils down to three features: (1) how you dress, (2) how careful you are about grooming, and (3) your presence, bearing, or poise. © Kay Chernush/Image Book

Message credibility refers to the logical completeness of the message. The **logical completeness** of a message exists to the extent that listeners think that a statement is warranted by the evidence and arguments presented. For example, if you were caught out in a pasture, standing under the shelter of an oak tree during a sudden summer shower, you would undoubtedly accept the logical completeness of these knowledge claims:

1. That shower came up in a hurry.
2. It's raining hard.
3. The shower won't last long.

EXHIBIT 15.4

THREE CHARACTERISTICS OF EFFECTIVE PERSUASIVE SPEAKING		
Characteristic	*Subdivision*	*Application*
Speaker Credibility	Trust	Trust boils down to two things: (1) ability to predict the other person's behavior and (2) belief in the other person's benevolence. To be trustworthy, make yourself predictable. Present facts honestly, play fair to both sides, maintain personal integrity, keep your mind open, and maintain your good reputation.
	Knowledge	To meet this criterion, a speaker must seem experienced, well-informed, trained, intelligent, and qualified to discus the topic.
	Appearance	Appearance is all about how you dress, how careful you are about grooming, and your presence, bearing, or poise. Dress appropriately, groom yourself carefully, stand up straight, hold your head up, and speak and move confidently—even if you don't feel confident.
	Audience Identification	Listeners identify with and invest credibility in people who confirm them and their ideas, or who share a common ground with them in terms of place, values, and beliefs.
Message Credibility	Propositions of Fact	Provide evidence and argument of sufficient quality to establish in the listeners the claim that something is as you say.
	Propositions of Value	Name and establish the criteria you will apply to the value judgment, then apply them to the object, phenomenon, or event about which you wish the listeners to share the value judgment.
	Propositions of Policy	Show why the policy is needed (harm, comparative advantages), then show how the proposed policy will address the need. Your answers to these questions must be compelling: (1) Is there a problem? (2) Is it serious? (3) Is it inherent in the status quo? (4) Will the proposal address the problem? (5) Will the proposal create new problems? (6) Will the proposal bring advantages sufficient to warrant approval of the proposal?
Message Strategies	One-sided vs. Two-sided Arguments	If you present only one side of an issue you might make a strong case for your position. However, you leave listeners unprepared for arguments from the other side. Research strongly supports offering both sides, then building up the side you support.
	Explicit vs. Implicit Conclusions	Research clearly indicates that drawing explicit conclusions—telling listeners precisely what you want them to do or believe—is more effective than implying or hinting at the goal you have in mind.
	Evoked Recall Appeals	Effective persuaders appeal to the emotional insecurities and drives of their listeners, but never to the exclusion of other logical arguments and attention to their personal credibility.

Exhibit 15.5

Pointers To Enhance Your Credibility	
Feature	*Pointer*
Well-Informed	Know what you are talking about. Show that you know by presenting facts, figures, names, dates, and so on.
Qualified	You must have the necessary academic and experiential background and listeners must know of your background. Either mention it yourself or have someone else mention it in writing or orally.
Experienced	To perceive you as experienced, listeners must believe that you have a history of involvement and concern with the topic. They learn of your experience when you or someone else tells them of it. Never try to manufacture experience you do not have.
Intelligent	In a speaking situation, intelligence includes both what you know and how clearly you articulate it. Thus, the marks of an intelligent speaker include organization of ideas and language usage.
Trained	Training involves both experience and credentials. While a scoutmaster with a bachelor's degree might be fully capable of setting a broken bone, a licensed physician has more credibility by reason of training. You or someone else must tell listeners that you have appropriate credentials and experience.

Each of these statements is a knowledge claim about what is. Such statements are called propositions. A **proposition** is an assertion of a speaker's general position on some subject. Its logical completeness depends on the weight of evidence and analysis that renders an audience willing to accept the knowledge claim as true. There are three kinds of propositions: (1) fact, (2) value, and (3) policy. Exhibit 15.6 defines and separates these three types.

Fact

Exhibit 15.7 shows, by example, how to develop propositions of fact. Remember, when the argument is logically complete enough, listeners will usually accept it.

If you wanted to support the argument that asphalt roads do not last as long as concrete highways further, you would compare the durability of concrete and asphalt as paving materials. You could support your case with examples of highways paved with asphalt and highways paved with concrete. You would want to show that, under

EXHIBIT 15.6

THE THREE TYPES OF PROPOSITIONS		
Type	*Features*	*Examples*
Fact	Something *is*	This is an oak tree.
		Most forest fires are caused by human carelessness.
		Asphalt highways don't last as long as concrete highways.
		Lake Superior is the deepest of the Great Lakes.
Value	Judgment terms, such as *good, right,* and *beautiful*	Swimming is the most effective form of total body exercise.
		People were wrong in boycotting McDonald's for selling animal meat.
		AIDS is the most frightening disease of our time.
Policy	Something or someone *should* or *ought*	We should lower tuition costs at this institution.
		The government should require all citizens to vote in national elections.
		Businesses ought to give a discount for cash purchases.

EXHIBIT 15.7

EXAMPLE PROPOSITIONS OF FACT		
The Knowledge Claim	*Supporting Argument*	*Evidence*
Most forest fires are caused by human carelessness or arson.	Natural causes account for only 10 percent of forest fires.	Statistics and cases from the national Park Service and the Department of Agriculture
Asphalt highways don't last as long as concrete highways.	Asphalt has a half-life of only five years, compared to twelve years for concrete.	Highway repair information from the US Department of Transportation.
Lake Superior is the deepest of the Great Lakes.	Water temperature is an accurate indicator of depth.	Report studies from the US Geological Survey.

similar traffic and weather conditions, concrete pavement lasts longer than asphalt.

Value

A **proposition of value** attempts to establish that something is good, bad, valuable, worthless, right, or wrong. Your job, as a speaker, is to introduce the information, the appeals, the criteria, and the evidence so that your audience arrives at the same conclusion you have.

Propositions of value may also have a component that you can discuss factually. A proposition of value should agree with what listeners *already* believe or feel. Otherwise, your audience probably will reject your position. Success here requires both rational and emotional appeals. You must be prepared with facts, but you should realize listeners will also judge you according to their personal feelings and values. Exhibit 15.8 illustrates by example how to develop a proposition of value.

EXHIBIT 15.8

EXAMPLE PROPOSITIONS OF VALUE		
Knowledge Claim	*Argument*	*Evidence*
Swimming is the most effective form of total body exercise.	Swimming yields better aerobic effect than any other physical activity and it does not damage joints or muscles.	Show research from sports medicine that compares running, agility sports, and swimming.
People were wrong in boycotting McDonald's for selling animal meat.	Eating red meat in moderation does not harm people. Moreover, each individual must take responsibility for her or his own choices about diet.	Show information from medical research and from the US Food and Drug Administration studies that support these arguments.
AIDS is the most frightening disease of our time.	AIDS is the fastest growing killer disease in modern times. Further, it is spread by means that cannot be eradicated.	Cite research about the growth of AIDS, and that compares it to such worldwide disasters as the Black Plague. Explain how it spreads with the exchange of body fluids, particularly as a result of sexual contact or carelessness, such as drug users sharing dirty needles.

Policy

A **proposition of policy** argues that some action should be taken. These propositions always involve both fact and value and, like the values discussed earlier in the chapter, typically contain the words *should* and *ought.*

Many situations require "should" and "ought" decisions: "Should I cut this class?" "Which outfit should I buy?" "Should I spend the rest of my money on a pizza or on a movie?" Any time you use the words *ought* or *should,* you are asking audience members to make a decision. If you want to persuade them that your position is the correct one, you need to provide them with evidence, while also considering their beliefs and attitudes. This task requires an appeal to both reason and emotion. Exhibit 15.9 shows by example how to develop a proposition of policy.

Message Strategies

Speaker credibility and message credibility should work together to evoke some kind of identification in listeners. Listeners process information using both sides of the brain.[4] The left side of the brain processes rational argument and evidence (what Aristotle called logos), while the right side of the brain deals more with feelings and emotions (pathos and ethos). When a persuasive message appeals and adapts to both sides of listeners' brains—to both the rational and emotional sides of audience members—persuasion is likely. But it will not happen unless you, as a speaker, choose wise message strategies.

The discussion that follows examines four kinds of message strategies for persuasion: (1) one-sided versus two-sided arguments, (2) explicit versus implicit conclusions, (3) appeals to evoked recall, and (4) organization in a motivated sequence.

One-Sided Versus Two-Sided Arguments

Speakers are sometimes tempted to presenting only one side of an issue. They think they can make a stronger case for their positions if they don't tell about the other side. However, this strategy is almost always a mistake because it leaves listeners unprepared for arguments from the other side. For example, a candidate for the U.S. Senate used the "one term" and "citizen on leave" argument in the campaign. The candidate asserted that there were too many career politicians and that he would serve only for six years and then return to life as a private citizen. A year after election, the senator took a different position. It was important, he said, for senators to have seniority to advance the interests of the nation and their constituents. The senator then acknowledged ignoring the other side of the issue during the campaign: "I was wrong. There is an advantage to the state and

EXHIBIT 15.9

EXAMPLE PROPOSITIONS OF POLICY		
Policy Proposition	*Argument*	*Evidence*
Every student in this room should see the showing of Rembrandt etchings at the art museum.	This is a rare opportunity to see the work of one of the greatest artists in the history of western art at bargain prices.	Quote the museum curator saying the 100 works have been collected from many different sources, have never been seen together before, and probably will never be together again. Quote an art history professor saying how important Rembrandt's work is to western art. Report the price for student admission into the show and remind the students that the exhibit is local.
The City Council should reconsider their earlier approval of money to attract a steel mill to our community.	New evidence shows the original decision was unwise for both economic and environmental reasons.	Show the new evidence to establish that the new jobs created will not cover the investment on a per-job basis, and that the plant will dump more pollution into the air and water than originally thought. Show new evidence that the pollution levels, in combination with pollution from existing manufacturers, will total more than the environment can tolerate.
Citizens of this county and city should vote for passage of a 10-mill increase in property levies to support the schools.	The money is truly needed. There is no fat in the current, overextended budget for the schools. The schools are understaffed, overcrowded, and less effective than they were ten years ago. Moreover, there is no other way to raise the money that is needed.	Give facts and figures from reliable sources to support these statements. Need has to do with both extant and future goals, including physical plant maintenance, student population growth, etc., compared to the revenue available. "No fat" refers to possible waste and graft. Expert, outside opinion would be needed to support this argument. School officials might have a biased position. Staffing patterns and overcrowded classrooms can be supported on the basis of research into optimum class sizes, and by testimony from education experts. "No other way to raise the money" must be supported by testimony about legal and practical constraints from expert and credible witnesses.

the nation that arises from experienced legislative representation." Naturally, this upset the senator's supporters. They had never contemplated this argument in favor of reelection. Support for the senator waned in his home state and the public criticized his position that citizens would benefit from the six years of experience in Congress. Many supporters of the senator became angry and the senator seemed genuinely surprised that people would question his change of heart. The problem was that the senator had failed to sketch for voters the other side of the issue—the arguments in favor of longevity. Not surprisingly, at the next election, the senator had the fight of a lifetime.

Two-sided arguments help increase the speaker's believability.[5] Most people realize that nearly every issue has more than one side and they like speakers to be honest in presenting a case. In fact, speakers gain an advantage if they present not only the arguments in favor of their position but deal also with the opposing point of view. Even in cases where listeners are not aware of the other side, the two-sided approach is more desirable.[6] Wise advocates prepare audience members for later situations when they may face the other side head-on. Listeners feel more confident of their position if they hear the opposition arguments presented and countered.

Finally, depriving listeners of information that will help them to reach an informed decision is difficult to justify ethically. The long-term results of two-sided presentations are also encouraging. When people encounter the other side at a later time, they understand the arguments.

Explicit Versus Implicit Conclusions

Should a speaker tell listeners what to do in the speech conclusion? Most research indicates that drawing explicit **conclusions** for listeners—that is, telling them precisely what you want them to do or believe—is more effective than implying or hinting at the goal you have in mind.

Some people have argued that intelligent, well-educated, or well-informed listeners might resent a suggestion about their actions, but research does not support that argument. In fact, research indicates that effective persuasive speakers specifically often tell listeners what information or conclusion the listeners should get from the speech and also describe any actions that are necessary. This makes the actions easy to perform.[7]

Drawing an explicit conclusion for listeners also has considerable ethical merit. If you are "open" with your audience about the fundamental goals of your message, listeners do not have to wonder what they are being asked to believe. If you only implied or hinted at your conclusion, different audience members could reach varying conclusions, based on information they already have and their interpretation of your message. An explicitly drawn conclusion leaves no room for varying interpretations.

It is important to remember, however, that some people resent being told what to believe and may be mistrustful of the message if you follow the explicit approach. These people feel they are capable of coming up with the proper conclusions themselves, rather than being directed by the speaker.[8] For an audience that has only a modest amount of information on the subject, explicit conclusion drawing has clearly been shown to be the most effective approach.[9]

Evoked Recall Appeals

Motivation research has provided information about eight compelling needs that drive humans to believe or act.[10] Some have called these needs "hidden persuaders." In this text, they are called **evoked recall appeals** because they stimulate listeners to bring their prior experiences and emotions to bear. Each man and woman has as well, a child ego state. Our emotions and our emotional responses reside in the child inside each of us. The evoked recall appeals all assume that child needs and wants nurturing. Exhibit 15.10 lists, defines, and illustrates eight evoked recall appeals.

A good deal of research has studied the effects of the need for emotional security. One especially interesting set of questions centered on the use of fear appeals. **Fear appeals** involve using evidence or argument designed to induce fear in listeners as a means of motivating them to some decision or action.

Although research in the use of fear appeals is inconclusive, it suggests at least two principles. First, messages that create a substantial level of fear or anxiety in listeners will have greater effects than messages that fail to arouse much fear.[11] However, you should not conclude that the more fear you can create, the greater your chances for success. It is difficult to manage the level of fear you may arouse in listeners. If you succeed in arousing a high level of fear, audience members may choose not to listen to your arguments simply because the material disturbs them. See Exhibit 15.11.

The second principle suggested by research on the use of fear appeals is that the message should offer reasonable solutions to the level of fear. Campaigns against AIDS or cigarette smoking often ask listeners to engage in behaviors that for them, are virtually impossible. Cigarette smokers crave nicotine, and sexually active young adults regard abstinence as incomprehensible. The solutions a speaker offers in these situations should be aimed at striking a resonant chord. A reasonable solution moderates the fear. For example, a reasonable solution for smokers might be to use the "nicotine patch," while for persons potentially exposed to AIDS, it might be always using appropriate protection from sexually transmitted diseases.

EXHIBIT 15.10

	EXAMPLES OF EVOKED RECALL APPEALS		
Appeal	*Definition or explanation*	*Appeal*	*Example*
Need for emotional security	We have learned to fear; to experience emotional distress and insecurity.	Do what I ask, buy my product, etc., and you will feel secure.	Ad shows woman driving alone at night through the rain. "Buy our brand because there's so much riding on your tires."
Need for reassurance of worth	People often feel personally unimportant and "not okay."	This product, or compliance with this request, will make you worthy.	Announcer tells you to buy an expensive hair dressing "because you're worth it."
Need for ego gratification	People need attention beyond mere reassurance of worth.	Do what I ask and you will be seen as very important.	Ad tells you it's time for you to buy a luxury car to show others how successful you have been.
Need for creative outlets	People need and desire to create and build things.	Compliance with this request, purchase of this product, etc., will let you be creative.	The entire "do-it-yourself" industry depends upon appeals to the need for creative outlets. Cookbooks are sold with this appeal.
Need for love objects	People need outlets for their affection and loving feelings.	If you do what I ask you will fill the gap in your life.	Ad uses images of puppies and babies to evoke affectionate feelings in hopes you will attach these feelings to the thing offered for sale.
Need for a sense of power	Children grow up feeling powerless. The society teaches us to need and strive for power.	Comply with this request, buy this product, etc., and you will be powerful.	Ad for a pickup truck shows it climbing a steep hill or going easily over rough countryside.
Need for roots	Mobility has caused people to lose their sense of place. People who feel displaced are uncomfortable.	This product, service, etc., will give you a sense of place. It will help you feel rooted. It will comfort you.	*Old-time* lemonade. Political call for a *return to traditional values*. Restaurant that advertises *good old-fashioned home cooking like grandma used to make*. Resort that advertises *escape to a slower time* while showing happy people walking near a barn.
Need for immortality	Death is the deepest taboo in our society. Our culture teaches us life must go on, even after death.	Compliance with this request will extend your life in some important way.	Ads for hair coloring, ads for plastic surgery to remove wrinkles, and the entire life insurance business rest on this need.

Source: Michael S. Hanna and Gerald L. Wilson, *Communicating in Business and Professional Settings, 4/E* (New York: McGraw-Hill, 1998), p. 388.

EXHIBIT 15.11

EXAMPLE OF MODERATE FEAR APPEALS		
Example	*Appeal*	*Explanation*
"It's hard to maintain your dignity when you're lying helpless in a hospital bed waiting for AIDS to steal your body."	"Practice 'safe sex.' Don't end up like me."	"AIDS can be transmitted only through bodily fluids and blood."
"I'm only 40 years old and I'm dying of cancer."	"I've had my larynx removed. I have to fight this cancer, so I quit smoking. Don't wait as long as I did. Quit today."	"The Surgeon General of the United States says smoking causes cancer."
"I lost all of my family savings playing the lottery."	"I should have realized that, eventually, I couldn't beat the odds."	"Addiction can take many forms: alcohol, drugs, and gambling."

As a persuasive speaker, you should ask yourself the following questions about using fear as an appeal:

1. Does your use of fear appeals overstate or exaggerate the danger to listeners?
2. Is your appeal based on the latest available evidence from reliable expert sources?
3. Have you allowed your personal biases to cloud the accuracy and completeness of the appeal?
4. Is there likely to be a negative consequence to listeners if you use these fear appeals?

Policy decisions often are made because someone has used the motivated sequence. © Janice Rubin/Black Star/PNI

Organizing in a Motivated Sequence

In Chapter 8, "Organizing the Body of the Speech," you read about the **motivated sequence,** a pattern for organizing persuasive speeches that works effectively when you want to persuade. The motivated sequence follows the pattern of thinking many people use to analyze a new idea. Exhibit 15.12 reviews and describes the five steps and provides a brief example of the desired audience response at each step. Refer to Chapter 8 for a more detailed discussion of the motivated sequence.

EXHIBIT 15.12

THE MOTIVATED SEQUENCE REVISITED		
Sequence Steps	*Purpose*	*Desired Listener Response*
Attention step	Get attention	"This is interesting. I will listen to this."
Need step	Show the need; show the problem	"Something needs to be . . . (felt, decided, changed)
Satisfaction step	Satisfy the need; show a solution to the problem	"Yes, this is what we ought to . . . (feel, decide, change)
Visualization step	Visualize the results of accepting the solution— or of rejecting it.	"I can see myself in the future, enjoying the benefits of . . . (feeling, deciding, changing) this."
		"I can see how bad things will be in the future if I reject this."
Action step	Ask for action or approval	"I will . . . (feel, decide, change) this."

SUMMARY

Persuasive speakers are ethically bound to communicate honestly, without misleading, oversimplifying, coercing, or presenting unsupportable arguments and emotional appeals.

Persuasive speeches that succeed in achieving their goals are characterized by three elements: The speaker must have a high level of credibility with listeners, (2) the message must be credible, and (3) the speaker's chosen message strategies should appeal to both the rational and emotional needs of listeners. Speeches that do not meet these criteria are not likely to be persuasive.

Of the many theories and models of persuasion available, this chapter presents four that are especially useful to speech students. Aristotle described how to use ethical, emotional, and logical proofs to persuade. Hugh Rank developed an intensification/downplay model that suggests we should play up our own strong points and our competitors' weak points or play down our weak points and our competitors' strong points.

The (3) evoked recall model of persuasion argues persuasion is something we do to ourselves. The persuader presents images in an effort to cause people to identify and respond. (4) Milton Rokeach described a hierarchy of beliefs and values, and showed how they influence the kinds of choices people make.

The bulk of this chapter reviewed these four theories and made specific recommendations for their use in persuasion.

KEY TERMS

Artistic proofs
Belief
Derived beliefs
Ethos
Evoked recall appeals
Evoked recall model
  of persuasion
Explicit conclusions

Fear appeals
Identification
Intensification/downplay
  model of persuasion
Logical completeness
Logos
Matters of taste
Pathos

Persuasion
Primitive beliefs
Proposition
Proposition of fact
Proposition of policy
Proposition of value
Shared beliefs
Value

APPLICATION QUESTIONS

1. When you listen to a public speech, how do you determine the credibility of the speaker? How important is speaker credibility in most of the speeches you have heard?

2. Which message strategies do most prominent speakers use? What is your usual reaction to fear appeals and one-sided persuasion? Why?

3. How important a role do you feel ethics plays in the communication strategy of most public speakers? Is it more important for prominent speakers to observe ethical procedures than for the average person? Why?

4. Have most of the persuasive speeches you have heard included propositions of fact, value, or policy? Which type of proposition seems to be appropriate for most of your discussions? Why?

5. What can audiences do when speakers present the appearance, not the reality, of trustworthiness? Often, advocates of a position, such as health-care reform, distort the "facts" of the other side. How can listeners know the difference between being "fair to both sides of an issue" and only appearing to be fair? The answer in the long run is that citizens in a free society have an ethical obligation to inform themselves about the issues. In the short run, listeners can ask the speaker to elaborate on such things as summary statistics, asking who did the study (to reveal possible biases), how the responses broke down into separate categories (very negative, somewhat negative, and neutral can all be claimed as "not supporting" an idea, issue, or proposal), and whether or not the questions suggested a particular answer.

IT'S MORE FUN TO KNOW

Ethical behavior is the foundation of responsible persuasion. See Richard Johannesen, *Ethics in Communication, Fourth Edition* (Prospect Heights, IL: Waveland Press, 1996), Chapter 3, for the most recent guidelines to ethics in communication. Another consideration is which appeals a speaker will use in addressing listeners. Research on how we process information in the brain is conducted in many fields, most notably psychology and marketing. For an example of such scholarship, see Chris Janiszewski, "The Influence of Nonattended Material on the Processing of Advertising Claims," *Journal of Marketing Research* 27 (August 1990): 263–78.

One of the most important elements in a persuasive situation is the character/believability of the speaker. Much has been written about the importance of speaker credibility but the work by J. M. Kouzes and B. Z. Posner, *Credibility*, (San Francisco: Jossey Bass, 1993) applies this concept to specific matters in the "real world." And when a speaker presents the ideas, one of the major concerns is whether to present both sides of the issue or only one side. Arguments and evidence on this issue abound, and it would be profitable to examine the writing of Allen, et al "Testing a Model of Message Sidedness: Three Replications," *Communication Monographs* (1990) 57:275–291 for evidence on both sides of the controversy.

Whether to draw your conclusions specifically or encourage the audience to come to their own decisions is another issue that is debated with some regularity. Again, it is useful to look at the research on both sides of the issue. It is discussed with clarity in Kardes, et al "Moderating Effects of Prior Knowledge on the Perceived Diagnosticity of Beliefs Derived from Implicit versus Explicit Product Claims," *Journal of Business Research,* (1994) 29: 219–224.

The art of persuasive speaking is a challenging experience. To explore the field in depth, the most recent work that examines all dimensions and literature in the field in a highly readable fashion is Robert H. Gass and John S. Seiter, *Persuasion, Social Influence, and Compliance Gaining,* (Boston: Allyn and Bacon, 1999). It will answer most basic questions about research and application in this field.

SELF-TEST FOR REVIEW

Mark each of the following as either true (T) or false (F).

1. Aristotle's artistic proofs are ethos, pathos, and probos.   T   F

2. "Income taxes are too high for the average American" is a proposition of policy.   T   F

3. Persuasion is the activity of attempting to change the behavior of at least one person through manipulation.   T   F

4. Explicit conclusion drawing is an effective strategy because it avoids confusion in the minds of listeners.   T   F

5. Fear appeals always increase the effectiveness of a persuasive speaker.   T   F

6. In the intensification/downplay model of persuasion, people emphasize their own strong points and their competitors' weak points.   T   F

7. The term *logos* refers to the use of emotional appeals in an argument.   T   F

8. If your audience is aware of contrary arguments, it is best to use two-sided persuasion.   T   F

9. According to Rokeach, primitive beliefs are harder to change than derived beliefs.   T   F

10. The persuasive speaker develops credibility primarily through the message.   T   F

Answers: 1. F, 2. F, 3. F, 4. T, 5. F, 6. T, 7. F, 8. T, 9. T, 10. F.

SUGGESTED READINGS

Engel, S. Morris. *With Good Reason: An Introduction to Informal Fallacies.* 3rd ed. New York: St. Martin's Press, 1986. This lively book in the field of reasoning is filled with contemporary illustrations, making it ideal for anyone interested in reasoning and especially fallacies in contemporary argument. The book is extremely interesting and informative.

Gass, Robert H. and John S. Seiter. *Persuasion, Social Influence, and Compliance Gaining.* Boston: Allyn and Bacon, 1999. The latest and one of the best comprehensive works for students of persuasion. This work emphasizes the social and psychological bases of persuasion and successfully utilizes much information from contemporary events to illustrate the application of principles.

Johnston, Deidre D. *The Art and Science of Persuasion.* Dubuque, Iowa: Brown & Benchmark, 1994. This recent offering views persuasion from the process perspective, with allied emphasis on the components of persuasion and its societal impact. It is an excellent contemporary source for research and application of theory and ethics in the persuasion process.

Larson, Charles U. *Persuasion: Reception and Responsibility.* 8th ed. Belmont, Calif.: Wadsworth, 1998. This latest edition of the roots and techniques of persuasion is especially strong in its analysis of the persuasive campaign and movements. For student speakers who are looking for a strong, contemporary understanding of applied persuasion theory, this book should be required reading.

O'Keefe, Daniel J. *Persuasion: Theory and Research.* Newbury Park, Calif.: Sage, 1990. This offering is a highly effective collection of the research findings and implications of contemporary investigations into persuasion. One of its interesting strengths is its thorough and heavily documented discussion of the factors that influence persuasive effects.

Reardon, Kathleen Kelley. *Persuasion in Practice.* Newbury Park, Calif.: Sage, 1991. This work is especially valuable for researchers pursuing persuasion theory and practice. It is aimed, to a substantial degree, at the application of persuasion to the contemporary business and industrial environment and is a fine source of summary research findings in interpersonal, mass media, organizational, and political settings.

INTERNET ACTIVITIES

1. To get an idea of how detailed the study of persuasion can get, check out the final examination for a 500-level course about persuasion at the URL: *http://www.ipfw.edu/comm/courses/com518/Final.htm* If the professor of that course has taken down the web page, then go to the URL: *www.excite.com* and type the word "persuasion" into the search box. You will undoubtedly locate a number of courses by scrolling down the page. Make notes of your impressions so you can exchange your ideas with your classmates.

2. *www.altavista.com* found 457 web sites for the words "source credibility." Go there and browse through some of these sites. Does a pattern of issues and concerns occur to you? Share your notes with your classmates.

3. Go to the reference desk of the Internet Public Library at the URL: *http://www.ipl.org/ref/* and click on the sign "Ask a question." How might the library staff be able to help you find information?

4. The AltaVista search engine (*www.altavista.com*) found nearly half a million "hits" when asked to search for "values and beliefs." If you wanted to find useful and informative materials for your study of this chapter you would want to *refine your search*. Click on that link, then experiment with turning on and off the various toggles you find. Continue to refine your search until you find something you like. Record how you found it, then return to class prepared to discuss what you did and what you found.

NOTES

1. Robert H. Gass and John S. Seiter, *Persuasion, Social Influence, and Compliance Gaining*, (Boston: Allyn and Bacon, 1999), p. 32.

2. Hugh Rank, "Teaching About Public Persuasion," in *Teaching About Doublespeak*, ed. Daniel Dieterich (Urbana, IL: National Council of Teachers of English, 1976), Chapter 1.

3. Tony Schwartz, *The Responsive Chord*, (Garden City, NY: Anchor Press/Doubleday, 1973). Also see Tony Schwartz, *Media: The Second God* (New York: Random House, 1981).

4. See *http://www/healtouch.com/level1/leaflets/aslha/aslha030.htm*.

5. J. Hale, P. A. Mongeau, and R. M. Thomas, "Cognitive Processing of One- And Two-Sided Persuasive Messages," *Western Journal of Speech Communication* (1991) 55:380–389.

6. *Ibid.*

7. For an excellent review of research on this issue see Robert H. Gass and John S. Seiter, *Persuasion, Social Influence and Compliance Gaining*, (Boston: Allyn and Bacon, 1999) pp. 183–184.

8. F. R. Kardes, J, Kim, and J. S. Kim, "Moderating Effects of Prior Knowledge on the Perceived Diagnosticity of Beliefs Derived from Implicit Versus Explicit Product Claims," *Journal of Business Research*, (1994) 29: 219–224.

9. *Ibid.*

10. Vance Packard, *The Hidden Persuaders*, (New York: Pocket Books, 1954).

11. K.Witte and M. Allen, "When Do Scare Tactics Work? A Meta-Analysis of Fear Appeals," Paper presented at the annual meeting of the Speech Communication Association, San Diego, 1996.

CHAPTER 16

SPEECHES FOR SPECIAL OCCASIONS

OBJECTIVES

After reading this chapter, you should be able to:

1. Explain how special occasion speeches differ from other types of speeches.

2. Name and separate into three subgroups nine different kinds of special occasion speeches.

3. Explain the purpose of each of the nine special occasion speeches discussed in the chapter.

4. Cite criteria for evaluating the nine special occasion speeches presented in the chapter.

5. Explain how to secure information for an introductory speech.

6. Define and explain five techniques of humor: satire, irony, exaggeration, parody, and reversal of values.

OUTLINE

Objectives

Outline

Abstract

Imagine

Introduction

    Speeches of Praise

      and Tribute

      Introductory Speeches

      Presentation Speeches

      Acceptance Speeches

      Eulogies

    Inspirational Speeches

      Commencement Speeches

Keynote Speeches

    Welcoming Speeches

Speeches for the

    Sake of Humor

      After-Dinner Speeches

Summary

Key Terms

Application Questions

It's More Fun to Know

Self-Test for Review

Suggested Readings

Internet Activities

Notes

ABSTRACT

The special occasions of life often call for speech making designed to praise or pay tribute, to inspire, or just to have fun. This chapter describes how to develop nine different kinds of special occasion speeches: (1) introductory speeches, (2) presentation speeches, (3) acceptance speeches, (4) eulogies, (5) commencement speeches, (6) keynote speeches, (7) welcoming speeches, and (8) after-dinner speeches. These speeches can be grouped into three categories: speeches of praise and tribute, inspirational speeches, and speeches given for the sake of humor.

IMAGINE

About two weeks before graduation, one of her professors approached Charlene and asked if she would present the "Most Likely To Succeed" Award to her friend Beth. The professor assured her that she only would need to speak for a couple of minutes and since Charlene and Beth were close friends it should be a relatively easy job. Charlene agreed.

But in the days that followed, she had second thoughts. What could she say about Beth that would be interesting? Yes, Beth had a high GPA, had been an intern with a nationally known business, and was one of the most popular seniors. But would that interest all the students and the people at Commencement? Should she tell the story about how Beth studied all night for her math final, was certain she had flunked the test, and ended up with the highest score in the class? And what about her willingness to work with the Special Olympics every year? Would these sound like too much praise? Charlene did not know how much material to include. She had to make some choices and she didn't want to ask Beth for help.

INTRODUCTION

Most of your public speaking will be informative or persuasive, but on occasion you may find yourself preparing to speak in a ceremonial setting.[1] For example, you might be asked to introduce Tim Arthur, whom you have known since high school, or you might be asked to present an award to Betty Simpson, who has worked with you for the last four years. In both cases, the ideas suggested in previous chapters for informative and persuasive speaking may seem somewhat inappropriate. Special occasion speeches call for a different approach.

The number of different kinds of ceremonial occasions defies description, and this chapter cannot tell you how to prepare a speech for each of them. However, the information in this chapter applies to speeches for numerous other special occasions not mentioned here. What you need to remember for all special occasion speeches is that the purpose of the special occasion always determines what you should do as the speaker. Adhere consistently to that purpose. Find out what function your speech has to contribute. Since you cannot say everything about anything, focus on the audience and occasion. That focus marks all of the better special occasion speeches. The quality of special occasion speeches also depends on brevity, appropriateness, timing, and pacing.

Finally, most people enjoy giving special occasion speeches because such occasions are usually rich in human warmth and caring. The best special occasion speeches reflect that warmth and caring as well.

Speeches of Praise and Tribute

Praise is an expression of your approval or admiration, while **tributes** are acknowledgments of your gratitude, esteem, or regard. Let these definitions guide your thinking when presenting any of the following speeches of praise and tribute: (1) introductory speeches, (2) presentation speeches, (3) acceptance speeches, and (4) eulogies.

Introductory Speeches

One day, someone probably will ask you to introduce another speaker—to present an **introductory speech**—to an audience. The speaker might be an old friend, a political figure, or a company or community dignitary. The frequency of such requests is why introductory speeches are discussed first in this chapter.[2]

Introductory speeches have two purposes. First, you want to focus listener attention on the person you are introducing. Second, you want to prepare listeners for the speech that will follow. For example, you might wish to help establish speakers' credibility by talking about their qualifications. Or you might want to change the mood or to "pump up" a group that has been together through a long session already.

Limit yourself to a few minutes when introducing a speaker. Your function as introducer is important, but secondary. Arouse anticipation, focus attention on the speaker, then get out of the way.

Exhibit 16.1 lists questions you may want to ask yourself as you prepare to introduce a speaker. The biographical and audience-centered information implied by these questions will provide you with the raw materials for your speech.

If you do not personally know the speaker, arrange for an in-person or over-the-phone interview to get vital information. Get as com-

EXHIBIT 16.1

QUESTIONS TO ASK AS YOU PREPARE TO INTRODUCE A SPEAKER

What are the speaker's qualifications?

1. What credentials does the speaker have in the field of his speech?
2. What do the speaker and the audience have in common?
3. How well do you know this person?
4. How long and in what way have you been acquainted?
5. What do you think is this person's most outstanding characteristic?
6. Why do you think this person has been so successful?
7. How is this person different from the average person?
8. What four words do you think best describe this person?
9. How do this person's contemporaries regard her?
10. Do you know any anecdotes that show the person's ability or character?

plete a picture of the total person as you can. If an interview is not possible, then ask the speaker's friends or relatives for information. Again, the questions in Exhibit 16.1 are helpful for these interviews.

Try to find out if the speaking situation contains any special conditions or expectations that might influence the speech. For example, in an introductory speech audiences usually expect the introducer to not mention the name of the person being introduced until the last moment. This technique creates suspense and allows the person making the introduction to emphasize the name of the speaker as the last information given. If that is what your audience expects, you should conform.

The great orator from Illinois, Senator Everett Dirksen, ignored this rule at the 1964 Republican convention. His job was to introduce presidential candidate Barry Goldwater. Early in the speech, he mentioned Goldwater's name. This error resulted in a demonstration by delegates that lasted more than ten minutes. Meanwhile, Senator Dirksen could only stand and wait for the tumult to subside. Although he resumed his speech after the demonstration, Dirksen never again captured listeners' attention. His early mention of Goldwater violated the basic expectation of his audience that the candidate's name would be mentioned only at the close of the speech. Exhibit 16.2 shows general criteria for an introductory speech.

Exhibit 16.3 presents a sample introductory speech that was given at a Rotary Club meeting. Notice how the introduction is brief, outlines the speaker's qualifications and credentials, and stresses the similarity of aspiration and accomplishment between the speaker and Rotary Club members. Thus, the speech meets all the criteria for successful introductory speaking mentioned in Exhibit 16.2.

EXHIBIT 16.2

GENERAL CRITERIA FOR AN INTRODUCTORY SPEECH

An introductory speech should:

1. Be brief.

2. Discuss the speaker's general qualifications.

3. Explain the speaker's credentials in the topic field.

4. Give audience members reasons to listen.

5. Demonstrate a thorough knowledge of the speaker.

EXHIBIT 16.3

SAMPLE INTRODUCTORY SPEECH

It's an honor for me to introduce the mayor of Centertown to you. At a time when everyone else seems to be calling for reductions in every kind of federal program, this man's enormous knowledge of the problems of rural people in our state has made him an outspoken advocate for increased government aid to the farmer. In fact, last year he led a delegation to Washington. He personally presented the petition many of you signed for more liberal farm loan conditions to the secretary of agriculture.

As a farmer himself, the mayor understands the needs of rural people. If ever there was a dynamic representative of farmers and their concerns, he's it. Join me in welcoming a successful farmer and a hard and dedicated worker whose primary concern is the future of the American way of life. It's my pleasure to introduce a man some have called "Mr. Rural America." He's here tonight to talk to us about promises of the future for agriculture in America and what that means to us here in Jefferson County.

Presentation Speeches

A **presentation speech** is the talk given almost every time a person receives an award or a gift in public. Exhibit 16.4 lists the chronological steps that nearly all presentation speeches follow.

Every year, the Student Government Association (SGA) at most colleges and universities holds an awards banquet. An SGA president gave the presentation speech in Exhibit 16.5 at one such banquet. Notice how the speech generally follows the steps suggested in Exhibit 16.4.

Presentation and acceptance speeches occur every day. © Bob Daemmrich/Stock Boston

Acceptance Speeches

A presentation usually calls for the recipient to make an **acceptance speech** to thank the presenter and the organization that gave the gift or award. Exhibit 16.6 lists the chronological steps in giving an acceptance speech.

The acceptance speech should be short and simple and should allow the recipient's warmth and gratitude to show. For examples of both good and bad, long and short acceptance speeches, watch any telecast of the Academy Awards. Exhibit 16.7 shows how Martha Williamson accepted the Student Government Association Outstanding Service Award.

EXHIBIT 16.4

CHRONOLOGICAL STEPS IN MAKING A PRESENTATION SPEECH

1. Name the reason for giving the gift or award.

2. Name and describe the criteria used in making the decision to present the gift or award.

3. Show how the person receiving the gift or award met the criteria.

4. If the award was made competitively, praise the other participants who were not selected.

5. Call the person forward to receive the award or gift.

6. If the award or gift carries an inscription, read it aloud to the audience.

EXHIBIT 16.5

SAMPLE PRESENTATION SPEECH

Ladies and gentlemen, every year the members of the Student Government Association honor the senior student who has done the most to foster good government and to advance the school.

So many people have done so much to advance student government and to make this university a great one, that this year we had a lot of trouble deciding upon the recipient. We looked at the service records of the nominees. We considered the overall grade point averages of the nominees. We collected letters of recommendation and support from faculty and staff and from students within and outside the Student Government Association. Then we talked and talked before we finally made our selection.

This year's recipient has been a member of the Student Senate for four years. She has served as president of SGA. She was vice president of SGA. She served as president of Jaguar Productions—the group that screens and coordinates all on-campus concert and theatrical productions brought in from outside.

She has been president of Delta Zeta sorority, as well as rush chairperson. She was a member of the Pan Hellenic Council for three years. She serves as a rape-crisis volunteer, giving one twenty-four-hour period each month to be on call to rush to the Medical Center when she is needed.

And this year's recipient is a fine student. She carries an overall grade point average of 3.85. She has been on the Dean's List or the President's List every semester that she has been a student at South.

I'd like to add that she has accomplished all of these things while working twenty hours each week to help pay her way through college.

Martha Williamson, will you please come forward to let us recognize you?

[Pause until the honored person is standing next to the presenter.]

Ladies and gentlemen, this award includes a plaque and a $350 honorarium. Her name will be inscribed on a permanent tablet that hangs in the University Center. I'd like to read the inscription on the plaque.

The Student Government Association Outstanding Service Award for 1998 is given to Martha Williamson in recognition of her unstinting service to the university and the community.

Congratulations, Martha.

EXHIBIT 16.6

CHRONOLOGICAL STEPS IN GIVING AN ACCEPTANCE SPEECH

1. Thank the people who gave you the gift or award.
2. Thank the people who helped you to achieve the goals that resulted in the award or gift.
3. If appropriate, express your intention to live up to the honor.

EXHIBIT 16.7

SAMPLE ACCEPTANCE SPEECH

How can I possibly tell you how grateful I feel right now? I am honored to receive this award. And I am completely surprised. What I did I did out of love. I love this university. I have loved every minute of my four years here. And I am so very grateful to the Student Government Association for giving me the opportunities to learn about government and to grow as a person. So I thank you all for this award. It really belongs to all of you.

But I would like to name some of the people here who have been especially helpful to me. Abby Ratcliff, you should share in this award. You have been there when I've needed you these past four years. Ladies and gentlemen, I met Abby during freshman orientation four years ago, and we've been friends ever since.

How could I have done anything without Michael Kim Wong? I think he lives in the SGA office. I'd like to tell you that Mike knows more about how this university works than anyone I know. Thank you, Mike, for your advice.

And thank you all, again, for this high honor.

Eulogies

The word **eulogy** means to praise or speak well of a person. Eulogies most commonly occur at a ceremony following a death—but not always.[3] Sometimes, we eulogize the living. To illustrate, the adult children of one family threw a surprise eighty-fifth birthday party for their father. One of his sons gave the eulogy in Exhibit 16.8.

Eulogies are always informative speeches. Listeners expect and want you to teach them something about the person being honored. But more than inform, eulogies seek to inspire others through careful use of language. As you plan a speech of this kind, try to move beyond mere history. Portray a sense of the core values listeners share with your subject. Paint an image with words. You want to arouse or heighten listeners' appreciation and admiration for your subject. Exhibit 16.9 shows the chronological steps to follow when giving a eulogy.

Do not give a eulogy for a person you do not know, or if you are not familiar with the person's accomplishments or character. Without that information, your speech will sound like an awkward series of empty generalizations.

EXHIBIT 16.8

SAMPLE EULOGY

Ladies and gentlemen, this happy occasion honors my father, Solomon Feldman. I have loved him, admired him, respected him, and feared him for slightly more than fifty years.

My father is something of an institution around here. He owned the first automobile dealership in this city. He was elected mayor when he was thirty-five, and again when he was approaching sixty. He has served on nearly every civic board it is possible for a person to serve on in our town. He was president of the Kiwanis Club three times. He was once Chairman of the Board of Education. And he was once even incarcerated in our local jail. His offense was that he didn't grow a beard during the Daniel Boone Days Celebration.

I could list everything I know about my father's accomplishments, and then you, his dear friends, could undoubtedly add to them. So I would like to pay tribute to the Sol Feldman who's not a local legend—Sol Feldman, ordinary man, Sol Feldman, extraordinary father.

I remember taking my father for granted. He was always there for us—steadfast and supportive. Now, looking back from my adult perspective, I am amazed when I recall how much time my father found to give his children. I will never forget my father's careful guidance in basic things that children must know. He taught us moral values by his example, by his engaging conversations. And, occasionally, he taught moral values by placing his hand firmly on one of our backsides. He taught us the value of work. He taught us the value of worship. He taught us the value of play, too. But he did all this teaching, it seems to me now, in a very low key, and with enormous patience. Mostly, he taught by example.

One day, I recall, the phone rang. It was Dr. Virtle's office. Could Daddy come right away to the hospital? And since we were alone in the house—I don't remember where Mama was—he said, "Come on. Now. There's been an accident. Someone needs blood." I asked him who it was, and he said, "I don't know, son. But God gave us each a special kind of blood. When they need our kind, we're the only place they can get it." That's the way my father has lived his life for eighty-five years—untiring, unstinting, selfless.

So, ladies and gentlemen, my father taught us what it means to love. It seems to me that one word, love, characterizes him more than any other. My father has always been, and still is, a great lover. He loves his family. He loves his community. He loves this place.

I know that you have all gathered here to honor Solomon Feldman on his eighty-fifth birthday, and I know you will all have a way to tell him that tonight. I'd like to speak for my family.

Daddy, we don't tell you enough that we love you back.

EXHIBIT 16.9

CHRONOLOGICAL STEPS IN GIVING A EULOGY

1. Identify your knowledge of the person.

2. Recognize the person's humanity.

3. Describe ways the person's life touched others, and give specific examples.

4. Restate the person's most basic characteristic.

Eulogies praise both the living and the dead. © John Coletti/Picture Cube

Listeners expect a tribute to focus on a person's human side. Point to your subject's significant, human characteristics. Discuss what made the person unusual or outstanding. And do not worry that the person may not have been a world leader or that you may not be a great orator. Plain, simple people and their basic goodness form the basis of our society. Plain, simple people usually give the best eulogies, too.

Inspirational Speeches

Inspirational speeches are meant to arouse, to animate, to quicken. Commencement speeches, keynote addresses, and welcoming speeches all fall into this category.

Commencement Speeches

A **commencement speech** is an address given during graduation ceremonies.[4] Perhaps the most common failing of commencement presentations is that they are long-winded. Audience members want to hear brief, glowing statements about their children, relatives, or friends. Their primary concern is with the ritual. They want to see the presentation of diplomas. Whatever precedes that presentation of diplomas should be brief, complimentary, and perhaps slightly challenging. Exhibit 16.10 lists the main criteria for a commencement speech.

EXHIBIT 16.10

CRITERIA FOR A COMMENCEMENT SPEECH
1. Comment on the nature of the occasion.
2. Acknowledge the contributions and sacrifices of the graduates and the audience.
3. Provide challenge or define the role of graduates, and suggest methods for success.
4. Avoid clichés.
5. Express sincere, simple feelings.
6. Be brief.

University President Ed Powers delivered the commencement speech shown in part in Exhibit 16.11. Applying the criteria in Exhibit 16.10 to this speech shows that Dr. Powers systematically met each standard. He acknowledged personal sacrifices and paid tribute to parents and students. He recognized the movement of the students into the work force. He suggested guidelines for career success. Best of all, he spoke for only ten minutes. Remember that, on ceremonial occasions like this, audiences want brevity, simplicity, and clarity.

Keynote Speeches

A **keynote speech** is given at the beginning of nearly every social or business function. An official, a celebrity, or perhaps a local dignitary addresses the audience to set the tone or mood for the meeting and the people attending. The speech can be inspirational, challenging, or problem oriented, as long as it sets the tone and gets things moving.

Most keynote speeches have the same objective—to generate enthusiasm and audience arousal. Like speeches of introduction, they should be brief and clearly stated. Unlike an introductory speech however, a keynote speech is a major focus of the meeting. The keynote speaker does not play second fiddle to the rest of the program or to the next speaker. Indeed, the keynote speech may receive more attention than any other part of the meeting.

Studies of conferences, conventions, business meetings, and the like show that getting off to a good start is essential. The keynote speech can establish the mood for the entire session. Thus, as a keynote speaker, you should state the theme or goals, and try to generate excitement and enthusiasm. Exhibit 16.12 suggests criteria for a keynote speech.

Exhibit 16.13 shows a portion of a keynote speech given at the annual sales meeting of a paper company. A study of this speech shows that the speaker integrated several of the Exhibit 16.12 criteria into his message.

Welcoming Speeches

Welcoming speeches occur most commonly when groups visit organizations and local businesses. Someone welcomes them to the company and may also conduct a tour of the facility. Similarly, groups of high school students and their parents often visit college campuses for "get acquainted days" that typically involve a number of welcoming speeches.

Welcoming speeches acknowledge the visitors and extend the hospitality of the organization. Thus, such speeches are usually brief and pointed. Exhibit 16.14 suggests the chronological steps to follow in making a welcoming speech. Exhibit 16.15 shows how one speaker welcomed a group of students and their parents to a "get acquainted day" recently.

EXHIBIT 16.11

SAMPLE COMMENCEMENT SPEECH

I want to be the first to applaud these graduates for their efforts and the sacrifices they made to be here today. I know the hours they've spent cracking the books when it would be much easier to play some hoops or listen to the latest CD. I know how tempting it is to put off the reading or writing assignment that is due until that last minute because the personal calendar is full of events that are much more attractive—watching a movie nominated for an Academy Award or heading out for some pizza.

I want to recognize the efforts so many of you have made in your personal quest for the degree. I applaud you, the part-time student. It's not easy to hold down a full-time job and succeed in classes. I applaud you full-time students whose major efforts are directed toward the beginning of a new career. For some of you, your education has been an enormous drain on your energies and meager financial resources. For many others of you, though, it was your folks who placed your needs for education ahead of their own desires. They had to dig deeply to pay the tuition bills, and skip the dinners out they thought they would be able to afford once you had gotten beyond high school. They suffered along with you about your goals for your life and your job opportunities after graduation. They have wanted for you the chances they never had. They're the model parents. Yes, they may have a fault or two, but they want for you a life just a bit better than they have had. And isn't that what you will want for your children? So this is an occasion for recognizing both the accomplishments of the graduates as well as the sacrifices of the parents.

Today, I want to challenge each of you graduates to be a success. And becoming a success is not easy. But I think I may be able to give you three suggestions about how you can be a success, regardless of what kind of job you choose to take.

Keep up-to-date in your field. The level of your job doesn't matter. You could be a customer service representative or a store manager. In any case, you must stay aware of developments in your field. You must know your job and the information needed to do your work effectively. Because your formal education may have ended does not mean you should stop being intellectually curious. Look, question, and read. New ideas are the best source for improving yourself and your work. You must know what others are doing or suggesting should be done.

Give it your best. There's no substitute for applying your efforts to your job. No one wants to hire or keep a lazy employee. All jobs become boring in one way or another, but you'll need to work your way through those times with the same energy and effort you show in the interesting and exciting moments. [Dr. Powers briefly discussed work and working. He then outlined how hard work and knowledge of the job are the keys to success.]

Finally, you need to believe in yourself and your talent. Let's call it self-confidence. You must believe you can perform. You must approach each task with a positive mental attitude. Your actions, attitudes, and accomplishments are significant if you trust yourself. You can succeed at your chores if you believe in yourself.

The road to success is difficult at best. Many people have made sacrifices to provide you graduates with the opportunity to succeed. But your degrees today are no guarantees of success. Society expects much from you. You are the leaders of this generation. You will be the experts in your field.

Your employers expect you to know your subject, remain abreast of new developments, and work hard with all the information available. They'll provide you with the place to work, the opportunities for success, but you must make your own contribution. And don't forget that you must believe in yourself, whether things are going your way or against you. Persevere.

I challenge you to be all that you and those who know you realize is possible. Can you meet that challenge? [Dr. Powers concluded with a restatement of his earlier formula for success.]

EXHIBIT 16.12

CRITERIA FOR A KEYNOTE SPEECH

1. Determine the purpose or theme of the meeting.

2. Use the theme as the central part of your speech.

3. Show the importance and relevance of the theme to listeners.

4. Gear the speech to the common concerns of the audience.

5. Show your personal concern for the central theme of the meeting.

EXHIBIT 16.13

SAMPLE KEYNOTE SPEECH

Fred Allen once defined the term conference to mean "a gathering of important people who singly can do nothing, but together can decide that nothing can be done." He could not have been thinking of this group.

As I look around this room this morning, I see dozens of success stories seated around me. I see people who have learned how important Shelter Paper and its products are to daily living. But their learning didn't stop there. You decided it was important that all those paper users needed to understand that we stand for quality and service more than any other company in our business.

That's not an easy job, but who ever said that Shelter Paper looked for the easy market and the easy sales? We've been leaders because we've taken on the opposition head-to-head for years and always come out the winner. Your attitude, your work, and your success are the reasons we continue to be the leader in paper product sales for the thirty-fifth consecutive year.

We're not here as a mutual admiration society. You and I are at this annual sales meeting to find out why we've been successful, why we lost some of those sales we really should have made, and to be updated on the latest products and techniques in our business.

But this is important. We need to remember that we are winners. What company in this business can claim to have larger sales, better paid salespeople and managers, or a more efficient home office staff? Your answer to that question is the same as mine: None. And no one will even come close if we continue to think and act like the winners we at Shelter have become over the years. Yes, it's the power of positive thinking. We're the best, and no one is going to take that position from us.

We work harder and have a better product. But most of all, we have the best people in the industry working for us. When you have the best people and the best product, you're going to be a winner.

That's what we have here today. Winners sitting next to winners. Our margin of victory is greater today than ever before and that is because each of you has thought, acted, and sold positively.

EXHIBIT 16.14

CHRONOLOGICAL STEPS IN GIVING A WELCOMING SPEECH
1. Greet the group, tell them who you are, and how you connect to the organization.
2. Express pleasure that the group has arrived for its visit.
3. Explain what will happen next, and offer to be of any service you can.

EXHIBIT 16.15

SAMPLE WELCOMING SPEECH
Good morning, ladies and gentlemen, and welcome to this get acquainted day. And especially to you students who are visiting us, welcome. My name is Tyrone Pate. I am a junior majoring in political science and I am one of the two junior class senators in the Student Government Association.
On behalf of everyone connected with the university, I'd like to say how happy I am that you have joined us today. You honor us by coming out today. I know you could be visiting a different college right now.
It's going to be a full day if you do everything we've planned. But of course, you don't have to do it all. You're welcome to come and go anywhere, of course, or just to hang around in the library or the University Center if you want.
If you'll look at the schedule that we placed in your chair, you'll see that our activities begin in about fifteen minutes with tours of the campus. That will take about an hour, maybe an hour and a half. Then you will meet some of our faculty. You have already indicated which departments you would like to visit. All the meetings are going to happen in two buildings, and the tour guides will show you where to go. After you meet the faculty, the tour guides will bring you to lunch. We've got a special music program for you at noon.
In just one more moment, Jack Reed will get you together with your student tour guide. They're all standing in the back, wearing red, white, and blue uniforms. Before we break up, let me say again, how glad I am to see you. We're proud of this school, and we'd like to share it with you. If there is anything I or any one of the tour guides can do to make your stay more pleasant, please speak right up. I'll see you at lunch.

Speeches for the Sake of Humor

So far, we have looked at what you must do to succeed when giving a speech of praise or tribute, or when you are trying to inspire others. Many special occasions, however, call for speeches that have humor as their primary goal. The word *humor* refers to a comic quality that causes amusement. Speeches in this category seek to be funny and comical, to show a sense of fun, and to produce laughter. After-dinner speeches are among the most common of this type.

After-Dinner Speeches

Nowadays, **after-dinner speeches** follow almost every kind of social meal. They are usually brief—no more than about ten minutes—and they often are designed to be entertaining.

Almost any subject can serve as the topic for an after-dinner speech if it lends itself to the light touch. Let your own good taste guide you.[5] But you obviously would not want to talk about cancer or herpes, child abuse, or the abortion issue.

Not everyone understands this commonsense suggestion. In one situation, a group of about 150 law enforcement officers and administrators had to sit through a tasteless presentation about automobile accidents immediately after they had eaten lunch. The speaker even showed full-color 35-millimeter slides. Many of the listeners simply got up and left the room.

The first thought most people have when someone invites them to give an after-dinner speech is that it must be funny. Humor, of course, plays an important part, but you do not have to be a stand-up comedian to succeed. Still, timing and a sense of the comical do not come readily to everyone. So after-dinner speaking can provide a special problem for people who do not easily poke fun. If you are one of these, and if you find yourself faced with having to give an after-dinner speech, either decline the invitation or focus your attention on *interesting* the audience. Before you take this option, however, double-check that taking an "interesting" (as opposed to "funny") approach will seem appropriate to listeners in that particular context. Discuss this matter with the person who invited you to give the speech.

Strip after-dinner speeches of technical detail and contentiousness. This is not the time to champion your point of view or to grind an ax. Rather, take a light-hearted, imaginative, stimulating approach. Make a point, but do it with consideration for the feelings and expectations of listeners.

Most after-dinner speakers prefer delivering either one-point speeches or pleasantry speeches. In the **one-point after-dinner speech,** the speaker states a central thought and then wraps stories, anecdotes, quotations, and the like around that central thought. In the **pleasantry speech,** the after-dinner speaker gently pokes fun. Almost anything can be a "target" for pleasantry: the audience, some institution, some person who represents a group or institution, some idea.

Pleasantry is not satire. **Satire** is the use of ridicule to expose, denounce, or deride. Thus, satire is negative and hurtful, and has a cutting edge. In contrast, pleasantry is usually expressed as (1) irony, (2) exaggeration, (3) parody, or (4) reversal of values.

Irony is saying one thing but meaning the opposite—on the condition that the result is a humorous insight. Be careful. When irony takes on a cutting edge, it is satire or sarcasm. For example, several people spoke at a retirement banquet honoring a local judge. They were generally full of praise for the judge's skill and insight over the course of her career. You can imagine the laughter, then, when the district attorney said, "She once handed down a judgment that was so subtle and cognitively complex nobody knew what she meant."

Exaggeration means blowing things up beyond the limits of truth, to increase or enlarge abnormally. For example, a school swimming coach made the following remark about his best woman freestyle swimmer—an Olympics contender—after a sports banquet: "She started her competitive career in swimming as a lifeguard at a car wash."

Parody is imitation for the sake of humor. This is a common form of humor on late-night television. An example of parody would be someone, for the sake of humor, imitating the president of the United States, but changing the content of what the president might say. Television's "Saturday Night Live" has used parody for years as a mainstay of its humor.

Reversal of values is a technique in which the speaker makes something significant out of the trivial, or something trivial out of the important. The fun is in the surprise turn. When a professor of geography was selected to give the Dean's Lecture—an honor that falls on some member of the faculty at the University of South Alabama once each year—the dean said:

How far is going too far in satire, irony, exaggeration, parody, or reversal of values?

> *He is not only a fine geographer with an enviable publication record, ladies and gentlemen, he's also a fine cartographer. His work in mapping the silt deposits flowing out of Mobile Bay and the Mississippi River have made him quite a reputation. He's published more than twenty separate maps over the past six years. Now if only he could show us how to refold them.*

A story is told of Supreme Court Justice Felix Frankfurter that also illustrates reversal of values. A friend asked Justice Frankfurter to officiate at her wedding ceremony. Justice Frankfurter explained that he did not have the authority to perform the ceremony. "What?" his friend exclaimed. "A Supreme Court Justice doesn't have the authority to marry people. Why not?" Frankfurter replied, "I guess it's because marriage is not considered a federal offense."

Exhibit 16.16 suggests steps in preparing an after-dinner speech.

> *Good evening ladies and gentlemen. The real challenge I face here after this wonderful meal is finding a way to keep all of you awake. Perhaps some of you feel a little like some of those passengers on Northwest Air Lines in Detroit who were trapped in their planes, on the runways, for up to eight hours with no food and very little drink. They were captives – you can always walk out.*
>
> *Sometimes each of us gets a little large for our real role. There's a story about Calvin Coolidge when we was Vice President and was living, for a time, in a hotel suite in Washington. Fire broke out in the building and everyone had to leave. Coolidge lost his patience after a while when nothing seemed to be happening and he tried to return to his rooms. But*

EXHIBIT 16.16

STEPS IN PREPARING AN AFTER-DINNER SPEECH

1. Determine the interests that audience members share in common.

2. Determine the approach you will take.

    A. If you decide to take the one-point approach:

    Select a central theme.

    Look for the fun in the theme.

    Select stories, anecdotes, quotations, and so on that bear on that theme.

    Organize your ideas so that they build to a high point.

    B. If you decide on pleasantry as your approach:

    Select a "target" subject.

    Look for irony, exaggeration, parody, and reversal of values.

    Tie the speech to a central theme that holds the various pieces together.

before he could go back upstairs he was stopped by the Fire Marshall who asked for identification. "I am the Vice President," Coolidge said, angry because he was being stopped. "Vice President of what?" asked the Marshall. "I am Vice President of the United States," Coolidge responded very sharply. "Then get back outside," the Fire Marshall said. "I thought you were vice president of the hotel."

This is the same man Coolidge, who later was President. When asked what he did for exercise replied, "I have my picture taken."

Now Coolidge was a man of few words, although not one of our outstanding national leaders. He was, as one of our great national philosophers said, "tight as a tick." Part of his thrift showed in a discussion of spending more money on military aviation. Coolidge is reported to have said to his cabinet in all seriousness, "Why can't we just buy one airplane and have all the pilots take turns?"

I guess the mood of Coolidge could best be summed up by his responses to a series of questions put to him by a reporter. To each question he answered, "No." After the interview ended he said, "Now don't quote me."

Most of you here this evening did not expect anyone to speak to you about Calvin Coolidge, but his brevity in speech is something all of us could learn. And Coolidge said he knew his role well, something that always is desirable. According to "Silent" Cal: "I always figured the American public wanted a solemn ass for President, so I went along with them."

I'm going to try to use some of his brevity tonight. When asked if he had something to say, Cal said: "Nope, I'm done." And so am I.

SUMMARY

Our lives include many special occasions that call for speech making. Speeches for special occasions require different approaches from the other types of public speaking situations discussed in this book. However, they share the need for effective and thorough preparation, knowledge of the audience, and speaker understanding of the person or occasion. All are audience centered and your success in these settings is largely determined by the carefulness of your preparation.

Speeches of praise and tribute include introductory speeches, presentation speeches, acceptance speeches, and eulogies. The introductory speech has two purposes: to focus listener attention on the person being introduced and to prepare listeners for the speech to follow. It is characterized by brevity and the presentation of basic biographical information about the speaker, such as qualifications and credentials. Gather facts and background information to create a picture of the total person. Remember that your purpose is only to introduce the main speaker. The audience is there primarily to listen to the other person, not you.

A presentation speech is the special occasion speech given when a gift or award is presented. The speaker names and describes the reason for giving the gift or award and the criteria used in deciding who should receive it. The speaker may then describe the recipient's personal qualifications for receiving the award. After the recipient has been called forward, the speaker reads any inscription on the award.

A presentation usually calls for the recipient of the gift or award to make an acceptance speech. The recipient thanks the people who gave the gift or award and the people who helped the recipient to achieve the goals that resulted in the presentation.

Eulogies are usually presented at ceremonies following a death, although the living are also sometimes eulogized. Eulogies require speakers to inform listeners about the person being honored—especially the person's significant human characteristics and specific ways in which the person's life touched others.

Inspirational speeches are meant to arouse and inspire. Commencement speeches, keynote speeches, and welcoming speeches fall into this category. Commencement speeches should acknowledge the personal sacrifices of parents and students and should define the role of graduates and suggest methods for achieving success. Such ceremonial occasions require speaker brevity, simplicity, and clarity.

A keynote speech is a special occasion speech that sets the tone or mood for the meeting and the people attending. It is the major focus of the meeting and is designed to create audience enthusiasm. To accomplish this emotional arousal, the speaker must determine the theme of the meeting, show how the theme is important to the speech and to listeners, gear the speech to the common concerns of listeners, and show a genuine interest in the topic and the audience.

Welcoming speeches are commonly presented when groups visit schools or organizations. The speaker briefly greets the group, expresses pleasure that the group has come, explains what will happen next, and offers to be of service.

Many special occasions call for speeches that have humor as their primary goal. Speeches for the sake of humor include after-dinner speeches. After-dinner speakers usually take a humorous approach, although some prefer to focus on interesting audience members rather than entertaining them. One-point after-dinner speeches and pleasantry speeches are commonly used formats. Successful after-dinner speakers often employ the techniques of irony, exaggeration, parody, and reversal of values.

KEY TERMS

Acceptance speech	Introductory speech	Pleasantry speech
After-dinner speech	Irony	Presentation speech
Commencement speech	Keynote speech	Reversal of values
Eulogy	One-point after-dinner speech	Satire
Exaggeration	Parody	Welcoming speech

APPLICATION QUESTIONS

1. What special occasion speech have you heard most recently? In what category would you place it? Using the criteria provided in the chapter, how well did the speech meet those standards?

2. Prepare a list of special occasion speeches that you have heard. What were the predominant strengths and weaknesses of each one? Given your reading of this chapter, could you suggest ways to improve the speeches? What changes would you recommend and why? Assume for the sake of this exercise that any meal is a special occasion. After a meal with friends or family members, make a little speech in which you praise the people at the table with you. Follow the suggestions in this chapter. Then report your experience to the class. What effect did your speech have on the people you praised? Would you judge the speech a success? Looking back, would you have changed the speech in any way?

3. Were you officially welcomed to campus when you arrived as a freshman? Was there an orientation period? Did an administrator make an official welcoming speech? Who was it? Can you remember the event well enough to evaluate what happened in terms of the guidelines for welcoming speeches presented on page 394?

IT'S MORE FUN TO KNOW

Speeches for special occasions always have represented an unusual challenge. The setting typically is either very happy or unusually sad. The speaker has challenges that are as difficult as any classroom assignment. For those occasions where a friend or relative is being mourned, an excellent source of illustrative material is Phyllis Theroux, *The Book of Eulogies: A Collection of Memorial Tributes, Poetry, Essays, and Letters of Condolences*, (New York: Scribner, 1997). For those situations where you must introduce or nominate others, you might consult Dianna Daniels Booher, *Executive's Portfolio of Model Speeches for All Occasions*, (Englewood Cliffs, NJ: Prentice-Hall, 1992) for excellent sample materials. Andrew Albanese (Ed) *Graduation Day: The Best of America's Commencement Speeches*, (New York: Scholastic Trade, 1996) is one of the best sources for specimen commencement materials. There is no substitute for examining models of the most effective presentations. Consider consulting one or more of these sources, as your needs require. Overall, the best single reference possibly is William Safire (Ed), *Lend Me Your Ears*, (New York: W. W. Norton Company, 1997).

SELF-TEST FOR REVIEW

1. Match the kinds of special occasion speeches in the left-hand column with the categories of special occasion speeches in the right-hand column.

    ____ a. Welcoming speech

    ____ b. Eulogy

    ____ c. After-dinner speech

    ____ d. Commencement speech

    ____ e. Keynote speech

    ____ f. Acceptance speech

    ____ g. Introductory speech

    ____ h. Presentation speech

1. Speech of praise or tribute

2. Inspirational speech

3. Speech given for sake of humor

2. Match the kinds of special occasion speeches in the left-hand column with the statements in the right-hand column that best describe them.

    ____ a. Welcoming speech

    ____ b. Eulogy

    ____ c. After-dinner speech

    ____ d. Commencement speech

    ____ e. Keynote speech

    ____ f. Acceptance speech

    ____ g. Introductory speech

    ____ h. Presentation speech

1. To focus listeners' attention on the speech they are about to hear

2. To give a gift or award in public

3. To thank a presenter or an organization for a gift or award

4. To praise or speak well of someone

5. To acknowledge contributions and sacrifices

6. To set the tone or mood of a meeting and to provide a challenge

7. To greet a group and extend the hospitality of the organization

8. To provide a light or humorous finish following a meal

3. Mark the following statements: 1 = Good advice about speaking for special occasions; 2 = Bad advice about speaking for special occasions.

    ____ a. It is usually not a good idea to ask people about themselves before introducing them. Instead, ask someone who knows them.

    ____ b. Try to understand if the speaking situation assumes expectations that can influence the speech.

    ____ c. Always name and describe the criteria used in deciding who should receive an award.

    ____ d. In an acceptance speech, it is a good idea to thank the people who helped you achieve the award.

    ____ e. Do not eulogize a living person.

____ f. Eulogies are always persuasive speeches, but the persuasion has to be subtle and in line with the achievements of the person you are eulogizing.

____ g. Keep a commencement address short and sweet.

____ h. Let the theme of a meeting guide your keynote speech.

4. Match the definitions in the left-hand column with the correct terms in the right-hand column.

____ a. Use of ridicule to expose, denounce, or deride

____ b. Pretending the trivial is significant

____ c. Imitation for the sake of humor

____ d. Blowing something up beyond the limits truth

____ e. Saying one thing and meaning another for humorous insight

1. Irony

2. Exaggeration significant is trivial

3. Parody

4. Reversal of values

5. Satire

Answers: 1. a. 1, b. 1, c. 3, d. 2, e. 2, f. 2, g. 1, h. 1, 2. a. 7, b. 4, c. 8, d. 5, e. 6, f. 3, g. 1, h. 2, 3. a. 2, b. 1, c. 1, d. 1, e. 2, f. 2, g. 1, h. 1, 4. a. 5, b. 4, c. 3, d. 2, e. 1.

SUGGESTED READINGS

Johannesen, Richard L., R. R. Allen, and Wil A. Linkugel. *Contemporary American Speeches.* 8th ed. Dubuque, Iowa: Kendall-Hunt, 1996. This book is a good source for model special occasion speeches. The authors explain each speech type, give the criteria, and outline the major features of the speeches they include.

Vital Speeches of the Day. Southhold, N.Y.: City New Publishing. This is the premiere source of contemporary speeches in American society. Published twice each month and found in nearly every college library, *Vital Speeches* contains speeches of all kinds about current national and international concerns.

INTERNET ACTIVITIES

1. You can see and hear some famous sample speeches at the URL: *http://www.history channel. com/speeches/index.html*

2. The Texas School Board Association provides sample speeches for its members at: *http://www.tasb.org/Education/speech3.html* Go to that address and see what you think of the speech samples.

3. Go to *http://www.Altavista.com* and type the language "Humor and stories for speakers." Browse through the many options, then come to class prepared to discuss what you found with your classmates.

NOTES

1. For perhaps the best examples see William Safire (Ed), *Lend Me Your Ears*, (New York: W. W. Norton Company, 1997).

2. Dianna Daniels Booher, *Executive's Portfolio of Model Speeches for All Occasions*, (Englewood Cliffs, NJ: Prentice-Hall, 1992).

3. Phyllis Theroux, *The Book of Eulogies: A Collection of Memorial Tributes, Poetry, Essays, and Letters of Condolence*, (New York: Scribner, 1997).

4. See, as examples, Harold Hill (Ed) *Life Isn't Fair: 300 Years of Advice from History's Most Memorable Commencements* (Gilbert, AZ: Perigee, 1997); Kimberly Colen (Ed), *Hold Fast Your Dreams: Twenty Commencement Speeches*, (New York: Scholastic Trade), 1996; and Andrew Albanese (Ed), *Graduation Day: The Best of America's Commencement Speeches*, (New York: William Murrow & Company, 1998).

5. John Davis Long, *After-Dinner and Other Speeches*, (North Stratford, NH: Ayer Co, Publishers, 1995).

Sample Speeches

Never Give Up: The Power of Perseverance

Address by WILLIAM R. CONROY, *Doctor of Dental Surgery, Delivered to the North Attleboro High School, North Attleboro, Massachusetts, June 7, 1998.*

Thank you Vice Principal Pickering. Superintendent Dr. DeGoes, Principal Whitty, Vice Principal Pickering, Members of the School Committee, Parents, Grandparents, Family, Friends, and the Graduates of 1998!

Before I begin I would like to thank all of you for giving me this opportunity to speak. It was just 20 years ago that I was sitting in your seats graduating from North Attleboro High School. It really does seem like yesterday. I even see some of my former teachers out there! What really blows me away when I think back on those years, is that many of you were just being born around the time I was graduating and going off to college. Wow! Time sure does fly. It is just amazing, isn't it? I wish we could bottle time!

I also wish I could remember more about my graduation day, but I have to admit it's a little hazy to me now. I can only remember bits and pieces of it. So this day won't be hazy to you, I would like all of you to take a moment and look at the person on your right and on your left. Write their names down in your YearBook and every so often remember them and this time and place. For this is a special moment and I don't want you to forget it! You know you will have many birthdays, Fourth of Julys, Thanksgivings, and other events and holidays, but you will only graduate once from high school. So recall this unrepeatable moment and remember all the special people who are here right now. Don't forget it. For this is an unrepeatable moment!

At this time I think we should thank your parents and all your loved ones for helping you achieve your diploma. Let's give them a hand! And I also think we should thank your teachers for helping you to grow and to learn your lessons. Let's give them a hand!

It's kind of funny to be standing here right now, because as I said, I graduated from North High just 20 years ago, and I never thought I'd be delivering the Commencement Address some day. I'm sure even some of my teachers are surprised! Is my English teacher Miss Bedard out there today? But I've often been told by former teachers and administrators that my class, the Class of 1979, was an exceptional one. I would like to acknowledge my classmates, some who are here today, and represent them as I speak this afternoon. And so many of my classmates went on to become business and professional people, teachers, and most importantly, responsible mothers and fathers . . . I'm so proud of my class and I know our teachers are too. I also know that it was not by accident that the success of my class is a direct result of their experience and growth at North High.

Honestly, I can tell you that I loved my days here and have many fond memories. I remember standing on this field because I was a member of the football team, and by the way, congratulations on your Super Bowl victory, I'm very proud of you and I applaud you for your achievement. And I played baseball right over there as a member of the baseball team, and in our gym right behind us, I played for our basketball team.

I participated in a number of different activities, and I enjoyed them all . . . I loved my experiences at North High and I am honored you invited me to speak today.

And I learned many important lessons in the classroom too. It was North High that prepared me for my future education. I recall a conversation we had as students with our chemistry teacher, who we had during our sophomore year. A number of us in the class were complaining about a tedious chemistry experiment that we were having a very tough time with. We argued that it wasn't important because we would never be using this material again. Our teacher explained to us that although this was true, the lab experiment was an experiment in thinking! That throughout the educational process the lessons learned would be forgotten and seemingly useless; however, the overall effect would be improvement in one's ability to think and reason out problems. He also explained that nothing learned is wasted! I recalled that conversation often after I left North Attleboro High. Just think of this: my lessons learned in high school were central building blocks towards a final goal . . . I was learning something well beyond my subjects . . . nothing learned is wasted.

After I graduated I went on to Bowdoin College to obtain my Bachelor's Degree and then on to Case Western Reserve for my dental degree. And I want to tell you that it wasn't easy. But I learned something very important at North High and that's what I want to talk about today. Don't give up when things seem tough . . . when you're stressed out or your problems seem insurmountable . . . don't quit . . . if you're ever at the end of your rope, tie a knot in the end and hang on . . . keep going . . . because it is possible to achieve your goals . . . your dreams . . . it is possible! But you must learn a special skill . . . the power of perseverance . . . because perseverance will get you around the walls and barriers and challenges that you are confronted with in life . . . and all of us will be challenged.

Believe me, it's a challenge right now just to speak to you and to leave you with an important message . . . really think about my challenge: I thought to myself, over a month ago, what in the world can I say that will help you today and leave a lasting impression? It is an awesome challenge, but I'm persevering! I would never quit! And you know what? There is an important message here today! That nothing in the world, including talent, genius, education, or money can take the place of persistence. Nothing!

And for those of you who like words, I must admit I even like the sound of that word, perseverance! Or, a root of the word, persist! Or, someone who is determined, immovable, and who doesn't quit to reach a goal, a persister. Say it right now to yourself silently . . . persist! Because perseverance is one of the most essential attributes for achieving a goal and realizing our dreams.

I think this true story illustrates my thesis perfectly. There was a basketball coach who was attempting to motivate his players to persevere through a difficult season. Their record was 6 defeats and 1 victory and they were very discouraged. Halfway through the season the Coach stood before his team and said: "Did Michael Jordan ever quit?" The team yelled back, "No!" He then screamed, "What about the Wright brothers? Did they ever give up?" "No way!" the team yelled. "How about John Elway?" They all responded, "No!" "What about Albert Einstein?" "No! No!" they screamed. "Did Elmer Smith ever quit?" There was a long silence. Finally one player was bold enough to ask, "Gosh, Coach, who the heck is Elmer Smith? We never heard of him." The coach snapped back, "Of course you never heard of him—he quit!"

Now I'm going to share something that may sound shocking to some of you. Perhaps you're questioning some of your accomplishments and pondering what the future holds for you . . . my answer is simple: Don't sweat it! To make it through North High, you are a persistor . . . you possess the power of perseverance. Granted, some are better at it than others, but there is no reason for any of us not to continue our growth, and to make adjustments when needed. Whether you are pursuing more formal education or entering the working world, or combining the two, you have to persist to grow. And I think we are put on earth to grow . . . to make adjustments . . . to persist so we will get better and better.

And I know we have a lot of success in this class and I know it has a lot to do with your persistence. I was speaking to your principal, Mr. Whitty, and he told me about a whole list of accomplishments: I know we won a number of science fairs over the years and this year we took Number 1 again! And I know it wasn't easy, because science can be a demanding field. But you made adjustments to achieve your goals and you persevered. I know our cheerleaders singled themselves out as the best in the state. And our drama club and band put on a number of wonderful plays and concerts. Again, I'm sure there were problems and challenges and yet you made adjustments and you persevered! And again I know our football team had to learn perseverance when they lost their first game against Xaverian High School, and came back to beat Bishop Feehan the next week, and then went on to win the Super Bowl. And I know there are many sitting here today who had to persevere because of challenges and stresses. It seems clear to me, that the members of the Class of 1998, like my own graduating class, are persistors.

Graduates, I am inspired by this thought from Celtics Coach, Rick Pitino, about mistakes. Coach Pitino said: "Failure is good. It's fertilizer. Everything I've learned about coaching, I've learned from making mistakes!" If things aren't going well, one sign of greatness is perseverance. I'm also reminded that Thomas Edison, in perfecting the light bulb, experienced 10,000 failures before he finally succeeded. A friend of Edison's remarked that 10,000 failures were a lot of failures, to which Edison replied: "I didn't fail 10,000 times. I successfully eliminated 10,000 materials and combinations that didn't work . . . Frankly, I have a lot of success with failure." Edison also said that genius is "1% inspiration and 99% perspiration!" I was thinking about Edison, and thought, here was a man who was a persister. He rolled up his sleeves and got to work. He would never quit!

But here's another insight that some might overlook. Part of the skill of the power of perseverance is to make those adjustments as you persist. A friend of mine has a great saying. He often says: "Bill, I can't keep making the same mistakes and expect to get different results." If you notice that things aren't going well as you persist, make some adjustments. I had to do that as I was going through North High and then on to college, to dental school, and now in my private practice. And even when I was first dating my wife, Alice, l had to make adjustments so I could develop a good relationship with her. Doing the same thing and not getting results makes no sense. Persist, but make the necessary adjustments!

Let me be honest: I did OK in high school . . . I wasn't the best student nor the worst student, but I would never quit when things went wrong. I made adjustments. I did OK in college . . . again, I wasn't the best student nor the worst student, but I would never quit when things went wrong. I made further adjustments. I did better in dental school and yet still would make adjustments when confronted with problems, walls, barriers, and some tall hurdles to jump . . . and yet I would never quit. And even now in private practice, I know sometimes someone could be afraid, a procedure could be difficult, or some other problem could arise, but I make adjustments to help relieve fear or pain. My patients need me to do my best and I do. I persevere so that my work truly helps others.

Now here's something that dawned on me as I was looking back over the past 20 years . . . as I was struggling and growing and trying to pass exams, establish my dental practice, enter into my marriage, and now raise my two children, I was really learning the habit of making adjustments and persevering. In other words, not quitting becomes a habit! And when I didn't quit, I began to see my challenges, burdens, and problems as a bridge and an opportunity for progress. As Einstein said, "In the middle of difficulty lies opportunity!"

I also think there are some wonderful examples of the power of perseverance in history. So let me quiz you. Can you tell me who this person is? And please, history teachers, hold your answers. He is often looked upon as an object lesson in growth and perseverance . . . this homely, awkward, self-conscious man.

> He failed in business in 1831.
>
> He was defeated for the Legislature in 1832.
>
> He saw his sweetheart die in 1835.
>
> He suffered a complete nervous breakdown in 1836.
>
> He was defeated for Speaker in 1838.
>
> He was defeated for Congress in 1843.
>
> He was defeated for the Senate in 1855.
>
> Then he was defeated for the Vice Presidency in 1856.
>
> But in 1860 he was elected President of the United States.

Can anyone tell me who he is? That's right, Abraham Lincoln. Just think of this: he must have learned some valuable lessons in his defeats and he developed the habit of perseverance. So can we!

Perhaps you're sitting there now and wondering why I spoke to you so "persistently" about persistence. Because too many give up when they could have succeeded, and frankly, some may even enjoy our lack of success and our failures. Don't ever indulge them! If someone hits you with the words. "I told you so! I told you you couldn't do it!" Well, please remember my words today and embrace them for as long as you live. Delete any negative self-talk and get in the habit of saying: I will persist! Yes, I'm a dentist, but I'm also someone who grew discouraged and could have quit many years ago, and that's what I don't want any of you to do. Promise yourselves one thing today, that you will never quit! That you will persist!

Anyway, I think a good speech is like a good filling. It gets the job done and it doesn't take too long. So I would like to conclude with some favorite thoughts that reinforce my message today.

> Today's mighty oak is yesterday's little acorn which made good . . . through perseverance!
>
> Big shots are only little shots who keep shooting . . . through perseverance!
>
> A diamond is a chunk of coal that is made radiant . . . through perseverance!
>
> When the tide is at its lowest, it turns . . . through perseverance!

And finally.

> Stopping at third base adds no more to the score than striking out. Perseverance bangs you home!

Congratulations graduates and remember this day! Persist!

DON'T QUIT When things go wrong as they sometimes will, When the road you're trudging seems all up hill, When the funds are low and the debts are high, And you want to smile, but you have to sigh, When care is pressing you down a bit, Rest if you must, but don't you quit.

Life is queer with its twists and turns, As everyone of us sometimes learns, And many a failure turns about When he might have won had he stuck it out: Don't give up though the pace seems slow—You may succeed with another blow.

Often the goal is nearer than It seems to a faint and faltering man, Often the struggler has given up When he might have captured the victor's cup, And he learned too late When the night came down How close he was to the golden crown.

Success is failure turned inside out—The silver tint of the clouds of doubt. And you never can tell how close you are. It may be near when it seems so far. So stick to the fight when you're hardest hit—It's when things seem worst that you must not quit. (Author Unknown)

Congratulations 1998 graduates of North Attleboro High School, and remember, persist!

Vital Speeches, LXII, No. 1 (October 15, 1998).

THE AMERICAN RED CROSS: PUBLIC RELATIONS AND COMMUNICATION

Address by ROBERT DILENSCHNEIDER, *CEO of The Dilenschneider Group*

Delivered to the Public Relations Managers of the American Red Cross, Washington, D.C., October 10, 1998.

I want to thank all of you at the American Red Cross for inviting me here today. It's flattering to be asked to share my thoughts with you. It's great to have an invitation like this so that we can stop and sort out what's important to us—and to our clients.

You're a perfect audience for this kind of review. In terms of public relations, you at the American Red Cross are the Mark McGwires and the Sammy Sosas. The heroes. You've accomplished so much. The world knows more about the American Red Cross than it does about most other charitable causes. Your logo is the symbol of hope in the face of despair; it symbolizes the generosity of the human spirit.

And it has been my privilege to have been involved with the American Red Cross for more than a decade. In that time, I have seen and been part of the Red Cross responding to the worst type of human tragedy.

You are the best.

You are pros in times of crisis. Remember when there was a question of accounting at the American Red Cross? You had your chief financial officer represent you—backed up by Elizabeth Dole and Norm Augustine, to be sure. But the CFO carried the water. That kept the media focused on the issue of accounting and not on the Red Cross per se. This is great positioning. Congratulations.

You are pros in motivation. Think of the commitment thousands of Red Cross volunteers make when disaster hits. Reflect on what you have done in the Caribbean in the wake of Hurricane Georges and consider how worse the suffering would have been, had you not been there. You brought compassion and expertise to a people in need. And while you didn't seek credit, you got it—because you deserved it. Congratulations.

You are pros in fund raising, one of the toughest areas for a non-profit. And let's not kid our-selves—it's going to get tougher in the volatile economic climate we are facing. "Help Can't Wait"—our motto—says it all. You display real empathy, and you tie it to resources that are vital to people who need help. Again, congratulations.

Yes, Red Cross communications people know what they are doing. Like the rest of those who toil in the communications trade, you have developed and constantly improved upon commu-nications strategies and techniques that get results.

But in your success, and in the success of others in the nonprofit and corporate fields, there lurks a growing problem. And I want to address that problem today because it is at the heart of the challenge we face over the next twenty years, and, indeed, it is truly at the heart of our democracy.

The problem manifests itself in the growing chorus of criticism of what we do. You and I are called flacks, spin doctors, and a half-dozen other names—one less flattering than the next.

Now, these are just labels, and I am sure being called names does not hurt you. But the sug-gestion behind the name-calling is that we are doing something wrong or that we are manip-ulating a naive public for nefarious purposes.

These ad hominem attacks come from the media, from lawyers, especially the plaintiff bar, from legislators, and dozens of other sectors who have their own agendas and are not shy in promoting them.

Why they do it is obvious. They do it because we are effective, and they don't like it.

And there is probably no stopping these attacks because they represent a strong tool our adversaries can use against us.

More of a problem, I submit, is the climate created by some of our number who feed the per-ception.

It's time to call a spade a spade in the communications business.

It's time to root out the people who over-promote stocks by advancing half-truths, by hold-ing back critical information, and timing the release of information so only a well-connected few benefit from disclosure.

It's time to bring up short those bigots who still, as we close on this remarkable century, work behind the scenes to retard the advancement of women and minorities in the workplace.

It's time to stop the negative political advertising and press leaks designed, not to advance positive programs and ideas that will help people, but to ruthlessly smear or damage oppo-nents.

Yes, it is time to bring to light the greedy practices of some non-profits, and fundraisers for non-profits, when the money and resources go to feather a profligate lifestyle and not to help people.

Let me tell you two short stories.

In 1997, I was called by a major American company to discuss a significant breakthrough they had achieved. It was, and is, big. But just like all breakthroughs, it had some problems—serious problems for the consumer.

Another consultant, a Washington pol actually, who has a very high-powered reputation and who is regularly on talk shows, was there. And there were several marketing managers from the Company. Their bonuses—not to mention careers—depended on the product's success.

Well, when the problems with the breakthrough were discovered, the question before the house was, "How do we present this?"

The high-powered consultant said, "However we want to," and went on to discuss a total dis-tortion that my 12-year-old would have seen through. The product managers winked at one another. They had brought in a slick Bill Barnum, and he was going to throw up enough smoke so everyone's paycheck would be safe and fat at Christmas.

My colleagues and I were stunned. We privately went to the company's senior officer. We told him we were prepared to lose the account, and we strongly urged him to tell the truth and iron out the problems before he went to market.

To his credit, he did just that, and today the product is a great success; the Company continues to do well, and the product managers got paid. Unfortunately, the high-powered consultant is still out there duping people right and left. You read about him in the news every day, as he works to distort the truth.

And now, a second story.

Some years ago, an editor of a second-rate publication came to me and said he would do a negative story on one of our clients unless that Company advertised in his publication.

We went to the editor's boss, who was outraged at his employee's behavior. The editor was fired. He has had a vendetta against us ever since. He has worked overtime to smear us. The good news is—no responsible publication will hire him

What do these two stories tell us?

They should tell us that there are plenty of people out there who pose as professionals in our field and get away with it.

I think we need to do something about that . . . NOW!

Item Number One on my list of reforms is an understanding of what positioning really is.

Has the line been crossed where positioning has become unethical? I'm convinced that it has.

In the 1970's, two smart men, Al Ries and Jack Trout, published a landmark book: POSITIONING. They explained how Mr. Clean—a detergent—was better known than George Bush. They told us that was because Mr. Clean was an "oversimplified" message. Mr. Clean cleaned. Mr. Clean was a fun guy. Period. Oversimplified message. Easy for people to understand. George Bush, on the other hand, was too complex. If George Bush wanted to be better known, he had to strip himself down to a handful of characteristics. Like Honest Abe. Like Camelot. Or like Help Can't Wait.

Well, some among us such as Dick Morris and Ed Rollins took that—positioning—too broadly. The spinners—the Morrises and the Rollinses—believed that you could oversimplify anything any way you wanted. And get away with it.

In the current scandal at the White House, the positioning is: "Clinton was a bad boy about sex. But he is a good President." This oversimplification, this spin doesn't account for the facts. The facts are: There may have been perjury. There might have been obstruction of justice. There might have been abuse of power. And last but certainly not least, what about the dignity of the Oval Office and the faith that the American people—and people around the world—have in its occupants?

Part of this White House positioning includes demonizing opponents. Ken Starr is a right-wing egomaniac bent on destroying the President. Henry Hyde is a hypocrite. Joe Liebermann is a traitor.

White House spinners and spinners at ADM, at Disney, at Harvard Law School—all those "positioners" reduce truth to a double function. To an either/or proposition. Either you're on our side and believe as we do. Or you're on "their" side. And if you're on "their" side, we are going to get you and destroy your reputation.

SPINNING ISN'T POSITIONING. Real positioning highlights positive characteristics. Real positioning shows Mother's Day as a sentimental time, as a time to show love. Real positioning shows getting a first-rate education as part of the American Dream. Real positioning shows that petting Muffy the Cat is a way for us to lower our blood pressure. Real positioning is what you do so well at the Red Cross.

Item Number Two is to raise our standards. You're constantly doing this at the Red Cross.

My mother grew up in a coal-mining town. To survive the atrocious conditions and go down into the mine every day, the workers had to turn off their brains. They didn't see the dripping water. They didn't hear those creaking, ominous sounds. They tried to ignore their chronic coughing. It took years for them to wake up. And years longer to wake up Washington to finally do something about health and safety in the mines.

Are we as a nation going brain-dead? Are we giving back all the progress we've made toward improving social conditions—improvements we've made in health, safety, education, and in social discourse?

Think about it. Why do we tolerate the likes of Jerry Springer? Why do we celebrate the garbage that passes for movies today? Why do we tolerate four-letter words as a matter of course today? Why do we take a view—well, everyone else does it, so it's OK? On the evening news recently there was a segment about the Hollywood stars who were supporting China. Now, everyone's entitled to their opinion. But really . . . what does that have to do with the price of tea in China? As the high priest of values, Bill Bennett asks, "Where's the Outrage?"

Indeed, where is our outrage?

Deceptive messages threaten our brand of capitalism. Capitalism is a tough system, but it must also be fair to survive, and that means reasonable regulation. American capitalism has created a large middle class. But American capitalism could go the way of communism in the former Soviet Union if we don't keep the game clean.

When deceptive messages determine the winners and the losers in our system, our brand of capitalism is in deep trouble. I am convinced: Unless we start reforming what we do, there will be a swing back to more onerous regulation. There will be more and deeper consumer mistrust. People's confidence will be shattered. Capitalism will become an empty dream.

Item Number Three—We need to do more self-policing of public relations.

Let's call on PRSA or IPRA or the IABC or someone else to get tougher.

Let's establish a vehicle like Marshall Loeb's splendid *Columbia Journalism Review* that will take a hard and objective look at what we do, with an eye toward raising standards. Let's get colleges or universities to call for tougher policing of our business.

Finally, with those three points in hand—understanding and positioning, raising the standards, start self-policing—let's find ways to demonstrate the importance of what we do. If we don't do it, no one else will.

On "Burden of Proof" Greta and John have taught us how the law works. On "ER" we've learned how to stabilize vital signs. On the old "Roseanne," we learned how a blue-collar housewife stays sane for two minutes. On "Thirty-something," we saw how an ad agency runs.

But there's no electronic forum for those of us in public relations to show and tell. What about a discussion program like "Burden of Proof"? We can debate the ethics of representing Bill Clinton or Ken Starr. We can examine what Disney is doing right—and wrong—in managing its image. We can backtrack and examine how a Studio 54 got so much buzz and how the buzz ultimately did it in.

As for a dramatic series, how about something like E. G. Marshall's "Defenders." A multi-faceted look at public relations. We could have had that kind of show if we lobbied for it. We know how to get that. We know how to get results. All of this will be healthy.

You certainly have a great story to tell of the day-in and day out heroics at the Red Cross. Don't be afraid to show the world how you tell it.

If you're a public relations person involved in area development, let people know what you are doing helps to build a tax base that leads to better schools and crime protection.

If you're involved in fundraising, let people know that awareness generates money to help those who can't help themselves.

If you're involved in recruiting, emphasize how communications helps to create jobs, and in advancing more women and minorities into leadership positions.

If you're involved in issues, celebrate the dialogue that brings out a side of the story that would otherwise not be told.

Is taking credit wrong? I cannot think of a professional field that does not seek credit in some way. And if you don't take some credit, no one's going to give it to you. That's the way of the world. You know that without your contribution, a positive result—big or small—would not have occurred. Be proud of that.

So, take some proper credit. Be modest, for sure. But don't hide because of what you have accomplished. Excessive modesty is also a form of egoism.

The Dick Morrises come and go. But in-the-trenches, public relations people such as you and I endure. And thrive. And we hit them out of the ballpark all the time. You certainly do that at the Red Cross. Celebrate what you do—don't brag—but celebrate. By doing that and by taking the steps I outlined earlier, you will help make this a profession everyone will admire and want to be a part of—just as so many thousands of people across the country are so proud to be a part of—indeed, the heart of, The American Red Cross. Thank you.

Vital Speeches, LXV, No. 5 (December 15, 1998).

American Sport at Century's End: An Overview

Address by D. STANLEY EITZEN, *Professor Emeritus of Sociology, Colorado State University Delivered to the Symposium: American Sport at Century's End: Consequences, Contradictions and Controversies, Colorado State University, Fort Collins, Colorado, November 12, 1998.*

We are here to consider sport through the assorted lenses of sociologists, sports journalists, and sports practitioners. For my contribution I will present a brief overview, focusing, on several paradoxes that are central to sport as it has come to be.

Paradox: While seemingly a trivial pursuit, sport is important. On the one hand, sport is entertainment, a fantasy, a diversion from the realities of work, relationships, and survival. But if sport is just a game, why do we take it so seriously? Among the many reasons, lets consider four: First, sport mirrors the human experience. The introductory essay in a recent issue of *The Nation*, which was devoted to sport, said this:

> Sport elaborates in its rituals what it means to be human: the play, the risk, the trials. The collective impulse to games, the thrill of physicality, the necessity of strategy; defeat, victory, defeat again, pain, transcendence and, most of all, the certainty that nothing is certain—that everything can change and be changed.

Second, sport mirrors society in other profound ways as well. Sociologists, in particular, find the study of sport fascinating because we find there the basic elements and expressions of bureaucratization, commercialization, racism, sexism, homophobia, greed, exploitation of the powerless, alienation, and the ethnocentrism found in the larger society. Of special interest, too, is how sport has been transformed from an activity for individuals involved in sport for its own sake, to a money-driven, corporate entity where sport is work rather than play, and where loyalty to players, coaches and owners is a quaint notion that is now rarely held. Also, now athletes are cogs in a machine where decisions by coaches and bureaucracies are less and less player-centered. I am especially concerned with the decisions made by big-business bureau-cracies (universities, leagues, cartels such as the NCAA, corporations, and sports conglomer-ates such as Rupert Murdoch's empire, which just in the U. S. includes ownership of the Los Angeles Dodgers, the Fox network, FX, 22 local cable channels, the New York Post, 20 Percent of L. A.'s Staples Center, a sports arena now under construction, and the partial rights to broadcast NFL games for eight years and major league baseball for five years). Another pow-erful sports conglomerate is the Walt Disney Corporation which owns the Mighty Ducks of Anaheim, 25 percent of the Anaheim Angels and the option to buy the rest from Gene Autry's estate, ABCIV, ESPY, and like Murdoch, partial rights for eight years of NFL games and five years of major league baseball. While we're at it, let's list the Time Warner sports empire, where Ted Turner is the major player. This sports empire includes ownership of the Atlanta Braves, Atlanta Hawks, Atlanta Thrashers, the Goodwill Games, World Championship Wrestling, Turner Field plus the Atlanta arena now under construction, *Sports Illustrated, Time Magazine*, CNN, HBO, TNT, TBS, and Warner Brothers. They have a four-year deal as the NBA's cable pawner. Obviously, sport is not a trivial pursuit by these media moguls.

A third reason why sports are so compelling is that they combine spectacle with drama. Sports, especially football involve pageantry, bands forming a liberty bell or unfurling a flag as big as the football field, and militaristic displays with the drama of a situation where the out-come is not perfectly predictable. Moreover, we see excellence, human beings transcending the commonplace to perform heroic deeds. There is also clarity—we know, unlike in many other human endeavors, exactly who won, by how much, and how they did it.

Finally, there is the human desire to identify with something larger than oneself. For ath-letes, it is to be part of a team, working and sacrificing together to achieve a common goal. For fans, by identifying with a team or a sports hero, they bond with others who share their alle-giance; they belong and they have an identity. This bond of allegiance is becoming more and more difficult as players through free agency move from team to team, as coaches are hired and fired and many times when coaches are successful they break their contracts to go to a more lucrative situation, leaving their players, assistants, and fans in their wake. The owners of many professional teams blackmail their cities for more lucrative subsidies or they'll move, which they sometimes do, leaving diehard fans without teams.

Paradox: Sport has the capacity to build character as well as encourage bad character. On the one hand, sports participation encourages hard work, perseverance, self-discipline, sacri-fice, following the rules, obeying authority, and working with teammates to achieve a common goal. Sport promotes fair play. Of the many examples of ethical behavior in sport, let me cite one. A month after Rockdale County (Georgia) won the state basketball championship in 1987, the coach Cleveland Stroud, found that he had unknowingly used an ineligible player. Although the player in question was in the game only a minute or two and had not scored, Stroud notified the authorities of the infraction. As a result, the only state championship in the school's history was forfeited. Coach Stroud said, "you've got to do what's honest and right. Peo-ple forget the scores of basketball games; they don't ever forget what you're made of." There are countless examples where competitors show respect for one another where sportsmanship rules.

But for all of the honor and integrity found in sport there is also much about sport that dis-regards the ideals of fair play. Good sportsmanship may be a product of sport, but so is bad sportsmanship. Let me cite a few examples: (1) trashtalking and taunting opponents; (2) dirty play (a recent article in *Sports Illustrated* documented dirty play in the NFL, citing the ten worst offenders, saying that "there's a nasty breed of players who follow one cardinal rule: Any-thing goes, and that means biting, kicking, spearing, spitting, and leg-whipping"); (3) coaches who teach their players how to hold and not get caught; (4) faking being fouled so that a referee who is out of position will call an undeserved foul on the opponent; (5) trying to hurt an opponent; (6) coaches rewarding players for hurting an opponent; (7) throwing a spitter or corking a bat; (8) using illegal drugs to enhance performance; (9) crushing an opponent (a Laramie, Wyoming girls junior high basketball team won a game a few years ago by a score of 81–1, using a full-court press the entire game); (10) fans yelling racial slurs; (11) coaches who, like Pat Riley of the Miami Heat, demand that their players not show respect for their opponents (Riley fines his players $1,500 if they help an opposing player get off the floor); (12) coaches who are sexist and homophobic calling their male players pussies or fags if they are not aggressive enough; (13) a male locker room culture that tends to promote homophobia, sexism, and aggressive behaviors, and (14) coaches who recruit illegally, who alter transcripts and bribe teachers to keep players eligible, and who exploit players with no regard for their health or their education.

What lesson is being taught and caught when a coach openly asks a player to cheat? Consider these two examples. A few years ago, the Pretty Prairie Kansas High School had twin boys on his team. One of the twins was injured but suited up for a game where his brother was in foul trouble at half time. The coach had the twins change jerseys so that the foul-plagued twin would be in the second half with no fouls charged to the player's number he was now wearing.

In another instance, a high school football coach in Portland sent a player into the game on a very foggy night. The player asked: "Who am I going in for?" "No one," the coach replied, "the fog is so thick the ref will never notice you."

My point is that we live in a morally distorted sports world—a world where winning often supersedes all other considerations, where moral values have become confused with the bottom line. In this in-your-face, whip-your-butt climate, winning-at-any-price often becomes the prevailing code of conduct. And when it does, I assert, sport does build character, but it is bad character. When we make the value of winning so important that it trumps morality, then we and sport are diminished.

Paradox: While the nature of sport is competition where ability tells, the reality is that race restricts. Just as in other social realms, we find in sport that the ascribed status of race gives advantage to some and disadvantage to others. Let's look at racism in sport, focusing on African Americans since they are the dominant racial minority in American sport.

At first glance, its seems impossible that Blacks are victims of discrimination in sport since some of them make huge fortunes from their athletic prowess, such as Michael Jordan, who makes an estimated $80 to $90 million a year in salary, endorsements, and public appearances, and Tiger Woods, who, although just beginning his professional career, makes $30 to $40 million annually. Moreover, it is argued that Blacks in sport are not victims of discrimination because, while only constituting 12 percent of the general population, they comprise 65 percent of the players in professional football, 80 percent of professional basketball players, and 18 percent of the players in major league baseball (and where Latinos constitute another 18 percent). Also about 60 percent of the football and basketball players in big-time college programs are African Americans.

Despite these empirical facts that seem to contradict racism in sport, it is prevalent in several forms. Let me cite some examples. First, Blacks are rarely found in those sports that require the facilities, coaching, and competition usually provided only in private—and typically racially segregated—clubs; sports such as swimming, golf, skiing, and tennis. Black athletes also are rarely found where it takes extraordinary up-front money, usually from corporate sponsors, to participate such as in automobile racing.

But even in the team sports where African Americans dominate numerically, there is evidence of discrimination. Sociologists have long noted that Blacks tend to be relegated to those team positions where the physical attributes of strength, size, speed, aggressiveness, and "instinct" are important but that they are under-represented at those playing positions that require thinking, leadership and are the most crucial for outcome control. This phenomenon, known as stacking, continues today, at both the college and professional levels in football and baseball. Using professional football as the example, African Americans are under-represented on offense and if on offense they tend to be at wide receiver and running back—the whitest positions are center, offensive guard, quarterback, punter, placekicker, and placekick holder. Blacks are over-represented at all positions on defense, except middle linebacker. The existence of stacking reinforces negative stereotypes about racial minorities, as Whites appear, by the positions they play, to be superior to Blacks in cognitive ability and leadership qualities but behind them in physical prowess.

African Americans are also under-represented in nonplaying leadership positions. At the professional level team ownership is an exclusively all-White club. In the league offices of the NCAA, major league baseball, the NBA, and the NFL, the employees are disproportionately White. The same is true, of course, for head coaches in big-time college and professional sports.

African Americans are also under-represented in ancillary sports positions such as Sports Information Director, ticket managers, trainer, equipment manager, scout, accountant, sportswriting, and sports broadcasting, especially play-by-play announcing.

Another consistent finding by sociologists is a form of discrimination known as "unequal opportunity for equal ability." This means that the entrance requirements for Blacks to college scholarships or to the professional leagues are more rigorous than they are for Whites. In essence, Black players must be better than White players to succeed in the sports world. In baseball, for example, Blacks consistently have higher statistics (batting average, home runs, stolen bases, earned run average) than Whites. What's happening here is that superb Black athletes are not discriminated against but the substars do experience discrimination. The findings clearly indicate that the undistinguished Black player is less likely to play regularly than the equally undistinguished White player. As sociologist Jonathan Brower has said, "in sport mediocrity is a white luxury."

Paradox: Schools emphasize sports because of the personal and social benefits for participants. Yet these same schools have generally resisted efforts by girls and women for participation and resources equal to that of boys and men. Research shows many benefits from sports for girls and women. When female athletes are compared to their non-athlete peers, they are found to have higher self-esteem and better body image. For high school girls, athletes are less likely than nonathletes to use illicit drugs; they are more likely to be virgins; if sexually active they are more likely to begin intercourse at a later age; and they are much less likely to get pregnant. These advantages are in addition to the standard benefits of learning to work with teammates for a common goal, striving for excellence, and the lessons of what it takes to win and how to cope with defeat. Yet, historically, women have been denied these benefits. And, even today, the powerful male establishment in sport continues to drag its collective feet on gender equity.

Title IX, passed in 1972, mandated gender equity in school sports programs. While this affected schools at all levels, I'll focus on the college level because this is where women have met the most resistance. Since 1972 women's intercollegiate programs have made tremendous strides, with participation quadrupling from 30,000 women in 1971 to 116,272 in 1996. Athletic scholarships for women were virtually unknown in 1972, now women athletes receive 35 percent of the athletic scholarship money that is distributed. These increases in a generation represent the good news concerning gender equity in collegiate sport. The bad news, however, is quite significant. Looking at the data for big-time schools for the 1995-96 school year, we find the following disparities by gender:

1. Head coaches of women's teams were paid 63 cents for every dollar earned by coaches of men's teams (and this inequity does not include many of the extras. The coaches of men's teams are more likely than the coaches of women's teams to receive lucrative radio and television deals, endorsements, cars, country club memberships, sweetheart business deals, and housing allowances).

2. Only seven schools met the proportionality test for equity—i.e., the number of women athletes should be within 5 percent of the proportion of women undergraduates enrolled. The average negative gap was 16 percent.

3. The average gender composition of an athletic department was 292 male athletes and 163 female athletes (65 percent male and 35 percent female), with a similar disproportionate distribution of scholarships.

4. The recruiting budget was skewed in favor of males with a 76 percent/24 percent ratio.

5. Operational expenditures were distributed even more unevenly at 78 percent/22 percent. And, most telling, it was not uncommon for a school with a big-time football program to spend twice as much on its football team as it spent on all its women's sports combined.

6. In a most ironic twist, in 1972, when Title IX was enacted, more than 90 percent of women's teams were coached by women. But now that participation for women has quadrupled, the percentage of women's teams coached by women has dropped to 48 percent.

7. At the administrative level, women hold 36 percent of all administrative jobs in women's programs and only 19 percent of all women's programs are actually headed by a female administrator.

Clearly, as these data show, gender equity is not part of bigtime college sports programs. In my view, universities must address the question: Is it appropriate for a college or university to deny women the same opportunities that it provides men? Shouldn't our daughters have the same possibilities as our sons in all aspects of higher education? Women are slightly more than half of the undergraduates in U.S. higher education. They receive half of all the master's degrees. Should they be second-class in any aspect of the university's activities? The present unequal state of affairs in sport is not inevitable. Choices have been made in the past that have given men advantage in university sports. They continue to do so, to the detriment of not only women's sports but also the so-called minor sports for men.

These are a few paradoxes concerning contemporary sport in the United States. There are more but I'll let my colleagues and the other panelists speak directly or indirectly to them. Let me conclude my remarks with this statement and a plea. We celebrate sport for many good reasons. It excites and it inspires. We savor the great moments of sport when an athlete does the seemingly impossible or when the truly gifted athlete makes the impossible routine. We exult when a team or an athlete overcomes great odds to succeed. We are touched by genuine camaraderie among teammates and between competitors. We are uplifted by the biographies of athletes who have used sport to get an education that they would have been denied because of economic circumstance or who have used sport to overcome delinquency and drugs. But for all of our love and fascination with sport and our extensive knowledge of it, do we truly understand it? Can we separate the hype from the reality and the myths from the facts? Do we accept the way sport is organized without questioning? Unfortunately for many fans and participants alike there is an superficial, uncritical, and taken-for-granted attitude concerning sport. Sportswriter Rick Reilly of *Sports Illustrated* has written that "sport deserves a more critical examination. We need to ask more probing questions about sport." That has always been my goal; it continues to be my goal; and I hope that it is yours as well.

Vital Speeches, LXVX, No. 6 (January 1, 1999).

WOMEN AND MEN COMMUNICATING: WHO'S FROM MARS?

Address by ANITA TAYLOR, *Professor of Communication and Women Studies, Executive Editor of Women and Language. Delivered to the University Old Town Lecture Series, Old Town Hall, Fairfax, Virginia, October 21, 1998.*

A decade ago I was fortunate to spend a spring living on the side of a Southern California mountain, a spot I shared with some interesting companions who adopted me. I'm not sure whether it was California New Age or mountain fog, but I experienced a heightened state of consciousness, and I made contact with representatives of another world. This is a group of beings whose resources were not expended in wars or civilizations continually set back from destruction of one war after another. Most of their research investment had not gone to weapons and destructive technology, so their communications and transportation technology are much advanced over ours. They could and were surveiling us . . . all the while eluding detection by those marvelous listening devices we've set up to know if there is intelligent life "out there."

They were trying to decide whether to drop their shields and make contact with us. So they had sent individuals to study our civilizations much as we once sent anthropologists all over the world studying "primitive" groups. I benefited then from sharing the report of their contact, She-he, who was studying the U.S. educational system. I shared much of that report with my colleagues and others in a lecture reprinted in Vital Speeches in 1988. At that time these beings decided against making contact with us. We were too violent (40 armed conflicts were occurring around the world at the time, not to mention the combat in the streets and homes of the U.S.) and too primitive. They couldn't take the chance of opening their worlds and technology to us.

But much has happened in 10 years. The Soviet Union is no more; the U.S. is now the undisputed world leader, in economics, industry and military. We're living in a dramatically altered world in which changes continue at an accelerating pace.

Then, this past year I spent time in our desert southwest . . . another world unto itself. There, where ancient Black Rock hunches on the horizon, watching over Spider Rock, home of Holy Spider Woman who taught the Navajos to weave, and where the centuries old petroglyphs of Monument Valley stand mute in awe of the power of wind and water to change earth's face, I again became aware of our visitors from outer space. On the night of a full moon amidst the hoodoos of Bryce Canyon, I heard a voice call my name. To my delight, my friend, She-he, was back. Those advanced beings are out there still, watching and listening to us. Once again I became an informant. I want to share with you part of She-he's report. I think you'll find it interesting.

She-he's report:

As you know, I'm a member of the team studying the changes during the last decade on planet earth's richest continent, which is known as North America. The three of us working on this project have divided the task. North America has three of the planet earth institutions known as the nation state, and while there are some superficial similarities among the states, there are some striking differences as well. He-she is reporting on the nation called Canada and They is studying Mexico and Central America. My focus is the United States.

Dramatic changes have occurred here in the last decade. To set them in context, we need to recall what He-she's report on gender showed. You'll recall that earthlings in the U.S. have a concept they describe in English as gender. Gender is an idea related to how they identify themselves. They have another concept they call sex, by which they divide the population into two groups, called male and female. They think that biology determines, at birth or conception, that a being is of either male or female sex. Moreover, they see this sex as an unchangeable characteristic. So, a person (which is what they call themselves) is thought to be male or female always and forever. Accepting such a rigid, unchangeable construct is not much of a problem for most earthlings—although it is quite a problem for some—to the extent that they will spent thousands of dollars and undergo quite invasive surgery to become the sex they think they should be.

In recent years it has become quite common to think these two sexes are "at war" with one another. Commonly, it's heard that another installment in the battle of the sexes has been fought. Indeed in the past few years a small industry has boomed around the idea that these two sexes are so different they come from different worlds. John Gray's book, *Men are from Mars Women are from Venus*, was on the best seller in the U.S. for more than two years. Gray has a booming consulting/speaking career and has launched a magazine built on the concept of two "opposite sexes."

Such a fuss over what researchers have identified as relatively small differences when actual behaviors are observed and measured is quite remarkable. Rigorous science based studies repeatedly demonstrate that men and women in the U.S. behave more similarly than not. Yet the belief in vast differences persists. What can be at work?

We have concluded that it is the concept of gender, which is quite troublesome for many earthlings. Gender is the term that English speaking earthlings apply to the whole complex of behaviors, dispositions, attributes, values, etc. that are supposed to go along with being either a male or a female. In a kind of shorthand, gender is often described is being feminine or masculine. In this idea called gender, major changes have occurred in the past 10 years, and I will be so bold as to predict that even greater changes are taking place right at this moment. Moreover, it's the cauldron of this rapid change that provides the context for the whole Mars/Venus phenomenon. As an aside, quaint isn't it that Earthlings' technology is so primitive that the planets of their solar system seem far away to them?

But, back to the point. Let's look at the nature of these changes in the gender system. You'll remember our previous report indicated that earthlings consider gender quite important. Male persons are expected to be masculine and that meant being aggressive, competitive, rational (which means not emotional), cool, logical, interested in cars, sports, business, and politics. And female persons were expected to be feminine, which meant being passive, noncompetitive, intuitive, nurturing, warm, compassionate, emotional, often irrational, not interested in sports, business or politics, but rather in appearance, children, and relationships. And when males are not masculine or females not feminine, they are considered odd, at best . . . deviants, evil or "sick" at worst.

And, just as U.S. earthlings think if you're male you cannot be female and somehow that makes male and female opposites, they thought this way about gender as well. So if one were masculine, it's believed they cannot also be feminine—and vice versa. What's especially curious about this way of thinking is that if they just describe the behaviors, the earthlings know quite well that they can be both cooperative and competitive, both aggressive and passive, both rational and emotional, etc. But somehow genders, the concepts that encompass and associate this range of behaviors with sex—i.e., femininity and masculinity—were seen as canceling each other out.

Among the most enduring gender expectations relate to what English speaking earthlings call love. It's thought to be natural that male persons will be sexually and/or romantically attracted only to female persons—and MOST attracted to very feminine female persons. And, of course, female persons are expected to be sexually and/or romantically attracted only to male persons—and MOST attracted to very masculine male persons. This attraction was supposed to be sealed with a contract (although usually the contract was unstated). One male person and one female person enter this contract, called marriage, meaning among other things they will have sexual relationships only with each other, and society expected them to reproduce each other. The unstated expectation of this contract were that they should be best friends with each other AND satisfy each other's needs for intimacy, social support, and self-realization—perhaps an impossible task.

Economic arrangements were such that the male person (the husband) had an occupation more important and financially rewarding than the female person (the wife), a condition that still holds. If the husband had a sufficiently rewarding occupation, the wife was expected to take an unpaid occupation called housewife—which meant that she did all the cooking, cleaning, primary child care and a lot of other things required to sustain the relationship and reproduction, tasks that one of their academics described as reproductive labor. If the husband's occupation was not sufficiently rewarding, the wife had to take a paid job in addition to her unpaid work, but she was still expected to do all or most of the reproductive labor. So she really did two jobs, but one of them wasn't paid for in cash and usually wasn't even thought of as a job. All of this economic environment provides fertile ground for significant communication difficulties due to the values placed on income generation, a point we discuss below.

First, we want to note the significance of the parallel between economic and political organization of the society and gender expectations. Business, politics, commerce and government at all levels, indeed, all of public life—are closely associated with the behaviors and values considered masculine. This is not, I suppose, surprising since until quite recently all important positions in U.S. public life have been held by males. But what does seem surprising is that the association has not been seen as having any relation to gender. It has been believed, by most people, that being logical, rational, unemotional, competitive (whether seeking to maximize one's returns in the market place or achieve high rank in a bureaucratic hierarchy) is the "normal" or "standard" way people "are" or should be. If these "normal" traits and values were also thought of as masculine, well, who noticed that? There's a corollary here: If one doesn't behave in these ways one is not "normal"—which presented a conundrum to female persons, they were supposed to be feminine—which also meant not be not normal. Only recently have female earthlings begun to identify this phenomenon, they call, after the title of a popular book, a *Catch 22*. Many now assert that to behave in a feminine way is not to be deficient, just different. But gaining acceptance for femininity in public life has not occurred. Women who gain high status do so by adopting behaviors that are male-identified: they compete, argue rationally, suppress emotionality, show little compassion for those who cannot compete, etc.

Another not-surprising corollary to the association of masculine with public life is association of feminine behaviors and traits with private and personal life. Hence female U.S. earthlings have been expected to be (and usually have been) better at doing and saying the kinds of things that contribute to effective interpersonal and family relationships.

Now, to mix my report with He-she's of a decade past: It often is argued that this division of traits and talents is "natural," meaning determined by nature—or to put it another way, by biology. Such dividing of talents, if it existed, could be seen as not problematic if certain conditions were met: First, if public life did not need or would not benefit from feminine qualities of compassion, nurturing, cooperation, or emotion. Or, if private life would not benefit from rationality, logic and control of emotions. In short, if public life didn't need femininity—or private life masculinity—dividing people and associated behaviors and values into two separate (and mutually exclusive) categories would be less pernicious for a culture. Such conditions, however, defy reality of life here.

The categories aren't mutually exclusive and the characteristics aren't neatly divided by sex. Before I continue, I want to point out complicating factors with the division of labor and values. The two sets of behaviors have not been equally valued—a problem in this culture that compulsively ranks any two elements seen as different. If two different sets of behaviors were seen as merely different, then rigid separation of what male and female are to do and be would have less serious consequences. There are cultural groups on earth with such separate but equal treatment of masculine and feminine. But in the U.S. portion of the planet, and indeed some of their scholars argue in all English speaking cultures, any two different items that are related are almost automatically ranked. This pattern has not changed in the past decade, and indeed, extends well beyond gender. Someone returning from holiday will be asked, what was your favorite place? One retiring from a lifetime at a career will be asked, what will you remember most? One senior professor at the University of Florida challenges her students to get through a single day without speaking in a way that makes ranking comparisons (better, best) and reports that she has only had one report success, a student whose native language is Thai.

As you will remember from my education report in 1988, the impulse to rank is pervasive throughout U.S. society. It's found in patterns of thought, institutions of government, arrangements in schools and even in interpersonal relations. Many U.S. scholars have noticed and commented on this impulse. Some defend it as "natural," being grounded in the biology of earthlings.

"Man" they claim is "naturally" competitive—and will always compete to be best, to win, to have more than others. When other scholars have identified societies in which such ranking does not occur, their work has been ridiculed and scholarly journals have refused to publish it. This issue of the competitive nature of "man" remains hotly contested.

Recently some earthlings, both male and female, have begun to say that the impulse to rank relates to gender. One writer whose books have become best sellers, Deborah Tannen, popularized a point that feminists have argued for years: Competitive, hierarchy creating and seeking are masculine behaviors and values—and here's where the confounding of behavior and biology becomes especially problematic. If it's masculine and thus identified with males, the easy conclusion is males do it because of biology. Even careful scholars like Tannen often talk in ways that suggest such causal conclusions, a careless inferring they otherwise explicitly reject. Tannen reported that males are more likely to engage in competitive communication than females because autonomy is more important to them, and they fiercely resist being on the bottom of a ranking comparison. Other academics grant that what is identified as competitive and hierarchy creating is male identified, but they contest the "naturalness" of the dichotomy.

Our observations do not support the conclusion that males are competitive while females are not. What we saw in 1988 was that U.S. society prescribed a different kind and type of competitiveness for women. We did see (and still do) considerable evidence that females are less physically violent in their competitions. But they displayed extreme competitiveness in vying for wealth, which females in the past could best achieve by marrying a wealthy male, which also often meant vying for being physically beautiful. That's competition, even if it isn't seeking to "win" in some sport or through intellectual agility in commerce, government, or warfare. And that hasn't changed much. What has happened in the last decade is that females have become much more comfortable adopting the openly competitive communication style of sport and business, a trend we believe likely to continue.

So long as male-identified (i.e., masculine) behaviors and values are thought more important and rewarded with higher compensation—hence helping people climb a rank ladder—they will be encouraged and female-identified communication (i.e., femininity) will not. We predict serious consequences both for individuals and cultures as a result. Family and interpersonal situations call for both males and females to demonstrate lots of feminine behaviors and qualities. Commerce, business, and government also benefit from more femininity.

All our conclusions of a decade ago remain partially accurate, but many changes are underway which could result in a very different situation within another ten years. Indeed, these changes are predicted to be dramatic, having been likened to tectonic plates clashing, similar to those driving up the San Bernardino Mountains along the San Andreas Fault in Southern California. We summarize some of those changes here.

First, women have and continue to dramatically expand the roles they play. Girls are now encouraged to think of growing up to careers in the workplace, not just doing jobs that may support or interfere with what used to be considered their primary (though unpaid) career, homemaking. Women are coming to define their success in much the same terms as do men, in terms of the public world. Overall, many, perhaps even most, women are now quite comfortable enacting many male-identified behaviors and values. Some similar increased flexibility in role enactments for men has also occurred, though much less than for women.

What has NOT happened is a revaluing of the feminine, in and of itself. Where the value of feminine things has been recognized and adopted by the public world, they have been renamed. For example, nurturing behaviors are now recognized as critical to successful organizations, only now they are described as cooperation, supportive behaviors or team building. Failure to revalue the feminine is important. Not only do boys and men fail to learn adequately important communicative skills, fewer women are now learning them. To appropriate the language of John Gray, fewer and fewer people from Venus will inhabit planet earth.

Also significant is that hierarchical thinking remains unchallenged. Even though the grounds of ranking systems may be changing, hierarchical thinking persists. Class, always important in the U.S. though seldom spoken of, seems to be increasingly so. Past identification of higher rank with masculine and white may be fading, but it still requires education and income to temper negative attitudes toward race and ethnicity. Thus, the ranking system that generates violent behaviors remains in place even though it is not so clearly identified with sex as it used to be. And, as evidence, the rates of violence within the culture continue to be very high, with increasing amounts of violence displayed by girls and women—not surprising of course as they adopt male-identified behaviors. High rates of international violence persist, with many states engaged in wars with each other and even more involved in some kind of internal or civil strife.

And, at this point, I stop quoting to you from She-he's report. They still support their decade old recommendation against contact with earth beings. We remain too violent. They fear that what is occurring may not be dramatic changes in gender itself, but simply flexibility within the roles that women are permitted to play. They believe that female-identified communication patterns and behavior are still undervalued, so that femininity is not available to all, especially not to men. Nor do they see truly egalitarian attitudes emerging either between women and men or between racial and ethnic groups, nor among nations and religions.

I wish I could report to you a more encouraging prognosis. It could happen. Times of dramatic change in gender roles, such as those in which we now live, often witness unexpected alterations in many parts of the culture. It could happen. Perhaps it will, if all of us committed to a more gender balanced, less violent world work toward really living the equality in which we profess to believe. If we can grow up as committed to equality in all aspects of our lives as we seem to have become to equal treatment of women and men, we might achieve that peaceful world we all claim to want. Perhaps then in a decade or so, She-he and their colleagues could send back a report recommending they make contact with this backward and violent planet. We can always hope.

Vital Speeches, LXV, No. 9 (February 15, 1999*).*

JOURNALISM: WORDS FROM A DINOSAUR

Address by JIM LEHRER, *Executive Editor and Anchor of the News Hour with Jim Lehrer. Delivered to the Town Hall Los Angeles, Los Angeles, California, October 20, 1998.*

My small message has to do with our line of work called journalism. It has to do with why, according to the polls, we are down there with lawyers, the congress, and the child pornographers in the public's respect and esteem.

And there is a long list of reasons, most of them obvious to anyone who has been paying attention.

New York Times columnist Russell Baker has been paying attention, if you didn't happen to see his recent column on the subject. Allow me to read the first three paragraphs:

> "Later, in one of those comically solemn conclaves at which journalists ponder the philosophy of their trade and eat high on the expense account, the news industry will struggle to understand the great media meltdown of 1998.
>
> If I am asked to contribute a monograph, it will tend toward the theory that something akin to road rage occurred in the Washington Press Corps.
>
> This produced actions that were variously foolish, shameful, dangerous to American democracy and destructive for the reputation of the news industry."

My own monograph would begin with the additional conclusion, that journalism has become something akin to professional wrestling, something to watch rather than to believe.

One of the reasons is the new savagery that has become part and parcel of some of the so-called new journalism. It is marked by predatory stakeouts. It is brutally coarse invasions of privacy, talk show shouting and violence, no-source reporting and other techniques.

Another reason is something I call the new arrogance. The fact that some in my line of work have developed an approach in words, sneers, body language that say loud and clear: only the journalists of America are pure enough to judge all others.

And judge we must. Because God really did die in the 1960s, and the journalists of America must take up the slack, because there are no others who can, no others out there who are pure enough to do it.

Another reason could be our new problem with entertainment. Garrison Keillor spoke of it a couple of years or so ago at a big dinner of Radio-TV journalists and semi-journalists in Washington.

He warned about the danger of trying to be fascinating rather than just informing.

> Quote: "When you slip into the field of entertainment, then you will be expected to be fascinating. This is going to shorten your careers. Nobody can be fascinating for long but people can be accurate and responsible for an entire career."
>
> End quote . . . Amen . . .

Another may be that trying to be fascinating has resulted in some confusing personnel moves. As Jim Squires, former editor of the *Chicago Tribune*, wrote recently:

> "News events spawn new celebrities, who show up at a later event with a microphone, pretending to practice the craft of journalism. Actors, comedians, politicians, lawyers, infamous criminals—and some who fit all five categories—now regularly masquerade as reporters on newscasts and talk shows. Watergate burglar G. Gordon Liddy and Clinton White House political adviser George Stephanopoulos are both now widely considered to be journalists. Former Nixon speechwriter Patrick Buchanan and civil rights activist Jesse Jackson go from being story subject one month to storyteller the next. Lawyer Johnnie Cochran may be on television standing beside a famous defendant one day and on another interviewing the same defendant from behind an anchor desk.

Worse, many of the people signing the pay checks of these pretenders and making the programming decisions can't see any difference between real news and celebrity news programming. They think that having been celebrated in one news event qualifies someone to cover another. It never crosses their minds that their position in charge of news organizations carries with it a responsibility to protect and preserve the values of real journalism.

On my list the most serious reason is the new blurring of the lines among what I believe are the three basic types of serious journalism: straight reporting, analysis, and opinion.

Here, folks, is what happened.

Here, now, is what it means.

And here, now, is what we, or I, think about it.

When I began in this business more than 30 years ago, each one of those "here" was a very separate function.

The reporting was done by reporters. The analyzing by carefully-labeled and credentialed analysis. And the "we" or "I" thinking by editorial writers, columnists and commentators.

The reader or listener or viewer knew the differences, because they were part of the contract, the basic one between all mainline news organizations and their audiences or customers.

Right before our eyes and ears that has changed, changed dramatically. And changed without much discussion or explanation.

My experience in recent weeks and months is that the public is very confused about what's going on. They see network reporters on the nightly news as straight reporters. And then on weekend programs as commentators or pundits.

And then hear them on various other television or radio programs giving their opinions about the news they reported.

They see network bureau chiefs, the people responsible for assigning reporters to stories, functioning also as analysts and pundits.

On the print side, they see editors of weekly public affairs type magazines, whose job it is to direct even-handed coverage, writing stridently—opinionated columns in newspapers and other publications about stories their own publications are covering.

They see straight news reporters for newspapers and other publications on television or radio acting as pundits.

They even see, from time to time, opinions, masquerading as angles, in so-called straight news stories in all of the media: TV, radio, and print.

It would be difficult for anyone to keep track of who is what, or what is who, without a scorecard. And there are no scorecards.

The result has been a problem for some of us still trying to operate under the old rules.

We had a situation at the beginning of the Lewinsky matter, when one of our regular straight-news contributors Stuart Taylor, then of *the American Lawyer and Legal Times*, covered the Supreme Court for us and did so brilliantly, in my opinion. But as the Lewinsky story broke, and then shook, rattled and rolled, he developed into a commentator about the story.

Not on our program but on other programs as well as print.

I felt there was some confusion about his roles being created, and we dropped him from his regular reporting slot.

We were attacked by many well-meaning people who saw my decision as being pro-Clinton, an effort to keep Taylor's strong views about the President off our program. I tried to explain it on the air, the differences of functions.

But I was truly swimming up stream, and I still am. Only one person in the press came to my assistance by the way.

Howard Rosenberg, the TV critic of the Los Angeles times helped me explain it in a column which I appreciated very much.

Everyone else who should care about such things remained silent.

And by their silence said loud and clear: You're a dinosaur, Lehrer. Journalism has changed, and you haven't.

I hereby plead guilty to that. And in doing so I do not wrap myself in some cloak of goodness and mercy, and accuse everyone who disagrees of being some kind of lesser person or professional.

There are no evil or wrong people involved in this change, this evolution into a new journalism. My point is that those who practice it have an obligation to explain what they are doing. To bring the public under the tent with them.

Because if they do not, it will continue to be one of those reasons our credibility and esteem will continue to sink.

And the problem with that is, simply that there is no room left down there to go.

Vital Speeches, LXV, NO.5 (December 15, 1998).

HAWAII—LAND OF VOLCANOES

Peggy Chiao—Student, *University of Missouri. Reprinted by permission of the author*

Good afternoon. Or, as we say in Hawaii, "Aloha." I bring you greetings from the 50th state, the islands of Hawaii.

There are many interesting and unusual features of Hawaii, but I'd like to share with you today some that you may not already know. My entire state was created by volcanic eruptions and the growth continues, even while we sit in this classroom.

We are a state where every racial and ethnic group is a minority. People from every race and color are represented in our population, and most of our citizens come from mixed origins. For instance, it is very common for a person to be the daughter of a Chinese mother and an Italian father. To get a better idea, just fill in the blanks. We have Portuguese immigrants, many citizens whose parents or grandparents came from Thailand, Japan, China, Spain, Germany, Ireland, Korea, and Canada. Mix them all together and you may have a better notion of the diversity of our people. Hawaii is a state of many mixed nationalities. But, just like any other state, we are all Americans first.

Finally, one of the more interesting features is the fact that in an all-island state, we have an interstate highway. I haven't figured out how it connects to the mainland, but on the island of Oahu there is Hawaii Interstate 1.

When you hear about volcanoes, you may think about Mt. Aetna or some location in Central America. The "big island," Hawaii, is the home of some of the most active volcanoes in the world. Let me give you a brief explanation of what happens when a volcano erupts.

In Hawaii, the process begins 60 miles under the earth surface where white-hot magma is created. The inside pressure of the earth forces this magma upward, toward the surface of the earth, to about 2 miles under the surface where it gathers in a large pool called a magma reservoir. Remember, all this is happening because of massive pressures deep inside the earth.

As more and more pressure develops, the magma reservoir seeks out areas of weakness in the surface. These are called "rifts." When there is enough pressure, the lava fountains erupt through these rift zones and we have a volcanic eruption. These eruptions are spectacular. Imagine, molten lava, fire and gasses rising suddenly 1500 feet into the air. And, at the same time, the lava begins to flow into the crater and then overruns the crater.

The result fills the air with toxic gases, and the lava soon forms a lava lake. As the eruption continues, more and more lava is pushed out of the magma reservoir. It is unstoppable by man. In 1983, when the Kilauea volcano erupted on the island of Hawaii, the lava flow, burning and burying everything in its path, came as close as 3 miles to the city of Hilo. All of this is a little like putting water into a balloon from a hose. After a while, the water will break the balloon and begin to flow everywhere.

As long as the buildup in pressure deep inside the earth continues, the volcano will continue to spew out its lava, the red-hot liquid from the magma of the earth. Just for your information and to show you how recently much of this has happened, you should know that during the 80's and 90's, eruptions have added over 600 acres to the coastline from the volcanic flows.

In fact, one of the most spectacular sights is the continuing lava flow from the Kileau volcano at this very moment. There, the reservoir drains into the east rift zone and this zone leads the lava to the sea. When the lava strikes the water, it is spectacular, especially at night. Remember, this lava flow has been active since 1983 when the volcano erupted.

Watching it from the sea makes you marvel at the wonder of nature. When the cool water touches the lava, it looks like a small city is on fire. The flames shoot nearly a hundred feet into the air, and the lava and water combine to create highly acidic steam and steam clouds. If you are downwind from the site, your eyes will burn from the acid fumes and you will feel as if you are witnessing the end of part of the earth.

Later, when the lava cools, you see a barren wasteland. But, the lava field is extremely fertile and, after a few years, you will see the return of small grasses followed by shrubs and later trees. Remember that all of the state of Hawaii was formed by these volcanic eruptions. When you consider how fertile our soil is, you have a clear notion of what happens years after the volcano becomes dormant.

If you're interested in seeing nature put on a fiery display, come to Hawaii. If you want to visit an area formed by volcanoes which are still active, come to Hawaii. If you want to see paradise, warm seas, sunny skies, temperatures in the 80's the year round, visit the Hawaiian archipelago. We're a long distance from the mainland, but the trip is certainly worth the effort. Where else could you see land formed before your eyes?

TROUBLESHOOTING GUIDE

Public speaking activity can continue throughout your lifetime. In school, at work, and in social, civic, and religious organizations, you will have many opportunities to give public speeches. Many people want a quick reference for refreshing their memory about public speaking or to give them new information about managing a public speaking situation. This book will serve as a helpful tool when those situations arise—helpful beyond the level provided by most public speaking textbooks.

At times, the typical book index, including the one in this book, is not a useful problem-solving tool because it is not problem oriented. To find solutions to your problems, you would ordinarily have to read through many sections of a book. This troubleshooting guide has been developed to provide something more. It is a problem oriented index based on the kinds of problems that speakers most often confront when called on to give a speech. Make a habit of using this guide. You will find *Public Speaking for Personal Success* a helpful resource for many years to come.

1. State the problem you are experiencing out loud or in writing.
2. Think of key words that describe the problem you have stated. Key words are listed alphabetically in the "Directory" that follows.
3. Locate those key words in the problem-solving index.
4. Find a question similar to yours and then turn to the referenced pages of the text for an answer.
5. If you do not find relevant key words for your problem in the "Directory," refer to the index at the back of this book to locate information related to your problem.

DIRECTORY

Anxiety
Argument
Audience analysis
Attending and attention
Audience adaptation
Brainstorm
Communication anxiety
Communication process
Comparison and contrast
Conclusion
Credibility
Definition of terms
Delivery
Demographics
Ethics
Evidence
Eye contact
First Speech
Gestures
Humor
Inform
Interview
Introduction
Language
Library
Listening
Logic

Meaning Agreement
Mistakes
Motivation
Narrow end focus
Needs
Notes
Organization of ideas
Outlining
Persuasion
Practice
Proving
Purpose
Questionnaire Reasoning
Remembering
Research
Signposts
Speaking
Specific purpose
Speech situations & problems
Stage fright
Supporting material
Testimony
Thesis
Topic
Transition
Visual aids

A

Anxiety

I am worried that I cannot succeed as a speaker. Is there any help or hope? Chapter 2, p. 26
Can I use notes in a speech to relieve anxiety? Chapter 2, p. 31
I feel afraid even when I think about giving a speech. What can I do to prevent this feeling or
at least deal with it? Chapter 2, p. 30
Why am I afraid of giving a speech? Chapter 2, p. 26

Argument (*See also* Logic, Reasoning)

What are the most common kinds of argument? Chapter 6, p. 112
I have to give a persuasive speech. What controls what a listener accepts and believes?
Chapter 6, p. 119
How do you prove a knowledge claim? Chapter 6, p. 124
Where can I find an overview of how people reason? Chapter 6, pp. 124, 127

I want to use evidence wisely to make an argument. But where do I find
evidence? Chapter 6, p. 126
How can I judge the accuracy or value of evidence? Chapter 6, p. 126
What is the best way to use statistics in an argument? Chapter 6, p. 128

Attending and Attention (*See also* Listening)

Sometimes when I am trying to listen, I cannot concentrate on what is being said. Is there
anything I can do? Chapter 3, p. 52
Sometimes, l find myself drifting off instead of paying attention. Is there anything I can do to
prevent this? Chapter 3, p. 52
How can I get attention from listeners when they are getting tired? Chapter 3, p. 53
What are the best ways to get the attention of my audience? Chapter 3, p. 53

Audience Adaptation

Suppose I know where my audience stands. How do I adapt to them? Chapter 5, p. 103
My listeners don't know much about the subject matter. What kind of argument should
I use? Chapter 6, p. 112
How can I know if my topic will be appropriate for my audience? Chapter 5, p. 103
I have a good idea, but I am not sure how to tie it into the interests of
listeners. Chapter 5, p. 99
I would like to know how listeners will respond to my speech. How can I predict their
reactions? Chapter 5, p. 94
What can I do to get the audience to empathize with my position? Chapter 3, p. 56

Audience Analysis (*See also* Demographics)

I would like to develop a questionnaire to test the audience position on my topic, but I do not
know how to begin. Any suggestions? Chapter 5, p. 94
Is there a way to analyze my class as though it were a real audience? Chapter 5, p. 94
I do not know anything about my audience. How do I begin an audience
analysis? Chapter 5, p. 94
What affect does the place where I speak and the time when I talk have on my chances for
success? Chapter 5, p. 93
What is inferential audience analysis? How does it work? Chapter 5, pp. 98, 102
How do I actually perform an audience analysis? Chapter 5, p. 94

B

Brainstorm

How can I brainstorm for speech topics? Chapter 4, p. 69

C

Communication Anxiety (*See* Anxiety)

Communication Process

What is involved in the communication process? Chapter 1, p. 16

Comparison and Contrast (*See also* Supporting Material)

How do comparison and contrast work as supporting material for a
speech? Chapter 11, p. 259

Conclusion

When I come to the end of my speech, I have trouble finishing it. What should I do? Chapter 10, p. 237

Credibility

I want listeners to trust me and have confidence in me. What can I do to increase my credibility? Chapter 6, pp. 124, 125/Chapter 15, p. 264

How can I make a speech more credible? Chapter 15, p. 364

D

Definition of Terms (*See also* Meaning Agreement)

What should I define, and what can I leave undefined? Why? Chapter 11, p. 249

Delivery (*See also* Visual Aids)

Is it ever okay to read a speech from a manuscript? Chapter 13, p. 306

I am thinking about writing out my speech and memorizing it. Is this approach okay? Chapter 13, 307

Should I worry about my speaking voice? Chapter 13, p. 312

Is there a style of delivery that is generally recommended? Chapter 13, p. 311

How do you select the right style of delivery? Chapter 13, p. 306

What should I do about gestures? Chapter 13, p. 316

Are there any pointers about delivery? Chapter 13, p. 319

Demographics

I know that demographics are important to audience analysis and marketing research, but what should I look for? Chapter 5, p. 99

What should I do with the demographic information that I collect about an audience? Chapter 5, p. 99

E

Ethics

What common ethical issues arise in public speaking? Chapter 1, p. 10

Are there ethical standards for public speaking? Chapter 1, p. 10

Evidence (*See also* Supporting Material)

What is a good definition of evidence? Chapter 6, p. 126

What are the various kinds of evidence and their strengths and weaknesses? Chapter 6, p. 126

Where can I find evidence? Chapter 7, pp. 140, 141

How can I know if the evidence is any good? What tests can I apply? Chapter 6, p. 126

Eye Contact

How important is eye contact with my audience? Chapter 13, p. 318

F

First Speech

How do I develop the first speech? Chapter 2, p. 32

G

Gestures

My gestures seem wooden and unnatural. What should I do? Chapter 2, p. 32

H

Humor

What kind of humor can I use to lighten the atmosphere? Chapter 16, p. 394

I

Inform

I'm supposed to give a descriptive speech. Does this book have any
pointers? Chapter 14, p. 337
I am supposed to give a speech to inform. What techniques will help me? Chapter 14, p. 329
What are the most common types of informative speech topics? Chapter 14, p. 332

Interview

How can I plan for and get the most out of an interview? Chapter 7, p. 141

Introduction

What strategies can I use to introduce a speech? Chapter 10, p. 230

L

Language

How can I use language more effectively? Chapter 11, p. 255
I want to avoid giving offense. How can I avoid language that offends? Chapter 11, p. 256
What does language mean? Chapter 11, p. 251
What language techniques can I use to make my speech vivid and
interesting? Chapter 11, p. 258

Library

What are the departments in a library? Chapter 7, p. 143
What are the most useful computertized databases in a library? Chapter 7, p. 146
Which are the most commonly used general indexes? Chapter 7, p. 149
Which are the most commonly used reference works? Chapter 7, p. 151
What criteria can I apply to judge the quality of information I find in a
library? Chapter 7, p. 158

Listening (*See also* Attending and Attention)

What are the key elements of listening that I must take into account as a
speaker? Chapter 3, p. 50
What can I do to help audience members listen if they have difficulty seeing or hearing?
Chapter 3, p. 51
People sometimes tell me I do not listen. I try to listen, but how can I improve my own
listening skills? Chapter 3, p. 57
Can I help audience members to listen more effectively? Chapter 3, p. 53

How can I help listeners remember my key ideas? Chapter Chapter 3, p. 56

I have been told that what I say is not always clear. What can I do to help listeners understand my ideas? Chapter 3, p. 54

Logic (*See also* Argument, Reasoning)

Something seems wrong with the logic of this speech, but I cannot figure it out. Any ideas? Chapter 6, p. 120

How can I strengthen the likelihood that listeners will accept the logic of my speech? Chapter 6, p. 119

M

Meaning Agreement

Sometimes, listeners think I mean something quite different from what I intended. What is the problem? Is there a solution? Chapter 12, p. 257

Sometimes, people misunderstand the words I use. What is the problem? Chapter 3, p. 54/Chapter 12, p. 260

Mistakes

What are the most common mistakes to avoid? Chapter 2, p. 32

Motivation (*See also* Persuasion)

What motivates people to do what they do? Chapter 5, p. 103

N

Narrow and Focus

People tell me not to "bite off more than I can chew"—to narrow and focus my topic. How do I do that? Chapter 4, p. 73

Notes

What is the best way to make and use notes? Chapter 7, p. 160

Can I use my outline for speaking notes? Chapter 9, p. 212

How can I use my visual aids for notes? Chapter 12, p. 277

O

Organization of Ideas (*See also* Outlining)

Why is organizing ideas so important? Chapter 8, p. 173

How should I organize the introduction of a speech? Chapter 2, p. 36/Chapter 9, p. 206

What characterizes good organization of ideas? Chapter 8, p. 174

Is there a surefire way to organize the ideas for my speech? Chapter 8, p. 176

How should I organize the conclusion of a speech? Chapter 2, p. 36

I want to give a speech about a problem that needs to be solved. Is there a best way to organize such a speech? Chapter 8, p. 178

I want to talk about a topic that is really interesting to me, but I am not sure how to organize it. Chapter 8, p. 184

I want to talk about a problem and propose a solution. How should I organize my ideas? Chapter 8, pp. 178, 183

I want to stimulate listeners to action. How should I organize this speech? Chapter 8, p. 184

Outlining

Can I get help on the Internet for outlining? Chapter 9, p. 195
How do I make an outline for a speech? Chapter 9, p. 201
What is the difference between a planning outline and a speaking outline? Chapter 9, p. 212
Are there sample outlines in this book? Throughout Chapters 8 and 9
How do I make a speaking outline? Chapter 9, p. 212

P

Persuasion (*See also* Organization of Ideas)

What makes a good persuasive speech? Chapter 15, p. 364
Should I give both sides of the argument in a persuasive speech? Chapter 15, p. 369
Should I use fear appeals to persuade? Chapter 15, p. 372
Is it okay to tell listeners what I want from them? Chapter 15, p. 371
I want listeners to feel they need my proposal. How can I create such a need in them? Chapter 15, p. 372

Practice

What is the best way to practice a speech without memorizing it? Chapter 2, p. 38/ Chapter 13, p. 319

Proving

How do you go about proving something? Chapter 6, p. 126

Q

Questionnaire

Can I use questionnaires in audience analysis? Chapter 5, p. 97

R

Reasoning (*See also* Argument, Logic)

How can I analyze a cause-effect relationship? Chapter 6, p. 115/Chapter 8, p. 178
Does it make sense to argue from example? Chapter 6, p. 115
What is the best way to test an argument from analogy? Chapter 6, p. 115
How can I judge the accuracy or value of evidence? Chapter 6, p. 126
What kinds of evidence are available, and how do I use them? Chapter 6, p. 126

Remembering

How can I help listeners to remember key ideas? Chapter 14, p. 346

Research

How do I conduct a key word search? Chapter 7, p. 147
Which are the most commonly used general indexes in a library? Chapter 7, p. 150
How can I use reference works? Chapter 7, p. 149
Can I use the Internet for research? Chapter 7, p. 153
How can I judge the quality of information I find? Chapter 7, p. 158

S

Signposts

I do not understand the purpose of signposts. What are they supposed
to do? Chapter 8, p. 187

Speaking

Why do people give speeches? Chapter 1, p. 8

Speaking Assignments

What kinds of assignments are most likely for the first speech? And what should I do?
Chapter 1, p. 26

Specific Purpose

What is the difference between a specific purpose and a thesis? Chapter 1, p. 38
Why is it important to have a specific purpose for a speech? Chapter 4, p. 13, Chapter 9, p. 202

Speech Situations and Problems

I have to give a speech soon. Where can I find an overview of what I have
to do? Chapter 2, p. 32
What should I do when I am called on for an impromptu speech? Chapter 13, p. 310
They are going to give me an award, and I'll have to make a speech.
Any advice? Chapter 16, p. 386
I'm supposed to make a welcoming speech for my company. Can you help? Chapter 16, p. 391
I am going to give the commencement address at my alma mater. What should
I do? Chapter 16, p. 390
I will deliver the eulogy at a friend's funeral. How should I prepare for it? Chapter 16, p. 388
I must give a speech of introduction. What should I do? Chapter 16, p. 384
I have been asked to give the keynote speech at a conference. What goes into such
a speech? Chapter 16, p. 391
I have been asked to make an award presentation. What should I do? Chapter 16, p. 386
I am supposed to give a speech to praise someone. I do not want to overdo it. What should
I do? Chapter 16, p. 388
I have been asked to give an after-dinner speech. How do I prepare? Chapter 16, p. 395

Stage fright (*See also* Anxiety)

I think I am suffering from stage fright. What are the symptoms? Chapter 2, p. 26
What can I do to handle my nervousness? Chapter 2, p. 28–32

Supporting Material (*See also* Evidence)

Is there a way to tell if a statement needs support? Chapter 2, p. 36
How do you support a thesis statement with main ideas and subpoints? Chapter 9, p. 203
How do I use examples wisely? Chapter 6, pp. 115, 129
Who is an authority, and who is not? Chapter 6, p. 119
Is there a set of do's and don'ts for using statistics as supporting material? Chapter 6, p. 126
How can I tell how much confidence to place in testimony? Chapter 6, p. 129

T

Testimony

How can I tell if the testimony I plan to use is believable? Chapter 6, p. 129

Thesis

How is a thesis statement different from a purpose? Chapter 2, p. 35
How do I develop a thesis statement that is correct? Chapter 4, p. 81

Topic (*See also* Narrow and Focus)

I am supposed to give a speech, and I have no idea what I should discuss. Any suggestions? Chapter 2, p. 32/Chapter 4, pp. 68, 69, 71, 73 and see, especially, Appendix C, p. 439
I am worried that my topic will not be interesting to listeners. What techniques can I use to hold their interest? Chapter 3, p. 56/Chapter 5, p. 103/Chapter 10, p. 229/Chapter 12, p. 272/Chapter 13, p. 306
How can I select a topic when I am out of ideas? Chapter 4, p. 69
How can I narrow a speech topic to manageable limits? Chapter 4, p. 72

Transition

What is a good transition? How can I develop it effectively? Chapter 8 p. 187

V

Visual Aids (*See also* Delivery)

What is a visual aid? Chapter 12, p. 270
What's involved in making visual aids? Chapter 12, p. 285
Do visual aids always improve a speech? Chapter 12, p. 272
When should I support my speech with visual materials? Chapter 12, p. 278
What should I support visually? Chapter 12, p. 278
How do I select the right visual medium? Chapter 12, p. 282
How do I judge the quality of a visual aid? Chapter 12, p. 284
I want my visual to be well-balanced. What criteria can I apply? Chapter 12, p. 293
How can I suggest action and tension with a visual aid? Chapter 12, p. 288
How can I suggest calm and peace with a visual aid? Chapter 12, p. 288
Visual aids can be text, graphics, or both. Are there any guidelines for choosing? Chapter 12, p. 272
How should I use visual aids when I'm practicing? Chapter 12, p. 294
What about using my computer to make visual aids? Chapter 12, p. 275
How can I make an effective visual aid? Chapter 12, p. 285
How much lettering should I use on a visual aid? Chapter 12, p. 291

POSSIBLE SPEECH TOPICS

Selecting a topic for a speech is often a challenging task for beginning speakers. As explained in Chapter 4, "Selecting and Narrowing Your Topic," an effective speech topic is one that you are knowledgeable about, that relates to your audience, that fits the occasion, and that can be discussed within the given time constraints.

This appendix lists titles from the Opposing Viewpoints® Pamphlets Series of Greenhaven Press. The Opposing Viewpoints® Series is a collection of books that present both sides of current issues. Each chapter of each Opposing Viewpoints® book is available in pamphlet form as a volume in the Opposing Viewpoints® Pamphlets Series. The pamphlet titles listed here may help you choose a speech topic. You may purchase Opposing Viewpoints® books ($9.95) or pamphlets ($3.50) by calling Greenhaven's toll-free number, 800–231–5163, or by writing to Greenhaven Press, Order Dept., PO Box 289009, San Diego, CA 92198–9009. Reprinted by permission.

Area Studies

Africa

What Are the Causes of Africa's Problems?
How Can Famine in Africa Be Reduced?
How Will the Dismantling of Apartheid Affect South Africa's Future?

Central America

Why Is Central America a Conflict Area?
Is U.S. Involvement in Central America Justified?
What Policies Would Strengthen Central American Economies?
What Role Does Christianity Play in Central America?
Is Peace in Central America Possible?

China

Historical Debate: How Should China Modernize?
Are China's Economic Reforms Significant?
Does China Guarantee Human Rights?
Is China a World Power?

Eastern Europe

Historical Debate: What Led to the Division of Europe?
Do Eastern European Revolutions Signal the Demise of Communism?
What Economic Policies Should Eastern Europe Adopt?
How Will a United Germany Affect Europe?
Is European Unification Possible?

Israel

Historical Debate: Is a Homeland for the Jews Necessary?
Does Israel Treat the Palestinians Fairly?
Should the United States Support Israel?
What Is Israel's International Role?
What Is the Future of Israel?

Japan

Is Japan a World Power?
Are Japan's Economic Policies Fair?
Is Japan an Internally Troubled Society?
Should Japan Increase Its International Role?
Is Cooperation Between the United States and Japan Beneficial?

The Middle East

Why Is the Middle East a Conflict Area?
Are Palestinian Rights Being Ignored?
What Role Should the United States Play in the Middle East?
How Does Religion Affect the Middle East?
What Is the Future of the Middle East?

Third World

Why Is the Third World Poor?
Why Are Human Rights Threatened in the Third World?
Does U.S. Foreign Aid Benefit Third World?
What Policies Would Promote Third World Development?
How Can Third World Debt Be Reduced?

Criminal Justice

America's Prisons

What Is the Purpose of Prisons?
How Do Prisons Affect Criminals?
How Can Prison Overcrowding Be Reduced?
Should Prisons Be Privatized?
What Are the Alternatives to Prisons?

Crime and Criminals

What Causes Crime?
How Should Criminals Be Treated?
How Can Crime Be Reduced?
How Should White-Collar Crime Be Controlled?
Would Gun Control Reduce Crime?

Criminal Justice

How Do Lawyers Affect the Criminal Justice System?
Should the Criminal Justice System Enforce Crime Victims' Rights?
What Reforms Would Improve the Criminal Justice System?

Do the Rights of the Accused Undermine the Criminal Justice System?
Do Police Abuse Their Authority?

The Death Penalty

Three Centuries of Debate on the Death Penalty
Is the Death Penalty Just?
Is the Death Penalty an Effective Punishment?
Does the Death Penalty Discriminate?
Do Certain Crimes Deserve the Death Penalty?

Violence in America

Is Violence in America a Serious Problem?
How Can Drug-Related Violence Be Reduced?
What Causes Family Violence?
What Causes Teen Violence?
What Motivates Serial Killers?
What Policies Would Reduce Violence?

Environment

The Environmental Crisis

Is There an Environmental Crisis?
How Should Pesticides Be Handled?
How Can the Garbage Problem Be Reduced?
How Should America Dispose of Toxic Waste?
How Serious Is Air and Water Pollution?
How Can the Environment Be Protected?

Global Resources

Are Global Resources Becoming More Scarce?
Is the Greenhouse Effect a Serious Threat?
Are Population Control Measures Needed to Protect Global Resources?
How Can Rain Forests Be Saved?
How Can Sustainable Agriculture Be Promoted?
What Policies Would Help Conserve Global Resources?

Water

How Should the Water Supply Be Managed?
How Can Water Pollution Be Reduced?
How Serious a Problem Is Acid Rain?
How Serious a Problem Is Ocean Pollution?

Foreign Policy

American Foreign Policy

How Should the United States Deal with the Former Soviet Republics?

Is U.S. Intervention in Other Countries Justified?

How Should the United States Deal With Its Allies?

What Should be the Goal of U.S. Foreign Policy?

What Are the Effects of U.S. Foreign Aid?

America's Defense

What Role Should the United States Play in World Defense?

Should Women Serve in the U.S. Military?

Should Defense Spending Be Decreased?

What Weapons Would Strengthen America's Defense?

The Breakup of the Soviet Union

Why Did the Soviet Union Collapse?

How Will the Breakup of the Soviet Union Affect the World?

How Should the United States Respond to the Breakup of the Soviet Union?

What Policies Would Strengthen the Republics' Economies?

What Measures Would Reduce Ethnic Conflict in the Republics?

Latin America and U.S. Foreign Policy

Is U.S. Intervention the Cause of Latin America's Problems?

How Should the United States Deal with Latin American Human Rights Conditions?

What Form of Government Is Best for Latin America?

How Serious Is the Latin American Debt?

The New World Order

What Will the New World Order Be?

What Role Will the United States Play in the New World Order?

What Role Will Economics Play in the New World Order?

How Will the End of the Cold War Affect the World?

What Role Will International Organizations Play in the New World Order?

Nuclear Proliferation

How Serious a Problem Is Nuclear Proliferation?

Which Nations Contribute to Nuclear Proliferation?

How Can Nuclear Proliferation Be Prevented?

Terrorism

Is Terrorism Justified?

Do the Superpowers Sponsor Terrorism?

Can Terrorism Be Eliminated?

What Are the Causes of Terrorism?

War and Human Nature

Are Humans Aggressive by Nature?

Government And Economics

American Government

What Is the Role of American Government?

Who Controls America?

Should the Constitution Be Revised?

How Can American Democracy Be Improved?

America's Elections

What Role Should the Media Play in U.S. Elections?

Censorship

Should There Be Limits to Free Speech?

Should the News Media Be Regulated?

Does National Security Justify Censorship?

Is School and Library Censorship Justified?

Should Pornography Be Censored?

Civil Liberties

How Should the Right to Privacy Be Defined?

Should Freedom of Expression Be Restricted?

Should Church and State Be Separate?

How Can Civil Liberties Be Protected?

Economics in America

What Is the State of America's Economy?

How Serious Is the Budget Deficit?

What Kind of Taxation Is Most Appropriate?

How Can America's Banking System Be Strengthened?
What Is the Future of American Labor?

Immigration

Historical Debate: Should Immigration Be Restricted?
How Do Immigrants Affect America?
How Should U.S. Immigration Policy Be Reformed?
What Policies Would Help Immigrants Adapt to the United States?

Politics in America

Does American Political Leadership Need Improvement?
Does the Two-Party System Effectively Represent Americans?

Space Exploration

What Should Be the Goal of Space Exploration?
Which Space Programs Should the United States Pursue?
Should NASA Be Eliminated?

Trade

Is Free Trade the Best Trading System?
Is the United States the Victim of Unfair Trade Practices?
Should Trade Be Restricted?
How Critical Is the U.S. Trade Deficit?
What Is the Future of the World Trading System?

Health

AIDS

How Serious is AIDS?
Is AIDS a Moral Issue?
Is AIDS Testing Effective?
How Can the Spread of AIDS Be Prevented?

Biomedical Ethics

What Ethics Should Guide Biomedical Research?
What Ethics Should Guide Organ Transplants?
What Ethics Should Guide Fetal Tissue Research?

Are Reproductive Technologies Ethical?
Should Animals Be Used in Research?

Chemical Dependency

What Are the Causes of Chemical Dependency?
Is Smoking Harmful?
How Harmful Is Alcohol?
Should Drug Laws Be Reformed?
Should Pregnant Women Be Prosecuted for Drug Abuse?
How Can Chemical Dependency Be Reduced?

Death and Dying

What Is the Best Treatment for the Terminally Ill?
How Can Dying Patients Control the Decision to End Treatment?
How Should One Cope with Grief?
Is There Life After Death?

Drug Abuse

How Serious a Problem Is Drug Abuse?
How Should the War on Drugs Be Waged?
Should Drug Testing Be Used in the Workplace?
How Should Prescription Drugs Be Regulated?
How Can Drug Abuse Be Reduced?

Euthanasia

Is Euthanasia Ethical?
What Policy Should Guide Euthanasia?
What Criteria Should Influence Decisions?
Who Should Make the Euthanasia Decision?
Is Infant Euthanasia Ethical?

Genetic Engineering

Is Genetic Engineering Beneficial?
Can Genetic Engineering Improve Health?
Does Genetic Engineering Improve Agriculture?
Is Genetic Engineering Adequately Regulated?
Will Genetic Engineering Lead to a Biological Arms Race?

The Health Crisis

Are Health Care Costs Too High?
How Can Health Be Improved?

Suicide

Is Suicide an Individual Right?
Should Physicians Assist Terminally Ill Patients in Suicide?
What Are the Causes of Teen Suicide?
How Can Suicide Be Prevented?

Sexuality

Homosexuality

What Causes Homosexuality?
Should Society Encourage Increased Acceptance of Homosexuality?
Can Homosexuals Change Their Sexual Orientation?
Should Society Legally Sanction Gay Relationships?

Male/Female Roles

Have Women's Roles Changed for the Better?
How Does Work Affect the Family?

Sexual Values

Have Sexual Values Changed in America?
Is Pornography Harmful?
How Should Society Treat Homosexuality?
Is Sex Education Beneficial?

Teenage Sexuality

What Kind of Sex Education Is Appropriate for Teenagers?

Social Issues

Abortion

When Does Life Begin?
Should Abortion Remain a Personal Choice?
Is Abortion Immoral?
Can Abortion Be Justified?
Should Abortion Remain Legal?

America's Children

What Education Policies Would Help Children?
How Can Children Be Protected from Abuse?
What Government Policies Would Help America's Poor Children?

How Can the Health of America's Children Be Improved?
Are Working Parents Harming America's Children?

America's Cities

Why Are America's Cities in Decline?
How Can Urban Homelessness Be Reduced?
How Can Urban Conditions Be Improved?
How Can Urban Crime Be Reduced?
What Measures Would Improve Urban Housing?

America's Future

Is America in Decline?
What Is America's Economic Future?
Is America Falling Behind in Technology?
How Can American Education Be Improved?
What Lies Ahead for America?

Animal Rights

Do Animals Have Rights?
Is Animal Experimentation Justified?
Should Animals Be Used for Food?
Does Wildlife Need to Be Protected?
How Can the Animal Rights Movement Improve Animal Welfare?

Child Abuse

Is Child Abuse a Serious Problem?
What Causes Child Abuse?
How Widespread Is Child Sexual Abuse?
How Should the Legal System Respond to Child Abuse?
How Can Child Abuse Be Reduced?

Culture Wars

What Cultural Influence Should the United States Perpetuate?
Are Diverse Traditions Fairly Represented in American Education?
Is American Culture Decadent?
Should Government Enforce Cultural Values?

Education in America

How Can Public Education Be Improved?
How Can the Teaching Profession Be Improved?

Should Education for Minority Students Emphasize Ethnicity?
What Role Should Religion Play in Public Education?

The Elderly

How Does Society View the Elderly?
Are the Elderly Poor?
Is Social Security Necessary for the Elderly?
How Should Society Meet the Elderly's Health Care Needs?

The Family in America

What Is the Status of the Family?
How Does Divorce Affect the Family?
How Are Two-Career Parents Affecting the Family?

The Homeless

Is Homelessness a Serious Problem?
What Are the Causes of Homelessness?
Should the Government Help the Homeless?
Can Housing Policies Reduce Homelessness?

The Mass Media

Is Advertising Harmful to Society?
Is Technology Ruining American Relationships?
Is Electronic Commerce Safe?

Poverty

What Are the Causes of Poverty?
Can Government Efforts Alleviate Poverty?
Why Does an American Underclass Exist?
Is Poverty a Serious Problem in the United States?
Why Does Poverty Disproportionately Affect Certain Groups?

Racism in America

How Serious Is the Problem of Racism in America?
Is Racism Responsible for Minority Poverty?
Does Affirmative Action Alleviate Discrimination?
Should Minorities Emphasize Their Ethnicity?
How Can Racism Be Stopped?

Social Justice

Is the United States a Just Nation?
Does America's Economy Promote Social Justice?
Does the United States Provide Equal Opportunities for Minorities?
What Policies Would Promote Social Justice for Women?
What Policies Can Promote Social Justice?

War on Drugs

Is the War on Drugs Necessary?
Can the United States Stop International Drug Cartels?

Values And Religion

American Values

What Are America's Social Values?
What Are America's Economic Values?
What Are America's Religious Values?
What Does America Need?

Constructing a Life Philosophy

How Do Others Make Moral Decisions?
What Is Life's Meaning?
How Do Religions Give Life Meaning?
How Should One Live?

Paranormal Phenomena

Do Paranormal Phenomena Exist?
Are UFOs Real?
Does ESP Exist?
Can the Future Be Predicted?
Can Humans Interact with the Spirit World?

Religion in America

Is America a Religious Society?
Should Religious Values Guide Public Policy?
Does Religious Discrimination Exist in America?
What Is the Future of Religion in America?

Science and Religion

How Did Life Originate?
Great Historical Debates on Science and Religion

GLOSSARY

A

abstract Brief summary of the contents of an essay or article.

acceptance speech A brief epideictic speech to thank the presenter and the organization that gave the gift or award.

accessibility Criterion for making a two-dimensional visual aid. The requirement that an audience must be able to understand the visual material.

activity dimension In connotation, a movement dimension which relates to a word's dynamics—to what a word does.

affect A combination of physical experience plus the language we use, either consciously or unconsciously, to describe the experience.

after-dinner speech A brief epideictic speech following a social meal, often are designed to be entertaining.

analogy The explanation of a particular subject by pointing out its similarities to another subject, usually one that is better known or more easily understood.

antonym A word having the opposite meanings from another word.

argument Reasoning in which one or more statements are offered as support for some other statement.

argument from analogy Argument that what is true of something known is also true of something unknown compared to it.

argument from cause Argument based on the assumption that something happened because of an earlier event.

argument from sign Assertion that certain characteristic features or symptoms suggest a state of affairs.

artistic proofs Three kinds of appeals described by Aristotle: ethos, logos, and pathos.

attending The process of selecting and then focusing on certain stimuli.

audience A collection of individual, unique human beings assembled for a purpose.

audience analysis The process by which a speaker tries to identify and understand the major characteristics of a group of listeners and the features of context and setting that render the group an audience.

B

backing Any additional evidence and argument that supports the principle in the warrant.

***because* test** Habit of following a knowledge claim with the word "because" to verify the ideas are arranged in appropriate superior-subordinate relationships.

belief A statement that something *is*.

body of the speech Major portion of a speech, in which the main ideas and arguments are developed.

brainstorming A timed procedure for generating a large number of ideas quickly.

C

causal order Pattern for organizing ideas that relies on either cause-to-effect or effect-to-cause reasoning.

cause-to-effect Organizational pattern that flows from the causal fabric to its effect. Pattern for organizing ideas to help listeners understand one set of conditions is responsible for a result.

channel In communication theory, the means of transmission.

claim Any expression of an opinion or conclusion a speaker wants accepted.

closing In speech, a statement designed to focus listeners' thinking and feelings on what was said or what was wanted from listeners.

code System of signs and symbols used to transmit messages.

cognition The act, power, or faculty of apprehending, knowing, or perceiving.

cognitive process: A mechanism used to handle information in the mind.

commencement speech A brief address given during graduation ceremonies.

communication apprehension Specific type of anxiety characterized by distress, worry, nervousness, and fear in a communication situation.

communication power Degree of potency and memorability of visual or other symbolic material.

comparison and contrast A figure of speech in which one describes how something is similar to or different from something else that is already know.

conclusion The end of a speech that focuses listeners' thoughts and feelings on the speech's main ideas. The unifying element for the ideas or tone you develop in the speech body.

concretion Act or process of using language to make something real, tangible, or particular.

conflict Antagonism or opposition between interests or principles; to be at variance.

connotation The affective value or meaning of a word.

context The physical, social, psychological, and temporal environment in which communication takes place.

credibility The degree to which a receiver (listener) believes in something.

credible Believable.

D

data In Toulmin's logical system, evidence, or grounds for accepting a claim.

decoder/receiver In communication theory, the target to which messages are sent. In public speaking, each listener.

decoding The process of drawing information from the rhetorical field, then interpreting that information.

deductive argument Opposite of inductive argument. Works from a general conclusion to specific instances that establish the conclusion.

definition The formal statement of the meaning or significance of a word or phrase.

delivery Use of the voice and the body to convey ideas to listeners. The vehicle speakers use to transmit ideas to listeners.

demographic analysis Statistical study of a population's vital characteristics, including income, marital status, age, sex, socioeconomic status, educational level, political background, and so on. In public speaking, part of audience analysis in which the vital characteristics of a population are used to make predictions about listener responses.

demonstrate To describe, explain, or illustrate by examples, specimens, experiments, and the like. To exhibit something.

denotation The definition of a word that can be found in a dictionary. Also refers to the associations usually called up by a word among members of a speech community.

derived beliefs Beliefs that emerge from a combination of other beliefs. Derived beliefs are less central than either shared or primitive beliefs.

derived interest Interest that flows from associating a new subject with something one already cares about.

description Use of language to picture some object, phenomenon, or event.

differentiation Technique of definition by separating or distinguishing something from other members of its class.

direct quotation Exact replication of an original written or spoken statement.

E

effect-to-cause argument Reasoning pattern that stresses the consequence first and the causes second.

emotional context The social and psychological portion of the communication event.

empathy Attempt to identify with another person and to respond appropriately (as the other person perceives appropriate) to that person.

enthymeme A syllogism based on probability and in which either the general case or the specific case is usually implicit and may be dropped from the stated argument. The power of an enthymeme comes from the listener's participation in completing it.

epideictic A speech for a special occasion, such as eulogy, commencement address, or after-dinner speech.

ethics The study of moral values, of rightness or wrongness.

ethos Aristotle's category of proof in which reputation and appearance create credibility for the speaker and the message. One of three artistic proofs.

etymology Study of the history of change in the meaning of a word.

eulogy An epideictic speech to praise or speak well of a person, or to blame her or him.

example As evidence, something selected to show the nature or character of the rest; a typical instance.

evaluative dimension In language, the overall positive and negative determinations stimulated by a word.

evidence The basic material of the argument, the data that are used as a base for an argument. Any informative statement that, because it is believed by a listener, can be used as a means for gaining the listener's support.

evoked recall Theory of persuasion that asserts people are driven by identification with stimulus materials which cause them to respond according to their need states, memories, experiences, attitudes, and opinions.

exaggeration Act of blowing things up beyond the limits of truth, to increase or enlarge abnormally.

example An instance used as an illustration. A form of support that uses one of a number of things to show characteristics of the whole number.

expert testimony Testimony from a prominent, qualified individual.

explanation To make clear by describing or interpreting how something works, how to evaluate it, or why it occurred.

explicit conclusion Message strategy characterized by telling listeners precisely what to think or do.

extemporaneous delivery Style of delivery that uses careful preparation but minimal notes—not memorized or read from a manuscript.

eye contact The rhetorical act of looking at or meeting someone else's eyes to establish a sense of relationship.

F

fear appeal Use of evidence or argument to induce fear in listeners as a means of motivating them to some decision or action.

feedback Messages listeners send back to speakers.

G

general purpose The broad intention that motivates a speech: to inform, to persuade, to entertain, to express oneself.

gesture Movements of the body or parts of the body to express ideas or emotions.

I

identification The process of responding to incoming messages with attitudes, values, and beliefs we hold now, or once held, in situations or contexts similar to those presented by the persuader.

illustrators Gestures that relate to and help clarify a speaker's words by showing what the words mean, as holding hands apart, palms facing each other, to show the length of something being described in language.

impromptu delivery Speaking without preparation or advance planning.

index Any alphabetized listing of names or topics.

inductive argument Argument that works from a series of individual cases to a conclusion.

inferential analysis The process of drawing inferences from demographic data about how listeners are likely to respond to a speech.

inflection Short-term change up or down in pitch of voice.

information-gathering interview Interview designed to acquire information about a subject, process, or person.

information structure How one has organized information in the mind.

informative speech Speech in which the speaker seeks to add to the general storehouse of knowledge an audience already possesses. To inform is one of the general purposes of speech.

intensification/downplay model of persuasion Model of the persuasion process in which persuaders play up their own strong points and their opponents' weak points, or play down their own weak points and their opponents' strong points.

internal summary Mini-summary used at the conclusion of a major point to remind listeners of the ideas just discussed.

introduction The beginning part of a speech, the purpose of which is to get attention, state the speaker's thesis, and prepare listeners for what is coming.

introductory speech Speech to introduce another speaker

irony Saying one thing but meaning the opposite with humorous intent.

K

keynote speech Speech given at the beginning of a social or business function designed to set the tone and focus of the function.

knowledge claim Any statement suggesting the speaker knows something.

L

language A system of signs and symbols used by a speech community to share meaning and experience.

lay testimony Testimony from the "man in the street."

logical completeness Extent to which listeners think a statement is warranted by the evidence and arguments presented.

logos Logical proofs. In Aristotle's system, one of three artistic proofs.

M

manuscript delivery Style of delivery in which the speaker reads from a written document.

matters of taste Arbitrary and rather insignificant beliefs about the world.

memorable Worthy of being remembered—easily retained and recalled.

memorized delivery Style of delivery in which the speaker commits the speech to memory and delivers a word-for-word progression of ideas.

message Whatever information a speaker sends into the rhetorical field. May be verbal or nonverbal.

message credibility The logical completeness of the message.

metaphor Implied comparison between two unlike things used to show some unexpected likeness between the two.

model Physical representation of an object or process.

motivation The needs and desires that drive or impel people to act as they do in their effort to achieve certain specific goals.

N

noise Any source of interference or distortion in message exchange. Anything that interferes with the fidelity of message exchange between two people.

O

observable behavior Any behavior you can see or hear.

occasion The context component in the communication process model. The particular time, place, and purpose of a speaking event. See, also, rhetorical field.

one-point after-dinner speech Epideictic speech in which the speaker states a central thought and then wraps stories, anecdotes, quotations, and the like around that central thought.

online catalog Holdings catalog stored as a computer database.

opening First part of a speech introduction, and designed to draw listeners' attention.

operational definition Defining something by describing what it does.

oral style A style of language usage characterized by short words, repetition of ideas, and use of contractions.

organizational link Transition, signpost, or internal summary that ties a speech together and keeps listeners headed in the right direction.

outline Framework for structuring ideas that consists of written phrases or sentences which show the structure or arrangement and relationships among ideas.

overhead projector (OHP) A machine that projects light through a transparent image onto a screen or the image generated by a computer onto a screen.

P

paraphrasing Putting another's ideas into your own words.

parody Imitation for the sake of humor.

pathos Emotional appeals. In Aristotle's system, one of three artistic proofs.

personal testimony Evidence provided from the speaker's own experience, usually presented in the form of a narrative.

persuasion The activity of attempting to change the behavior of at least one person through symbolic interaction.

physical context The physical and temporal surroundings in which a communication event occurs.

physical noise Noise that occurs in the channels.

planning outline Document used in planning discourse to determine the most appropriate organizational sequence for a given audience, and to determine what evidence and arguments are needed to support knowledge claims.

pitch The level of the vocal sound at which the voice mechanism works with maximum efficiency and ease.

plagiarism Taking another person's ideas or language and claiming them as your own.

potency dimension Part of the connotative meaning of a word. A power dimension, involving such judgments as *strong-weak, hard-soft,* and *heavy-light.*

praise is an expression of approval or admiration.

presentation speech The talk given when a person receives an award or a gift in public.

preview In a speech introduction, a brief description of the analysis, a hint at the main ideas of the speech.

primitive beliefs Beliefs people have about themselves, about existence, and about our personal identities.

problem-to-solution Pattern for organizing ideas that identifies a difficulty and then presents a solution that solves the elements of the problem.

process model Model of communication showing dynamic, interactive process.

proofs Artistic elements that provide a reason to support an argument or change one's attitudes or behaviors.

proposition Assertion of a speaker's general position on some subject. Its logical completeness depends on the weight of evidence and analysis that renders an audience willing to accept the knowledge claim as true.

proposition of fact A statement that something is true.

proposition of policy A statement that some action should be taken.

proposition of value A statement that something is good, bad, valuable, worthless, right, or wrong, etc.

psychological noise Noise that occurs inside people

public speaking Oral communication in a one-to-many setting, usually occurring face-to-face.

public speaking course The course that focuses most or all of its attention on the public speaking activity.

Q

qualifier The part of Toulmin's logical system that tells how much confidence the speaker has in the claim.

R

rate The speed at which a person speaks.

receiver Person or thing that takes in messages.

relational meaning The part of language, usually nonverbal, that tells people how speakers define their relationships with listeners.

remembering Bringing back to consciousness those things that are stored in our minds.

reservations In Toulmin's logical system, any statements that might undermine or diminish the claim.

reversal of values A technique in which the speaker makes something significant out of the trivial, or something trivial out of the important.

rhetorical field The combination of context, setting and occasion in which an audience understands itself to exist. Comprised of four elements: (1) *when* you plan to speak, (2) *where* you will be speaking, and (3) the *events that precede and follow* your appearance. (4) *Why* the audience is gathered. The elements, including the audience, the occasion, the speaker and his/her behavior, the language, topic, organization of the message, and strategies of presentation which contribute to the success of a communication experience.

rhetorical question A question, etc. asked for effect. One that implies its own answer. The power comes from listener participation in answering the question.

rule of thirds Principle of design for two-dimensional visual aids in which the visual plane is divided into thirds, both horizontally and vertically, and the major design components are located at or near the intersections of the dividing lines.

S

satire Use of ridicule to expose, denounce, or deride.

search engine Any of a large number of Internet tools that can be used to search the World Wide Web because it treats the WWW as a database.

selective perception Act of choosing, unconsciously, to focus on one idea or one person to the exclusion of others.

sensing Receiving stimuli through the senses.

shared beliefs Beliefs that result from experiences we are willing to discuss with others.

shared meaning Both speaker and listeners have a similar perception of an idea or an object.

signpost Unit of speech that announces or points to some new or important idea.

simple Basic, uncomplicated, not complex, readily understood, without superfluous materials, fundamental, and easy to follow.

simplicity With reference to a visual aid, plain, immediately obvious, easy to see from a distance, unmistakable even to a person who is not familiar with the subject.

source Location of an idea or the originator of a message.

space pattern of organization Pattern of organizing ideas that relies on geographical relationships.

speaker credibility The degree to which listeners believe in you as a source.

speaking outline Outline made to be used as notes. Its purpose is to help a speaker stay on track during a presentation.

specific purpose The particular action goal of a speech. What you want from the audience as a result of your speech.

speech community All of those who use the same language system.

speech to entertain A speech that seeks to hold audience attention agreeably, to divert or amuse.

statistics As evidence, the use of numbers to support ideas. A shorthand method of summarizing a large number of cases.

summary A brief recapitulation of the main ideas developed in a speech.

supporting material Any verbal or nonverbal material used to develop credibility or to win acceptance for knowledge claims.

suspense Mental uncertainty and excitement.

syllogism Formal argument having three parts: a generalization, a specific case, and a conclusion.

synonyms Words that have the same, or nearly the same, meanings as other words.

T

testimony Using the words of another person as evidence for an argument.

thesis statement Sentence that tells listeners what the speaker wants from them or what the speaker plans to discuss.

time pattern of organization Pattern for organizing ideas based on some sequence of events through time.

topical divisions organizational pattern Pattern for organizing ideas according to the natural divisions of a topic.

transition A sentence or two designed to move listeners smoothly from one part of a speech to another.

tributes Acknowledgments of one's gratitude, esteem, or regard.

understanding Interpreting and evaluating what comes in through the senses.

U

understanding Interpreting and evaluating what comes through the senses.

V

value A statement containing the words *should* or *ought,* or such subjective terms as *good, beautiful.*

visual aid Any object, photograph, chart, graph, sketch, or lettered image that supports a speech or the speaker.

volume The loudness of a voice.

W

warrant In Toulmin's logical system, the line of reasoning that connects the data and the claim.

welcoming speech A speech that acknowledge visitors and extends the hospitality of an organization to them.

written style A style of language usage that may be fairly complex, rather abstract, and formal in expression.

APPENDIX E

INDEX

A

Acceptance, 420, 441, 87, 36, 236, 272, 382–383, 386, 388, 398, 400–401
Active listening, 142
Aggressiveness, 416
Allness, 114
Apprehension, 26, 40, 46, 308
Attraction, 420, 264
Attribution, 46

B

Business, 405, 408, 410, 412, 417, 419–420, 422, 424, 7, 10, 82, 52, 60, 62, 101, 107, 111, 133, 139, 150, 158, 167, 180, 182, 210–212, 214, 216, 220, 222, 230, 234, 271, 301, 307, 311, 313, 343–344, 373, 378–380, 382, 391, 393

C

Channels, 414, 3–4, 14–15, 19–21
Communication, 409, 418, 420–422, 428–429, 3–4, 6–7, 12–17, 19–22, 84, 87, 26, 28, 42, 44, 46, 49, 60, 62, 99, 105, 108, 125, 131–135, 149, 155, 165, 189, 191, 219, 229, 243–244, 248, 256, 262–263, 265, 268–271, 274, 282–284, 296, 298–299, 301, 306, 313, 315, 317, 322–324, 342, 350–351, 356, 360, 377–378, 380
Competence, 28, 44, 46, 209, 348
Confidence, 412, 430, 434, 5, 17, 41, 116, 121, 123, 126, 133, 159, 210, 250, 298, 309–310, 319, 321, 345

Contact, 418, 422–423, 428, 430, 18, 30, 32, 40, 117, 181–182, 303–305, 307, 310, 315, 318–319, 321–323, 368
Context, 419, 3–4, 12–13, 20–21, 49–50, 54–56, 59, 91, 94, 100, 120, 142, 356, 395
Conversation, 406, 16–17, 76, 48, 139, 236, 305, 311, 314, 316, 318, 361
Credibility, 425, 428, 430, 6, 11, 17, 20, 36, 41, 53, 109–112, 120, 124–126, 128, 131–133, 165, 174, 224, 271, 283, 310, 328, 331–332, 345–346, 348, 350–351, 353–354, 364–366, 369, 376–380, 384
Critical thinking, 87, 134–135, 195, 350
Criticism, 410, 6, 22, 142, 231
Culture, 415, 421–422, 441, 26, 373

D

Decoding, 15, 20
Depression, 35, 43
Dress, 16, 40, 128, 307, 364–365

E

Effects, 439, 20, 87, 42, 46, 49, 62, 108, 132, 165, 181–182, 255, 270, 301, 324, 362, 372, 378–380
Empathy, 410, 48, 56–58, 60
Errors, 15, 158, 223
Ethical issues, 430, 4, 11, 140, 185
Ethnocentrism, 413
Evaluating, 50, 133, 165, 349, 351, 381
Examples, 408, 414–415, 434, 3, 5, 8, 15, 71–73, 77, 82, 27–28, 33, 36, 39, 53–56, 95–96, 98, 101, 109–110, 112–117, 125–127, 130–132, 134–135, 142, 151, 154, 173, 177, 187, 196, 201, 227, 230,

232–233, 235, 237, 243, 249, 258, 260, 298, 330, 334, 349, 353, 360, 362, 366–367, 373, 386, 389, 403

Experience, 406, 413, 416, 424, 6, 8, 13, 17, 70, 23–26, 28–30, 34, 38–39, 42, 44, 57, 101, 107, 128, 130, 196, 198, 230, 234, 242, 249–253, 261–263, 265, 280, 290, 320, 333, 340–341, 343, 348, 358–359, 366, 371, 373, 378, 400

F

Feedback, 3–4, 15, 19–21, 29, 51, 56–60, 195, 309–310, 318, 321

G

Gender, 416–417, 419–422, 87, 90, 99, 101, 104–106, 108, 256

Groups, 418–419, 421–422, 442, 5, 7, 9, 20, 23, 30–31, 90, 92–93, 100–101, 106, 108, 141, 159, 314, 391, 399

H

Hearing, 431, 75, 51, 56, 255–256, 331

Homosexuals, 441

Honesty, 19–20, 126, 165, 331, 357

I

Illustrations, 8, 19, 55, 135, 215, 228, 248, 254, 258, 260–261, 267–268, 288, 290, 295, 297, 330, 379

Illustrators, 316

Imagery, 255

Informative speeches, 34, 37, 234, 327–329, 332, 346–348, 350, 388

Internet, 433, 18, 66–67, 72, 87, 24, 44, 90, 99, 107, 110–111, 135, 137–142, 146, 149, 152–158, 162–165, 182, 185, 194, 196, 221, 225, 228, 244, 248, 265, 268, 277–278, 282, 290, 300, 304, 324, 328, 351, 354, 380, 382, 402

Intimacy, 420

Involvement, 437, 37, 123, 196, 199, 351, 366

J

Judgments, 69, 249, 253, 324, 363

L

Language, 418, 421–423, 428, 431, 11, 15, 18, 22, 71, 73, 76, 82–83, 86, 40, 54–55, 57, 60, 102, 145, 147–148, 152, 161, 167, 172, 174, 202, 209–210, 236, 244, 247–265, 267–268, 271–272, 288, 291, 298, 300, 305, 307, 309, 311–312, 316, 319–321, 328, 335–336, 345–346, 349, 356, 366, 388, 402

Leadership, 413, 416, 440, 4, 29, 126, 231–232

Listeners, 429–430, 432–433, 435, 9, 11, 13–19, 21–22, 66, 68, 71, 73–83, 85–87, 26–27, 29–38, 40–43, 47, 49–57, 59–60, 90–95, 97–106, 108, 110, 112, 114–118, 120, 124–130, 162, 165, 172–174, 176–177, 179–182, 184–188, 196–197, 199, 202–203, 209, 211, 213–216, 220, 228–230, 232–235, 237–241, 243, 247, 249–252, 254–256, 258–261, 263–264, 268–275, 277–278, 280, 282, 284–285, 288, 290–297, 305–306, 308–316, 318–322, 327–343, 345–350, 353–354, 356, 358, 362–366, 368–369, 371–372, 374, 376–378, 384–385, 388, 390, 393, 395, 398–399, 401

Listening, 1, 9, 17, 19, 76, 24, 27, 29, 31, 42, 47–55, 57, 59–62, 91, 99, 104, 115, 120, 142, 189, 252, 269, 272, 312, 315, 335, 338–339, 345, 349, 418, 428–429, 431

M

Maintenance, 94, 206, 370

Messages, 412, 3–4, 14–15, 18–19, 21, 50, 53, 56–57, 251–252, 255, 304–305, 315, 321–324, 351, 357, 372, 380

Nonverbal messages, 3, 18, 56–57, 304–305, 315, 321, 323–324

Noise, 3–4, 15, 19–21, 49, 51, 60, 93–94, 101, 314

N

Nonverbal messages, 3, 18, 56–57, 304–305, 315, 321, 323–324

O

Organization, 420, 428, 432–433, 8, 22, 30, 33, 38, 58, 62, 97, 101, 157, 160, 171–174, 178–182, 188–189, 191, 215, 219, 273–274, 279, 329, 346, 366, 369, 386, 391, 394, 401

P

Paraphrasing, 57
Perception, 410, 48, 52, 54, 60–61, 132–133, 313, 328, 332, 349
Persuasive speeches, 188, 208, 346, 353–354, 363–364, 375–377, 402
Physical context, 13, 20
Power, 405–408, 411, 418, 437–438, 5, 19, 22, 42, 250, 253, 257, 260–262, 268–269, 282–284, 288, 296, 298–299, 343, 356, 373, 393
Problem solving, 271
Propositions, 353, 365–370, 377

R

Racism, 413, 415, 442, 362
Relationships, 413, 419–420, 441–442, 13, 34, 37, 42, 178–179, 182, 195–196, 213, 218, 220, 243, 261–262, 264, 271, 279, 351
Repair, 206, 234, 242, 274, 339, 367

S

Secrecy, 224
Self-concept, 53
Self-confidence, 4–6, 392
Self-disclosure, 3, 21
Signals, 14, 58
Silence, 406, 425, 12, 40, 142, 234, 308
Small groups, 5, 9
Speakers, 427, 437, 9, 14–17, 19–20, 66, 72, 81, 23, 25, 29, 33, 42, 49, 51–54, 57–58, 92–94, 103–104, 111–112, 119–120, 124, 127, 131, 172, 191, 208, 228, 235, 237, 239–240, 242, 251, 255, 261–262, 264, 270–271, 290, 293–295, 304–305, 308, 311–314, 316–318, 320–322, 324, 328–329, 332, 336, 338, 340, 346, 348–350, 353–354, 363, 369, 371, 376–377, 379, 384, 395, 398–399, 402
Speeches, 405, 407, 409, 411, 413, 415, 417–419, 421, 423, 425, 427, 434, 8–10, 14, 17–19, 69, 72, 79, 87, 24–25, 33–34, 37, 39, 42–43, 45, 94, 130, 140, 162, 178, 187–188, 190–191, 195, 208, 219, 229, 232, 234, 253, 255, 261, 268, 271–272, 293, 295, 304, 307–308, 310, 317, 319, 325, 327–329, 332, 334–336, 338, 346–348, 350, 353–354, 360, 363–364, 375–377, 381–391, 393–395, 397–403
Statistics, 416, 429, 434, 15, 53, 109, 111, 126–128, 130–132, 135, 285, 367, 377
Status, 415, 420, 442, 78, 90–91, 100–101, 104, 365
Stereotyping, 215–216

T

Testimony, 428, 434–435, 37, 109–111, 126–127, 129–132, 134–135, 165, 216, 314, 351, 370

U

Understanding, 411–412, 4, 6, 15, 22, 44, 48–50, 54–55, 57, 59–60, 62, 105, 119, 250, 257, 261, 264, 272, 280, 290, 313, 329, 360, 379, 398

V

Visual aids, 428, 430, 432, 435, 18, 33, 39, 41, 44, 51, 127, 213, 267–275, 278, 280–282, 284–286, 291, 293–296, 299–301, 309–310, 320–321, 330, 334, 336, 345–347

W

World Wide Web, 153–154, 300